Communism and Political Systems in Western Europe

Other Titles in This Series

Ideology and Politics: The Socialist Party of France, George A. Codding, Jr., and William Safran

The Spanish Political System: Franco's Legacy, E. Ramón Arango

Westview Special Studies in West European Politics and Society

Communism and Political Systems in Western Europe
edited by David E. Albright

Developments of the 1970s suggest the need for a new approach to the analysis of communism in Western Europe. During the early years after World War II, Western observers tended to look upon the West European Communist parties as fundamentally an extension of communism in the USSR—as national only in the narrow, formal sense. With the growing signs of disunity within the international communist movement during the late 1950s and early 1960s, however, a shift in perspectives took place. Most Western analysts sought to assess the extent to which the West European parties had asserted their independence of the Soviet party and the attendant degree of pluralism manifest in the European context. A widely accepted assumption was that a loosening of bonds between the West European parties and Moscow would probably mean the evolution of the former back toward left-wing democracy and their reabsorption into the prevailing West European order.

Whatever merit these approaches may have had in previous years, they are clearly inadequate today to yield a true picture of communism in Western Europe. This book provides fresh insights by focusing on the roles of the West European Communist parties in the specific political systems in which they operate. The introductory essay offers a broad overview of the West European situation; eight chapters deal with the most important individual parties; and the final chapter explores the interaction between the roles of the West European parties in their own political contexts and their relations within the international communist movement.

David E. Albright is senior text editor of the journal *Problems of Communism*. Dr. Albright was formerly research associate and editor of the Council on Foreign Relations' project on the United States and China in world affairs.

Communism and Political Systems in Western Europe

edited by David E. Albright

Westview Press / Boulder, Colorado

Westview Special Studies in West European Politics and Society

Published in 1979 in the United States of America by
Westview Press, Inc.
5500 Central Avenue
Boulder, Colorado 80301
Frederick A. Praeger, Publisher

Library of Congress Cataloging in Publication Data
Main entry under title:
Communism and political systems in Western Europe.
(Westview special studies in west European politics and society)
Bibliography: p.
1. Communism—Europe—Addresses, essays, lectures. 2. Communist parties—Addresses, essays, lectures. 3. Europe—Politics and government—1945- —Addresses, essays, lectures. I. Albright, David E.
HX239.Z7C63   335.43'094   78-19054
ISBN 0-89158-308-4

Printed and bound in the United States of America

Contents

Tables

Figures

Preface

The genesis of this volume was fairly simple. During the course of my work on the editorial staff of *Problems of Communism* in the 1970s, I became convinced of the need for a volume that would take a comprehensive look at the complex phenomenon of communism in Western Europe. As a result, I was highly receptive when Fred Praeger broached the idea of such a book to me in late 1976, and I immediately set about putting together a group of contributors.

The actual production of the volume, however, has proved a tortuous process. To some extent, this difficulty reflected the fact that little serious work had been done on a number of important parties. More critically, events since the conception of the book have not only underscored the need for such an undertaking but have also moved at a pace that makes up-to-date evaluations difficult. I would be remiss if I did not pay tribute to the way in which the contributors have performed in the face of these problems—and their demanding and relentless editor.

Several of the chapters draw upon material published earlier in *Problems of Communism*. These include the ones on Italy, Portugal, Greece, Finland, and interparty relations. All, however, are revised and updated contributions prepared expressly for this volume.

Aside from those whose work appears in the succeeding pages, a number of other persons rendered valuable service to the project. As I have already noted, Fred Praeger stimulated me to launch the venture, and he has shown infinite patience in awaiting the ultimate product. Ronald Tiersky, Erik Willenz, Pio Uliassi, Joan Barth Urban, Robert Putnam, and Joergen Rasmussen shared their thoughts with me on a variety of issues. In a more general sense, Alexander Dallin, with whom I studied during the years I was pursuing my doctorate at Columbia University, has helped to shape my perceptions of the international communist movement. Kimberly Johnson-Smith found time in her crowded schedule to retype many of the chapters after the completion of the editing, and James Smith, her husband, bore my impositions on them with unfailing good humor and understanding during the period when the volume was coming to fruition.

David E. Albright

About the Contributors

David E. Albright is senior text editor of the journal *Problems of Communism*. He has contributed articles on Soviet and Chinese politics and foreign policies as well as on the international communist movement to a number of journals and symposia. In addition, he has edited a forthcoming volume on *Communism in Africa*, and he is author of another forthcoming book entitled *The Dilemmas of Courtship: The Soviet Union, China, and Ghana*.

William J. Davidshofer is associate professor of political science at the University of Maine, Presque Isle. He has specialized on French politics and especially on the French Communist Party. Moreover, he did doctoral research at the Foundation Nationale des Sciences Politiques in Paris.

Kevin Devlin is a political analyst for Radio Free Europe in Munich. He has published extensively on Europe's Communist parties, and he is now involved in a collective research project to produce a volume entitled *Imperium und Ideologie*.

Trond Gilberg is professor of political science at Pennsylvania State University, University Park. Born in Norway, he has specialized on politics in both Western and Eastern Europe, particularly the Nordic countries and Romania. His publications on the Nordic countries include *The Soviet Communist Party and Scandinavian Communism: The Norwegian Case*.

John H. Hodgson is professor of political science at Syracuse University. He has written widely on both the Soviet Union and Finland. Among his works on Finland are *Communism in Finland: A History and Interpretation* and *Escape to Russia: A Political Biography of Otto W. Kuusinen*.

Dimitri Kitsikis is professor of the history of international relations at the University of Ottawa in Canada. Born in Athens and educated at the Sorbonne, he has been a research scholar at several prominent European academic centers. His writings include *Propagande et pressions en politique internationale—La Grèce et ses revendications à la Conférence de Paix, 1919-1920; Ê Ellas tês 4ès Augoustou kai ai Megalai Dunameis, 1936-1941; Ellas kai Xenoi, 1919-1967—Ta Arheia tou Ellênikou Upourgeiou Exôterikôn;* and *Sugkritikê Istoria Ellados kai Tourkias ston 20° Aiôna.*

Eusebio M. Mujal-León is a doctoral candidate in political science at the Massachusetts Institute of Technology. He has contributed articles on Iberian politics to several journals and symposia, and he spent 1977 in Madrid working on a study of the Spanish Communist Party.

David Lynn Price is a consultant and political analyst based in England. He has published on a wide range of topics connected with the Middle East, but he has also followed the activities of the Communist Party of Great Britain closely over a number of years. His writings on the latter subject have appeared in such publications as the annual *Yearbook on International Communist Affairs* put out by the Hoover Institution on War, Revolution, and Peace at Stanford University.

Giacomo Sani is professor of political science at The Ohio State University in Columbus. Born in Italy, he has written extensively on Italian politics and the Italian Communist Party. He has concentrated particularly on the analysis of mass politics.

Abbreviations

This list includes only abbreviations used in this book. It does not, therefore, afford a complete rundown on either the Communist parties mentioned in the discussion or all the Communist parties that exist in the area.

AB	*Altydubandalagid* (People's Alliance) of Iceland
AKP(m-1)	*Arbeidernes Kommunistiske Parti—Marxistisk-Leninistisk* (Workers' Communist Party—Marxist-Leninist) of Norway
APK	*Arbetarepartiet Kommunisterna* (Workers' Party—Communist) of Sweden
BR	*Bandera Roja* (Red Flag) of Spain
CPGB	Communist Party of Great Britain
CPI	Communist Party of Ireland
CPM	Communist Party of Malta
CPN	*Communistische Partij van Nederland* (Communist Party of the Netherlands)
DKP	*Danmarks Kommunistiske Parti* (Communist Party of Denmark)
DKP	*Deutsche Kommunistische Partei* (German Communist Party) of West Germany
DP	*Democrazia Proletaria* (Proletarian Democracy) of Italy
EDA	*Eniaia Dêmokratikê Aristera* (United Democratic Left) of Greece

EKKE	*Epanastatiko Kommounistiko Kinêma Elladas* (Revolutionary Communist Movement of Greece)
FSP	*Frente Socialista Popular* (Popular Socialist Front) of Portugal
KAK	*Kommunistisk Arbejdskreds* (Communist Labor Circle) of Denmark
KFML	*Kommunistisk Forbund-ML* (Communist League—Marxist-Leninist) of Denmark
KFML(r)	*Kommunistiska Förbundet Marxist-Leninisterna-R* (Communist League of Marxist-Leninist Revolutionaries) of Sweden
KKE-Exterior	*Kommounistiko Komma Elladas* (Communist Party of Greece—sometimes referred to as Communist Party of Greece—Exterior)
KKE-Interior	*Kommounistiko Komma Elladas Esôterikou* (Communist Party of Greece—Interior)
KPÖ	*Kommunistiche Partei Österreichs* (Communist Party of Austria)
KU	*Kommunistisk Ungdom* (Communist Youth) of Sweden
KUF	*Kommunistisk Ungdoms Forbund* (Communist Youth League) of Denmark
KUML	*Kommunistisk Ungdom—ML* (Communist Youth—Marxist-Leninist) of Denmark
LDE	*Läike Dêmokratikê Enotêta* (People's Democratic Union) of Greece
MLK	*Marxist-Leninistiska Kampförbundet* (Marxist-Leninst League of Struggle) of Sweden
M-L KKE	*Marxistiko Leninistiko Kommounistiko Komma Elladas* (Marxist-Leninist Communist Party of Greece)
NCP	New Communist Party of Great Britain
NKP	*Norges Kommunistiske Parti* (Norwegian Communist Party)

OMLE	*Organôsê Marxistôn Leninistôn Elladas* (Organization of Marxist-Leninists of Greece)
ORT	*Organización Revolucionaria de los Trabajadores* (Revolutionary Workers' Organization) of Spain
PCB	*Parti Communiste de Belgique/Kommunistiche Partij Van België* (Communist Party of Belgium)
PCE	*Partido Comunista de España* (Communist Party of Spain)
PCE-ML	*Partido Comunista de España—Marxista-Leninista* (Communist Party of Spain—Marxist-Leninist)
PCF	*Partito Communiste Français* (French Communist Party)
PCI	*Partito Comunisto Italiano* (Italian Communist Party)
PCL	*Parti Communiste de Luxembourg* (Communist Party of Luxembourg)
PCOE	*Partido Comunista de Obreros Españoles* (Spanish Communist Workers' Party)
PCP	*Partido Comunista Português* (Portuguese Communist Party)
PCS	*Partito Comunista di San Marino* (Communist Party of San Marino)
PdA	*Partei der Arbeit/Parti du Travail/Partito del Lavoro* (Labor Party) of Switzerland
PDUP	*Partito di Unità Proletaria* (Party of Proletarian Unity) of Italy
POCH	*Progressive Organisationen, Schweiz* (Progressive Organizations, Switzerland)
PRP-BR	*Partido Revolucionario do Proletarido—Brigadas Revolucionarias* (Revolutionary Party of the Proletariat—Revolutionary Brigades) of Spain
PT	*Partido de Trabajo* (Labor Party) of Spain

SEW	*Sozialistische Einheitspartei Westberlins* (Socialist Unity Party of West Berlin)
SIS	*Samtok Islenzkra Sosialista* (Organization of Icelandic Socialists)
SKA	*Sveriges Kommunistiska Arbetarförbund* (Communist Workers' League) of Sweden
SKP	*Suomen Kommunistinen Puoloue* (Communist Party of Finland)
SKP	*Sveriges Kommunistiska Parti* (Swedish Communist Party)
SUF	*Socialistisk Ungdoms Forbund* (Socialist Youth League) of Denmark
SWP	Socialist Workers' Party of Great Britain
VPK	*Vänsterpartiet Kommunisterna* (Left Party—Communists) of Sweden
WRP	Workers' Revolutionary Party of Great Britain

Communism and Political Systems
in Western Europe

An Introductory Overview

David E. Albright

During the early years after World War II, Western analysts tended to approach communism in Western Europe as fundamentally an extension of communism in the USSR. Although they acknowledged that the West European parties sought to capitalize on local social, economic, and political conditions—and, indeed, had succeeded in doing so to a certain extent in some countries—they looked upon these parties as national only in the narrow, formal sense. That is, they regarded the parties as instruments of Moscow's will, irrevocably committed to the destruction of all aspects of the existing order in the West European states and firmly resistant to integration into local societies and polities.[1]

However, the growing signs of disunity within the international communist movement during the late 1950s and early 1960s—especially the turmoil generated by the Sino-Soviet dispute—produced a switch in approach. Most analysts now sought to assess the extent to which the West European parties had asserted their independence of the Soviet party and the attendant degree of pluralism manifest in the European context.[2] This new approach, it is important to note, implicitly embodied some of the assumptions of the old one, for there was a widespread belief that a loosening of bonds between the West European parties and Moscow would probably mean the evolution of the West European parties back toward left-wing social democracy. One leading observer of the European scene even went so far as to predict that "it is doubtful if, five years hence, the parties out of power will be distinguishable except in name from the Social Democratic formations of the period between the two world wars, albeit that they will probably not have to

The views expressed in this essay are those of the author and do not necessarily reflect the perspectives of the International Communication Agency or the U.S. government.

fear the conversion into mass parties of the Stalinist-minded, pro-Chinese sects that have come into being since 1961."[3]

Whatever merit these two approaches may have had in previous years, recent developments clearly suggest that neither is now adequate to yield a true picture of communism in Western Europe. For example, the relations of the French and Italian Communist parties (PCF and PCI) with Moscow have grown increasingly contentious, but it is not at all certain that these parties are undergoing a transformation into social democratic parties. Nevertheless, both have managed to retain their popular support, and the PCI has even expanded its mass base. Both have also appeared to be moving nearer to participation in the governments of their respective countries. Indeed, the PCI since August 1976 has exercised substantial influence on national policy in Italy even without representation in the cabinet. Because its at least indirect backing in parliament has been crucial to the formation and survival of a government, it has had a say in what to do about critical problems facing the country. On the other hand, close ties with the Communist Party of the Soviet Union (CPSU) have not prevented some West European parties from registering major successes within their local environments. For instance, the loyalist Portuguese Communist Party captured nearly 13 percent of the popular vote in the April 1975 elections to Portugal's Constituent Assembly and held various posts in the cabinet in 1974-1975. Although its position has weakened as a result of its connection with an abortive coup d'etat in November 1975, it demonstrated that it is still a force to be reckoned with by winning about 15 percent of the ballots in the parliamentary elections of 1976 and by consolidating its grip on the Portuguese labor movement during the course of 1976.

In short, there is need for a fresh approach to the subject of communism in Western Europe. The present book attempts to respond to that need.[4] It looks at the West European Communist parties in terms of their roles within the specific political systems in which they operate.[5] Eight chapters deal with the more important and more unorthodox of the individual parties, and the final chapter explores the impact of the interaction of the parties with their local political milieus on interparty relations within the world communist movement. This introductory essay will attempt to provide an overview to set the ensuing analyses in a broad framework. In the process, it will also touch briefly on those parties not covered in separate chapters.[6]

At the outset, it is important to recognize that a party's role in the political system in which it functions depends on the interplay of several factors. First, there are the opportunities that circumstances in the society and polity afford the party. These derive from a variety of considerations, but the key ones include the objective social and economic conditions in the country and the attitudes of the populace toward these conditions, the political history and traditions of the country, the constellation of political forces in the country, and the attitudes of other political forces toward the Communist party. A second factor is the image that a party has of itself and seeks to project to others. Although attitudes toward the USSR and the CPSU figure prominently among the determinants of a party's self-image, they are not the sole influence involved. Such things as national radical traditions and the personal history of a particular leader enter in as well. Finally, there is the party's strategy. Strategy grows out of a party's answers to a host of critical questions. To what range of social forces should the party address its efforts? Under what conditions should the party engage in parliamentary politics? What should the purpose of parliamentary activity be? With what political forces should the party seek to ally, and to what end? Under what circumstances should the party come to power? And so on.

Since such factors entail many variables and since the number of precise situations that can result from differences in these variables is, in turn, enormous, it almost inevitably follows that the role of each West European party in its political system is in large measure unique. Consequently, most of the meaningful generalizations that one can make about the roles of the parties throughout the area concern the factors that shape these roles. It is to such generalizations, then, that we shall turn initially.

Opportunities

Bearing in mind that the opportunities confronting the Communist parties of Western Europe have grown out of a multiplicity of circumstances, let us look briefly at the impact in regional terms of the most relevant of these. On balance, the ethnic and linguistic makeups of individual West European countries have provided relatively few openings that Communist parties could seek to exploit, for the great bulk of the countries boast a high degree of homogeneity on these counts. However, there are five notable exceptions— Belgium, Great Britain, Malta, Spain, and Switzerland. In Belgium, Flemish constitute 55 percent of the total population; French-speaking Walloons, 33 percent; and persons of mixed or other background, 12 percent. Though 83 percent of the British populace are of English extraction, 9 percent come from Scottish stock, 5 percent from Welch stock, and 3 percent from Irish stock. Malta has a population that is highly heterogeneous—including Arabs, Sicilians, Normans, Spanish, Italians, and British. Although better than 70 percent of the Spanish population speak Castilian Spanish, the rest speak a number of regional dialects. Specifically, 17 percent use Catalan; 7 percent, Galician; and 2 percent, Basque. The native population of Switzerland is composed of 74 percent Germans, 20 percent French, 10 percent Italians, 1 percent Romansch, and 1 percent "other."[7]

Of these exceptions, Malta appears to have a sufficiently diverse population that ethnic considerations have not assumed great importance in the politics of the island, and Switzerland has long maintained a confederal type of government that allows each ethnic group a large measure of autonomy in the areas of its concentration. The other three countries, however, have in recent years experienced growing demands for regional autonomy by those who feel themselves inadequately represented at the center. In Belgium, these demands have come primarily from the Flemish; in Great Britain and Spain, from the minority groups. This dissatisfaction with the existing political order has enhanced the potential appeal to the disgruntled groups of parties dedicated to reshaping that political order.

Religious differences have not afforded many of the Communist parties grounds upon which to make political capital either. Most of the parties, of course, confront difficulties in trying to take advantage of any such opportunities because of their own strong commitments to atheism. But in any case there are few West European countries where religious conflict has been even potentially of much significance. One religious group enjoys overwhelming dominance in each of the countries except West Germany, Great Britain, the Netherlands, and Switzerland. In West Germany, the Netherlands, and Switzerland, Roman Catholics and Protestants command the loyalties of roughly equal portions of the local populace, and in Great Britain the Protestants predominate, with the Catholics constituting a fairly strong minority.[8] Only in the Northern Ireland region of Great Britain has religious identification actually loomed of great moment in political terms, and even here it has gotten intertwined with other social and economic considerations.

Socio-occupational status appears to have had diminishing importance throughout the region as a source of major openings for the Communist parties. Many West European societies traditionally displayed sharp social cleavages, but the pace of economic development since World War I and especially in the post–World War II era has considerably reduced these, for it has led to high rates of social mobility in the area. The most dramatic evidence of such mobility comes from the drop in the percentage of the work force engaged in agriculture. Of the thirteen countries for which prewar data are available, only Great Britain has registered a decline of less than 10 percent of the total work force since the end of the war, and the figure in this case reflects the fact that the country already had a low percentage of the laboring population in agriculture before the war— about 6 percent. For the remaining states, the decrease ranges from 12 percent for Belgium to 37 percent for Finland.[9] Data on inter- generational mobility from manual to nonmanual jobs reinforce the picture of societies in substantial flux. Although the evidence here is not as comprehensive or as up to date as that on the transfer of peasants to worker or white-collar occupations, information on eight countries in the postwar years indicates rates of mobility ranging from 17.1 percent for Italy in 1963-1964 to 27.4 percent for Sweden in 1950.[10]

Economic conditions, on the other hand, seem to have been highly productive of opportunities. In assessing these, it is essential to distinguish between Northern Europe, or Europe north of the Alps, and Southern, or Mediterranean, Europe.

With the exceptions of Ireland and Iceland on the periphery, all the countries of Northern Europe had already attained high levels of industrialization before World War II, and after recovering from the ravages of the war, they underwent major economic development in the 1950s and 1960s. As a consequence, the per capita national incomes in the area by the mid-1970s had reached $5,000 to $6,000 everywhere except in Austria, Great Britain, Iceland, and Ireland. In Austria and Iceland, the figure stood at about $4,500; and in Great Britain, a little more than $3,500. Only in Ireland did it remain comparatively low—at just over $2,000.[11] No less important, the gap between rich and poor has narrowed. Indeed, available evidence suggests that in all the countries of the area except West Germany, incomes are distributed less unequally than they are in other economically advanced countries.[12] Finally, many of the govern- ments in Northern Europe set up welfare states in the years immediately preceding or after the war, and those that did not go so far soon put into effect measures designed to ease the lot of persons at the lower end of the economic scale. This combination of circum- stances has tended to minimize or at least soften economic cleavages in the area. As a matter of fact, economic-related grievances since the mid-1960s—particularly in the Nordic lands—have stemmed from the deleterious impact of modernity and industrialization on traditional ways of life and from the heavy burdens of the welfare state.[13]

In Mediterranean Europe, quite a different situation has prevailed. Before World War II, industrialization had barely begun in some countries, and it had been partial and limited in the rest. Though all the countries in the area registered substantial progress in economic development during the 1950s and 1960s, national income per capita had still not risen beyond $1,000 to $2,500 in Greece, Italy, Malta, Portugal, and Spain by the mid-1970s. Only in France had it reached a level comparable to that in Northern Europe—more than $5,500.[14] Of perhaps even greater consequence, the gap between wealthy and poor, though it has narrowed somewhat, appears to have stayed quite large almost everywhere. This is especially true with regard to France, Spain, and probably Greece.[15] In the absence of major government programs to improve the lot of those on the lower rungs of the economic ladder, sharp cleavages have emerged. These have been exacerbated in some countries by the fact that tax dodging by the wealthy, low taxes on inheritances, and other benefits for the rich have meant that white-collar and industrial workers contribute the lion's share of the revenue that the government derives from income taxes.[16]

Despite the disparities in the underlying economic states of affairs in Northern and Mediterranean Europe, however, both regions have experienced some common travails in the mid-1970s, and these have enhanced the potential for economic-based conflict throughout Western Europe generally. The travails have stemmed from the major economic recession that descended upon Western Europe—indeed, upon much of the world—in the wake of the Arab oil embargo in 1973 and the subsequent decision of oil-producing countries to quadruple the price of crude oil. According to official national figures, all the West European countries except Greece, Malta, Norway, Spain, and Sweden registered negative growth rates in 1975. Although virtually none of them failed to move back onto the positive side of the growth ledger in 1976, the British, Finnish, Icelandic, Spanish, Swedish, and Swiss economies remained sluggish with growth rates of less than 2 percent.[17] During the same period, inflation and unemployment climbed to levels unknown since the early postwar years. In 1975, for example, consumer prices went up by percentages ranging from 6.0 for West Germany to a whopping 48.9 for Iceland.[18] Since then, a few countries such as Switzerland, West Germany, Great Britain, and

Iceland have made some headway in reducing their rates, but most states have been unable to do anything but hold the line or watch their rates go higher.[19] As for unemployment, only Luxemburg, Switzerland, Norway, and Sweden could boast a figure of less than 2 percent at the end of 1975, and Portugal topped the list with a figure of more than 15 percent. Moreover, most countries recorded essentially the same or higher percentages in 1976. Only in Denmark, West Germany, Greece, Malta, and Sweden did the figure drop at least marginally.[20]

To the extent that one can identify common elements in the political histories and traditions of the West European states, these have both worked to the advantage of and constrained the Communist parties. In a number of countries, certain segments of the population or certain areas have radical heritages, and these heritages have rendered them particularly open to communist appeals. The best examples are the far northern, "wilderness" portions of Finland, Sweden, and Norway; the small fishing villages along the eastern and northern coasts of Iceland; the rural Alentejo region of southern Portugal; and the rural areas of central Italy. Of some importance as well has been the anarchist tradition among workers in Italy, France, Spain, and Portugal.[21]

Fairly recent controversy over the relationship between church and state has by and large improved the chances of the Communist parties to win support among those elements of the population favoring secularism and even among certain circles of devout believers. This factor has been of greatest consequence in France, where the residual effects of traditional anticlericalism are still felt. But it has increasingly entered into the picture in Italy, Spain, and Portugal as well. In Italy, growing numbers of persons have reacted to the presence of the Vatican enclave and the Catholic church's rather blatant support for the Christian Democratic Party by urging that politics be divorced from religion. Perhaps more important, others have grown to feel that religious beliefs do not preclude radical political views. Similar trends have become evident in Spain and Portugal. The Catholic church's record of fairly close ties with the authoritarian Franco and Salazar-Caetano regimes has had a major bearing on the situation, but changing attitudes with regard to the compatibility between religious convictions and leftist politics have played a substantial role, too, especially in Spain.[22]

Although all the countries of Western Europe today boast democratic political systems, these systems have far deeper roots in some countries than in others, and how deeply these roots go has decidedly affected the opportunities of the local Communist parties. Here again, there is a broad distinction between Northern Europe and Mediterranean Europe. With the exceptions of West Germany, which went through a fascist period in the 1930s and 1940s, and Iceland, which gained its independence only in 1944, the countries of Northern Europe have enjoyed representative institutions during most of the twentieth century. Indeed, some have had such institutions for centuries. These institutions, furthermore, have shown themselves generally responsive to the demands and needs of the societies in which they function. In Great Britain and the Scandinavian countries, welfare states have come into being; elsewhere, social and economic programs of substantial proportions, if less total in scope, have been enacted. Such circumstances have clearly limited the openings available to the Communist parties of Northern Europe to exploit.

In Mediterranean Europe, democratic institutions are relatively new and lack the legitimacy that they possess in the North. Only in the mid-1970s did Spain and Portugal establish representative governments after decades of authoritarian rule. Greece returned to civilian rule in 1974 after an interlude of military dictatorship; however, over the last fifty years it has experienced military control for two lengthy periods, foreign occupation for three years, and a prolonged civil war. Italy set up a parliamentary democracy after World War II, but it had spent the prior twenty years under Fascist rule. Moreover, its postwar history has been marked by governmental instability and bureaucratic inefficiency in handling pressing issues. Although Malta has been self-governing since 1947, it acquired independence only in 1964; thus, it has no time-tested political traditions to speak of. Even France, with its strong democratic heritage, suffered from constant cabinet turnovers prior to Charles de Gaulle's advent to power in 1958 and barely averted a civil war over the decolonization of Algeria in the 1960s. Such contexts have provided many potential opportunities for the local Communist parties in Southern Europe.

The constellation of political forces in all the West European countries has restricted what the local Communist parties could conceivably do; however, the degree of constraint entailed has by no means been uniform everywhere. Throughout the post–World War II era, no Communist party has ever captured a majority of either the popular vote or the parliamentary seats in the country in which it operates. Indeed, it was not until the mid-1970s that one even obtained more than a third of the ballots or the legislative seats. (The

PCI got 34 percent of the votes and 227 out of 630 seats in the House of Deputies in the 1976 Italian elections.)[23] At the same time, most of the West European states have multiparty political systems in fact as well as form.[24] Only Austria, Great Britain, Greece, West Germany and West Berlin, Ireland, and Malta have experienced periods during the postwar years in which one or two non-Communist parties dominated local political processes, and these periods have been sporadic in Greece, West Germany, and Ireland. This widespread fragmentation of political forces has, on balance, created some room for the Communist parties to maneuver in most West European countries.

The degree of maneuver available to them, however, has varied from context to context. In terms of the overall lineup of political forces, the situation in Italy in recent years has afforded the Italian Communist Party (PCI) the greatest potential leeway of any of the Communist parties. The PCI has constituted one of two large parties on the Italian scene, neither of which has had enough seats in parliament to control the government without cooperating with smaller parties or with each other. In several other countries, circumstances have provided significant, if more limited, openings for action. The Finnish Communist Party (SKP), the French Communist Party (PCF), and the San Marino Communist Party (PCS) have each been one of four major parties in their respective polities.[25] All the parties in Finland have commanded about the same political strength for years. Up until 1978, there had been greater disparities among those in France and San Marino, but the March 1978 elections in France produced a situation there roughly comparable to that in Finland. In fact, the four French parties are now more tightly bunched than the four Finnish parties.[26] As of early 1978, substantial disparities remain in San Marino, and the PCS ranks second on the list of parties. The People's Alliance (AB) in Iceland, the Portugese Communist Party (PCP), and the Spanish Communist Party (PCE) each have also qualified as one of four leading parties in their respective countries, with the Icelandic and Spanish parties holding third position and the Portugese party fourth. Yet all three have stood fairly far behind the front-running parties. Elsewhere, the general constellation of forces has offered relatively few opportunities of note for the local Communist parties.

Of perhaps greater import in determining the exact margin for maneuver that has confronted individual Communist parties, of course, have been the status and makeup of the Left in the particular contexts in which the parties function. During the whole of the postwar era, only in Austria, Finland, France, West Berlin, Great Britain, Malta, Norway, Portugal, San Marino, and Sweden have political forces to the left of center at any time enjoyed preeminence, as measured by share of the popular vote or by seats in parliament or by both. If one bases the list on the 1968-1978 decade, it consists merely of Austria, West Berlin, France, Great Britain, Malta, Portugal, and Sweden. In most instances, this leftist hegemony has not been continuous—even in the more recent period. West Berlin, which has experienced uninterrupted leftist dominance throughout the postwar years, constitutes the prime exception. During the periods of leftist sway, moreover, the chief political force in most of these lands has been a non-Communist Socialist or Labor party. The SKP in Finland has overshadowed its local competitors at such times, and the PCF in France had always boasted a similar ascendancy until 1978. But of the remaining Communist parties, only the PCP in Portugal and the PCS in San Marino have even posed credible challenges to Socialist or Labor supremacy.

Although the Left has remained consistently in the minority elsewhere, in none of these portions of Western Europe has it ever suffered from such weakness as to render it an inconsequential force. However, the PCI in Italy and the AB in Iceland are the only two Communist parties in any countries here to have managed preeminence on the left at any time during the period since World War II. Both parties have now boasted such a position for better than two decades. In the other states, a Socialist or Labor party has always predominated; furthermore, in some instances additional non-Communist leftist parties have on occasion claimed second and even third spot. Recently, of the Communist parties in these countries, only the PCE in Spain, the Communist Party of Greece (KKE-Exterior), and the Communist Party of Luxemburg (PCL) have come close to passing muster as serious competitors of their prime local non-Communist rivals.

The extent to which the attitudes of non-Communist political forces have offered openings for the West European Communist parties to exploit has differed over the years.[27] Immediately after World War II, many non-Communist groups had relatively favorable images of their local Communist parties because of mutual cooperation in the antifascist resistance during 1941-1945, and there was also widespread recognition among non-Communists that most Communist parties had succeeded in building up their strength during the wartime years. As a consequence, Communists participated in the initial postwar governments of ten polities—Austria,

Belgium, Denmark, Finland, France, Iceland, Italy, Luxemburg, Norway, and San Marino. Indeed, only in Portugal and Spain, where authoritarian and rigidly anticommunist regimes held the reins of power, did Communists find themselves official outcasts.

The onset of the cold war in 1947-1948, however, drastically altered this general state of affairs. A combination of Communist takeovers in Eastern Europe, particularly the coup in Czechoslovakia in 1948, and Communist promotion of civil strife in a number of West European countries raised fears among non-Communists about Communist intentions. The show trials that took place in Eastern Europe prior to Josef Stalin's death in 1953, the rebellions in Poland and Hungary in 1956, and the bloody Soviet suppression of the Hungarian uprising merely served to reinforce these feelings. In such an atmosphere, it is hardly surprising that most West European Communist parties wound up isolated.

Only the Communist parties of Iceland, Italy, and San Marino managed to salvage something out of the debacle. Although the Icelandic party had to go into the opposition in 1947, it retained enough credibility as a national entity—because it operated in a context far removed from the Soviet Union and succeeded in keeping its distance from the Soviet party—to be invited to become a junior partner in a center-left coalition government in 1956. This government remained in office until 1958. In San Marino, a coalition of Socialists and Communists held the reins of power without interruption until 1957, and even after that the Socialists retained ties with the Communists for several years. Despite the fact that the Italian Communist Party had withdrawn from the government in 1947, the Socialist Party formed an alliance with it to contest the 1948 parliamentary elections. In ensuing elections, the Socialists ran a separate slate of candidates, but they continued to honor a unity-of-action agreement at the national level until 1957. Even then, Socialist-Communist cooperation was still the rule at the local level in many portions of the country.

The 1960s brought new circumstances that ultimately produced a far more complex situation. As the Sino-Soviet conflict heated up, it became increasingly apparent that the international communist movement was fragmenting. Furthermore, a number of West European Communist parties evinced a growing desire to assert their individuality by launching out on new courses, while others seemed content to follow traditional paths. The responses of non-Communist forces in Western Europe to this evolving state of affairs have varied, not only from country to country but also within the same country. To make matters even more complicated, there has been a proliferation of Communist parties in virtually every polity in the area, and non-Communists have tended to adopt differentiated attitudes toward those of local relevance.

Although the non-Communist Left in Western Europe has by no means exhibited unanimity on the issue, segments of it in a number of states have shown a willingness to contemplate some form of cooperation with at least the dominant Communist parties in local contexts. In certain instances, these elements have been merely individuals with ties to leftist parties; in other cases, they have held the leadership posts of their political organizations. Moreover, there has been considerable diversity in the degree of cooperation that they have envisioned.

Perhaps the greatest Communist opportunities stemming from the attitudes of the non-Communist Left have emerged in Finland, Italy, San Marino, and France. Here Socialist parties have advocated the inclusion of, respectively, the SKP (through its electoral front, the SKDL), the PCI, the PCS, and the PCF in coalition governments at the national level. In France, the Radicals of the Left have taken a position similar to that of the Socialists. However, the situation in France may have entered a state of flux in the wake of the March 1978 elections. The Socialists have officially attributed the Left's failure to win a legislative majority to the PCF's attacks on them before the elections, and at least certain elements of the Left Radicals seem to have become sufficiently disillusioned with the PCF to have lost any desire to participate in an alliance with it.

Yet openings worth mentioning have developed in several other places as well. In Iceland, the Organization of Liberals and Leftists in the early 1970s favored a coalition government embracing the AB. From 1970 to its ouster from power in 1976, the Social Democratic Party in Sweden at times solicited the parliamentary support of the Left Party—Communists (VPK). In Luxembourg, the Socialist Workers' Party in 1969 endorsed the formation of a municipal coalition government involving the Communist Party (CPL) in Esch-sur-Alzette, the country's second largest city. Although this move provoked a split in the Socialist Workers' Party in 1970, at least certain Socialist elements continued to back such an arrangement. In Norway, the Socialist People's Party and dissidents from the Labor Party sought the participation of the Communist Party (NKP) in an electoral alliance for the 1973 parliamentary elections, and they subsequently urged the NKP to become an element of the single party that they intended to establish. During the mid-1970s, the Social

Democratic Party in Switzerland has on occasion evinced a disposition to join forces with the Communists of the Labor Party (PdA) and/or the Progressive Organizations, Switzerland (POCH) to wage specific cantonal elections. In Greece, two social democratic parties— the Party of Socialist Initiative and the Movement of the Socialist Way —manifested a desire for an electoral coalition with the Communist Party of Greece "of the interior" (KKE-Interior) and the United Democratic Left (EDA) before the November 1977 parliamentary elections. Moreover, Andreas Papandreou and his Panhellenic Socialist Movement have proposed a united front of "democratic forces," which would encompass all three factions of the Greek Communist movement—the KKE-Exterior, the KKE-Interior, and the EDA—as well as the opposition parties of the Center. In Ireland, the Marxist wing of the Sinn Fein (which pushes for the immediate unification of all Ireland) has encouraged the Communist Party of Ireland (CPI) to work closely with it. The Socialist People's Party in Denmark has sanctioned some types of mutual undertakings with the Danish Communist Party (DKP) in the trade union movement. Individual members of the Socialist Party in Austria and the Labour Party in Great Britain have insisted on the wisdom of joint ventures with the Communist Party of Austria (KPÖ) and the Communist Party of Great Britain (CPGB), respectively, even though their own parties oppose such enterprises.

Two additional cases of a special nature should also be noted. Before the establishment of parliamentary democracy in Portugal and Spain in the latter half of the 1970s, the non-Communist opposition—composed mainly of leftist groups but including some centrist forces as well—tended to look upon the PCP and the PCE as potential allies against the authoritarian regimes in the two countries. In Portugal, there was even substantial support in the initial period after the April 1974 military coup for representation of the PCP in the new provisional government. But the flowering of democracy in the two states removed the raison d'être for these attitudes and brought other considerations to the fore. Accordingly, the openings available to the PCP and PCE decreased significantly.

As might be anticipated, the forces of the Center and the Right in Western Europe have by and large remained much more suspicious of local Communist parties than have leftist elements, and their perspectives have thus afforded the Communists far fewer bases for maneuver than have those of the Left. Nonetheless, there has not been a total lack of opportunities. In Iceland, the Progressive Party in the early 1970s deemed the AB worthy of participation in a center-left coalition government. In Finland, groups such as the Center (formerly the Agrarian) Party have favored the incorporation of the SKP (or, more precisely, the SKDL) into the ruling coalition. In Italy, the centrist Social Democrats and Republicans have recently adopted the same position with respect to the PCI. Although the Christian Democrats have not been willing to go so far, they have proved amenable to accepting PCI support in parliament in order to form a minority cabinet under their control. In Greece, Christian Democracy, a party of national-socialist inclinations, expressed a desire to form a coalition with the KKE-Interior and EDA for the November 1977 parliamentary elections; furthermore, Premier Konstantinos Karamanlis and his rightist New Democracy have spoken positively about the notion of cooperation with the KKE-Interior and EDA.

Self-identifications

Defining an identity has been simplest for the Maoist and Trotskyite parties in the area.[28] Nearly every country in Western Europe now has groups of both stripes, and with the fragmentation of the extreme Left since the early 1960s, there are a number of countries where several such parties exist. Some of these constitute groups that have split off from local Communist parties at various times over the years; others have formed de novo. For both types of parties, the critical commitment is to permanent revolution. In their eyes, parliamentary and electoral activity may be useful for propaganda purposes, but the triumph of socialism will inevitably require a resort to violent means. More important, they feel that the CPSU has betrayed the cause of world revolution for the sake of its own selfish national interests—by emphasizing the necessity to construct socialism in the USSR as a bulwark for the international communist movement, by endorsing the peaceful road to socialism, etc. Thus, they look to other mentors for their inspiration. The Trotskyite elements subscribe to Leon Trotsky's teachings that states in which a communist breakthrough has occurred can be protected against counterrevolutionary forces only by the triumph of the world revolution, and that the interests of the world revolution must take precedence over narrow national interests. Although the Maoists recognize the many differences between the political situation in Western Europe today and the situation Mao Tse-tung confronted during his rise to power and during his rule in China, they regard Mao as the prime defender of the world revolution in the post–World War II era; hence, they associate themselves with his global revolutionary vision. Both kinds of groups still retain a firm theoretical commitment to the Leninist concept of a disciplined elitist party that operates on the basis of "democratic centralism"; however, it should be noted that as far as discipline is concerned, their practice not infrequently belies their "principled" stand.

For the other Communist parties, the task by and large has proved relatively complicated. On the international front, for instance, they have felt called upon to decide whether to break off relations with the CPSU entirely, to insist on their right to adopt an independent posture while still retaining fraternal ties with the CPSU, or to accept the primacy of the CPSU in the world communist movement. With regard to domestic matters, they have had to assess the merits of the peaceful road to socialism, to determine the applicability of the Soviet model of socialism for their countries, and, if they have rejected the Soviet model as unsuitable, to articulate one of their own.

Since different combinations of answers to such dilemmas are possible, it is not surprising that one finds a variegated set of identifications. As of early 1978, the biggest group of parties falls into what might be termed the "orthodox Communist" mold. This group now includes the Communist parties of Austria (KPÖ), Belgium (PCB), Denmark (DKP), the Federal Republic of Germany (DKP), Ireland (CPI),[29] Luxembourg (PCL), Malta (CPM),[30] Portugal (PCP), Switzerland (PdA), and West Berlin (SEW). It likewise includes the largest party in Greece (the KKE-Exterior) and minority parties in Great Britain (the "New Communist Party"),[31] Iceland (the Organization of Icelandic Socialists, or SIS), Spain (the Spanish Communist Workers' Party, or PCOE), and Sweden (the Workers' Communist Party, or APK)—five countries where over the years disputes among the non-Maoist and non-Trotskyite Communist forces have led to formal ruptures and the establishment of separate national parties.

All these parties not only maintain relations with the CPSU and most other ruling parties but also defer to the USSR as the head of the international communist movement. However, the Austrian, Belgian, Danish, and Swiss parties have not always followed a straightforwardly Soviet line. All, for instance, denounced the invasion of Czechoslovakia by the Warsaw Pact nations in 1968—although the Austrian and Danish parties later backed off from this heresy, the former doing so after the expulsion of "autonomist" elements in 1970. The Belgian party has also shown a greater tendency through the years to be conciliatory toward the Chinese than Moscow has.

As regards domestic matters, all these parties today speak of charting "national paths to socialism" and endorse the peaceful, parliamentary road to power as the best available course under existing conditions in their countries. But in accordance with general Soviet disquisitions on the subject, they decline to rule out an ultimate resort to force. They agree with Moscow that whether the transition to socialism takes place peacefully will depend in the final analysis on the attitudes and responses of "counterrevolutionary" forces. Moreover, all these parties clearly accept the Soviet model of socialism as the one to be emulated when the revolution that they see as inevitable over the long term comes about, although the Belgian party in early 1978 did commence to criticize the USSR's treatment of dissidents. All, too, subscribe to Leninist norms for party structure and operation.

Despite the basically pro-Soviet orientations of these parties, it would be a great error to view them as nothing more than surrogates of the CPSU. However circumscribed their options may have been, these parties have quite plainly exercised conscious choice in delineating their identities. The factional fights that most of them have carried on with dissidents both within and outside their ranks attest that they could have adopted a self-image different from the one they project today. The reasons that they have not done so, of course, are varied and complex. These include such considerations as the character of their rank-and-file memberships and their domestic constituencies, the nature of the competition they confront within their own individual political contexts, and the local political value they may derive from association with the global power of the Soviet Union. But the essential point is that they have weighed these considerations in defining their identities—they have not merely succumbed to coercion.

Six of the remaining parties may be described as "autonomist, revisionist" entities. This group includes the PCF in France, the PCI in Italy, the PCS in San Marino, and the dominant Communist parties in Great Britain (CPGB), Spain (PCE), and Sweden (VPK). The San Marino party is really an offshoot, or branch, of the Italian party, so one can for all practical purposes speak of a total of five.

These parties share two elements of self-perception. First, although they believe in the value of links with fraternal Communist parties, they regard themselves as sovereign bodies with the right to make their own decisions on matters of relevance to them without interference from other parties, especially from the CPSU. Second, denying the validity of any attempts to distill a universal model from Soviet experience, they view themselves as the creative appliers of

Marxist-Leninist precepts to the realities and traditions of their own local politics and societies. Not all segments of the five parties, of course, endorse such positions, for each party has its factions. Nevertheless, these positions do reflect the outlooks of the majority forces in the parties, particularly at the leadership level.

On other matters, however, there are variations in emphasis and nuance among the five. For example, the PCE clearly makes the strongest effort to dissociate itself from the USSR, though it has thus far eschewed a formal break with Moscow. Party spokesmen, notably Secretary-General Santiago Carrillo, have talked openly about the absence of democracy in the Soviet Union and have contrasted "totalitarian" socialism in the East with their own version of socialism. At the other end of the spectrum, the PCF and PCI have evinced the greatest caution in this regard. Both have condemned Moscow's treatment of dissidents, but both have also been selective in their criticisms, and neither has embarked on any full-blown examination of the faults of the current Soviet regime. The CPGB and VPK fall between these two poles, with the former closer to the Spanish position and the latter closer to the French and Italian position.

As for foreign policy more generally, the Italian, Spanish, and French parties show a distinctly more nationalistic bent than do the British or Swedish parties. For instance, the Italian party has long upheld Italian participation in the European Economic Community (EEC), and it has recently argued against Italian withdrawal from NATO without commensurate changes in the Warsaw Pact forces. The Spanish party has urged its country's entry into the EEC and has indicated that it would not challenge U.S. bases in Spain as long as Europe remained divided into two power blocs. The French party deplores the attempts of President Giscard d'Estaing to move away from some of the Gaullist postures in foreign affairs—and roundly chastises Moscow for its benign attitude with respect to these "deviations." It should be underscored, however, that the foreign policy positions of all five parties do not differ greatly from those of the USSR.

Although all these parties see themselves as carrying forward the Leninist tradition—in fact if not necessarily in label—the Swedish party has appeared the most committed to a "progressive" interpretation of that heritage. Indeed, the statutes it adopted in 1967 loosened up its operations to an extent that raised fears among hard-line party members that it would soon lose all semblance of a Leninist body, but a subsequent radicalization of its leading elements prevented further erosion of this nature. How the splintering off of the pro-Soviet faction in the spring of 1977 will affect the situation remains unclear even in early 1978. The French party's concept of internal life, by contrast, still diverges little from Stalinist norms. The perspectives of the Spanish and Italian parties—particularly the former—seem to lie toward the Swedish end of the continuum, and those of the British party, toward the French end.

In the realm of domestic politics, the PCE shows the greatest dedication to the pursuit of a course rooted in Western liberal traditions and time-honored values, although even its vision of the future pluralist, socialist society contains distinct circumscriptions on political rights for nonsocialists. No doubt the Spanish Communists' need to validate their "democratic" credentials to ensure their legal participation in the political life of post-Franco Spain has figured in their behavior, but the statements and actions of at least the party secretary-general suggest that it cannot be ascribed wholly to tactics or opportunism. The PCI approaches the Spanish party in terms of zeal in this area, and the Swedish party follows close behind. In the first case, present attitudes are the product of more than twenty years of evolution in outlook; in the second, their origins date from at least the mid-1960s. The French and British parties have thus far displayed the least enthusiasm about the merits of such a path. Neither, for instance, endorsed it even equivocally until the mid-1970s.

Three parties—the largest group in Iceland (AB) and the two minority parties in Greece (KKE-Interior and EDA)—fit into a category best labeled "national Communist." None of them maintain formal ties with the CPSU, and none of them took part in the Conference of European Communist Parties in June 1976, though the Icelandic party had on previous occasions sent "observers" to some gatherings of the world communist movement. For the AB and the EDA, this standoffishness is clearly a matter of principle. As far as the KKE-Interior is concerned, it derives from more complicated considerations. The party has contacts with a few other Communist parties such as the PCI in Italy and the PCE in Spain and might welcome the broad international recognition that ties with the CPSU and the world communist movement would entail; but Moscow views the rival orthodox Communist party, the KKE-Exterior, as the only legitimate Communist group in the country, and it has not appeared at all disposed to alter that position. Under such circumstances, a "national" stance makes a virtue of necessity and at the same time prevents any blurring of the line between the KKE-Interior and KKE-

Exterior on domestic matters. On other issues of foreign policy, the AB, KKE-Interior, and EDA all likewise assume a highly nationalistic posture. In the case of the Icelandic party, this has been most evident in its vociferous backing of a fishing limit zone of 200 miles around the country; in the case of the Greek parties, it has been manifest particularly in their proposal for the formation of a "government of national unity" to meet the threat that many Greeks feel Turkey has posed in recent years.

The domestic "national roads" of the three parties, as one might expect, differ markedly. Fundamentally, the cleavage is between the Icelandic party on one hand and the Greek parties on the other. The Icelandic party describes itself as a leftist alliance on a Marxist basis, and it has long adhered to that basic stance. Furthermore, it is in actuality an electoral front that, though under Communist domination, contains elements not essentially Communist in outlook. The commitment of its Communist component to alliances has also rendered the party receptive to cooperation with other diverse political forces for purposes of forming a government. Although the party favors state ownership of industry and other major economic ventures, it by and large plays down the collectivist elements of Marxist-Leninist doctrine, and it focuses its attention on bread-and-butter social and economic issues.

Although the EDA in Greece bears at least a superficial resemblance to the AB, both the EDA and the KKE (Interior) retain much more of a Leninist flavor than does their Icelandic counterpart—even though the two Greek parties stress the "democratic" side of "democratic centralism" in their statements. Both seem to opt, too, for the "Westernization" of Greece, along the lines of the models currently being set forth by Italian, French, and Spanish Communists, from whom the parties derive much of their intellectual inspiration. Although both joined with the KKE-Exterior in a United Left coalition for the 1974 parliamentary elections (the first postwar balloting in which Communists were allowed to run openly as Communists and not as candidates of a front organization), they followed a different course for the November 1977 elections. They formed an alliance—known as the Alliance of Progressive and Leftist Forces—with two small social democratic parties and a national-socialist party. Furthermore, the two parties now advocate a coalition with the conservative New Democracy party of Prime Minister Konstantinos Karamanlis and the establishment of what they call a "government of national unity."

Five parties—the Communist parties of the Netherlands (CPN)

and Norway (NKP); the Party of Proletarian Unity (PDUP) and the Proletarian Democracy (PD) in Italy; and the Progressive Organizations, Switzerland (POCH)—are so highly idiosyncratic as to defy easy classification. For more than a decade, from 1964 to 1975, the Dutch party roundly denounced the CPSU leadership as revisionists and insisted on pursuing its own autonomous course. In keeping with its stance, it maintained almost no contacts whatsoever with other Communist parties, including the CPSU, and it sharply criticized many aspects of Soviet behavior—from the USSR's willingness to accept a limited détente with the West to Moscow's expulsion of the dissident writer, Aleksandr Solzhenitsyn. Nonetheless, its posture on a number of critical foreign policy issues coincided with that of the Soviet Union. For instance, it advocated the dissolution of NATO and a status of neutrality for the Netherlands, and it urged the country to withdraw from the EEC because of that body's domination by "monopoly capitalism." With respect to domestic affairs, it proposed the formation of an alliance of all socialist and progressive forces as a prelude to the installation of a "truly progressive" government that would launch the country on its own distinctive path to socialism. At the same time, the party did not depart from Leninist prescriptions regarding party organization and modus operandi. It continued to uphold "democratic centralism" and the retention of its own integrity within any political alliance or coalition.

Beginning in 1975, the Dutch party began to modify its self-image somewhat. It did not abandon its claims to autonomy, but it professed no longer to see its position and that of the CPSU as essentially antithetical to each other. Indeed, it now stressed their elements of commonality. In accordance with such a line, it toned down its critiques of Soviet policy, moved to normalize relations with the Soviet party, and attended the June 1976 conference of European Communist parties as a full-fledged participant. The shift of view's impact in the domestic sphere was far less pronounced. Although the party eschewed disparaging comments about the USSR's internal policies, it held staunchly to the primacy of Dutch circumstances as the basis for determining its own domestic course.

There is now a serious question, however, as to whether these modifications will endure. In the national parliamentary elections of May 1977, the party experienced a major setback, with its share of the popular vote falling from 4.5 percent in the last election to 1.73 percent this time and with its seats in parliament dropping correspondingly from seven to two.[32] This setback has produced ferment within the CPN, including a feeling by some that the weakening of the party's nationalistic stance had a lot to do with the disaster.

Since the early 1960s, the Norwegian party has stoutly defended its right to conduct its affairs according to its own assessments of its best interests and has refused to treat the USSR as the leader of the international communist movement. With respect to specific issues of foreign policy, it has been highly critical of Soviet efforts to force parties to take sides in the Sino-Soviet dispute and of the Soviet invasion of Czechoslovakia. On questions where its positions have coincided with those of Moscow—for instance, opposition to Norwegian entry into the EEC—the similarity has reflected common perspectives, not Soviet influence.

As for domestic politics, the outlook of the NKP has undergone major change in recent years. During the late 1960s and early 1970s, the party increasingly took a "revisionist" stance and opened up lines of communication with elements of the non-Communist Left in the country, although it maintained an overall commitment to the Leninist model of party organization. After a major intra-party fight in 1975, however, the "revisionist" forces that had been leading the party found their authority wrested from them, and many of them left the organization. Thus, the NKP has now returned to orthodoxy in its domestic political line and reaffirmed its view of party life. That is, it adheres closely to the Soviet model as the harbinger of Norway's future, and it upholds Leninist party norms.

Although a party has existed under the PDUP label since 1972 in Italy, it assumed its present character in 1977 as a result of a split in its ranks. The original party came into being as a union of elements of the disbanded Socialist Party of Proletarian Unity (PSIUP) and a group associated with the publication *Il Manifesto* who had been expelled from the PCI in 1969 for attacking the PCI's "reformist" policies. From the outset, this body was an uneasy alliance of forces, and in 1977 the vast majority of the former PSIUP contingent broke away from it, leaving it largely in the hands of the *Manifesto* faction.

In keeping with the backgrounds of its members, the PDUP espouses a militant political line. Although it engages in parliamentary activity and holds four seats in Italy's House of Deputies, it seriously questions the viability of a peaceful, parliamentary road to power. For this reason, it criticizes both the PCI and the Soviet Union. Furthermore, it displays a highly nationalistic bent and eschews any kind of international ties, although its foreign policy stances—to the extent that it defines any—tend to coincide with those of the Soviet

Union. Insofar as it articulates a vision of the kind of society toward which it is striving, this resembles Soviet reality more than it does the pluralistic model that the PCI endorses. By and large, the party operates as a loose association of individuals and groups and has little formal structure. What institutional coherence it boasts derives from *Il Manifesto* and the parliamentary caucus.

The DP emerged in its present form only in 1977. But it represents an amalgamation of elements with much longer histories, and these histories have much to do with the party's current image of itself. Basically, the party joins two groups—Vittorio Foa's faction of the original PDUP and the Workers Vanguard (AO). The first group initially belonged to the Italian Socialist Party (PSI) and then entered the ranks of the PSIUP when the latter split off from the PSI in 1963 over the PSI's participation in a coalition government with the centrist Christian Democrats. After the PSIUP dissolved in July 1972, the bulk of its members went into the "autonomist, revisionist" PCI, some others returned to the PSI, but the rest—essentially Foa and his followers—coalesced with the *Manifesto* group to form the PDUP. In 1977, Foa and his supporters deserted the PDUP and, in conjunction with the AO, established the DP. The AO, founded in 1968 by a number of Trotskyite labor organizers, had been one of the PDUP's partners in a leftist coalition set up to wage the 1976 parliamentary elections.

Like the PDUP, the DP preaches militancy. Although it carries on electoral campaigns and even has two seats in the House of Deputies, it expresses doubt about the possibility that a transition to socialism will take place by peaceful, parliamentary means. It therefore denounces both the PCI and the USSR for helping to create illusions on this score. On the whole, the DP chooses to devote its energies to national domestic matters. What foreign policy positions it articulates have much in common with those of the Soviet Union; however, it maintains no discernible links with forces abroad. In calling for "authentic democracy," it looks toward the creation of a society dominated by "the proletariat" and offering little scope for action by other social elements. At the same time, it speaks favorably of workers' self-management. As for internal party life, the very heterogeneity of its makeup works against an extensive hierarchy and a high degree of discipline. However, the DP does have a substantial apparatus in the labor movement in certain areas of Italy.

The POCH also came into existence quite recently, and its origins have likewise colored the way in which it views itself. It was established in 1972 by a congress of local and cantonal groups, the oldest of which dated from 1968. These groups, made up essentially of young people, had grown dissatisfied with the leadership of the orthodox Communist party of Switzerland, which they regarded as overcautious and rigid. They advocated, in contrast, a militant posture, although they never seem to have rejected the possibility of attaining power by the parliamentary road.

Since its founding, the party has focused almost entirely on local, regional, and national questions—in that order. It has dealt with foreign policy issues only marginally. To the extent that it has taken any foreign policy stances, these conform basically to Soviet positions, but it maintains no ties or formal affiliations with the CPSU. Furthermore, it has refused either to endorse or condemn the so-called "Eurocommunist" policies of the "autonomist, revisionist" Communist parties, notably the Italian, French, and Spanish parties. It has maintained that "Eurocommunism" is a tactical matter, one that concerns overage, top-heavy parties.

In line with its emphasis on the local milieu, the party remains a rather loosely coordinated series of groups with bases in particular cities and cantons. It lacks any real national structure or apparatus. At the same time, it has managed to generate pressure on a countrywide basis for the enactment of at least certain measures that it has deemed "progressive."

The last party, the Finnish Communist Party, suffers from such pronounced factionalism at the moment that it can only be described as having a split identity. It has been dominated since the mid-1960s by elements who, though they support fraternal ties with the CPSU, insist on defining and pursuing their own policies. Not only have they criticized some of Moscow's actions in the international sphere—particularly the Warsaw Pact invasion of Czechoslovakia in 1968—but they have also charted a "reformist" course in internal politics, indicating, among other things, a willingness to accept political pluralism under socialism and a desire to place more emphasis on the "democratic" aspect of "democratic centralism" than on the "centralization" aspect. However, a substantial group within the party retains an orthodox communist orientation. This group accords the Soviet Union recognition as the leader of the international communist movement, and although it accepts the peaceful road to power as the only viable alternative in Finland at present, it regards the Soviet model of socialism as the genuine one and therefore the one that Finland must eventually adopt.

Strategies

The formulation of a political strategy has required the Communist parties of Western Europe to address a host of specific questions, but these have clustered around two fundamental issues. The first is what road to power one should pursue. All the parties remain committed to radical transformation of the societies and polities in which they operate. To carry out such a transformation, however, the parties must acquire power in some way. Hence, how to do so becomes a key matter. The second issue is with whom one should ally. None of the parties at present have enough strength to assume power on their own. Consequently, each must determine whether to wage its battle in "splendid isolation" or to seek allies, and if it opts for the latter course, it must identify its desired collaborators and define the terms of cooperation.

On both these broad issues, the West European Communist parties as of early 1978 manifest a diversity of positions.[33] With respect to the path to power, the Maoist and Trotskyite groups hold that it cannot be peaceful—the "bourgeoisie" will never relinquish control voluntarily, so it is necessary to take power by force. To the extent that these parties engage in parliamentary political activities, they do so to spread their revolutionary message and to radicalize the populace. There are, however, some differences in emphasis between these groups. All of them adhere to the principle of violent revolution, but only a few maintain that violent undertakings are the proper course at the moment. Some of this minority argue that the preconditions for revolutionary transformation already exist; others contend that terrorist acts help to create such preconditions. These groups are to be found essentially in Spain (e.g., certain of the Basque separatist factions of Euzkadi ta Askatizuna, the Grupo de Resistencia Antifascista de Mayo), Portugal (the Movimento Reorganizativo do Partido do Proletariado, the Partido Revolucionario do Prole- tarido—Brigadas Revolucionarias), Italy (the Red Brigades, the Armed Proletarian Nuclei), and Germany (the Spartacus League, the Second June Movement, the Revolutionary Cell). Most of the Maoist and Trotskyite groups, in contrast, insist that the populace is not yet sufficiently awakened to make conditions ripe for revolution and that their major effort must be directed at remedying this situation.

All the rest of the parties accept the proposition that it is possible to attain power by nonviolent means, and they acknowledge that the parliamentary road represents the concrete way to achieve this end in current West European circumstances. But beyond this point disagreements crop up.

The orthodox Communist parties cling to the notion that the parliamentary road is merely the best available path in light of prevailing conditions in Western Europe—not the only legitimate path. If the "bourgeoisie" refuses to adhere to democratic procedures and seeks to prevent Communists from taking power, these parties maintain, "counterviolence" may prove necessary. In effect, then, their commitment to the parliamentary road is carefully hedged so as to preserve all options.

By and large, the maverick parties—the CPN in the Netherlands, the NKP in Norway, the PDUP and the DP in Italy, and the POCH in Switzerland—adopt the same stance as the orthodox Communist parties. However, the Italian and Swiss groups exhibit a stronger inclination toward militancy than do the orthodox parties or the Dutch and Norwegian parties. That is, they seem less disposed to put their faith in the ultimate efficacies of the parliamentary path than do their orthodox and maverick counterparts.

The six "autonomous, revisionist" parties (including the San Marino party), the three "national Communist" parties, and at least the dominant wing of the "schizophrenic" Finnish party formally endorse the parliamentary path as *the* legitimate path to power in Western Europe. At the same time, they hold divergent views about what restraints this position imposes on them once they assume power. The PCF stands at one extreme on this issue. Although it has verbally accepted the principle of alternation of socialist and nonsocialist forces in the government, it has also underlined the importance of moving swiftly to render "the revolution" irreversible. Moreover, once "the revolution" is irreversible, it would greatly restrict the nonsocialist forces' freedom for maneuver. In short, it foresees fairly rapid curtailment of political liberties.

The PCI provides the most articulate statement of the opposite extreme. Drawing a lesson from the Chilean experience under Salvadore Allende, the PCI contends that the attainment of power by a bare numerical majority does not insure the irreversibility of "the revolution." That can only come about when the great bulk of the population agrees that the implementation of socialism is the desirable course, and the emergence of such a consensus will require a gradualist approach and much effort at building confidence. In line with this position, the party not only explicitly accepts the principle of alternation of socialist and nonsocialist forces in government, but also urges governmental cooperation between socialist and non-socialist parties. Furthermore, it grants the need for retaining democratic political rights unfettered long after acquiring authority. Thus, although it would undoubtedly find even a temporary loss of power distasteful, it considers such a possibility preferable to increased polarization of the country, perhaps leading to a "counter-revolutionary" coup.

It should be pointed out that this divergence between the two parties concerns methods of moving toward socialism and not necessarily the shape of the future socialist society. Both anticipate a major restructuring of social and political life in their countries, and there are indications that each believes this will ultimately bring about limitations on the political rights of at least some elements of the population. Just how those limitations might compare in the two cases remains unclear at the moment—primarily because the Italian party, arguing the inevitability of a lengthy transition period, has been rather vague on the subject.

On balance, the rest of the parties would appear to fall toward the Italian, rather than the French, end of the spectrum. The CPGB has not defined its position with great precision—probably because the chance that it might acquire a share of power in the foreseeable future has seemed so remote. However, the others have left little room for speculation about their perspectives. Indeed, the "national Communist" Icelandic party and the "schizophrenic" Finnish party have in recent years provided concrete demonstrations of their views by participating in governmental majorities and then going into the opposition when political tides shifted.

On the issue of allies, several parties take a "principled," sectarian stand. That is, they do not seek collaboration with any other groups but prefer to operate on their own to advance their individual causes. This category includes most Maoist and Trotskyite groups and the orthodox parties of Austria, Great Britain, and Sweden. It may encompass the orthodox groups in Malta and Spain as well, but as of early 1978 there is not enough information available on either to permit a definitive judgment.

Although the bulk of Maoist and Trotskyite groups have preferred "splendid isolation" to coordinated action, a few have demonstrated a willingness to collaborate with one another or even with other groups that espouse ultraleftist views. For example, two French Trotskyite parties—Lutte Ouvrière and Ligue Communiste—joined forces to contest the 1973 parliamentary elections in France. The basis of such cooperation has been agreement on general revolutionary goals, and this has in turn imposed limits on what parties constitute suitable allies. In short, these groups have demonstrated no interest in cooperation with those not of a similar revolutionary persuasion.

The two maverick parties in Italy and the maverick party in Switzerland have taken a highly idiosyncratic position with regard to alliances. Since the PDUP and DP in Italy emerged in their present forms in 1977, they have both adhered to the line endorsed by their PDUP forebear, although the commitment of the rump PDUP has tended to be somewhat stronger than that of the DP. The original urged a broad alliance of the Left including even the Socialist Party, but it had constant disagreements with both the PCI and the Socialist Party over goals and tactics. Hence, at the national level the PDUP chose to work essentially with other elements of the extreme Left. For example, it waged the 1976 parliamentary elections in coalition with three such groups. From 1975 on, however, the PDUP cooperated with the PCI and the Socialists to form Left local governments in a few specific places. The POCH in Switzerland has followed a similar "two-level" course.

Of the remaining parties, most advocate an alliance of all local socialist forces except the Maoists and Trotskyites. In some cases, this means merely the Communists and the Social Democrats; in others, it may involve three parties, or even more. Among those Communist parties that favor such an alliance are the orthodox parties of Denmark, West Germany, West Berlin, Greece, Ireland, Luxemburg, Portugal, and Switzerland; the "autonomist, revisionist" parties in Great Britain, Spain, and Sweden; and the maverick Norwegian party. It should be noted, however, that the splits in the British and Swedish parties in 1977 have made the rump organizations in practice reluctant to work closely with the new orthodox groups as well as with Maoist and Trotskyite groups. Moreover, the "autonomist, revisionist" party in Spain, for essentially tactical reasons, has evinced a willingness to collaborate with portions of the non-socialist Center in addition to various socialist groups on a number of matters.

This group of Communist parties favors cooperation with the aim of "building socialism." Although they are acutely aware that definitions of "socialism" differ, they believe that sufficient elements of common purpose exist to hammer out a program that will serve as a basis for united action for at least a temporary period. However, they tend to set minimum criteria that others must meet, rather than to negotiate the terms of collaboration from scratch, for they seem more interested in drawing other parties toward them than in moving toward these parties.

Three parties—the orthodox Belgian, the maverick Dutch, and the "autonomist, revisionist" French parties—champion an alliance of the Left, embracing all "progressive" elements, nonsocialist as well as socialist. All exclude the Maoists and Trotskyites from the pale of acceptability in this regard, but there is some variation in outlook among the three with respect to desirable collaborators. All urge the inclusion of the local Socialist or Labor party, but the Belgian and Dutch parties want the alliance to encompass somewhat different nonsocialist forces than does the French party. The former court the more left-wing elements in the generally conservative Catholic parties in their countries; the latter concentrates on left-wing secular groups such as the Left Radicals.

As these three parties see things, the goal of cooperation is the establishment of an "advanced democracy," to use the French formulation. This implies the implementation of major structural reforms in the economy, the society, and the polity, but it does not mean the dawn of socialism. Commitment to the course of reform serves as the basis for incorporation into the alliance. However, the three parties recognize that the substantial diversity of forces involved ensures differing opinions on what the nature of the reforms should be, and they have shown some willingness to negotiate and compromise on an immediate reform program—as long as the measures do not fall short of the threshold that they feel must be passed to open the way for a future advance to socialism. The PCF has been particularly insistent on such a proviso. Despite the rigidity on this point, the general terms of collaboration that these parties define tend to be much less stringent than the terms that those parties who seek a straightforward "socialist" alliance lay down.

The "schizophrenic" Finnish party and the "national Communist" party of Iceland opt for a center-left coalition in some form. Each bans Maoist and Trotskyite elements from such an alliance, and each strives to give the grouping as leftist a coloration as possible. Yet in most respects both seem to be relatively pragmatic with regard to the composition of the coalition. Indeed, the Finnish party has served in the government with varying sets of parties at different times.

In both cases, the terms of cooperation that the Communists establish have a leftist orientation but fall short of anything like a commitment to sweeping structural reforms. As a matter of fact, they by and large involve specific issues rather than a general, comprehensive program. This approach, of course, ties in closely with the high degree of pragmatism that the parties display in respect to the makeup of the alliance.

The "autonomist, revisionist" parties of Italy and San Marino and the "national Communist" parties of Greece endorse a "national coalition." In Italy, this would include the six "antifascist" parties of the "constitutional arc"—the Communists, the Socialists, the Social Democrats, the Christian Democrats, the Liberals, and the Republicans. Of these, of course, the Communists and Christian Democrats would be the most important. In San Marino, the collaboration would also encompass all parties but those of the extreme Left and the extreme Right, although there would be somewhat fewer of them. Here, too, the Communists and Christian Democrats would constitute the pillars of the alliance. In Greece, the situation is a bit more complicated. The KKE-Interior and EDA speak of a "national coalition," and they actually entered into an electoral alliance with two minor social democratic parties and a small national-socialist one for the November 1977 balloting for parliament. But they seem most concerned about establishing cooperation with the conservative New Democracy party of Prime Minister Konstantinos Karamanlis. Indeed, they have engaged in fairly bitter polemics with the orthodox Communist party on a whole range of issues, and they have quarreled with Andreas Papandreou's Panhellenic Socialist Movement over their flirtations with Karamanlis and his supporters.

Participation in the coalitions that these four parties seek to put together requires agreement only on fundamental steps to deal with certain overriding national problems. In the cases of Italy and San Marino, these have to do with the economic and social crises in which the two lands have found themselves in recent years as a result of the impact of modernization, the increase in international oil prices, the world economic recession, inefficient state bureaucracies, and a host of other related considerations. As for Greece, the critical issue is the persistent conflict between Greece and Turkey since the Turks invaded Cyprus in 1974. The conditions of alliance that these parties propose, then, represent the least demanding that any of the parties set.

Comparison of the Parties' Roles

As pointed out at the beginning of this essay, the mix of opportunities, self-identification, and strategy differs so much from Communist party to Communist party in Western Europe that the role of each party in its individual political system is to a substantial degree unique. Nonetheless, one can discern some commonalities or broad patterns with respect to specific aspects of the parties' roles. These have to do with the contributions that the parties make to the functioning of the particular political systems in which they operate and the influence that they exercise within those systems.[34]

As regards the former, it can be argued, first, that today virtually all the parties except the Maoist and Trotskyite groups that resort to violent undertakings act as legitimators of their local political systems.[35] The acceptance of legal status and visible efforts to carry on political work within the confines of an existing system—whatever a party's long-range intentions vis-à-vis that system—lend weight to claims that the system can be altered and is not so rigid and oppressive that it must be entirely dismantled. And with the extension of parliamentary democracy to the whole of Western Europe in recent years, there are only a few nonterrorist Communist groups in scattered places that do not enjoy such a status and engage in such work.

To be sure, the degree to which these parties serve as legitimators of their individual systems varies. For example, those Maoist and Trotskyite parties that preach violence, even though they do not practice it at the moment, do not have the legitimating force of the orthodox and maverick parties, which acknowledge the possibility that a transition to socialism may take place by the parliamentary road. By the same token, the orthodox and maverick parties exert less legitimating impact than the "autonomist, revisionist" and "national Communist" parties, which endorse the parliamentary road as the only genuine path to socialism in Western Europe. Since the 1960s, it should be underscored, the number of parties in the last two categories has risen appreciably.

Second, the great bulk of the parties perform a "tribune" function for at least segments of the populations of their countries. The "national Communist" party of Iceland; the "autonomist, revisionist" parties of Italy, France, and San Marino; and the orthodox party of Portugal—all boast sizable representations in their local parliaments and labor assiduously to defend the interests of their constituencies. In addition, the "national Communist" parties in Greece; the "autonomist, revisionist" parties in Spain and Sweden; the maverick parties in Italy, the Netherlands, and Switzerland; the orthodox parties in Belgium, Greece, Luxembourg, Denmark, and Switzerland; and even a few Maoist and Trotskyite groups have a small number of delegates in their individual parliaments; they, too, display great zealousness on behalf of their supporters. The orthodox parties of Austria and West Germany hold no seats in their national parliamentary bodies, but they do control some seats on a number of municipal councils in their countries. These afford the two parties the opportunity to serve as spokesmen for elements of the populace on, at minimum, matters of parochial concern. Although lacking any sort of governmental representation, the "autonomist, revisionist" British group does exercise a limited "tribune" role through its strong positions in certain trade unions. For the rest of the parties, the link between their activities and an identifiable popular base is so tenuous as to be insignificant. However, only the maverick Norwegian party; the orthodox parties of West Berlin, Great Britain, Iceland, Ireland, Malta, and Spain; and the vast majority of Maoist and Trotskyite groups belong in this category.

Third, all the parties provide a radical critique of the political systems in which they operate. In this sense, they help to insure constant reexamination of the tenets of the system and to generate pressure to correct deficiencies and inequities. Some parties, however, have proved more effective in this "opposition" role than others. For many years, for example, the dominant Communist parties in Italy, France, San Marino, Iceland, and Finland have been the chief critics—regardless of whether they have had some form of governmental responsibility or not—of their local political systems, and their clout in their individual political contexts has caused others to pay attention to what they say, if for no other reason than to find ways to weaken their popular appeal. Although the PCF lost its preminence as critic in the March 1978 French elections, it still runs a close second to the local Socialist Party in this regard. With the establishment of parliamentary democracy in Portugal, the orthodox Communist party there has come to join the select group of main critics. The "autonomist, revisionist" party in Spain aspired to do the same, but the results of the country's first national elections in forty-one years in June 1977 dashed its hopes in this respect. It emerged as a decidedly secondary force to the Socialist Workers' Party, which still views itself as a revolutionary Marxist party and employs such a rhetoric. All the rest of the parties have more or less functioned from the sidelines of the political arena. Either they have found themselves overshadowed by other radical forces, or they have lacked sufficient political weight to command much of a hearing.

In terms of influence, the West European Communist parties at present fall into four different groups. One—numerically the largest —operates on the fringes of the local systems and has only a marginal impact within them. To the extent that these parties affect domestic politics, they do so through such means as the assassination of a national political figure, a campaign in a municipal council for more housing for workers, agitation for restructuring institutions of higher education, etc. This group includes all the Maoist and Trotskyite parties; the orthodox parties of Austria, Belgium, Denmark, West Germany, West Berlin, Great Britain, Greece, Iceland, Ireland, Malta, Sweden, and Switzerland; the maverick parties of Italy, the Netherlands, Norway, and Sweden; the "autonomist, revisionist" party of Sweden; and the "national Communist" parties of Greece. Perhaps equally important, this group has for many years—or at least since the parties came into being—encompassed all the lot except the Swedish "autonomist, revisionist" entity.

The second category of parties lacks a sufficient mass base to give it any real political clout, but it exercises some influence on national politics because it holds consequential positions in certain social and political institutions. In early 1978, this category consists of the "autonomist, revisionist" party in Great Britain and the orthodox party in Luxembourg. From 1970 to 1976, however, it also embraced the "autonomous, revisionist" party in Sweden. The British party falls into this classification as a result of its strength in the trade unions. Its leaders have figured prominently in all the union-government confrontations of recent years. The foundations of the Luxembourg party's strength lie in the trade unions and in municipal government. A member of the party secretariat, for example, serves as mayor of Esch-sur-Alzette, the second largest city in the country. Before the defeat of the ruling Social Democratic Party in the 1976 parliamentary elections, the "autonomous, revisionist" Communist party in Sweden for six years held the balance of power in the Riksdag between the government and the more conservative opposition. Social Democratic dependence on Communist votes was at its height during the 1973-1976 period.

The third set of parties functions at center stage in the national political drama and helps to shape the fundamental dynamics of national political life. All these parties enjoy a substantial amount of popular support, and this backing gets translated into at least a fair number of seats in parliament. The parties also wield influence in other important social and political institutions—trade unions, neighborhood and professional organizations, regional and munici-pal governments, etc. In some cases, they even operate, or at least have operated, in alliance with other forces in the local political spectrum, thus enhancing their overall clout. As of early 1978, this group embraces the "national Communist" party in Iceland; the "auto-nomist, revisionist" parties in France, Spain, and San Marino; and the orthodox party in Portugal. Until 1976, it included the "autonomist, revisionist" party in Italy as well, and from time to time in the last few years it has encompassed the "schizophrenic" party in Finland too.

The final category of parties has some direct say about the nature of governmental policies, although it does not enjoy unchallenged sway over the government. These parties belong to ruling coalitions of either a de facto or de jure sort, but they do not constitute the dominant elements within the coalitions. As of early 1978, the "autonomist, revisionist" party in Italy provides the critical backing that keeps a Christian Democratic minority government in office, and gets consulted about proposed governmental initiatives; however, it remains outside the cabinet and bears no formal responsibility for governmental undertakings. In a somewhat different situation, the Finnish party has seats in the cabinet yet constitutes a junior partner of the Social Democrats. At the moment, this category comprises just the Italian and Finnish parties. In the early 1970s, however, it also took in the "national Communist" party in Iceland, and if one goes back to the late 1950s, the present "autonomous, revisionist" party of San Marino once qualified for inclusion in it.

Two aspects of the foregoing analysis deserve particular emphasis. To begin with, all the kinds of systemic contributions and all the influence described presuppose the existence of democratic, parliamentary political systems. It is such systems that have afforded the local Communist parties the chance to operate openly and that have at the same time established "rules of the game" to which the parties have responded in one way or another. This concrete linkage between roles and democratic, parliamentary systems has several important corollaries. On the one hand, it is a major distortion to speak of a distinctive form of European communism—or, to use the currently fashionable label, Eurocommunism. What distinguishes West European communism from many other forms of communism today is its specific political setting and the impact that this setting has had on the parties concerned. But neither is unique to West European countries. One can find comparable contexts and effects on Communist parties in other states—Japan and Venezuela, for example. By the same token, some West European countries— notably Portugal, Spain, and Greece—lack strong traditions of democratic, parliamentary rule; hence, the present political sysems in these countries can hardly be represented as outgrowths of some distinctly "European" impulse. On the other hand, the disappearance of a democratic, parliamentary system in any West European country would almost inevitably bring profound changes in the roles of the Communist parties there. What the precise nature of those changes would be, of course, would depend heavily on the character of the systems that emerged.

Second, although the systemic contributions and influence of the parties have undergone change—especially in recent years—the change involved has been evolutionary and incremental, not swift and dramatic. No party, for instance, has moved from perpetrator of violence to strong legitimator of its local political system, or vice versa, during the entire postwar period. Similarly, no party has captured popular imaginations to the point where it has risen from oblivion to national prominence in just a few brief years; nor has one suffered a precipitous decline in fortunes during at least the last two decades.

Prospects

Thus far, our discussion has treated the existing political systems in Western Europe more or less as "givens." In turning now to a brief consideration of the future outlook with regard to the roles of the local Communist parties in their individual systems, it is important to recognize that not all of these systems display a high degree of stability at present. Indeed, those in several countries have come into being only recently and as yet have quite shallow roots in their local soil. Moreover, there is substantial evidence of emerging social bases for political realignments in many states, and these could, in turn, lead to efforts to revamp the local political systems there.[36] Should major systemic changes occur in one or more of these countries, such changes might drastically alter the roles of the Communist parties in those particular systems. The nature of the new Communist roles, of course, would vary according to the shape of the political system that emerged.

Whether developments of this sort take place will depend largely upon how the non-Communist forces in West European countries respond to the concrete circumstances facing them, for no Communist party in the area seems likely to find itself in a position to substantially alter the character of its local political system on its own. Although the "autonomist, revisionist" party in Italy already has considerable say in the determination of governmental policy and might even enter the cabinet in the next few years, the constellation of political forces in the country imposes great constraints on radical initiatives. Aside from the Communists, the other elements of the Left are relatively weak, and the Christian Democrats and other forces of the Center and Right retain significant strength. The same holds true in Iceland. Although the Left in Finland enjoys a good deal more clout than it does in Italy and Iceland, the Social Democrats predominate, and they look to the parties of the Center as their main collaborators. The Left in France edged out the parties of the ruling coalition in the first round of balloting in the March 1978 parliamentary elections, but it fell considerably short of winning a majority of parliamentary seats in the second round. Furthermore, not only did the PCF lose its status as the largest party of the Left to the Socialist Party in the elections, but its quarrels with the Socialists and Left Radicals in the months prior to the elections have even left in doubt its long-term ability to retain an alliance with these non-Communist forces. Indeed, some of the Left Radicals have already given signs in late March 1978 of an inclination to turn toward the center. In Portugal, the Left holds the majority of the seats in parliament; however, the Socialist Party has rejected cooperation with the orthodox PCP, preferring instead to operate, first, with a minority cabinet and, then, in alliance with the centrist Social Democratic Center party. The June 1977 elections in Spain gave the Left only a minority of the popular vote and the seats in parliament, and the PCE wound up far behind the Socialist Workers' Party in terms of both. For other Communist parties, local situations offer even less promise of an opportunity to carry out major systemic changes alone.

In the absence of far-reaching transformations of the West European political systems, the roles of the Communist parties in the area may still undergo some modifications, but these will probably fit the pattern that has prevailed over the last two or three decades. That is, they will be small and gradual in character.

Notes

1. See, for example, Mario Einaudi, Jean-Marie Dominach, Aldo Garosci, *Communism in Western Europe* (Ithaca, N.Y.: Cornell University Press, 1951); Franz Borkenau, *European Communism* (New York: Harper and Brothers, 1953).

2. For typical products, see Alexander Dallin, ed., with Jonathan Harris and Grey Hodnett, *Diversity in International Communism* (New York: Columbia University Press, 1963); William E. Griffith, ed., *Communism in Europe*, 2 vols. (Cambridge, Mass., MIT Press, 1964-1966).

3. R. V. Burks, "Transmutation of European Communism," in *The Future of Communism*, ed. R. V. Burks (Detroit: Wayne State University Press, 1968), p. 238. For similar statements by other prominent commentators, see Richard Lowenthal, *World Communism: The Disintegration of a Secular Faith* (New York: Oxford University Press, 1964), p. 267; William E. Griffith, "European Communism, 1965," in Griffith, *Communism in Europe*, vol. 2, pp. 7, 25.

4. For earlier full-scale efforts along similar lines, see Ronald Tiersky, *French Communism, 1920-1972* (New York and London: Columbia University Press, 1974); and Donald L. M. Blackner and Sidney Tarrow, eds., *Communism in France and Italy* (Princeton, N.J.: Princeton University Press, 1976). As the titles indicate, however, these pioneering volumes deal only with communism in France and Italy. Neil McInnes's *The Communist Parties of Western Europe* (London: Oxford University Press for the Royal Institute of International Affairs, 1975), contains much useful information on the West European parties, but instead of looking at the relationships between these parties and the societies and polities in which they exist, it merely describes the parties and their outlooks.

5. Lest any misunderstanding arise, it is essential to clarify the meaning of *role* here and throughout this volume. To begin with, the term is basically descriptive in character and does not refer to the kind of system-maintenance imperatives posited by the school of structural-functional analysis. Second, it implies a dynamic relationship between party and system, not a fixed and immutable one. Lastly, it often stands for a complex reality, a mix of several different, perhaps even conflicting, types of function—e.g., that of a counterculture and that of a governing party.

6. For purposes of this book, I have defined Western Europe as all the non-Communist states on the European continent and the islands associated with the continent, from Finland in the northeast counterclockwise around to Greece in the southeast. It should be noted that this definition does not correspond exactly to that of the organizers of the European Communist conferences of 1967 and 1976, for they invited representatives from the Communist parties of Cyprus and Turkey as well. Yet most analysts tend to see these two states as more Middle Eastern than West European in nature. Indeed, as Dimitri Kitsikis suggests in his chapter on the Greek Communist movement in the present volume, it may even be stretching a point to include Greece in the analysis.

7. See *National Basic Intelligence Factbook, July 1977*, GC BIF 77-002 (U) (Washington, D.C.: Central Intelligence Agency, July

1977). This document, which is one of a semiannual series put out by the Central Intelligence Agency, is available to the general public through the Documents Expediting Project of the Library of Congress.

8. Ibid.

9. For data on the pre-1945 period, see United Nations, *1948 Statistical Yearbook* (Lake Placid, N.Y., 1949), pp. 240-251. These are in absolute figures, and I myself calculated the percentages. For 1970 data (the latest available), see World Bank, *World Tables 1976* (Baltimore: Johns Hopkins University Press, 1976), p. 516.

10. See Walter D. Connor, *Socialism, Politics, and Equality* (New York: Columbia University Press, forthcoming), Chapter 4, for presentation and discussion of the data. The countries include Denmark, France, Great Britain, Italy, the Netherlands, Norway, Sweden, and West Germany. Most of the studies were carried out in the late 1950s and early 1960s.

11. United Nations, *1976 Statistical Yearbook* (New York, 1977), p. 691.

12. See Malcolm Sawyer, "Income Distribution in OECD Countries," *OECD Economic Outlook* (Paris), July 1976, pp. 16-17.

13. See the contributions to this volume and the annual volumes of the *Political Handbook of the World* put out by the Council on Foreign Relations in New York.

14. United Nations, *1976 Statistical Yearbook*, p. 691.

15. Sawyer, "Income Distribution," pp. 16-17.

16. See, for example, the contributions to this book; Sabino Acquaviva and Mario Santuccio, *Social Structure in Italy* (Boulder, Colo.: Westview Press, 1976); articles by Jacqueline Grapin, Stanley Meisler, and Jim Hoagland, *The Washington Post*, July 17, August 24, and October 23, 1977, respectively; the statements of Greek opposition leaders and the government's reply in *Ê Kathêmerinê* (Athens), December 25, 1977, in Foreign Broadcast Information Service, *Daily Report: Western Europe* (Washington, D.C.), December 28, 1977; speech of Spanish Prime Minister Adolfo Suárez on February 4, 1978, as reported by Radio Madrid in Spanish, February 5, 1978, in Foreign Broadcast Information Service, *Daily Report: Western Europe*, February 9, 1978.

17. See United Nations, *World Economic Survey 1975* (New York, 1976), Supplement, p. 70; "International Economic Survey," *New York Times*, January 30, 1976; *National Basic Intelligence Factbook, July 1977; OECD Economic Outlook*, July 1977.

18. *World Economic Survey 1975*, Supplement, p. 71.

19. See the contributions to this book; "International Economic Survey," *New York Times*, January 30, 1977; ibid., January 21, 1978; *The Washington Post*, July 16, August 24, October 16, November 27, and December 20, 1977, and February 13, 1978; Richard F. Starr, ed., *Yearbook on International Communist Affairs 1977* (Stanford, Calif.: Hoover Institution Press, 1977).

20. United Nations, *Monthly Bulletin of Statistics* (New York), December 1977; *Yearbook on International Communist Affairs 1977.*

21. See, for example, the contributions to this book; McInnes, *The Communist Parties of Western Europe;* Tierksy, *French Communism, 1920-1972;* Sidney Tarrow, "Communism in Italy and France: Adaptation and Change," in Blackmer and Tarrow, *Communism in Italy and France,* pp. 575-640; *Sociologie du communisme en Italie* [Sociology of communism in Italy] (Paris: Armand Colin, 1974); Rona M. Fields, *The Portuguese Revolution and the Armed Forces Movement* (New York: Praeger, 1976); the various annual volumes of the *Yearbook on International Communist Affairs* put out by the Hoover Institution Press.

22. See, for instance, the contributions to this book; Tarrow, "Communism in Italy and France"; *Sociologie du communisme en Italie;* Fields, *The Portuguese Revolution;* Eusebio Mujal-Leon, "The Domestic and International Evolution of the Spanish Communist Party," in *European Communism in the Age of Détente,* ed. Rudolf L. Tökés (New York: New York University Press, forthcoming).

23. For data on the electoral performances of West European Communist parties, see the contributions to this book; McInnes, *The Communist Parties of Western Europe,* pp. 21-28; the annual volumes of the *Yearbook on International Communist Affairs;* the annual volumes of the *World Strength of the Communist Party Organizations,* issued by the U.S. Department of State up through 1973; the semiannual volumes of the *National Basic Intelligence Factbook;* Foreign Broadcast Information Service, *Daily Report: Western Europe,* June 22 and 24, 1976; Howard Penniman, ed., *Italy at the Polls: The 1976 Parliamentary Election* (Washington, D.C.: American Enterprise Institute, 1978); *Le Monde* (Paris), February 17, April 1, and May 27, 1977, and March 14, 1978; *The Economist* (London), June 25, 1977; *New York Times*, March 20, 1978.

24. The following discussion draws upon all the sources cited in note 23 except McInnes.

25. The SKP in Finland, it should be noted, participates in elections through a Communist-dominated front known as the

Finnish People's Democratic League (SKDL).

26. The breakdown for France is based on the results of the first round of voting in the elections. For the complete returns of this phase, see *Le Monde*, March 14, 1978. The second round of balloting, which determined the actual number of seats in parliament, yielded greater differentiation among the parties, with the PCF coming in distinctly fourth. See the *New York Times*, March 20, 1978.

27. For information on historical and contemporary non-Communist attitudes toward the West European Communist parties, see the contributions to this book; Tiersky, *French Communism, 1920-1972;* idem, "French Communism in 1976," *Problems of Communism,* January-February 1976, pp. 20-47; Blackmer and Tarrow, *Communism in France and Italy;* Donald L. M. Blackmer, *Unity in Diversity: Italian Communism and the Communist World* (Cambridge, Mass., MIT Press, 1968); Sidney G. Tarrow, *Peasant Communism in Southern Italy* (New Haven, Conn.: Yale University Press, 1967); Roy Macridis, *French Politics in Transition: The Years after De Gaulle* (Cambridge, Mass.: Winthrop, 1975); Frédéric Bon, *Le communisme en France* [Communism in France] (Paris, A. Colin, 1969); Frank L. Wilson, *The French Democratic Left, 1963-69: Toward a Modern Party System* (Stanford, Calif.: Stanford University Press, 1971); Daniel Tarschys, "The Unique Role of the Swedish CP," *Problems of Communism,* May-June 1974, pp. 36-44; Per Egil Hegge, " 'Disunited' Front in Norway," ibid., May-June 1976, pp. 49-53; A. F. Upton, ed., *Communism in Scandinavia and Finland* (New York, Anchor Press/Doubleday, 1973); Richard Cornell, "Communism in Scandinavia," *Survey* (London), Autumn 1975, pp. 107-120; Walter Kendall, "The Communist Party of Great Britain," ibid., Winter 1974, pp. 118-131; the annual volumes of the *Yearbook on International Communist Affairs;* and the annual volumes of the *Political Handbook of the World.*

28. The discussion in the following section on self-identifications draws upon data in the contributions to this book; McInnes, *The Communist Parties of Western Europe;* Tiersky, *French Communism, 1920-1972;* idem, "French Communism in 1976"; Blackmer and Tarrow, *Communism in France and Italy;* Penniman, *Italy at the Polls;* Heinz Timmerman, *I Comunisti italiani* [The Italian Communists] (Bari: De Donato, 1974); Eusebio Mujal-León, "Spanish Communism in the 1970's," *Problems of Communism,* March-April 1975, pp. 43-55; idem, "The Domestic and International Evolution of the Spanish Communist Party"; Upton, *Communism in Scandinavia and Finland;* Cornell, "Com-

munist Party of Great Britain," pp. 118-131; the annual volumes of the *World Strength of the Communist Party Organizations;* the annual volumes of the *Yearbook on International Communist Affairs;* the *World Marxist Review* and its *Information Bulletin* (Toronto—English-language versions of the Prague-based *Problems of Peace and Socialism* and its *Information Bulletin*); Foreign Broadcast Information Service, *Daily Report: Western Europe,* for recent years; and the background reports on West European parties in *Radio Free Europe Research* (Munich).

29. During most of the postwar years, Northern Ireland, which still remains a part of the United Kingdom, and the southern Republic of Ireland had separate Communist organizations, but the two bodies united to form a single party in 1970.

30. Insofar, at least, as there is information available on the party. The Maltese Communist Party was founded in 1970, but Paul Agius, the party secretary, has seemed to be the only overtly active member. In 1972, he was elected secretary and general manager of the Farmers' Cooperative, the island's largest single farm group. See *World Strength of the Communist Party Organizations*, 25th Annual Report, 1973 ed. (Washington, D.C.: Bureau of Intelligence and Research, U.S. Department of State, July 1973).

31. This party came into being in July 1977. See *Morning Star* (London), July 18, 1977.

32. See *Le Monde*, May 27, 1977.

33. The ensuing analysis is based on information in the contributions to this book; McInnes, *The Communist Parties of Western Europe;* Blackmer and Tarrow, *Communism in France and Italy;* Tiersky, *French Communism, 1920-1972;* idem, "French Communism in 1976"; Jean Kanapa, "A 'New Policy' of the French Communists?" *Foreign Affairs*, January 1977, pp. 280-294; Timmerman, *I comunisti italiani;* Penniman, *Italy at the Polls;* Donald L. M. Blackmer, "Italian Communism: Strategy for the 1970's," *Problems of Communism*, May-June 1972, pp. 41-56; Sergio Segre, "The 'Communist Question' in Italy," *Foreign Affairs*, July 1976, pp. 691-707; Mujal-León, "Spanish Communism in the 1970's"; idem, "The Domestic and International Evolution of the Spanish Communist Party"; Upton, *Communism in Scandinavia and Finland;* Cornell, "Communism in Scandinavia"; Tarschys, "The Unique Role of the Swedish CP"; Kendall, "The Communist Party of Great Britain"; the *World Marxist Review* and its *Information Bulletin;* the annual volumes of the *Yearbook on International Communist Affairs;* the 1973 edition of *World Strength of the Communist Party Organiza-*

tions; Foreign Broadcast Information Service, *Daily Report: Western Europe,* for recent years; and the background reports on West European parties in *Radio Free Europe Research.* It also owes an intellectual debt to Pierre Hassner.

34. The following discussion draws upon the contributions to this volume; Blackmer and Tarrow, *Communism in France and Italy;* Tiersky, *French Communism, 1920-1972;* idem, "French Communism in 1976"; Upton, *Communism in Scandinavia and Finland;* Cornell, "Communism in Scandinavia"; Tarschys, "The Unique Role of the Swedish CP"; Hegge, "'Disunited' Front in Norway"; Kendall, "The Communist Party of Great Britain"; Foreign Broadcast Information Service, *Daily Report: Western Europe,* for recent years; the annual volumes of the *Yearbook on International Communist Affairs.*

35. For the conceptual framework of the analysis in the next few paragraphs, I am indebted in large measure to Georges Lavau. See especially his "The PCF, the State, and the Revolution: An Analysis of Party Policies, Communications, and Popular Culture," in Blackmer and Tarrow, *Communism in France and Italy,* pp. 87-139. Unlike Lavau, however, I do not contend that the enumerated contributions relate to *essential needs* of even particular political systems. I believe that it is possible to talk about these contributions without making judgments on that score.

36. The growth of social bases for political realignments has been documented in several national opinion studies. For interesting presentations of some of the data, see Ronald Inglehart, "The Silent Revolution in Europe: Intergenerational Change in Post-Industrial Societies," *The American Political Science Review,* December 1971, pp. 991-1017; and his more extended *The Silent Revolution: Changing Values and Political Styles among Western Publics* (Princeton, N.J.: Princeton University Press, 1977). It should be pointed out, however, that Inglehart's conclusions imply a less open-ended future than the data themselves suggest.

1
Italy: The Changing Role
of the PCI

Giacomo Sani

June 1975: the Italian Communist Party (PCI) scores impressive gains in nationwide municipal and regional elections. *June 1976:* parliamentary elections bring the Communists forty-eight additional seats in the House of Deputies and twenty-two additional seats in the Senate.[1] *August 1976:* the PCI parliamentary group abstains in the vote of confidence on a new government, thereby making possible the inauguration of a minority Christian Democrat cabinet led by Giulio Andreotti. *July 1977:* after months of negotiations the PCI signs an agreement for a limited policy program with the Christian Democrats (DC), the Socialists (PSI), the Social Democrats (PSDI), the Republicans (PRI), and the Liberals (PLI). *September 1977:* some 30,000 youths affiliated with radical Left groups march through the streets of Bologna—the showcase of Italian communism—chanting slogans openly hostile to the PCI.[2] *January 1978:* the PCI indicates that it will no longer support the Andreotti cabinet indirectly by abstaining on crucial votes, and Andreotti resigns. *March 1978:* the PCI reaches an accord with the DC, the PSI, the PSDI, and the PRI that makes it part of the official parliamentary majority for a new minority Christian Democrat cabinet, again headed by Andreotti.

Part of the research for this work was carried out during the 1976-1977 academic year under a Guggenheim Fellowship. The author wishes to thank his colleagues Alberto Marradi and Giovanni Sartori for sharing with him data from their 1975 survey of the Italian electorate. He also wishes to thank the Polimetrics Laboratory and the Computer Center of The Ohio State University (Columbus) for their assistance and *Problems of Communism* for permission to reproduce several tables and charts that appeared in his "The PCI on the Threshold," *Problems of Communism,* November-December 1976, pp. 27-51.

These events mark some of the high points in the evolution of the Italian Communist Party in recent years. The changes *in* the PCI and attitudes *toward* the PCI have captured the attention of observers and politicians not only in Italy but elsewhere as well. Thus, the political experiment now under way in Italy may have a significance far beyond the boundaries of that political arena. Indeed, it could influence developments elsewhere and possibly even affect the balance of forces at the international level.

It is hardly surprising, given the fluidity and the ambiguity of the situation, that there have been different interpretations of what is going on and contrasting projections for the future. For some, the changes that have taken place within the PCI and the party's new role in governmental affairs constitute a positive development, one that will strengthen the democratic Left and benefit Italian society. For others, the developments of the last few years represent a dangerous turning point, the beginning of a realignment of forces that will eventually threaten the survival of democracy in Italy. Still others regard the PCI's strategy and behavior as being too accommodating and as signaling the abandonment of the radical goals that the party has espoused in the past.

Although commentators of different political persuasions reach different conclusions about the "Communist question" in Italy, most of their analyses touch upon three major, and interrelated, aspects of it. These are: (1) the increase in the level of popular support for the PCI in the mid-1970s and the factors associated with that development; (2) the broad strategy and the specific conditions that led the PCI to support a DC cabinet after thirty years of uninterrupted opposition; and (3) the changed role of the PCI within the Italian Left and the emergence of forces challenging the party's traditional hegemony in this sector of the political spectrum.

The present chapter will address itself to these three major dimensions of the issue. It will describe the growth of the PCI at the mass level and interpret the phenomenon in light of the broad sociocultural changes that have affected Italian society in the last decade. Then it will discuss the strategy that the PCI has elaborated and pursued (the "historic compromise"), and examine the consequences of this strategy in regard to the party's role in the political system. Finally, it will look briefly at the tensions and dilemmas that the recent changes have created for the PCI.

The Pattern of Growth

When democratic political life resumed in Italy at the end of World

Figure 1: Trends in the Electoral Strength of the Three Major Italian Parties, 1946-76

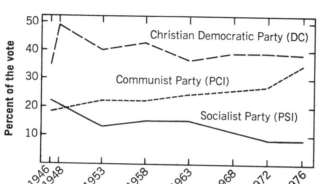

SOURCES: Data for 1946-72 were taken from Mario Caciagli and Alberto Spreafico, Eds., *Un sistema politico alla prova* (A Political System Under Trial), Bologna, Il Mulino, 1975, page 61, Table 7. Data for 1976 were from election results published in the Italian press; see, for example, *Corriere della sera* (Milan), June 23, 1976. Points in the figure represent percentages of total vote polled by the respective parties in the 1946 Constituent Assembly election and in subsequent elections to the Italian House—elections with the broadest voter franchise. In 1948, the PCI and PSI ran on a joint ticket, which polled 31 percent of the vote. In 1968, the PSI united with the Social Democrats under the banner of the Unitary Socialist Party (PSU), which polled 14.5 percent of the vote.

War II, the PCI emerged as the third largest party (after the Christian Democrats and the Socialists), receiving 18.9 percent of the popular vote for the Constituent Assembly in the election of June 2, 1946 (see Figure 1). The party's strength, however, varied considerably in different areas of the country (see Figure 2). In general, the party was considerably stronger in the central regions, especially in Emilia-Romagna and Tuscany, than in the Northeast and in the South, with intermediate strength in the industrialized areas of the Northwest. The ensuing thirty years have brought major alterations in this picture. In the parliamentary election of June 20, 1976, the PCI garnered 34.4 percent of the total popular vote (Figure 1). Moreover, it made substantial gains in all regions, consolidating and expanding its support base in the areas where it had its initial strongholds and successfully penetrating other regions (see Figure 2). Although there is still a certain unevenness in the distribution of its strength, the disparity is considerably less pronounced than in earlier years. As a consequence of this expanded electoral base, the PCI now occupies

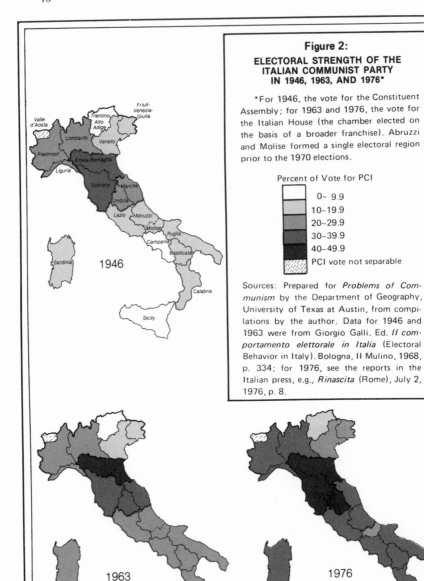

Figure 2:

**ELECTORAL STRENGTH OF THE
ITALIAN COMMUNIST PARTY
IN 1946, 1963, AND 1976***

*For 1946, the vote for the Constituent
Assembly; for 1963 and 1976, the vote for
the Italian House (the chamber elected on
the basis of a broader franchise). Abruzzi
and Molise formed a single electoral region
prior to the 1970 elections.

Percent of Vote for PCI

	0– 9.9
	10–19.9
	20–29.9
	30–39.9
	40–49.9
	PCI vote not separable

Sources: Prepared for *Problems of Communism* by the Department of Geography,
University of Texas at Austin, from compi-
lations by the author. Data for 1946 and
1963 were from Giorgio Galli. Ed. *Il comportamento elettorale in Italia* (Electoral
Behavior in Italy). Bologna, Il Mulino, 1968,
p. 334; for 1976, see the reports in the
Italian press, e.g., *Rinascita* (Rome), July 2,
1976, p. 8.

1946

1963

1976

RJH - 76

Table 1: Increase in the Electoral Strength
of the PCI by Region, 1946-76

Region	Difference between PCI's percent of vote in 1946 and in 1976	Rate of increase (in percent)
Northwest		
Piedmont	+14.6	70.2
Liguria	+10.7	37.7
Lombardy	+11.5	57.2
Northeast		
Trentino-Alto Adige	+ 5.1	63.0
Veneto	+10.1	73.7
Friuli-Venezia-Giulia	+13.4	101.5
Central		
Emilia-Romagna	+11.0	29.3
Marche	+18.1	83.0
Tuscany	+13.9	41.4
Umbria	+19.3	68.9
South		
Lazio	+21.8	154.6
Campania	+24.9	336.5
Abruzzi-Molise[a]	+23.0	227.7
Puglia	+17.0	115.6
Basilicata	+20.3	156.0
Calabria	+20.8	170.5
Sicily	+19.6	248.1
Sardinia	+23.1	184.8

[a] While Abruzzi and Molise formed separate regions in 1976, they constituted a single region in 1946. Therefore, they are treated as one region for purposes of this particular analysis.

SOURCES: Calculated by the author on the basis of data in Giorgio Galli, Ed., *Il comportamento elettorale in Italia* (Electoral Behavior in Italy), Bologna, II Mulino, 1968, p. 334, and in official reports of the results of the June 1976 election, published, *inter alia*, in *Rinascita* (Rome), July 2, 1976, p. 8.

positions of power at the subnational level in a large number of political domains—including seven regions, almost all of the large cities (Turin, Milan, Venice, Bologna, Genoa, Florence, Rome, and Naples), more than thirty-five próvincial capitals, and countless smaller communities.[3]

An analysis of the pattern of growth of PCI electoral strength leads to several conclusions. First, the increase in the PCI's strength has been gradual but steady over time (Figure 1). Until the elections of the mid-1970s, the support base of the party had been widening slowly, without sudden expansions. The overall gain reflects a series of small increments from election to election rather than massive surges followed, and partially offset, by sudden declines. To be sure, in certain areas the party has occasionally suffered some losses, but these reversals have generally been modest in size and have been more than made up in subsequent elections.[4]

Second, the expansion of the party's base of support has been general in geographical terms. Growth has been more pronounced in the regions where the party was initially weaker, but it has by no means been confined to these areas (Table 1). If the PCI has made greater strides in the South and in the Northeast, doubling and even tripling its share of the vote, it has also registered considerable gains in the areas where it was originally strongest. For example, the growth of support was such that in 1976 it came very close to polling a majority of the votes in Emilia-Romagna (48.5 percent), Tuscany (47.5 percent), and Umbria (47.3 percent).

Third, the expansion of the PCI has not taken place along narrow class lines. The party has succeeded in attracting the support of voters from different social groups, as Palmiro Togliatti had envisioned it might when he put forth the strategy of the "new party" in the early postwar period.[5] A precise assessment of the social composition of the Communist electorate is difficult; however, studies based on both survey and aggregate data indicate that although the PCI receives a disproportionately high share of support from less privileged social groups, it also attracts significant support from segments of other social groups that cannot be considered "working class" in the traditional sense of the term—that is, from white-collar workers, teachers, shopkeepers, artisans, and the like.[6] Thus, in terms of the social composition of support, the PCI's profile is not much different from that of Italy's other major party, the DC, and it is reasonably close to the profile of the electorate as a whole (see Figure 3). In 1944, Togliatti urged the party to move beyond the recruitment of workers and to attempt to attract "the peasantry, the masses of intellectuals, ... professional men, technicians, clerks;" after the electoral successes of the mid-1970s, it would appear that the PCI has come close to achieving that goal.[7] Today, from the point of view of its base of support, the Italian Communist Party can be described more accurately as a "catchall" party—or, as Sidney Tarrow has recently proposed, as a "populist" party—than as a "party of the working class."[8]

Finally, the growth of the PCI has taken place concurrently with

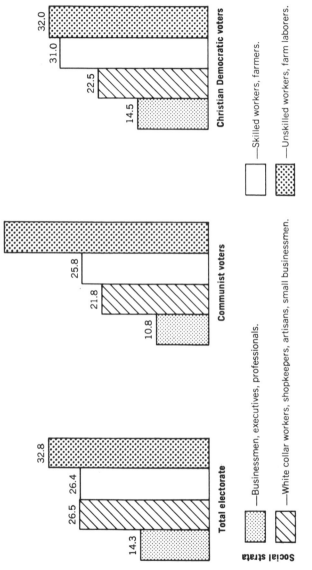

Figure 3: Social Composition of the Italian Electorate, 1975

(in percent)

Total electorate — 32.8, 26.4, 26.5, 14.3

Communist voters — 41.6, 25.8, 21.8, 10.8

Christian Democratic voters — 32.0, 31.0, 22.5, 14.5

Social strata

—Businessmen, executives, professionals.
—White collar workers, shopkeepers, artisans, small businessmen.
—Skilled workers, farmers.
—Unskilled workers, farm laborers.

SOURCE: The three profiles were prepared on the basis of 1975 survey data made available to the author by Giovanni Sartori and Alberto Marradi. Respondents were assigned to social strata by the author on the basis of their occupation or that of the head of the household.

the gradual decline of the Socialist Party (see Figure 1). At the beginning of the postwar period, the two major parties of the Left had approximately equal support, with the Socialists enjoying a small lead. By 1953, when the two parties contested the national election separately after an unsatisfactory experience with a Fronte Popolare in 1948, the Communist Party had taken a sizable lead. Ten years later, the PCI's share of the vote was approximately twice as large as that of the Socialists. By 1972, there were three Communist voters for every Socialist voter, and the 1976 election tilted the balance even more in favor of the PCI (34.4 percent to 9.6 percent for the PSI).

These two opposition trends should not, of course, be taken to mean that the growth of the PCI is due entirely to shifts in the allegiance of Socialist voters. Although such shifts have occurred, internal shifts within the Left are, as we shall see, only one component of the PCI's success. The point here is that as a result of its gradual gains, and the concomitant decline of the Socialists, the PCI has established itself as the leading force of the Italian Left. Hence, it has become a rallying point for many progressive voters who desire the implementation of social and economic reforms and who do not see a viable and realistic alternative to the PCI.

As suggested earlier, the gains the Communists made in the 1976 election (3.5 million votes more than they received in the preceding parliamentary election in 1972 and an increase of 7.2 percent in share of the total vote) were considerably higher than the gains they had registered in past elections. One might therefore wonder whether the response of the electorate in the mid-1970s signals a departure from the pattern of the past. For insight into this question, it is essential to look at the specific factors that have contributed to these overall results. The present author has set forth a detailed analysis of such factors elsewhere,[9] and it may be summarized here.

In the interval between the last two parliamentary elections, seven cohorts of new voters, or approximately 5.5 million people, came into the electorate (three as a consequence of the extension of suffrage to people eighteen years of age). During the same period, the names of more than 2 million older electors were removed from the electoral registry because of death. Thus, there was a very large turnover of voters, with a net increase of the electoral body roughly twice as large as the mean increase recorded in the past. The import of these changes in the composition of the electorate becomes obvious when another fact is taken into consideration—namely, that the distribution of party preferences among the younger and the older generations differs substantially. Among the younger electors, sympathies for the parties of the Left and especially for the PCI are much more common than they are among voters over fifty years of age. This, of course, means that the electoral turnover did not affect all parties equally. Some parties acquired a disproportionately large share of the new votes available, and they lost fewer votes because of the passing away of electors from the older generations. The PCI appears to have been one of the main beneficiaries of the turnover, with a net gain of about 1.5 million votes—a figure of some consequence. However, the PCI's total gain was 3.5 million, so one must still account for 2 million votes. Survey data and the electoral results themselves suggest that approximately half these votes represented defections from parties of the Center-Right, and the other half reflected internal shifts within the Left, i.e., transfers of allegiance from the Socialist Party or other minor leftist parties.[10] Of the increase of 7.2 percent in the PCI's share of the total vote, then, 3.2 percent can reasonably be attributed to turnover of the electorate, 2.0 percent to defections of moderate voters, and another 2.0 percent to internal shifts within the Left. In short, the PCI would clearly have increased its strength without the beneficial impact of turnover, but its success would have been less spectacular.

Further and more detailed investigations might necessitate some modification or revision of these estimates, but it seems unlikely that they would produce major alterations in the picture. The chief sources of the PCI's growth in recent years have been, in combination with the high stability of the Communist vote, the party's ability to attract a disproportionate share of younger voters and the success of its appeals to segments of both moderates and Catholics in the electorate. These last two factors provided the element of novelty in the 1976 election.[11] They can best be understood in the light of the new image of the PCI that has been emerging over the last few years.

The Decline of Anticommunism

For most of the post–World War II period, the PCI suffered from a negative image among the non-Communist segment of the electorate. This image had—and has—several components. Perhaps the most important of these was that the PCI, despite its pronouncements, was not truly committed to the rules of representative democracy—that its conception of democracy differed from the Western tradition and that its acceptance of the democratic creed was a tactical ploy rather than the expression of a genuine and profound belief. The fear that once in power the PCI would institute systemic changes (or, as Giovanni Sartori put it, that it "would replace the system as well as the people")[12] was reinforced by the PCI's close ties with the international communist movement, particularly the Soviet Union. This linkage was generally interpreted as signifying subservience to Moscow's dictates and the party's intention to transform Italian society to conform with the general pattern of Communist societies in Eastern Europe. That this transformation was likely to be revolutionary and violent in nature added a third dimension of apprehension and suspicion, particularly poignant for those who could remember the confrontations and violence of the early 1920s or the mid-1940s. Additional negative aspects of the PCI, with perhaps different degrees of significance for different segments of the electorate, were (1) its anticlericalism (combined with the general limitations on religious freedom under all existing Communist regimes) and (2) implicit threats to private property in its programs of economic reorganization and redistribution. Finally, the PCI's strong organization, its possession of able leaders and a large number of committed militants, its reliance on the theory and practice of "democratic centralism," and its crushing of internal dissent—all made the PCI appear to be a powerful and well-oiled machine, a dangerous foe that could not be taken lightly.

This multifaceted image of the PCI reflected, as the present author has tried to show elsewhere, the debates, polemics, and confrontations that had taken place among parties during the first two decades of the republican regime.[13] In short, it embodied many echoes from the past: the political violence of 1945-1946, the anticlerical posture of the Popular Front during the 1948 campaign, the accounts of terror in the Soviet Union under Stalin, the Soviet interventions in Hungary and Czechoslovakia, and so on.

The anticommunist barrier remained strong for almost a quarter of a century. By the early 1970s, however, popular attitudes toward the PCI were growing increasingly differentiated. Not all electors from the Center and the Right displayed major misgivings about the party; furthermore, different segments of the voters objected to the PCI on different grounds.[14] Thus, although the anticommunist barrier had not collapsed, it no longer appeared to be as formidable as it had once been. More recent evidence, as well as impressionistic observations, indicate that the weakening trend has continued at an accelerated pace in the mid-1970s and that the preclusions against the Communist Party have diminished, at least in certain sectors of the electorate.

Let us briefly review some of this evidence. In doing so, it is important to bear in mind that changes in mass attitudes tend to lag behind modifications of ideas and beliefs among the elite and the

Figure 4: Trends in Religious Practice and in Perceived Compatibility of Communism and Catholicism

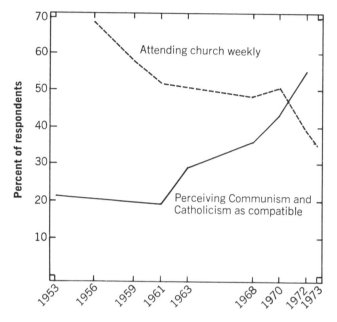

SOURCES: Data on weekly church attendance are from various surveys reported in *Bollettino Doxa* (Milan) and *Ricerche demoscopiche* (Milan), from a 1959 survey by Gabriel Almond and Sidney Verba, and from 1968 and 1972 surveys by the author and Samuel Barnes. Data on the compatibility issue are from surveys reported in *Bollettino Doxa* and from the 1972 survey by the author and Samuel Barnes; points on the solid line are the percent of respondents answering "Yes" to the question "Can one be a good Communist and a good Catholic at the same time?"

relatively small strata of the attentive public. Large segments of the electorate are poorly informed and insulated from the mass media, so their images of parties change very slowly.

If we begin with objections to the PCI based on the ground that the party is hostile to religion, we can see a fall over the last fifteen years or so in the portion of the public that perceives an incompatibility between communism and Catholicism (Figure 4). This trend reflects the growing secularization of Italian society, evidenced also by the decline of "clericalism"—i.e., a greater unwillingness on the part of

segments of the Catholic electorate to be guided in political matters
by the directives of the church. There are reasons to believe that the
trend has become even more pronounced in recent years. During the
1974 campaign preceding the referendum on the divorce issue, there
emerged a group of dissenting Catholic intellectuals. No wholly
reliable estimates exist on the number of practicing Catholics who
voted against the guidelines of the church and the DC in the
referendum, but survey data collected during the campaign prior to it
indicate that as many as 30 percent of the Christian Democratic
electorate might have cast their ballots in favor of the divorce law.[15] It
is even more difficult to estimate the impact of the weakening of the
religious preclusion against the PCI in the regional elections of 1975
and in the parliamentary elections of 1976, but it is noteworthy that in
the latter elections, several well-known Catholic intellectuals
were included on the Communist electoral lists, though they were
elected as independent deputies. Although claims made by these
people that the bulk of the voters who shifted to the PCI in 1976 were
Catholics are probably exaggerated,[16] their own candidacies and the
switches of Catholic voters to the PCI that did occur are a clear
indication of the erosion of the Catholic tradition and of the church's
growing inability to channel the electoral choices of the Catholic
masses away from the parties of the Left.[17]

A similar evolution has taken place with respect to other negative
components of the PCI's image. Looking at the answers to a question
on the nature of the Communist Party posed to a sample of Italian
electors toward the end of 1975, we find that the party was viewed as
"revolutionary" by approximately half of the non-Communist
respondents; the rest either were uncertain about (24 percent) or
denied the validity of (25 percent) the statement. Furthermore, only 47
percent of the non-Communist voters interviewed in the same study
accepted the characterization of the party as "nondemocratic." Of the
remainder, 25 percent rejected it, and the rest did not express an
opinion.[18] The significance of such findings is highlighted by the fact
that these are not the answers of voters who had already switched to
the PCI, but of electors who, as of 1975, still preferred other parties.
This suggests that the image of the Communist Party is improving
not only among converts but also among other, larger segments of the
electorate.

Additional data from other studies confirm this gradual transformation of the party's image at the mass level. In 1970, 45 percent of the
people interviewed by the Demoskopea Institute agreed with the
statement that "the Communists are still a serious danger for our

Table 2:   The Changing Image of the PCI, 1967-76

	1967	1974	1975	1976
Communists . . .	(In percent [a])			
"are honest"	22	28	29	45
"have many good ideas"	21	34	45	60
"are 'simpatici'"	15	24	27	34
"are against violence"	16	26	31	43
"are competent"	..[b]	43	44	65
"are young, youthful"	32	39	54	..[b]
"are modern"	23	41	46	..[b]
"are united"	60	56	59	..[b]
"defend people like us"	29	39	45	..[b]

[a]Figures represent percent of respondents in a nationwide sample agreeing with the statements.
[b]Question was not asked.

SOURCE: *Bollettino Doxa* (Milan), Sept. 1, 1976.

freedom, no agreement with them is possible"; by 1974, only one-fourth of the respondents interviewed in another survey by the same organization chose that statement as the best description of the PCI.[19] From 1972 to 1974, opposition to a "historic compromise" between the PCI and DC and the entry of the Communists into a governmental coalition with the Christian Democrats dropped significantly. Correspondingly, between 1972 and 1975 there was a decrease in the general level of hostility expressed toward the Communists on questions having to do with the degree of sympathy with the PCI.[20] Finally, recent surveys have shown an increased willingness on the part of the public to attribute positive traits—such as "efficiency," "capacity to maintain order," and "honesty"—to the party.[21] In September 1976 the Doxa Institute of Milan published figures drawn from surveys conducted between 1967 and 1976 that summarize this evolution of the electorate's views of the PCI rather well.[22] As one can readily see from Table 2, during the period covered the image of the Communist Party has generally improved with respect to virtually all of the traits about which respondents were queried. The only one where there has been little change—and perhaps even a slight

Table 3: Perceptions of the Italian Populace Concerning
Party Attitudes toward the Preservation of Freedom, 1976

(in percent[a])

| | Italian Parties[b] | | | | | | | |
	PCI	PSI	PSDI	PRI	DC	PLI	MSI
The party wants to defend freedom	39	62	56	56	60	48	12
The party wants to limit freedom	45	18	20	11	25	25	66
Don't know, no answer	16	20	24	33	15	27	22
TOTAL	100	100	100	100	100	100	100

[a]Figures represent percent of responses in a nationwide sample.

[b]Initials, from left to right, stand for the Communist Party, the Socialist Party, the Social Democratic Party, the Republican Party, the Christian Democratic party, the Liberal Party, and the Social Movement.

SOURCE: *Bollettino Doxa* (Milan), Sept. 1, 1976.

Table 4: Popular Evaluations of the July 1977 Agreement
Reached by Six Major Italian Parties, Summer 1977

(in percent[a])

	DC Voters	PCI Voters	Sample
The consequences of the agreement will be:			
"certainly positive"	20.2	27.6	20.5
"probably positive"	40.7	47.9	43.1
"probably negative"	23.4	12.2	19.0
"certainly negative"	12.9	9.8	14.0
other answers, no answer, does not know	2.8	2.5	3.4

[a]Figures represent percent of respondents in a nationwide sample.

SOURCE: *La Discussione* (Rome), August 8, 1977.

reversal—is the party's unity (a point to which we shall return later). Because of the large number of nonresponses, these data must be approached with great caution; nevertheless, they appear to confirm the observations already made on the basis of other studies. And the improvement in the image of the PCI stands out even more in light of the concomitant deterioration of the popular image of other parties, particularly that of the DC.

Can one conclude from this brief review that the PCI has won its long struggle to make itself acceptable to wider segments of Italian society? There can be little doubt that in the late 1970s Italian voters look at the PCI with different eyes and that they see a party considerably different from that of the late 1940s. However, not all reservations have vanished, and the preclusions that once constituted a formidable barrier to the PCI have not entirely disappeared. Perhaps the aspect of the party's negative image that has persisted most tenaciously relates to its dedication to the preservation of freedom. Of all the major parties in the Italian political spectrum, only the Neofascists (MSI) inspire less confidence on this score than does the PCI (see Table 3). Other lingering misgivings about the Communists arise from the possibility that their advent to power might bring about serious disorders, the collapse of the economy, the confiscation of private property, and the nationalization of all industry.[23] In sum, then, although the attitudes of the mass public toward the PCI have changed, fairly sizable segments of the electorate still harbor many doubts about the party.

Perhaps the best testimony to both the change in attitudes and the lingering suspicions and reservations vis-à-vis the PCI comes from data gathered in the summer of 1977, shortly after the six major parties reached an agreement on a limited program of government.[24] Asked to pass judgment on this agreement and to evaluate its likely consequences for the country, the voters replied in the manner summarized in Table 4. Although the data in themselves do not provide direct information on attitudes toward the PCI, it is not unjustified to suppose that the voters' responses reflect, at least to some degree, their orientations toward the PCI, since the presence of the PCI in this broad "informal coalition" represented the major novelty of the situation. And, as one can see, a majority of the DC voters—who traditionally have been hostile to communism—express positive or somewhat positive feelings about the arrangement. There is little doubt that these data signal shifts in popular attitudes, for such a distribution of responses would have been rather unlikely only a few years ago. However, the same data also show that within the Christian Democratic electorate, sizable subgroups are presumably still motivated by the hostile feelings of the past and hence do not look with favor on a state of affairs in which a DC cabinet has to accept the explicit support of the PCI.

Thus, one must conclude that although popular attitudes have changed, and will probably continue to evolve in future years, the orientations of the past have not entirely disappeared.[25] Nor can the possibility of a reversal of the recent trend be entirely discounted. In a transitional phase such as the present one, attitudes toward political entities are not deeply rooted; consequently, they are highly susceptible to influence by events or developments of various sorts.

The Legitimation of the PCI

How does one account for these important, if still not total, changes in the mass image of the PCI? Since, on the one hand, a party is a complex and nonhomogeneous social phenomenon and since, on the other, a societal image in a sense represents the aggregation of a large number of individual "visions," answering this question is a very difficult task. Nevertheless, it would appear that four developments have contributed to the evolution of mass attitudes toward the PCI.

First, there is no doubt that the statements made by the Communist leaders and the positions taken by the party in the last few years represent a departure from the past. Even before the decision to abstain on the vote of confidence on the Andreotti cabinet, the PCI had been progressively softening its opposition to successive DC-dominated governments. It has moderated its anticlerical polemics and endeavored to reach a compromise with Catholics, first, on the divorce issue and, later, on legislation concerning abortion. It has repeatedly stressed its autonomy vis-à-vis the Soviet Union. It has explicitly indicated its acceptance of political pluralism, fundamental freedoms, and individual rights. It has offered reassurances to the non-Communist elements of society in the areas of economic plans, social reforms, and private property. It has argued for acceleration of the process of European integration. It no longer objects to Italy's membership in NATO and, more generally, in the Western "camp."[26]

Scholars who follow PCI developments closely might argue that these steps are not really innovations and that the party has essentially been traveling the path charted earlier by Antonio Gramsci and Palmiro Togliatti. But apart from the fact that the recent pronouncements are far more explicit than those of the past, one must bear in mind that previous statements buried in abstruse party documents are quite a different matter from recent declarations such as those made by Berlinguer at the 25th Congress of the Communist Party of the Soviet Union, or in joint communiqués with Georges Marchais (of the French CP) and Santiago Carrillo (of the Spanish CP), or from the rostrum of the Berlin Conference of European Communist Parties. In other words, the PCI is for the first time taking advantage of events widely covered by the mass media to try to reach broad audiences. This effort is itself a departure from the past.

The second development has to do with the attitudes of the mass media and with the content of the political messages they transmit to the mass public. In a recent debate on the Italian situation, political scientist Giovanni Sartori pointed out that an assessment of the PCI's current stances depends in part on the position of the observer, and he ventured the opinion that observers have changed more than the party.[27] One might disagree with his conclusion, but Sartori's basic point underscores the significant role played by the channels through which society receives information about parties and politicians. A party could drastically change its policies, but if messages transmitted to the public through channels of political communication do not reflect the changes, it is unrealistic to expect the public to become aware of modifications in the party's stance. In this connection, it should be noted that for a considerable portion of the postwar period, most mass media in Italy were under the control of industrial groups or the Christian Democratic party;[28] moreover, the general picture of the PCI painted by the government-controlled radio and television network and by large segments of the press was a negative one. Although the PCI had over the years built up an imposing network of political communication of its own,[29] the messages that the PCI's official daily and its other newspapers, popular magazines, and highbrow journals diffused reached primarily people who were already sympathetic to the Communist Party. Thus, the non-Communist electorate was largely insulated from the PCI network and thus not exposed to, or influenced by, messages conducive to positive orientations toward the party.[30]

In the last few years, however—let us say since the late 1960s—there have been considerable changes in this picture. Many intellectuals, critics, and journalists who work for radio, television, and the mass-circulation press have shown a more sympathetic attitude toward the PCI. Union-controlled committees of journalists and printers have increased their power vis-à-vis editors and publishers and now have more control over what is written and printed; consequently, coverage of the PCI has become more extensive, and interviews with party leaders are now quite commonly found in publications that in the past tended to ignore the party. Moreover, the PCI and its leaders now have greater access to radio and TV than they did previously. In short, much, if not all, of the negative bias has disappeared and has been replaced by at least a neutral, and in some cases a positive, orientation.[31]

This observation should not be taken to mean that the changes in the popular image of the PCI are due simply to the new attitude of the media. Among other things, the circulation of newspapers is still fairly limited, and even the radio and television network reaches only a portion of the electorate. Furthermore, the mass media probably reinforce, or erode marginally, mass attitudes more than they bring about sudden conversions. Nevertheless, it seems safe to say that the images that the channels of communication have projected have had some positive impact on popular orientations toward the PCI.

The third development contributing to changes in the public image of the PCI is that segments of the non-Communist political, social, and religious elite have changed their behavior toward the Communists. We would expect Socialist or moderate voters, for example—at least those who are reasonably well informed about interparty dialogue—to perceive the Communist Party differently to the extent that Socialist and DC leaders treat the Communists differently. For these people, party leaders constitute significant reference groups; they are sources of cues, explanations, clarifications, hints of future developments; etc. And there can be little doubt that many of the political, social, and religious elite who for most of the postwar period had stressed hostility and total opposition to the PCI have in recent times modified their attitudes, at least to some extent. For example, the Socialist Party has called for greater assumption of governmental responsibilities by the PCI; the Christian Democrats have put forward the notion of a *confronto,* a constructive dialogue with the PCI; segments of the clergy have evinced considerably diminished hostility toward the party; and sectors of the business world have demonstrated an unprecedented willingness to enter into dialogue with the PCI on matters of mutual concern.

One might be tempted to see these new postures as natural consequences of the PCI's increased bargaining strength resulting from the advances that it has made. But non-Communist as well as Communist elites actually softened their stands before the PCI's successes of 1975 and 1976. In any event, the point is that the acceptance of a dialogue with the PCI by segments of the non-Communist elite tends to accelerate the process of legitimation of their party at the mass level. It helps to weaken the preclusions against the PCI that the non-Communist elite had in the past reinforced by its behavior and pronouncements.[32]

The last development that has helped alter the PCI's image has been changes in the electorate—changes in the political audience, so to speak—which have facilitated the acceptance of new ideas and, conversely, diminished the efficacy of the political appeals of the past. It is impossible to discuss at length here the political implications of the sociocultural transformations that have occurred in Italy over the last twenty years, partly as a result of the "economic miracle," but several quick comments about these transformations are in order. To begin with, there has been a dramatic turnover in the composition of the electorate. About half of the voters who witnessed the harsh political confrontations and the bitter polemics of the mid-1940s are no longer around. More important, 60 percent of the 1975 electorate has been added to the electoral registry since 1946. Many people who voted for the first time in the mid-1970s had not yet been born when Stalin died; others were too young to remember the Soviet intervention in Hungary or even the building of the Berlin Wall. The political memories of these voters thus differ significantly from those of the older cohorts. To the youth of 1978, communism is no longer the subversive, anticlerical force that frightened their fathers. It is not difficult to see why the political messages that are effective with the generations socialized in the 1940s and 1950s might be less relevant to those who have come of age politically during the years of Vietnam.[33]

One must also take into account the impact of the social changes that have accompanied the modernization of Italian society: higher levels of education, massive internal migrations, increasing urbanization. All these phenomena tend to break down the ties between individuals and their traditional political subcultures, rendering them open to new political appeals. Similarly, the widespread perception of social inequalities, coupled with rising expectations deriving from a period of substantial prosperity, cannot help but strengthen the appeals of those political forces that emphasize the ideal of a just and fair society and whose record is not marred by a credibility gap between promises and accomplishments.

Finally, secularization has increased, with a consequent decline of the Catholic tradition in political matters. The proportion of people who regularly attend mass and perform the religious injunctions of the church is shrinking. Among those who still engage in religious practice, many no longer heed the precepts of the clergy in political matters. Catholic organizations, which in previous periods played an important role, are either less effective or less flexible. The clergy's influence on political socialization appears to be declining.

In sum, it seems that many of the trends in Italian society over the last decade or so, together with the other factors mentioned above, have provided a favorable climate for change in the popular perceptions of the PCI and, consequently, for new directions in political behavior. One might offer a final observation that helps to explain why the continuous erosion of the moderate electorate has benefited primarily the PCI rather than other parties of the Left, such as the Socialists. To put things simply, the PCI has a number of positive assets that even its enemies have long recognized. It has performed reasonably well in the cities, provinces, and regions where it has held positions of governmental responsibility. It has a sizable core of competent party officers and a large number of committed militants. It enjoys the support of most intellectuals. It has fashioned, maintained, and expanded a strong and efficient organizational network, which is of great significance for harnessing popular support. The party's leadership is of high quality, and it has not so far been paralyzed or pulled in contradictory directions by the factionalism that has plagued other parties. Moreover, the weakening of preclusions against the PCI has brought with it an emphasis on the party's strength, unity, efficiency, and commitment. It is under-standable, therefore, that voters who no longer have doubts about the PCI's democratic character, its autonomy from the Soviet Union, and its commitment to preserve the nation's fundamental freedoms and to live by the rules of pluralistic democracy might see good reasons to cast their ballots for the Communists rather than for the Socialists.

The "Historic Compromise" Strategy

Whatever the reasons for its success at the polls in 1976, the PCI interpreted that success as confirmation of the correctness of the strategy that it had adopted in the early 1970s. The leadership could argue that the party's mass following had endorsed the strategy, that the strategy had helped attract new voters, and that it had increased the party's strength to a point where, in light of the distribution of seats in parliament, the PCI had greater bargaining power than ever before. The long-standing claim to be a party destined to govern (*un partito di governo*) began to seem more valid. Given the balance of forces resulting from the election, the Christian Democrats enjoyed little room for maneuver; conversely, the PCI had an excellent opportunity to press its traditional antagonist to take steps toward the broad coalition that the Communist leadership had been proposing since 1973: the "historic compromise."

Few expressions in Italian political discourse have elicited as many comments, polemics, and debates as has "historic compromise." Not unexpectedly, interpretations of the PCI proposal bearing this name differ. For some, it amounts to little more than another version of the "opening to the left" that the PCI has long advocated; for others, it represents a momentous change. Some believe that its realization would mark the triumph of Marxism in Italy; others see it as definitive proof that the PCI has accommodated itself to the existing system and has abandoned its original goal of a drastic transformation of Italian society. It is impossible to analyze here all the different interpretations that have been propounded—in part because the debate is still in progress—but it is useful, in order to discuss the implications of the current situation and prospects for the future, to look briefly at the arguments on which the Communist leadership has grounded its strategy and at the responses of other political elites to this strategy.

Although the term *historic compromise* appeared for the first time in a series of three articles Enrico Berlinguer wrote for the party's weekly *Rinascita* in the fall of 1973,[34] the main components of the PCI proposal can be found in earlier documents and pronouncements by party leaders (most notably those stemming from the 13th Party Congress in March 1972). Indeed, Berlinguer himself has stressed the continuity between his proposal and ideas that have been part of the PCI philosophy for a good many years and which can be traced back to the theoretical works of Gramsci and Togliatti.

At the core of Berlinguer's argument in 1973 for a "historic compromise" were the following propositions: To be successful, a Communist party's strategy must be realistic—i.e., it must take into account the particular conditions of the country in which the party operates, the history of the country, the internal distribution of social and political forces, and, last but not least, the international context. If leftist movements in the capitalist world attempt to transform their respective societies without considering powerful conditioning factors—both domestic and international—they are likely to suffer major defeats, as Greece in the 1940s and the recent example of Chile demonstrate.[35] Great changes cannot be brought about by antagonizing powerful oppositions, by splitting, as it were, society into two hostile "camps." Rather, such changes can be accomplished only by forging alliances with a variety of different social groups and with the mass parties that represent them. In Italy, the progressive-oriented proletarian class constitutes only a minority of the population. Between the working class and its antagonist, the bourgeoisie, there are intermediate strata whose support is crucial to Communist efforts to change society.[36] Hence, the Italian party should strive to promote a convergence of interests between these intermediate groups and the working class—that is, it should seek reforms that will improve the position of the latter without harming the position of the former.[37] In this regard, considerable attention must be paid to the "priorities and timing of social transformations . . . , not merely in order to prevent the collapse of the economy but, rather, to insure its effectiveness during the critical phase of transition to a new socialist order."[38]

Social alliances, Berlinguer went on, cannot be brought to fruition without the involvement of all political forces that represent the broad masses. Despite its connections with the bourgeoisie and its hostility to socialist movements, the Christian Democratic party is a force with considerable influence not only among the intermediate strata but also among Catholic members of the working class. Therefore, the DC, regardless of its ambiguous and contradictory nature, must not be excluded from the new and effective social bloc that the PCI is endeavoring to weld together. To exclude it would be to encourage conservative elements within the DC to push their party and the intermediate groups it represents further away from the working-class movement.[39] Eventually, this would divide the country into two blocs, a polarization of political life that would entail serious risks for the survival of a democratic regime. Under such conditions, it would be an illusion to think that even if the parties of the Left were to obtain 51 percent of the seats in parliament, a leftist government could survive and prosper after taking power.[40] The conclusion is inescapable: "The seriousness of the country's problems, the ever-present threats of reactionary groups, and the necessity to open the way for economic development, social change, and democratic progress of the nation" underscore the need "for that which can be defined as a new, great 'historic compromise' between the forces that represent the great majority of the Italian people."[41]

In the course of the debate, both within and outside the PCI, that followed the publication of Berlinguer's articles, other aspects of the party's strategy came into focus. Was the encounter with Catholic forces to result in an agreement between the DC and the PCI that would exclude other parties? The answer was a clear "no," since the PCI had always considered the Socialists "an essential component" of any alliance, having, like other "democratic forces" (Social Democrats and Republicans), "a peculiar and irreplaceable role to play."[42]

To the charge that the strategy was in effect a PCI acceptance of the DC "as it was," with all its defects, ambiguities, and hostility toward the Left, the reply was that the "historic compromise" did not imply that the PCI would renounce its right to criticize the Christian Democrats. To the contrary, the party would use its critiques to stimulate growth of the popular, democratic, and antifascist elements within the DC and to isolate its reactionary segments.[43] In this connection, Berlinguer contended that when groups of the New Left shouted slogans proclaiming that unity of the working class should take place against the DC, they only appeared to be revolutionary and were in fact taking a meaningless "sectarian" posture. According to Berlinguer, this approach played into the hands of domestic and international forces that stood to benefit from a deep division of Italian society.[44]

What did the encounter with the Catholics imply for PCI relations with the church? On this point, it was argued that an alliance between the PCI and the church was out of the question, but that at the same time the party had to recognize the role and needs of the church in Italy. Therefore, the party should follow a line designed to prevent a "break between believers and nonbelievers, Catholics and non-Catholics, between the church and the state"—a development that would have tragic consequences for the country and, above all, for the working-class movement.[45]

What relationship did the "historic compromise" have to the development of socialism in Italy? The leadership maintained that domestic and international constraints made it unrealistic to expect that Italy could become a socialist society in the short run. Hence, the immediate task was the introduction "into the general functioning of society of elements of socialism."[46] This was possible because certain social and economic reforms that could be supported by forces outside the socialist movement would inevitably bring about changes in "production relationships, distribution of wealth, consumption patterns, and life-style" along socialist lines.[47]

What were the implications of the "historic compromise" for foreign policy, specifically for Italy's position within NATO and the European Economic Community? On this point, the premise of the PCI's argument was the continuation of détente, with less rigid juxtaposition of the two political and military blocs in Europe making possible more autonomy for individual countries. However, since the blocs still exist and progress in negotiations on arms reduction depends on the maintenance of parity in military strength, "it is not realistic to think that single countries can unilaterally leave either one of the two camps."[48] In this situation, the PCI no longer objected to Italy's participation in the NATO alliance, although it insisted that its acceptance of the alliance must be accompanied by sustained efforts to improve relations between the two blocs and ultimately to make military alliances unnecessary. Similarly, with reference to the EEC, the leadership stated: "Certainly Italy cannot leave the European Economic Community; but within it there is a need for a democratization of its organs, and there is also a need to diminish the power of the large national and multinational groups which operate within the community."[49]

Finally, to answer those who objected to the term *compromise* (including the PCI's President Luigi Longo), Berlinguer said the expression did not necessarily have a derogatory connotation, that compromises are not all alike, and that as Lenin had shown, compromises at certain critical historical junctures can have revolutionary consequences.[50] In any event, he maintained, the "historic compromise" was not to be a narrow pact, a mere device for sharing power and its spoils, but rather "the result of efforts of mutual understanding, of an encounter and agreement reached by different popular democratic forces on issues of fundamental importance for the future of the country."[51]

Berlinguer's avowed intention was to provoke a debate on the PCI's proposal, and he succeeded in doing just that. Among the points made by politicians and non-Communist elites, the following were the most common. First, the basic philosophical tenets and *Weltanschauungen* of the PCI and DC are fundamentally opposed to each other and hence incompatible.[52] Second, an agreement involving the two major parties and the intermediate political forces (Socialists, Social Democrats, Republicans) would for all practical purposes eliminate legitimate, democratic opposition to the government, with serious consequences for the future of pluralistic democracy in the country.[53] Third, the PCI was seriously miscalculating in assuming that the "historic compromise" would make possible significant changes in Italian society in a socialist direction. Those who attributed primary responsibility to the DC for the national crisis that had developed could not believe that the process of systemic decay could be halted without smashing the mechanisms on which the DC had built its power base—that is, without replacing the Christian Democratic–dominated government entirely with a coalition of the Left.[54] To these and other observers, the "historic compromise" smacked of "transformism," an operation designed to make possible a sharing of the spoils by the two major parties.[55] Fourth, the PCI proposal would alter the existing balance of forces at the international level; hence, it would not be welcomed by the United States or the USSR, both of which, according to this line of argument, have an interest in preserving the division of Europe into two spheres of influence. Fifth, at least in the short run, there were questions about the feasibility of the PCI proposal. According to some commentators, the DC could not afford an encounter with the PCI without risking the loss of a sizable portion of the moderate electorate; by the same token, the PCI would run a risk—although to a lesser extent—of delivering a shock to, and causing a trauma for, many Communist militants if it entered a government coalition with the Christian Democrats.[56] Finally, in a future situation of severe economic crisis and mounting social unrest, the PCI would have primary responsibility for insuring the survival of the country but might not be able to restore order and revitalize the economy without recourse to strong methods. Projecting the final consequences of this scenario, Giovanni Sartori wrote: "The DC will lose its power; the PCI will lose its soul (or will find again its Stalinist soul); and 99 percent of Italians will lose whatever they still have."[57]

The Transition

The debates over the meaning of the "historic compromise" and the discussions about the changes in the Italian political system that it would entail were largely speculative and theoretical at this juncture, for in 1974 the role of the PCI, despite its overtures, remained unchanged. That is, the Communists were still an opposition force. And even after the municipal elections of June 1975, when the party improved its position in many areas of the country and acquired control of a number of large cities, the PCI role at the national level did not essentially change. To be sure, after the gains of 1975 the party loomed larger on the political scene, and the speculations about its future role were much less remote than they had been. But there were still some very important "ifs."

By January 1976, however, when the PSI withdrew from the center-left coalition, it was becoming clear that the alignments of the past were no longer viable and that a new political phase was in the making. And the results of the 1976 parliamentary elections brought the discussions of the role of the PCI down from the realm of abstract possibilities to the very concrete level of negotiations among the parties.

The events that followed the 1976 election have been widely reported and need not be recounted here in detail. With utter adamancy, the Socialists refused to support another government based on the center-left formula of the past, and they pressed for greater involvement of the PCI in governmental responsibilities. The Communists, for their part, insisted that a broad ruling coalition including the PCI was indispensable to the tackling of the serious economic and social crisis facing the country in the aftermath of the 1973 Arab oil embargo and the ensuing world economic recession. Although the verdict of the polls had not proved as unfavorable as some observers had predicted, the Christian Democrats discovered, much to their dislike, that they had little room for maneuver. The formula that eventually emerged was a DC minority cabinet led by Giulio Andreotti. This arrangement was a precarious one, resting as the prime minister noted, on a "lack of no confidence."[58] But it was palatable if not fully satisfactory. The Socialists had succeeded in involving the PCI, at least indirectly, and the Christian Democrats could argue that they had not reneged on their campaign pledge not to accept a coalition with the Communists. And, finally, the PCI could claim that it had at least achieved a role commensurate with its strength in the political system. Party Secretary Berlinguer, speaking in parliament, summed things up with some pride: "everybody knows by now that if we voted against, this government would fall immediately."[59]

There can be little doubt that the events of the summer of 1976 represented a victory for the PCI. They marked the first time that a prime minister designate had openly consulted the party; the first instance in which Communist action in parliament had been crucial to the survival of the cabinet; and, most important, the first occasion on which a Christian Democrat prime minister had not rejected as unwanted, or unnecessary, the votes of the PCI. The goal that the party had pursued for many years, to leave the "ghetto" of permanent opposition, had finally been achieved. To be sure, the interparty negotiations had fallen short of finding a fully satisfactory solution, as PCI leaders made quite clear in their comments and pronouncements. Yet from the party's standpoint, it certainly represented a step in the right direction, the achievement of a "more advanced position."[60]

The new role of the PCI was reinforced by the results of long and complex interparty negotiations, which took place in the spring of

1977 and which led to a limited agreement in July 1977 on the policies to be followed by the Andreotti cabinet. This agreement was certainly not a major breakthrough. It did not bring about a reshuffling of the cabinet, and it did not produce a formal transformation of the PCI's abstention into a vote of confidence. But it was an unprecedented development that had considerable symbolic significance and hence clearly represented another incremental gain for the PCI.[61]

A significant breakthrough did come, however, in March 1978. Early in 1978, after the Socialist and Republican parties had been insisting for several weeks that the Communists be admitted to the cabinet to enable the government to deal with pressing economic issues and terrorist activities, the PCI withdrew its indirect support of the DC minority government. Andreotti then submitted his cabinet's resignation. The protracted negotiations that followed produced an agreement whereby the PCI became a part of the parliamentary majority backing a reconstituted DC minority cabinet headed by Andreotti. The program approved by the five parties also included a number of proposed reforms that the Communists particularly wanted, such as an end to the military status of Italian police (which would permit them to unionize) and increased indirect taxes to finance industrial expansion.[62]

The developments of 1976-1978 had a number of consequences for the PCI's role in the political system. First of all, the party made further progress toward the goal of full legitimacy. The very fact that non-Communist elites had to consult, confer, and come to terms with the PCI weakened the traditional argument that the party is an "antisystem" party. Thus, it helped to undermine, in the eyes of moderate public opinion, the preclusions and objections that had in the past been at the core of anticommunism. As a leading Socialist intellectual has recently observed:

> If the Christian Democrats negotiate with the Communists, if they make joint important decisions with the PCI, if they form a parliamentary majority with the Communists, if this happens, the DC can no longer tell the Italian people that the PCI is a totalitarian party subservient to Moscow. On the contrary, the result will be that Italians will consider the PCI a party like the other ones, a party that can be in the government. And this would be a result of considerable political significance for the Communists.[63]

A second consequence of the PCI's new role in the political system is that the Communists have held more positions of both symbolic significance and considerable power. Pietro Ingrao, a leading PCI figure, holds the very prestigious office of chairman of the House of Deputies. Other members of the Communist parliamentary groups in the two houses head a number of important committees. Because of the advances made at the local level, PCI officers hold positions of substantial influence on the boards of directors of a large number of public organizations, such as hospitals, public transportation agencies, housing development agencies, and other significant municipal institutions.[64] Finally, the PCI has begun to benefit from the distribution of political appointments in financial institutions such as banks, and it has obtained some positions of considerable influence in the state-controlled radio and television networks.[65]

One could argue, of course, that these developments were long overdue and that the new positions the Communists have acquired represent only a modest gain for the party. Nevertheless, although the gains might be limited, they certainly have expanded the network of power positions that the party controls.

By the same token, there cannot be many doubts, in this author's opinion, about the PCI's enhanced influence in policymaking at the national level—a third consequence of the developments of 1976-1978. On this point, a number of other observers would tend to disagree. Indeed, some of the tensions that have emerged within the PCI since 1976, as well as the criticism directed at the party from outside, have been predicated on exactly the opposite notion, namely, that the PCI has not managed to exercise much influence on governmental policies. The critics point to the slow pace, even the lack, of tangible policy outcomes and to the Communists' support of measures that at least in the short run have not been beneficial to the working classes. Clearly, however, these negative and pessimistic evaluations of the PCI's role are strongly colored by what the critics believe the party might have accomplished. That these people feel not enough has been achieved is hardly proof that the party's influence has not grown. It cannot be denied that in 1976-1978 the PCI was openly consulted on most major policy decisions; that leaders of other parties attempted to anticipate the PCI's reactions to proposals for legislation; and that appointments to politically significant offices were made in consultation with Communist leaders. Such involvement in the governmental process might not be enough to satisfy critics, but it certainly represents a departure from the pattern of the past, when there were far fewer consultations and deals and when these took place in arenas of "invisible politics."[66]

The fourth consequence of the changing role of the PCI concerns the posture of the party vis-à-vis the cabinet and, more generally, vis-à-vis the Christian Democratic party. According to critics, the PCI has become too accommodating and has toned down its polemics against its traditional antagonist; in other quarters, the judgment is that the PCI is acting "responsibly." The PCI's behavior reflects the fact that it has a stake in the preservation of the current alignment, which it regards as a significant improvement over the past. This does not mean that the Communists have stopped pushing for a "more advanced" solution, but it does mean that they proceed very carefully, well aware that a harder stance might jeopardize retention of their recent gains. PCI leaders know that segments within the DC are fundamentally unhappy with the developments of the last few years, and the PCI certainly has no interest in providing these groups with more ammunition. To the contrary, the Communist leadership would like to bolster the elements within the DC whose cautious and perhaps reluctant moves have made possible the beginning of a new opening to the left.[67]

Such a cautious tactic is very much in line with the overall PCI strategy of the "historic compromise." Despite the unhappiness of the Socialists and other forces at the Communist emphasis, the DC remains the central target of the PCI efforts. From the PCI's standpoint, if the goal is a long-standing collaboration with the Catholic masses, it follows that one should avoid antagonizing the party that represents them. This precept has at least in part underlain the PCI's relative restraint on such issues as economic austerity measures, "fair rent" legislation, and changes in provisions governing cost-of-living increases for wage earners.

The last consequence of the PCI's new role is that the party can no longer blame government actions—and, even more, lack of government actions—entirely on other political forces. This situation is precisely what the Socialists had wanted,[68] and even the DC has recently come to appreciate its virtues.

Since the PCI's involvement in government at the national level is a recent development and since mass attitudes change slowly, the costs that it has entailed for the Communist Party to date have probably not been very high; but as time goes on, its impact in all likelihood will grow. To be sure, PCI leaders will argue, as indeed they already have, that some progress has been made; that problems are complex, and their solution takes time; and, lastly and most important, that responsibility for the delays, the inefficiencies, and the modest results achieved rests primarily with their reluctant partners, with those conservative sectors of society that do whatever they can to slow down the pace of change.[69] It is hard to predict whether these arguments will be effective and whether they will prevent an erosion of the popular support that the PCI now enjoys. But clearly the new role that the PCI assumed in 1976-1978 has spawned tensions and dilemmas that did not exist when it was in full-fledged opposition. It is to these that we now turn.

The PCI and the Left

In some respects, the situation in which the PCI finds itself in the late 1970s is similar to the situation that confronted it in the mid-1940s. Indeed, there are even striking parallels between the pronouncements of the party now and then. The recent characterization of the party as a *partito di lotta e di governo* ("party of struggle and governance") is hardly a new concept. It had been articulated by Palmiro Togliatti as early as 1944.[70]

According to Togliatti, the party, in order to be effective, had to operate both at the top, i.e., to participate in the government and play a leading role in it, and at the grass roots, i.e., to organize the masses and exert pressure from below. This dual approach maximized opportunities. "We participate in the government," said Togliatti, "but at the same time we reserve the right to criticize governmental action whenever it does not correspond to our program or to the needs of the people and to the aspirations of the masses."[71]

But, as Togliatti himself recognized, such an approach also opened up possibilities for tensions. The PCI's participation in the government imposed upon it the burden of justifying certain policies, or the lack thereof, to the masses. And it was obviously not easy to go to the masses and ask them to wait and be patient, or to attribute the government's shortcomings to the behavior of others.[72]

Although there are certainly differences between the 1940s and the 1970s, some fundamental structural similarities exist between the two situations. In both cases, the party reoriented its strategy, adopting Togliatti's *partito nuovo* in the first instance and Berlinguer's *compromesso storico* in the second. In both cases, strategic considerations required the party to tone down its polemics against former adversaries and to treat these ex-antagonists as partners in government. In both cases, there were expectations and demands for rapid change on the part of the working masses.[73] In both cases, the realities of having to share power with other forces constrained what the party could accomplish. In both cases, the Communist leadership saw the balance of forces at the international level as a key, limiting factor.[74]

Table 5:   Italian Voters' Preferences
for Alternative Governmental Coalitions,
Summer 1977

(in percent by party preference[a])

Kind of Cabinet	Party	
	PCI	DC
Present Andreotti cabinet without changes in the composition	0.7	29.0
A DC minority cabinet including independent ministers chosen with the consent of the PCI	14.3	34.1
A new cabinet with representatives of PCI, PSI, PSDI, PRI, DC, and PLI	41.3	21.5
A cabinet of the Left (PCI and PSI) possibly open to other parties but without the DC	34.6	1.6
Other answers, no answer, does not know	6.0	13.8

[a]Figures represent percent of respondents in a nationwide sample.

SOURCE: *La Discussione*, August 8, 1977.

It should not be surprising, then, that the latter half of the 1970s has witnessed increased tensions between the party and the working masses. Despite the PCI's efforts to dampen excessive optimism when it took on its new responsibilities, there is evidence of the emergence of a mood of frustration and impatience among PCI followers, as party leaders have explicitly admitted.[75] There is evidence, too, of uneasiness among party officials over what they regard as the slow progress of reform and the lack of significant, tangible results from the PCI's new role.[76] Although it is difficult to assess how intense and widespread mass dissatisfaction is—and even more to project its likely impact—the implementation of the PCI strategy in the second half of the 1970s has clearly complicated the relationship between the party and the masses much in the same way that it did in earlier times.

That such conditions have also generated strains within the PCI seems fairly clear. To begin with, the party leadership appears to have had difficulties in persuading the party rank and file to accept its new course. A majority of PCI voters evidently supports the "historic compromise" line, but there is hardly unanimity on the subject. Recent surveys have shown that a segment of the PCI electorate does not fully approve the party's official stance.[77] Indeed, as Table 5 indicates, approximately one out of three Communist voters in the summer of 1977 preferred a coalition of the Left that would exclude the Christian Democrats from office—a formula certainly not contemplated by the leadership. Perhaps in time those PCI followers who are now skeptical and uneasy will develop more positive attitudes about the realignment that the party leaders envisage, but such a shift in outlook may not come quickly.

The major reason for this state of affairs is the considerable residue of hostility toward the Christian Democratic party among the Communist rank and file. In the mid-1970s, few Communist sympathizers attributed positive qualities to the DC. The large majority of PCI voters saw the Christian Democrats as inefficient, old, conservative, clerical forces tainted by corruption (see Table 6). Given this image of the DC, it is hardly surprising to find much skepticism at the grass-roots level of the PCI about agreements and coalitions with the Christian Democrats.[78]

In part, these negative perceptions of the DC reflect the polemics and the political vicissitudes of the past. That is, there are many echoes of the charges of corruption, malpractice, and inefficiency that the PCI has hurled at the DC over the years. But these attitudes also stem in part from the ambiguous posture that the PCI now takes in this period of transition. The DC is no longer the antagonist, but it

Table 6: Italian Communist Voters' Views of Christian Democracy, 1975

(in percent)

The DC is...	Yes	No	No opinion, no answer
"The party of the rich and powerful"	69.1	15.7	15.2
"A clerical party"	76.7	7.1	16.1
"An old party"	78.6	9.9	11.6
"A progressive party"	13.0	66.9	20.1
"An efficient party"	11.9	74.3	13.8
"An honest party"	7.6	75.7	16.7

SOURCE: Data were drawn from the 1975 survey conducted by Giovanni Sartori and Alberto Marradi. The percentages reported are based on the answers of 658 Communist respondents.

has not yet become a partner. Hence, it has to be criticized and pressured to move in the "right" direction. At the same time, to attack the DC frontally, as in the past, is no longer appropriate. Nowhere is this ambiguous posture more evident than in the PCI's view of the Italian crisis. Communist statements typically contend that the DC is fundamentally responsible for the crisis, but they likewise depict the DC as an indispensable force, along with the PCI, for pulling the country out of its predicament.[79] Such contradictory cues from the party leadership tend to encourage selective perception and retention of negative attitudes at the mass level.

In addition to having trouble getting some of the PCI rank and file to go along with the new party line, the party leadership has been encountering substantial dissatisfaction among party faithful with the results of its policy. Although few if any Communists believed that the new role of the PCI would signal the arrival of the millennium, many did have fairly high expectations when the party assumed a greater governmental role, and these continue to exist. To a major extent, such expectations grow out of party pronouncements and behavior in past years. While in the opposition, the PCI blamed government policies—at times with good reason—for the sad state of the country and for the many unresolved problems that had accumulated over the postwar years; it argued that things would change once it brought its influence and expertise to bear on matters. Indeed, the relegation of the PCI to opposition status and the requirements of electoral competition reinforced the party's inclination to be critical of other forces, to articulate demands, and to make implicit or explicit promises to the electorate. This is not to say that all current expectations flow out of the earlier behavior and pronouncements of the PCI. Many have their roots in objective realities, and some are the consequence of the behavior of other parties. But certainly the PCI has played a significant role in stressing problems and in identifying and magnifying aspects of popular dissatisfaction with the outputs of the political system.

It is hard to tell how deep and pervasive the feelings of frustration and disillusionment are at this writing. However, we do have some evidence that the desire for change and the conviction that change must be radical have been growing among the masses in recent years. During the first part of the 1970s, popular dissatisfaction with the outputs of the political system increased sharply, and there was a corresponding increase in the percentage of voters who felt that only a fundamental transformation of society could turn things around.[80] A 1976 study commissioned by the PCI showed that a substantial

Table 7:   Views of Young Italians Favoring Parties of the Left
on the Kind of Change Needed to Solve the Problems
of Italian Society, Summer 1977

(in percent)

Party Preference

Kind of Change	Ultra-Left	Radical Party	PCI	PSI
Gradual	14.0	34.7	49.2	55.8
Radical	64.0	57.1	47.4	39.1
Revolution	22.0	6.1	2.3	0.0
Other answers, no answer	0.0	2.0	1.1	2.2

SOURCE: Data are drawn from Table 10.2 and comments on p. 122 of *Bollettino Doxa*, September 12, 1977.   They are part of the results of a nation-wide survey of Italian youth in the summer of 1977.

number of electors wanted drastic change.[81] This evidence suggests that substantial portions of the PCI may harbor deep feelings of frustration and disillusionment at the moment.

The PCI leadership is certainly aware of the dangers implicit in the chasm between expectations and accomplishments.[82] Given the party's self-consciousness, its careful monitoring of social dynamics, and its effective and pervasive organizational network, one would hardly anticipate otherwise. And the leadership's concern about these dangers has manifested itself most plainly in a preoccupation with the party's standing among youth.[83] The party even organized a number of special meetings in the spring and fall of 1977 to discuss the youth problem—meetings that revealed a variety of perspectives on the issue.[84]

A combination of factors accounts for the PCI leadership's worries about the attitudes of youth. First, the young generation of voters made a significant contribution to the party's electoral advances in the mid-1970s, and the PCI must retain this support if it is to consolidate its gains and make further progress.[85] Second, the party knows that segments of leftist youth are susceptible to the appeals of the ultra-Left. The student riots in Communist-run Bologna in March 1977 and the massive demonstration of leftist youth in the same city a few months later have made this susceptibility all too clear. Although party officials blamed a few provocateurs for the violence, the spectacle of sizable groups of students openly attacking the PCI obviously troubled the party. Lastly, the young have experienced unemployment and social dislocation to a greater degree than older segments of the population.

Data gathered by the Doxa Institute in the summer of 1977 indicate that the concern of party leaders about the attitudes of youth is justified. Although these data do not specifically demonstrate the unhappiness of the young with the PCI, they do attest that many within the younger generations are broadly dissatisfied with the situation in the country and worry about the future.[86] The same survey also shows that many youth feel that only a radical change will solve the problems of Italian society. This point of view is particularly pronounced among those who sympathize with the parties of the Left. Table 7 breaks down this segment of the sample. These data suggest two conclusions relevant to the present discussion. First, if the PCI adopts too moderate a course of action, it could in the long run alienate a sizable portion of its backers among young voters. Furthermore, given the present orientations of the supporters of the radical Left (i.e., the Radical Party and the ultra-

Giacomo Sani

Table 8:   Partisan Preferences
of Young Leftist Voters, Summer 1977

(in percent)

Ultra-Left groups	11.7
Radical Party	10.7
Communist Party	57.2
Socialist Party	20.4

SOURCE: Data were drawn from *Bollettino Doxa*, September 12, 1977, but were recomputed by the author.

Left), there is little chance that the PCI will succeed in recapturing this segment of the electorate.

Because of the small size of the radical Left at present, the latter situation does not in itself constitute a serious problem at this writing. But there is no doubt that in time it could. For groups of the radical Left attract greater sympathy from young voters, and from future voters, than from the electorate as a whole. Most commentators on the 1976 election have agreed that this is the case,[87] and recent survey evidence has corroborated this judgment. Table 8 gives the distribution of party preferences among youth who favored the Left in a poll of young voters taken in the summer of 1977. For a variety of technical reasons, this breakdown must be considered a tentative estimate rather than an accurate picture of reality; nevertheless, the figures do have some significance. If the radical Left continues to gain strength among leftist youth, the PCI in the future could face a serious challenge from its left.

It is significant, then, that in the 1970s the Communists have lost their monopoly over the extreme left of the political spectrum, a monopoly they held during the first twenty-five years of the postwar period. During the 1970s several political groups that compete with the PCI for this position have come into being. These new radical forces lack any mass base to speak of, enjoy only minuscule

Table 9: Attitudes of Young Leftists on Actions and Ideas
of the Ultra-Left, Summer 1977

(in percent by party preference)

Approve actions/ ideas of the ultra-Left	Radical Party		PCI		PSI	
	Actions	Ideas	Actions	Ideas	Actions	Ideas
Always	8.2	22.4	1.5	4.9	2.1	4.2
Often	10.2	24.5	3.8	10.9	3.2	12.6
Sometime	22.4	24.5	10.9	26.3	8.4	25.3
Never	53.1	26.5	76.7	48.5	80.0	51.6
No answer, other answer	6.1	2.0	7.1	9.4	6.3	6.3

SOURCE: *Bollettino Doxa*, September 12, 1977, p. 151.

representation in parliament and local bodies,[88] and are badly divided among themselves. But they have political visibility and influence considerably beyond what their numerical strength would suggest. And the fact that they attack the PCI from the left with arguments that have a traditional leftist flavor magnifies the challenge.

Whether these groups will succeed in attracting greater support among those who sympathize with the Left remains to be seen. In the summer of 1977, a Doxa Institute survey found that an overwhelming majority of Italian youth still reacted negatively to the unorthodox and sometimes violent *actions* of the groups of the ultra-Left. However, the tendency to condemn the *ideas* of these groups was far less pronounced. In fact, as Table 9 shows, a considerable segment of young Communist and Socialist sympathizers expressed at least occasional approval of the ideals and positions of the groups of the radical Left. Although it would be unwise to extrapolate from these findings and draw inferences about future electoral returns, it does seem legitimate to say that in pursuing its current strategy, the PCI risks alienating those segments of the electorate that look with at least some sympathy on more radical alternatives, and thus to some extent eroding its support base.

The International Dimension

Interestingly enough, the PCI's expanded responsibilities have not, up to early 1978, raised the level of tension in one realm where they might conceivably have done so—namely, in the party's relations with the international communist movement and particularly with the Communist Party of the Soviet Union (CPSU). Before the formation of an Italian cabinet not explicitly "closed" to the PCI, strains had already developed between the Italian Communists and Moscow. The PCI had long asserted its right to autonomy and to define an explicitly "Italian way to socialism." Indeed, Berlinguer had even gone so far as to suggest that such a course was possible only so long as Italy remained outside the "socialist camp."[89] As a result of this perspective, the PCI had expressed not only a willingness to tolerate Italian membership in NATO but also a desire to accelerate the process of European integration. Moreover, Italian Communists had more and more frequently given vent to criticism of the Soviet Union and Eastern Europe—especially on the issues of civil rights and individual freedom—as the party attempted to emphasize aspects of its "road to socialism" that might reassure an uneasy public opinion.[90] Such manifestations of the PCI's primary concern with its own interests had predictably irritated Soviet leaders.

The PCI's enlarged role in the governmental affairs of Italy opened up possibilities for even more discord. Having bettered its position but having fallen short of its goal of entry into the cabinet, the PCI might have sought to improve its image among the supporters of the Christian Democrats by selective measures to demonstrate its independence of the USSR. Aspects of the party's composition tended to enhance the likelihood of such a development. For example, most PCI militants and low-level cadres, according to statements of PCI officials reported by the press, have joined the party since 1968,[91] and the younger generations of PCI leaders and party members are far less attached to the "myth of the Soviet Union" and less restrained by the ties of the past than the older cohorts they are gradually replacing. Thus, they are not so reluctant to engage in confrontation with the USSR. In the face of the PCI's clear determination to pursue its "heresies" in order to effect a "grand coalition" including the Christian Democrats, furthermore, Moscow might have reacted vehemently.

Neither of these potentialities, however, has come to pass as of the beginning of 1978. By and large, the Soviet Union has responded positively to the PCI's acquisition of greater influence in governmental affairs in Italy. It is conceivable, to be sure, that Moscow's June 1977 attack on Santiago Carrillo, secretary-general of the Spanish Communist Party, for the views expressed in his *Eurocommunism and the State*[92] may have been meant in part as a warning to the PCI not to use its growing influence in Italy to further the formation of an anti-Soviet bloc of West European "socialist" states. Nevertheless, Moscow has eschewed any frontal assault on the PCI for undertaking new responsibilities. The PCI, in turn, has tried to uphold its line without being unduly provocative to the USSR. This approach emerged clearly during the controversy over Carrillo's *Eurocommunism and the State*. Instead of rising strongly to the Spanish leader's defense, the PCI attempted to serve as a mediator of differences. That is, it defended the right of the Spanish Communists to chart their own course, but it refrained from endorsing all of Carrillo's arguments.[93]

No appreciable evidence of additional strains in PCI-CPSU relations has cropped up as yet, but new tensions may still arise. One can set forth various scenarios according to which this potential might become a reality, but what seems most critical—in the author's view—is not so much the willingness of the PCI to increase its distance from Moscow as the emergence of international issues that might force the party to take positions antagonistic to the USSR. Even then, the PCI leaders know that an outright break would be costly in terms of the party's standing with other Communist parties and many of its own constituents, and they would clearly be reluctant to accept the unpleasant consequences unless forced to do so.[94] For this reason, the likelihood of an open break between the PCI and CPSU appears fairly low.

Prospects

As we have seen, then, the developments of the mid-1970s have greatly increased the strength of the PCI and have expanded the Communists' role in the political system. But these very same developments have also given rise to tensions within the PCI and have complicated life for the party leaders.

These problems would for the most part disappear if the PCI returned to the opposition. There are segments of the party that favor such a course, and it cannot be entirely ruled out as a possibility. But it would entail heavy costs—especially since it would create doubts about the PCI's commitment to the "historic compromise" that the party has pursued so tenaciously for the past few years. As Berlinguer argued at a meeting of the party's Central Committee in October 1977, such a move would be a step backward, not a solution to the party's difficulties.[95] Therefore, there seems a fairly low probability that the PCI will take this path.

Nor is it likely that new elections would decisively alter the balance of forces among parties. The results of some local elections in the spring of 1977 suggest that the PCI's fortunes may experience some ups and downs,[96] but neither a collapse nor a great surge in its electoral strength appears in the cards.

All things considered, it seems probable that the "transitional" phase of Italian politics inaugurated in 1976 will persist, with all its uncertainties and ambiguities, for some time to come.

Notes

1. These figures include a number of seats won by independent candidates running on PCI lists.

2. This march represented a continuation of the confrontation between the PCI and several groups of the radical Left. In March 1977, elements of the radical Left had staged violent demonstrations in the

same city. The demonstrators had accused the PCI of cooperating with the police in suppressing the movement; the PCI, in turn, had severely reprimanded those who had engaged in looting and political violence. For a radical Left interpretation of the March events, see the collectively authored *Bologna Marzo 1977* [Bologna, March 1977] (Verona: Bertani Editore, 1977). For the PCI evaluation of these events and the problems posed by the "movement," see Angelo Bolaffi and Paolo Franchi, "Il partito della lotta armata" [The party of armed struggle]; Enrico Menduni, "Gli studenti e la democrazia" [The students and democracy]; and the interview with Renato Zangheri, mayor of Bologna—all in *Rinascita* (Rome), March 18, 1977. See also Renzo Imbeni, "Qual'è il pericolo" [What the danger is], and Biagio de Giovanni, "Riflessioni sul nuovo sovversivismo" [Reflections on the new political agitator], in ibid., March 25, 1977; Fabio Mussi, "Immagini e discorsi del convegno di Bologna" [Sights and words of the meeting at Bologna], and Renzo Imbeni, "Che cosa hanno imparato ma anche insegnato la città' e i communisti" [The lesson that the city and the Communists have learned and also taught] in ibid., September 30, 1977.

3. Information on the changes in local governments resulting from the 1975 regional, provincial, and communal elections can be found in *Almanacco PCI 1976* [PCI almanac 1976] (Rome, January 1976), especially pp. 178-181.

4. Analysis of returns at the regional level for pairs of adjacent elections shows that in the 1946-1976 period only three regions posted two consecutive losses: Liguria (in 1946-1953 and 1953-1958), Basilicata (1963-1968 and 1968-1972), and Sicily (1963-1968 and 1968-1972).

5. For discussion of the PCI strategy in the postwar period, see Sidney Tarrow, *Peasant Communism in Southern Italy* (New Haven, Conn.: Yale University Press, 1967); Donald L. M. Blackmer, *Unity and Diversity: Italian Communism and the Communist World* (Cambridge, Mass.: MIT Press, 1968); idem, "Italian Communism: Strategy for the 1970s," *Problems of Communism*, May-June 1972, pp. 41-56; idem, "Continuity and Change in Postwar Italian Communism," in *Communism in Italy and France*, ed. Donald L. M. Blackmer and Sidney Tarrow (Princeton, N.J.: Princeton University Press, 1975), pp. 21-68; and Giuseppe Mammarella, *Il partito comunista italiano: 1945-75* [The Italian Communist Party, 1945-75] (Florence: Vallecchi, 1976).

6. For analyses of the social composition of the electoral base of the PCI, see Mattei Dogan, "La stratificazione sociale dei suffragi"

[The social stratification of the voters], in *Elezioni e comportamento politico in Italia* [Elections and political behavior in Italy], ed. Alberto Spreafico and Joseph LaPalombara (Milan: Edizioni di Comunità, 1963); Lawrence E. Hazelrigg, "Religious and Class Bases of Political Conflict in Italy," *American Journal of Sociology*, January 1970, pp. 496-511; Samuel H. Barnes, "Italy: Religion and Class in Electoral Behavior," in *Electoral Behavior: A Comparative Handbook*, ed. Richard Rose (New York: Free Press, 1974); Paolo Sylos Labini, *Saggio sulle classi sociali* [Essay on the social classes] (Bari: Laterza, 1975); Giorgio Galli, *Dal Bipartitismo imperfetto alla possible alternativa* [From imperfect bipartisanism to a possible alternative] (Bologna: Il Mulino, 1975); Livio Maitan, *Dinamica delle classi sociali in Italia* [The dynamic of the social classes in Italy] (Rome: Savelli, 1975); Giacomo Sani, "Mass Level Response to Party Strategy: The Italian Electorate and the Communist Party," in Blackmer and Tarrow, *Communism in Italy and France*, pp. 456-503.

7. The quotation is from a speech by Togliatti, "I compiti del partito nella situazione attuale" [The tasks of the party in the current situation], delivered October 3, 1944, in Florence and reprinted in *Critica Marxista*, (Rome), nos. 5-6, September-December 1963, p. 336. A recent survey commissioned by the PCI and conducted by the Demoskopea Institute of Milan appears to confirm the general picture presented in Figure 3. See Chiara Sebastiani, "Un paese insoddisfatto e politicamente maturo" [A dissatisfied and politically mature country], *Rinascita*, May 13, 1977, pp. 6-7.

8. For a characterization of the PCI as a "populist party," see Sidney Tarrow, "The Italian Party System between Crisis and Transition" (Paper delivered at the panel of the Conference Group on Italian Politics, American Political Science Association meeting, Chicago, Illinois, September 2-5, 1976). PCI commentators frown upon the use of the expression *catchall* to designate their party, yet they stress that support for the party comes from a broad range of social strata. See, for example, Celso Ghini, *Il terremoto del 15 giugno* [The earthquake of June 15] (Milan: Feltrinelli, 1976), pp. 270-271; and similar comments by the same author in *L'Italia che cambia* [Changing Italy] (Rome: Editori Riuniti, 1977).

9. Giacomo Sani, "Le elezioni degli anni settanta: terremoto o evoluzione" [The elections of the '70s: earthquake or evolution], in *Rivista Italiana di Scienza Politica* (Bologna) vol. 6, no. 2, 1976. The interpretation is summarized in English in idem, "Mass Support for Italian Communism: Trends and Prospects," in *Italy and Euro-communism*, ed. Giovanni Sartori and Austin Ranney (Washington,

D.C.: Hoover Institution and American Enterprise Institute, forthcoming).

10. Shifts of votes within the Left were facilitated by the fact that between 1972 and 1976 a number of political groups disappeared (i.e., Partito Socialista Italiano di Unità Proletaria, Movimento Politico dei Lavoratori) and others emerged (Democrazia Proletaria, Radical Party).

11. If it is important to stress the novel elements of the vote for the PCI, it is equally important not to lose sight of the contribution made by the PCI's traditional supporters. Without an extremely high rate of loyalty on the part of electors who had already voted for the PCI in previous elections, the successes of the mid-1970s would not have been possible. Analysis of the returns and survey evidence suggest that only a tiny portion of the PCI electorate defected in 1975 and 1976. On this point, see my "Mass Support for Italian Communism," Table 5.

12. Giovanni Sartori, "European Political Parties: The Case of Polarized Pluralism," in *Political Parties and Political Development*, ed. Joseph LaPalombara and Myron Weiner (Princeton, N.J.: Princeton University Press, 1966), pp. 137-176.

13. Giacomo Sani, "Mass Level Constraints on Political Realignments: Perceptions of Anti-System Parties in Italy," *British Journal of Political Science*, vol. 6, 1976, pp. 1-31.

14. This point is documented in Table 15 of my "Mass Level Response to Party Strategy," p. 488.

15. According to data released by the Demoskopea Institute, some 30 percent of the Christian Democratic electorate polled opposed repeal of the divorce law. See *Ricerche demoscopiche* (Milan), May-June 1974.

16. See, for example, Raniero La Valle, "Il travaso è di voti cattolici" [The shift involves Catholic votes], *Rinascita*, June 25, 1976, p. 4.

17. For a discussion of several aspects of dissent within the Catholic groups, see Arturo Parisi, "La matrice socio-religiosa del dissenso cattolico in Italia" [The socioreligious characteristics of Catholic dissent in Italy], *Il Mulino* (Bologna), vol. 20, 1971, pp. 637-657; and idem, *Referendum e questione cattolica: L'inizio di una fine* [Referendum and the Catholic issue: the beginning of the end] (Bologna: Il Mulino, 1974). For an evaluation of the role of the church in the 1976 election, see Arturo Parisi and Gianfranco Pasquino, "20 giugno: struttura politica e comportamento elettorale" [June 20: political structure and electoral behavior] in *Continuità e mutamento elettorale in Italia* [Continuity and electoral

change in Italy], ed. Arturo Parisi and Gianfranco Pasquino (Bologna: Il Mulino, 1977), pp. 11-66.

18. See Tables 6 and 7 of my chapter "La nuova immagine del PCI e l'elettorato Italiano" [The new image of the PCI and the Italian electorate], in *Il Comunismo in Italia e in Francia* [Communism in Italy and France], ed. Donald Blackmer and Sidney Tarrow (Milan: Etas/Libri, 1976).

19. These findings appeared in the bulletin of the Demoskopea Institute, *Ricerche demoscopische*, nos. 1-2, 1975.

20. Sani, "La nuova immagine del PCI e l'elettorato Italiano," Tables 8 and 9.

21. A study conducted by Alberto Marradi and Giovanni Sartori in 1975 showed that many moderate voters attributed these positive qualities to the PCI. The results of this study were made available to the author personally by Marradi and Sartori.

22. Data published in *Bollettino Doxa*, September 1, 1976.

23. See *Ricerche demoscopiche*, nos. 1-2, 1975.

24. The survey was commissioned by the Christian Democratic party and conducted by the Demoskopea Institute. Some preliminary findings are presented in *La Discussione* (Rome), August 8, 1977, p. 2.

25. This conclusion is supported by other recent surveys. See, for example, *Rinascita*, May 13, 1977, pp. 6-7.

26. Changes in the PCI's position on a number of issues have been widely reported by the press. For an overall picture of the party line in the mid-1970s, see Enrico Berlinguer's report to the 14th PCI Congress, which took place in Rome on March 18-23, 1975. This speech is reprinted in *XIV Congresso del Partito Comunista Italiano* [The 14th Congress of the Italian Communist Party] (Rome: Editori Riuniti, 1975), pp. 15-76. The PCI's official position at the June 1976 Berlin Conference of European Communist Parties is summarized in Sergio Segre, "La conferenza di Berlino" [The Berlin conference], *Rinascita*, July 9, 1976, p. 1. See also Antonio Rubbi, "Berlino oltre le polemiche" [Berlin behind the polemics], ibid., July 30, 1976, p. 9. On the international positions of the PCI, see Donald L. M. Blackmer, "The International Strategy of the Italian Communist Party," in *The International Role of the Communist Parties of Italy and France*, ed. Donald L. M. Blackmer and Annie Kriegel (Cambridge, Mass.: Center for International Affairs, Harvard University Press, 1975). For a review of changes in the PCI line over time, see Mammarella, *Il Partito comunista italiano*. A recent PCI document summarizing the party's view of issues and outlining solutions is *Proposta di progetto a medio termine* [Proposal of a

medium-range plan] (Rome: Editori Riuniti, 1977), with an introduction by Giorgio Napolitano.

27. Giovanni Sartori, "Revisitando il pluralismo polarizzato" [Reviewing polarized pluralism], in *Il caso italiano* [The Italian case], ed. Fabio Luca Cavazza and Stephen Graubard (Milan: Garzanti, 1974), p. 210.

28. Studies of the press include Ignazio Weiss, *Politica dell' informazione* [The politics of information] (Milan: Edizioni di Comunità, 1961); Paolo Murialdi, *La stampa italiana del dopoguerra* [The Italian press of the postwar period] (Bari: Laterza, 1973); Vittorio Capecchi and Marino Livolsi, *La stampa quotidiana in Italia* [The daily press in Italy] (Milan: Bompiani, 1971); Gaetano Fusaroli, *Giornali in Italia* [Newspapers in Italy] (Parma: Guanda Editore, 1974); Valerio Castronovo and Nicola Tranfaglia, eds., *La stampa italiana del neo-capitalismo* [The Italian press of neocapitalism] (Bari: Laterza, 1976).

29. *La presenza sociale del PCI e della DC* [The social presence of the PCI and the DC] (Bologna: Il Mulino, 1968); Giorgio Galli and Alfonso Prandi, *Patterns of Political Participation in Italy* (New Haven, Conn.: Yale University Press, 1970).

30. Giacomo Sani, "Canali di comunicazione politica e orientamente dell'elettorato" [Channels of political communication and the orientations of the electorate], *Rivista italiana di scienza politica,* no. 2, 1974, pp. 371-386.

31. Discussing changes in the press, Luca Pavolini speaks of "steps forward" and "more objective information," in "Stampa e democrazia" [The press and democracy], *Rinascita,* August 27, 1976. For other evidence of changes and discussion by different political observers, see the debate in *Panorama* (Milan), no. 488, 1976; and Peter Lange, "What Is to Be Done—About Italian Communism?" *Foreign Policy,* Winter 1975-1976, pp. 224-240.

32. On this point, see the observations made by a leading Socialist intellectual, Giuseppe Tamburrano, in an interview published in *Il settimanale* (Milan), September 1977.

33. For a study of values among Italian youth, see Carlo Tullio Altan, *I valori difficili* [The difficult values] (Milan: Bompiani, 1974).

34. The texts of Berlinguer's articles "Reflessioni sull'Italia dope i fatti del Cile" [Reflections on Italy after the Chilean events] are now reprinted in a collection of speeches and other documents edited by Antonio Tato, *La "questione comunista"* [The "Communist question"] (Rome: Editori Riuniti, 1975), vol. 2, pp. 609-639.

35. Ibid., pp. 618-619.

36. Ibid., p. 629.

37. Ibid., p. 631.

38. Ibid., p. 632.

39. Ibid., p. 636.

40. Ibid., p. 633.

41. Ibid., pp. 638-639.

42. Enrico Berlinguer, "Per transformare la scuola e l'istruzione, per rennovare l'Italia" [For the transformation of the schools and education, for the renewal of Italy], speech delivered in Bologna on October 27, 1973, in ibid., p. 647.

43. See ibid., pp. 657-658.

44. Ibid., pp. 648, 643.

45. Ibid., pp. 656-657.

46. Berlinguer's report to the Central Committee in preparation for the 14th Congress, December 10-12, 1974, reprinted in ibid., p. 868.

47. Ibid.

48. Ibid., p. 877.

49. Ibid., p. 879.

50. Ibid., pp. 626-627.

51. Ibid., p. 649.

52. See, e.g., Giuseppe De Rosa, "Un'operazione suicida" [Operation suicide], in the discussion of the "historic compromise," *Biblioteca della liberta* (Turin), July-August 1974, pp. 38-42.

53. See, e.g., Nicola Matteucci, "Salvare la componente liberal-democratica" [Preserving the liberal democratic model], in ibid., pp. 65-67.

54. This is the central thesis advanced by a group of intellectuals who have formed an association to promote a "left alternative" (Azione e Ricerca per l'Alternativa). Reports presented at a meeting of the association in Milan on April 18-19, 1975, are reprinted in Massimo Teodori, ed., *Per l'alternativa* [For the alternative] (Milan: Libreria Feltrinelli, 1975).

55. See, e.g., Gianfranco Pasquino, "Il sistema politico italiano tra neo-transformismo e democrazia consociativa" [The Italian political system between neotransformism and consociational democracy], *Il Mulino*, July-August 1973; and idem, "Compromesso e ordine" [Compromise and order], *Biblioteca della libertà*, July-August 1974, pp. 81-85.

56. See, e.g., Giovanna Zincone, "Una maggioranza inquietante" [A worrisome majority], in ibid., pp. 118-121.

57. Ibid., p. 98.

58. Andreotti used the expression in his speech in parliament on August 4, 1976.

59. *L'Unità*, August 11, 1976, p. 12.

60. This was the language that party commentary employed. See, for example, *Rinascita*, August 20, 1976, p. 3.

61. Emanuele Macaluso, "Il peso e l'unità delle masse" [The influence and unity of the masses], *Rinascita*, July 22, 1977. The July 1977 agreement did not cover foreign policy matters; however, the six parties that supported the Andreotti cabinet signed a joint statement on foreign policy in the fall of 1977. See *Corriere della Sera*, October 19, 1977, and December 3, 1977.

62. See, for example, *Corriere della Sera*, March 8-13, 1978.

63. Guiseppe Tamburrano, in *Il settimanale*, September 21, 1977, p. 17. An example of what Tamburrano had in mind is provided by the headline "Christian Democrats and Communists Agree," on the first page of *Corriere della Sera*, November 7, 1977.

64. Data on the distribution among the three largest parties (DC, PCI, PSI) of such key positions in the different regions are presented in *La discussione*, September 19, 1977, p. 2.

65. The PCI's apparent acceptance of the principle of the division of the spoils, which the party had criticized in the past, gave rise to a polemic within the party as well as between the party and its outside detractors in the summer and fall of 1977. See *Corriere della Sera*, October 21, 1977, p. 1.

66. For a recent and comprehensive analysis of this aspect of the behavior of parties in different arenas, see Giuseppe Di Palma, *Surviving without Governing* (Berkeley and Los Angeles: University of California Press, 1977).

67. There is evidence of this position in a number of recent statements by PCI leaders. See, for example, Emanuele Macaluso, "La sinistra, la DC e i nodi del confronto" [The Left, the DC, and the issues], *Rinascita*, October 28, 1977, pp. 1-2.

68. The PSI's insistence on the formal association of the PCI with the government grew out of a desire to make the Communists subject to popular dissatisfaction with austerity measures along with other parties. To use an expression widely reported in the press in 1976-1977, the PSI would no longer be left to "shake the tree while the PCI collected the apples."

69. See, for example, the interview given by Gerardo Chiaromonte in *Rinascita*, November 11, 1977.

70. Togliatti's concept of the "new party" was set forth in a series of speeches: "La politica nazionale dei comunisti" [The national

policy of the Communists], Naples, April 1944; "Per la libertà
d'Italia, per la creazione di un vero regime democratico" [For the
freedom of Italy, for the creation of a truly democratic regime], Rome,
July 9, 1944; "Avanti verso la democrazia" [Onward to democracy],
Rome, September 1944; "I compiti del partito nella situazione
attuale" [The tasks of the party in the present situation], Florence,
October 1944. These speeches were published individually in
pamphlet form by the party after the liberation of the entire country
in 1945. Subsequent citations come from these pamphlets. In 1963-
1964, *Critica marxista* (Rome) reprinted not only these speeches but
also many others that Togliatti had made during the mid-1940s.

71. Togliatti, "I compiti del partito nella situazione attuale," p.
30.

72. Togliatti, "Avanti verso la democrazia," p. 18.

73. On the existence of widespread expectations for change in the
immediate postwar period, see Giuseppe Mammarella, *L'italia dopo
il fascismo* [Italy after Fascism] (Bologna: Il Mulino, 1970),
especially pp. 93-99.

74. That the connection between the "historic compromise" and
the international situation is very strong is demonstrated by
numerous references to the latter in Berlinguer's famous article
"Riflessioni sull'Italia dopo gli eventi del Cile." The linkage between
the international situation and the domestic strategy of the PCI is
discussed in Donald L. M. Blackmer, *Unity and Diversity: Italian
Communism and the Communist World.*

75. See, for example, the statement by Lucio Libertini at a meeting
of the Central Committee of the PCI on March 14-16, 1977, reprinted
in *I comunisti e la questione giovanile* [Communists and the youth
question] (Rome: Editori Riuniti, 1977), pp. 43-48.

76. *Rinascita*, November 11, 1977, p. 3.

77. For other evidence not covered in the ensuing discussion, see
Table 4 of this chapter and *Bollettino Doxa*, November 7, 1977, Table
5-1, p. 198.

78. One should add that Christian Democratic electors had
essentially symmetrical, largely negative views of the PCI.

79. See, for example, Paolo Franchi, "Popolo minuto e popolo
grasso" [The bourgeoisie and the common people], *Rinascita*,
October 14, 1977, pp. 9-10.

80. In May 1971, only 17.5 percent of a sample of electors agreed
with the proposition that the Italian political system was radically
wrong, but by 1974 the figure had climbed to 34.6 percent. See *Ricer-*

che demoscopiche, nos. 1-2, 1975, p. 35. In 1977, 47 percent of the people interviewed by the Doxa Institute said that a radical change of the social and political system was needed to solve the country's most important problems. See *Bollettino Doxa,* November 7, 1977, p. 192.

81. According to this study, 71 percent of the respondents had a negative view of the social and political system; 45 percent believed that "deep reforms" were needed; 25 percent felt that the system was radically wrong and should be changed altogether. See the report by Chiara Sebastiani, "Un paese insoddisfatto ma politicamente maturo" [A dissatisfied but politically mature nation], *Rinascita,* May 13, 1977, p. 7.

82. Pronouncements by party leaders are full of cautionary statements about what party supporters can realistically expect, in at least the shortrun, e.g., "militants should have no illusions," "the process will be painful," etc.

83. The PCI Central Committee devoted its entire session of March 14-16, 1977, to the "Tasks and Activities of Communists vis-à-vis the Condition of Youth in the Present Crisis of the Country." This session's proceedings appear in *I comunisti e la questione giovanile.*

84. For example, a party seminar on this subject took place at the Gramsci Institute in Rome on October 7-9, 1977.

85. For a discussion of this point, see Sani, "Mass Support for Italian Communism."

86. The major results of the survey are presented in *Bollettino Doxa,* September 12, 1977.

87. For analyses of the 1976 elections, see Arturo Parisi and Gianfranco Pasquino, eds., *Continuità e mutamento elettorale in Italia* [Electoral continuity and change in Italy] (Bologna: Il Mulino, 1977); and Howard Penniman, ed., *Italy at the Polls: The 1976 Parliamentary Election* (Washington, D.C.: American Enterprise Institute, 1978).

88. Proletarian Democracy (DP), a coalition of leftist groups, has six representatives in the House of Deputies, and the Radical Party (PR) has four. Several other groups identified with the radical Left are not represented in parliament.

89. In a July 1976 interview, Berlinguer said "I feel that since Italy does not belong to the Warsaw Pact, . . . we are absolutely certain that we can proceed on the Italian road to socialism without any constraint. . . . I want Italy not to leave the Atlantic Pact 'also' because of this. . . . I feel safer being on this side." Interview with Gianpaolo Pansa, *Corriere della Sera,* July 15, 1976.

90. See, for example, *Rinascita*, July 2, 1976, p. 17.

91. See *Corriere della Sera*, September 30, 1976.

92. For the attack, see *New Times* (Moscow), no. 26, June 1977, pp. 9-13.

93. See, for example, the speech to the PCI Central Committee by Gian Carlo Pajetta, head of a party delegation that went to Moscow in the wake of the Soviet denunciation of Carrillo. This is reported in *l'Unità*, July 22, 1977.

94. See, e.g., a 1976 exchange between Alberto Jacoviello, a Communist journalist who has criticized the USSR, and *l'Unità* editor Luca Pavolini. Jacoviello argued that the PCI should strive to improve its relations with the Chinese Communist Party even if such an effort led to a confrontation with the CPSU. Pavolini argued for maintaining "friendship" with all Communist parties. See *Corriere della Sera*, September 30, 1976.

95. His statements were widely reported by the press. See, for example, ibid., October 24, 1977.

96. Local elections took place in a handful of communities on April 17, 1977. In some areas, the PCI fared well; in others, it suffered rather serious losses.

2

France: The Evolution of the PCF

William J. Davidshofer

The establishment of the Fifth Republic in France in 1958 confronted the French Communist Party (PCF) with a highly unfavorable political setting. Not only did the party now have to operate under a constitution that greatly strengthened the role of the executive and potentially that of the president in particular, but the return to single-member voting districts also brought an immediate and heavy drop in Communist representation in the National Assembly—from 150 out of 596 seats to 10 out of 578 seats.[1] Moreover, the party could do little to change this situation as long as it remained confined to the political ghetto in which it had found itself ever since the dismissal of Communist ministers from the Ramadier government in 1947. Yet it lacked all credibility with the rest of the Left. After the formation of the Cominform in 1947, it had showed itself to be as servile to Moscow's foreign policy considerations as it had been during the years of the Comintern (i.e., before 1943).

The first real opportunity for the PCF to make any headway in altering its situation arose in the period preceding the second round of balloting in the 1962 National Assembly elections. At this juncture, Socialist Party leader Guy Mollet played a pivotal role in putting together a makeshift voting alliance of the Radical, Socialist, and Communist organizations to oppose a Gaullist constitutional amendment providing for the direct election of the president, and to diminish Gaullist voting strength in the National Assembly.

Capitalizing on this opening, the Communists managed to expand cooperation with the then Federation of the Left (Socialists, Radicals, and Convention of Republican Institutions) during the mid-1960s. In February 1968, the PCF and the Federation of the Left, headed by François Mitterand, even signed a Common Declaration, whereby they pledged to rid France of Gaullist presidentialism and return the country to a more strictly parliamentary system of government.[2]

To have moved beyond this document would have been to exceed the parameters of a "purely defensive alliance" against Gaullism. Yet such a step is precisely what the party seems to have had in mind from a very early date, although its resolve to take such a step increased after the 17th Party Congress in May 1964 and the death of Maurice Thorez later the same year. As early as 1961, the Communists called upon the Socialists to join together with them to "build socialism" in France.[3] Shortly after the National Assembly elections in 1962, the PCF followed up this initiative by urging that a common program of government be drawn up.[4] And before his death even Thorez depicted the notion of the *parti unique*—i.e., that the PCF was the only political force that could set the country on a socialist path—as mistaken Stalinist doctrine.[5] By the time of the 17th Party Congress, it was quite clear that the party intended that a common program of government would serve as the basis of a transitional regime, one whose program of economic transformations would only begin to launch the country along the road to socialism but would nonetheless constitute a "bridge" to socialism. At this congress, the party adopted the term *true democracy (démocratie véritable)* to identify the type of regime that it had in mind. Four years later, it restated its strategy in a more dramatic and elaborate fashion. This time, it characterized the transitional model of government as a regime of "advanced democracy."[6] It is this concept, the party maintains, that made possible the conclusion of the Common Program of Government of the Communist and Socialist parties of France on June 27, 1972.[7]

To the extent that the Common Program reflected the Communist strategy for obtaining a governmental role in the French political system, the document represented the culmination of what one might call a "grand design" of the party leadership spanning a decade. But the concessions that the Socialists eventually extracted from the PCF, especially pronouncements impinging upon the Soviet version of the role of the dictatorship of the proletariat in the evolution of socialist society, simply would not have been possible while Maurice Thorez, or any other leader similarly steeped in Comintern and Cominform tradition, continued to head the party.

What this chapter would argue at the outset, therefore, is that at some point in a series of exchanges with the Socialists on the terms of a common program of government, the dominant voices in the French Communist leadership resolved to embark upon a course that moved the party further and further away from the subservience to Moscow that had so marked its previous history. This decision stemmed from the express desire to reach an understanding that would permit the Communists and Socialists to work in partnership to capture control of the government and then to set France on the road to socialism. To achieve such a goal, the PCF recognized, Socialist cooperation was essential. And eliciting that cooperation, it also realized, entailed grappling with some fundamental theoretical issues. That the party sought to address these issues was evidence of its evolution and of its seriousness about an alliance with the Socialists.

The considerations involved were threefold. First, precisely what was the distinction between a regime of advanced democracy and socialism, and what was the link between them? Second, to what extent would the PCF's role in such a regime be consistent with its traditional claim to constitute the revolutionary vanguard? And third, what impact would the answers to the foregoing questions have in efforts to reconcile the doctrine of the dictatorship of the proletariat with the practical requirements for effecting a political under-standing with the Socialists to govern together? An analysis of the PCF's approach to these matters not only reveals how the party succeeded in reaching an agreement with the Socialists on the Common Program of Government, but also sheds light on the party's subsequent behavior, behavior that has surprised many observers.

The Concept of "Advanced Democracy"

To grasp the PCF's interpretation of "advanced democracy" and, still more, to appreciate the policy implications embodied in it, one must first understand the party's characterization of state monopoly capitalism. As early as 1966, at an International Communist Conference on State Monopoly Capitalism at Choisy-le-Roi, the PCF advanced a series of key propositions on this subject. The Economic Section of the Central Committee by this juncture was already well along in a study of the Marxist notion of the "overaccumulation of capital" as the starting point for a new analysis of state monopoly capitalism, and Paul Boccara served as spokesman for the section's work.[8]

In keeping with Marxist tradition, Boccara held that capital accumulates "in excess" and that the excess of capital produces a situation in which the mass of surplus value does not grow as quickly as the capital employed. There occurs, then, the onset of the Marxist "law of the tendency of the rate of profit to fall." What distinguished Boccara's presentation of this well-known Marxist theorem was his treatment of Marx's analysis of the "internal contradictions" of the law.[9] Boccara argued that Marx saw certain "countertendencies" at work in the capitalist system, countertendencies that afford periodic "solutions" and keep the rate of profit from falling. To describe these "solutions" generically, Boccara used the term *dévalorisation,* which he pictured as counterposed to *suraccumulation* in line with Marx's own presentation of the opposing tendencies at work with respect to the "law of the tendency of the rate of profit to fall."

According to Boccara, *dévalorisation* is a situation in which a certain portion of total social capital is forced to forgo its claim to the limited surplus value available for the whole of capitalist society in any given period—and hence is forced to operate at a reduced profit, no profit, or even a loss. This situation in turn permits the rest of existing capital to claim the standard rate of profit. Thus, the process of accumulation continues. Under classical capitalism, Boccara maintained, *dévalorisation* occurred as a result of periodic recessions triggered by market crises. These recessions brought about depreciation of the value of various elements of fixed and variable capital. In this fashion, the blind forces of the market historically produced a periodic restoration of the standard rate of profit to the capitalist system, until a new round of overaccumulation once again threatened the profit rate.

Boccara went on to contend that the more developed an economy becomes, the greater the tendency for the overaccumulation of capital to generate acute and long-lasting recessions. What emerges from his analysis is a picture of a series of crises of spiraling dimensions beginning at the end of the nineteenth century and culminating in the "Great Depression" of the 1930s. Moreover, each successive crisis is represented as having given rise to increasing social pressure against the capitalist system, with the *dévalorisation structurelle* of capital being the consequence. It is this last phenomenon that is said to explain the development of state monopoly capitalism.

As defined by Boccara and subsequently by other PCF sources, state monopoly capitalism means the establishment in developed capitalist nations of a public economic sector that serves not only to help stabilize these economies but also to maintain the standard rate of profit for private capital belonging to the monopolies, thereby encouraging the continued accumulation of capital by the monopolies.[10] In this perspective, surplus value in effect gets transferred from the public economic sector to the monopolies by a pricing policy that favors the monopolies in the exchange of goods between the two sectors. A two-volume textbook of the Economic Section of the Central Committee published some five years after Boccara's original exposition of the theory of overaccumulation declared:

It is the state that assumes the cost of financing (partially at a loss) of railway, air, and maritime transport and that finances almost all basic research and a large part of applied research and development. It is the state that today underwrites the investments of the principal branches of industry; metallurgy just as aeronautics, chemistry as well as electronics, armament as well as naval construction. It is the state that facilitates self-financing and fixed investments by a complex system of fiscal deductions and accelerated amortizations.

By investing at a loss, by not calling for profit or only requiring for public capital a profit inferior to the mean rate, the state thereby grants to the monopolistic groups the main part of the mass of profits realized within the framework of capitalist society.[11]

In the 1960s, the PCF's analysis continues, the long postwar period of accumulation by the monopolies, in this case with the aid of public financing, led to a new stage of overaccumulation. Again, therefore, the problem of obtaining sufficient surplus value to restore the standard rate of profit has arisen.[12] Rather than permit another massive *dévalorisation* of private capital (a depreciation in the value of fixed capital), state monopoly capitalism is said to have resorted to the expedient of inflation. That is, it has simply reduced the real wages paid to labor—or, in Marxist terminology, it has intensified the rate of exploitation. According to the *Traité marxiste*, "The expansion of the value of monopolistic capital in the present conditions of the development of the forces of production lies at the heart of inflation. Everything that happens to lower the value the monopolies need, in terms of a certain rate of profit, is the cause and pretext of inflation and of the reinforcement and extension of capitalist exploitation."[13]

Given the negative impact that the diminished purchasing power of the masses has on the sale of goods, the PCF goes on to contend, state monopoly efforts to offset the overaccumulation of capital lead to "stagflation"—chronic high-level inflation accompanied by underconsumption and high-level unemployment. It is from the onset in 1967 of the symptoms of this phenomenon that the PCF dates the "crisis" of state monopoly capitalism.

Thus far, we have essentially a Marxist critique of the capitalist method of expanding the forces of production through a market economy, capped by a picture of chronic stagflation, a state of affairs that signals the crisis of state monopoly capitalism (the most recent stage of capitalism). From this point on, PCF theorists become more speculative but at the same time relevant to policy.

Following Marx, the PCF holds that accumulation under the

capitalist system raises the productivity of labor by continuously expanding the forces of production, and this continuous accumulation of fixed capital in turn brings about a further expansion of monied capital. Such a process, the argument runs, suppresses self-development on the part of human labor. However, the PCF maintains, the age of automation, and the conditions of a highly developed industrial society such as now exists in France, has changed the principal requirement of productivity. The party claims that in the age of automation, characterized in the French Communist press as the "scientific-technological revolution," productivity has more and more become a function of high-level technology and, particularly, the all-around development of the abilities of human labor to apply this technology effectively. But here the party argues that the capitalist system is unable to satisfy the requirements of automation, for it is founded on a logic that makes profit and accumulation dependent on diminished expenditures for human labor.[14] Thus, the crisis of state monopoly capitalism takes on far-reaching implications from the standpoint of a Marxist dialectical perspective on history: the industrial revolution, which is rooted in the development of the machine tool, must give way to the scientific-technological revolution, which is rooted in the development of man.[15]

What precise solution, then, does the party propose for the "crisis" of state monopoly capitalism? As Boccara has put it:

> It is a question henceforth of moving away from the *prevailing* aim of capitalist accumulation and profit. Without yet suppressing private accumulation and profit, it is a question of reducing them to a sector that will be subordinate and the relative weight of which will keep on diminishing with the progressive nationalization of the key sectors of industry and of the financial sector. These nationalizations, combined with the direction and transformation of the state by the working and democratic forces, provide the conditions for public intervention with a purpose other than capitalist accumulation and profit. The aim of responding to the needs of the diverse categories of laborers can begin to prevail.[16]

The term *new economic logic* has gained currency in the party literature to characterize the thrust of this statement. Such a logic entails a twofold preoccupation: first, that "man produce for himself and not for the profit or accumulation of a tiny minority" and, second, that "investment for man, for the laborer has become . . . the sine qua non for development of production at the dawning of the scientific-technical revolution."[17] Once these imperatives are accepted as fundamental principles of economic development, the party contends, not only will the crisis of state monopoly capitalism growing out of the *dévalorisation* of capital be amenable to resolution, but in production attention will immediately focus on the human self-development of labor. Given the latter condition, the resolution of the crisis of state monopoly capitalism in France will thus begin to bring about the eradication of the "technological foundation of the contradiction between constant capital and variable capital."[18] In classical Marxist terms, this means that the separation between physical and mental labor will commence to disappear. Hence, the PCF claims, France confronts the prospect of a "developed socialist society."[19]

It is precisely these two preoccupations of the new economic logic that are to lie at the heart of a regime of advanced democracy. Therefore, the PCF has always conceived such a regime to be a "form of transition to socialism."[20] Indeed, the *Traité marxiste* insists that carrying out a transition to socialism is the sole purpose of a regime of advanced democracy:

> The aim—and especially the one of advanced democracy—is not to "manage" capitalism in order to render it "supportable" (what every reformist policy moreover vainly tries to do). It is, quite to the contrary, a question of creating (by nationalizations and—of principal importance—by the democratization of all economic and social life) a new relationship of economic and political forces that would render socialism necessary and possible.[21]

In short, a regime of advanced democracy is to spearhead a frontal attack on state monopoly capitalism by dealing directly with the problem of overaccumulation in the fashion described above. It differs in concept, then, from the *front populaire* of the 1930s and the *tripartisme* of the immediate post–World War II period, for it affords an economic model to begin the transition to socialism immediately.

But launching a regime of advanced democracy entails freeing a critical mass of investment capital from the logic of capital accumulation. To achieve this, the party has insisted, a certain "minimum threshold" of nationalizations is necessary. During the negotiations with the Socialists leading to the Common Program signed in 1972, the Communist leadership greatly reduced the original threshold of nationalizations it had in mind, but the Common Program did call for the nationalization of banking, insurance, and credit agencies still under private ownership, and of the following industrial "groupes": Dassault, Roussel-Uclaf, Rhône-Poulenc, I.T.T.-France, Thomson-Brandt, Honeywell-Bull, Péchiney-Ugine-Kuhlman, Saint-Gobain-Pont-à-Mousson, and Compagnie Générale d'Electricité.[22] According to Communist statistics, these firms, when combined with the existing state enterprises, would expand the public sector to the point where it accounted for more than 50 percent of the country's industrial investment.

From the PCF's standpoint, however, a minimum threshold represents merely a starting point, a point of departure; for in order for the new economic logic to prevail in the struggle against the accumulation of capital by the monopolies, a regime of advanced democracy will constantly have to strengthen the leverage that it exercises over the rest of the economy. As one Communist author has put it: "What is irreversible in the revolutionary process of advanced democracy is that it will necessarily have to expand until socialism or fail by returning to state monopoly capitalism; it cannot be a phase of the capitalist mode of production in the sense in which we employ the word phase with respect to state monopoly capitalism."[23] Since the initial package of nationalizations ensuring the minimum threshold of the new economic logic will not in itself suffice to establish socialism, additional nationalizations will be required.

The political support to move forward, according to the Communists, will be generated by the results of the first set of "structural economic reforms" introduced by the new economic logic. Indeed, the whole idea behind advanced democracy is linking up subjective political and objective economic forces to extend the new economic logic to full-fledged socialism. As the PCF sees things, moreover, the possibility of effecting such a linkage gives political immediacy to the struggle to carry out the transition to socialism.

The notion of advanced democracy thus embodies a revolutionary strategy. This strategy had already been fully worked out by the time of the PCF's 19th Congress in 1970. George Marchais's report to the congress stated:

> It goes without saying that an advanced democracy, in realizing these antimonopolistic measures, still will not suppress the exploitation of man by man. But it will progressively and systematically reduce the power of monopolies; it will augment the authority of the working class and its political weight in the life of the country; it will contribute to the isolation of reaction and the rallying of all the forces of progress; and it will create the best conditions for the majority of the French to declare themselves favorable to the passage of France to socialism.[24]

Marchais reiterated the same theme in his report to the 22d Party Congress in 1976: "Nothing changes if men themselves, if the popular masses themselves do not decide to change. So much the less can Communists be content to await the disappearance of capitalism, so much the less to speculate on the crisis that, if an obsolete system, an obsolete policy, is maintained, the consequences of it are more and more harmful for the laborers, for the country." Then, in addressing PCF policy, he concluded: "But one is more and more forced to acknowledge: in order to get the country out of the crisis, in order to obtain a perceptible and enduring amelioration of the fate of each, in order to provide France with a new élan, a genuine and profound change is necessary, a change of policy, a change of power, a change of society."[25]

In sum, the PCF expressly intends that "structural economic reforms," far from "rendering the capitalist system supportable," will immediately launch the economic and political transition to socialism. To complete the picture, one need only recognize that with respect to a regime of advanced democracy, the PCF continues to claim for itself the role of revolutionary vanguard. In exercising this role, the party is both to make the masses conscious of the necessity of the new economic logic and to assure that the required political linkage exists to move the country progressively toward socialism.

It should be noted that the concept of the new economic logic filled a certain theoretical void by offering a perception of the concrete economic requisites of socialism, an issue to which no West European Communist party had devoted any real attention since the late 1940s. Over the intervening years, socialism in the people's democracies of Eastern Europe had come to be defined in essentially political terms, i.e., as proletarian dictatorships based on the political hegemony of the respective Communist parties.

The French Communist leadership was plainly aware of the utility of filling this void, for it realized that the principle of Communist political hegemony as a sine qua non of socialism would figure vitally in the discussions with the Socialists about a common program of government. If the Communists made concessions on this principle by formally renouncing the notion of the *parti unique*, then the PCF's theoretical concept of the foundations of socialism would need some serious reshaping. The new economic logic of advanced democracy facilitated the renunciation of the notion of the *parti unique* by affording a consistent economic theory of socialism that was wholly discrete from the notion of the *parti unique*. Consequently, the party could claim that the renunciation of the notion of the *parti unique*, with all of its attendant concessions, in no way signified that it was surrendering its role as revolutionary vanguard. In fact, it could argue that the closer the political collaboration it established with the Socialists, the greater the need there was for it to exercise its role as revolutionary vanguard.

Communist-Socialist Negotiations

As the negotiations between the Communists and Socialists proceeded, it became evident that only one type of Communist renunciation of the notion of *parti unique* would satisfy the Socialists. Such a renunciation must include a renunciation of the intention to dominate any other party in the French political system, including those opposed to socialism. But the Communists were inclined to distinguish between the political rights of Socialists as their governing partners and the political rights of opposition parties.

Fairly early on, the Communists provided a reasonably acceptable explanation of what they meant by offering to govern together with Socialists on the basis of "equality in rights and duties." In his last work, for example, Waldeck Rochet wrote: "They [the Communists and Socialists] will elaborate solutions acceptable to all and will replace clashes by discussions and useful compromises. In certain cases, perhaps it will not be possible to reach a compromise. Then, according to the democratic rule, the majority will decide, and the minority will have to submit to the law of the majority."[26]

The Communists, however, showed considerable obstinacy on the question of the rights of opposition parties, at least insofar as the possibility of *alternance*—that is, the ouster of Socialist parties by non-Socialist parties through the ballot box—was concerned. This was apparent in a document published in late 1970 after some nine months of discussions between the two parties. The "First Balance Sheet" recorded many areas of agreement between the two parties, but it indicated that a critical disagreement still existed on the question of *alternance*. At one point in the document, the Socialists affirmed that "if the confidence of the country, freely expressed, were refused to the majority parties, the latter would give up power and resume the struggle in the opposition."[27] The Communists, on the other hand, declared: "The Communist party considers that the democratic power, the existence of which involves the support of a popular majority, will have the satisfaction of the laboring masses as its principal task and will therefore be strengthened by the trust that they will ever more actively bring to it."[28] Even though the Communists had promised to respect the verdict of popular elections, this statement contained no direct reference to the *alternance* and consequently raised misgivings about how they would weigh the "trust" of the "laboring masses."

It was thus clear from the "First Balance Sheet" that the two parties had not reached an agreement on the question of *alternance.* That the Communists remained committed to Marxist categories of thought and presumably to a class concept of democracy that precluded *alternance* was brought out in more pointed terms in the last of a series of public exchanges between the two parties under the rubric "Week of Marxist Thought." The topic of this session was "Problems of the Socialist Revolution in France 100 Years after the Commune." When Denis Cépède of the Socialists posed the question of *alternance,* François Billoux, representing the Communist delegation, stated: "It is true that the passage to socialism will be definitive once you have put an end to the capitalist regime. If you will excuse the word, it will be, I believe, a one-way ticket without return to the capitalist regime."[29] Billoux later added that he viewed the concept of *alternance* as a false one to the extent that it posited an actual reversal of socialism.[30] However, he did suggest that if Communists and Socialists could agree that socialism, once definitively established, would put an end to the question of the capitalist alternative to it, then it was still possible to discuss the question of *alternance* with respect to the transitional period of advanced democracy.

This suggestion that the question of *alternance* during the transitional period of advanced democracy was open to discussion eventually permitted the parties to circumvent their ideological impasse and reach agreement on the Common Program in 1972. Although many Socialist leaders did not wish to distinguish between a regime of advanced democracy and socialism in discussions with the Communists on *alternance,* such a distinction was clearly apparent in the motion that carried by a narrow margin at the "Congress of Socialist Unity" at Epinay-sur-Seine in June 1971—a congress that elected a new party leadership under François Mitterrand.[31] The Common Program, which emerged after three months of new discussions and compromises, followed the same line. In an introduction by the Communists, Marchais specified that the objective of the Common Program was the establishment of a regime of advanced democracy as "a form of transition to socialism." Then the document itself proclaimed:

The regular organization of elections by universal, direct, and secret suffrage allows the people to express their judgment on what the elected do and how the government is run. The parties of the majority like those of the opposition will respect the verdict expressed by universal suffrage.

If the confidence of the country were refused to the majority parties, the latter would relinquish power in order to resume the struggle in the opposition. But the democratic power, the existence of which involves the support of a popular majority, will have the satisfaction of the laboring masses as its principal task and will therefore be strengthened by the trust that they will ever more actively bring to it.[32]

The second paragraph, it will be noted, reflected the divergent Communist and Socialist statements in the "First Balance Sheet," but spliced them together into a single perspective.

The fact that the Communists signed a document containing the explicit language of the Socialist Party on the question of *alternance* was indeed remarkable. Yet its application remained limited to a transitional regime of advanced democracy. Furthermore, as the wording of the particular passage in question indicated, the Communists still showed a marked inclination not to concede that *alternance* could lead to the ouster of a "progressive" government.

In subsequent statements, the party has not distinguished between advanced democracy and socialism when speaking of the rights of the political opposition. In a widely circulated work published in 1973, Marchais declared: "We will *in all cases* respect the verdict expressed by universal, direct, secret, and proportional suffrage, whether it be favorable or unfavorable to us. How, for example, could we envision undertaking or pursuing construction of a socialist society in France without the support of the majority of the French people?"[33] In another section of the same work, Marchais added:

I have already indicated that we intend, at all stages of our work, to respect *all* liberties. Among them naturally figures the freedom of association. And consequently the freedom of formation and activity of political parties, *including parties of the opposition.* In a socialist France, the rights of the minority will be strictly respected so long as they will be exercised, according to the democratic rule, in the framework of legality. The right of the parties of the opposition to rally a new majority will thus find its guarantee in the liberties of which they will dispose like all other groups, and also in the application of proportional representation in all the elections.[34]

The political resolution of the 22d Party Congress in 1976 addressed the question as follows: "At each stage of the construction of the new society, the assent of universal suffrage will be the condition of the continuation of the transformations undertaken. All the parties will have to respect its verdict. The proportional vote will guarantee to each current and political organization, both of the majority and of the opposition, a representation that conforms to its real influence and will assure a viable substance to the right of minorities."[35] And in March 1977, the French, Italian, and Spanish Communist parties issued a joint communiqué that said:

> The crisis of the capitalist system demands that ever greater effort be made for the development of democracy and for the advance toward socialism. In the building of this new society, the Spanish, Italian and French communists are resolved to work within the pluralism of the political and social forces and to respect guarantees and develop all individual and collective freedoms: Freedom of thought and of speech, of the press, of association and meeting, of demonstration, of free circulation of persons within the country and abroad, trade union freedom, independence for the trade unions, the right to strike, inviolability of private life, respect for universal suffrage, *prospects for the democratic alternative of the majorities*, religious freedom, cultural freedom, freedom of expression for different trends of opinion, philosophical, cultural and artistic.[36]

Nonetheless, since as recently as 1971 François Billoux was still speaking of socialism as a one-way ticket, it remains debatable how firm the party's resolve to respect the principle of *alternance* would be if *alternance* meant a reversal of "definitively constituted" socialism. Under such circumstances, the party might, of course, choose to proliferate the stages of advanced democracy in order to avoid a confrontation on the question of *alternance* under socialism. One could read the political resolution of the 22d Party Congress as an effort to lay the groundwork for such an approach. The resolution spoke of the reforms of the Common Program as "taking democracy a step forward" and then went on to assert: "The French Communist Party in effect considers that *at all stages of this democratic conquest, which will be so many markers along the road to socialism*, it will be up to the French people to choose its future. The Communists will in all circumstances respect its verdict."[37] But what ultimate course of political action the party would pursue if the French expressed the wish to reverse socialism as definitively constituted is still open to conjecture, and there may well be divisions of opinion within the Politburo itself on this question.

For the present, however, the leadership is primarily concerned with the party's public image on the matter of democracy. The leadership clearly realizes that the party's chances of future political success, in terms both of maintaining an alliance with the Socialists and of helping to attract the necessary votes to install the Common Program partners in power, are vitally dependent on its professions of commitment to democracy. Dramatic evidence of this realization came in Marchais's injunction to the 22d Party Congress to eliminate the term *dictatorship of the proletariat* from the party program.[38] Actually, the term *dictatorship of the proletariat* had already almost completely disappeared from official party literature after 1970, and in 1975 the party had even gone so far as to draw up a "Draft Proposal of Constitutional Law Bearing upon a Declaration of Freedoms," with the hope that after a general public debate the document might be inscribed as a preamble to the existing French constitution.[39]

Significantly, the PCF has felt compelled to carry the campaign to represent itself as a defender of democratic freedoms into the international arena. Central Committee member Pierre Juquin, one of those who had worked on the Draft Proposal, attended a meeting on October 21, 1976, at the Mutualité in Paris organized by a group of mathematicians to protest the treatment of six political dissidents, two of whom were Soviet citizens and one a Czechoslovak. Although making every effort to distinguish the Communist regimes in the Soviet Union and Czechoslovakia from the three Latin American governments that were the other targets of the protest, Juquin, speaking directly in the name of the French Communist Party, nevertheless stated: "We cannot accept therefore, that there be, in the Soviet Union or in Czechoslovakia, citizens prosecuted, imprisoned, interned for having expressed their views. We will never accept that, in whatever country it might be, one resort, in the name of socialism, to methods that violate the rights of the human individual."[40]

The Soviet government reacted immediately in a TASS communiqué, which declared that "Soviet public opinion does not understand how the representatives of the French Communist Party have been able to participate in a sordid understanding of this kind." It added that such efforts "only lent support to the forces absolutely hostile to the ideals of freedom, democracy, and of socialism."[41] What seemed to anger Soviet officials the most was that the PCF chose this particular meeting at which to voice a protest against political suppression, thus allowing the possible inference that the status of political freedoms in the Soviet Union resembled that of political freedoms in Uruguay, Bolivia, and—most offensive—Chile.

When Soviet dissident Vladimir Bukovskii, one of the chief subjects of the protest, was finally released from prison and simultaneously exiled from the Soviet Union, the PCF Politburo sharply denounced the alternative of "prison or banishment."[42] In a biting rejoinder to the earlier TASS communiqué, it also contended that genuine respect for the principle of the "struggle of ideas" would "avoid being placed in situations where the class adversary does not hesitate to liken actions of a socialist country to the practice of a fascist country." Then, plainly addressing itself as much to a domestic as a foreign influence, it added that the Bukovskii episode underlined the "capital importance of the policy defined by the 22d Congress of the French Communist Party" that "the French people go to socialism by the democratic way and that [they] construct an authentically democratic socialism, in the colors of France."

A sequel to this exchange occurred soon afterward. When the Czechoslovak government began to crack down on the signers of "Charter 77,"[43] *l'Humanité* commented that French Communists could not conceal their "astonishment at the accusation brought by Czech authorities that the signatories of 'Charter 77' were acting, according to *Rudé Právo*, 'on the instructions of anti-Communist and Zionist centers.'" The commentary went on: "We [French Communists] cannot allow practices that imply that with socialism, every divergent voice would be condemned either to silence or to repression. French Communists categorically exclude these attacks on individual and collective rights and freedoms from their political perspective. They declare them [these attacks] to be foreign to the ideal of socialism."[44]

Nor did the PCF let the issue of Charter 77 rest there. When four prominent Czechoslovak citizens, three of whom had signed Charter 77, drew heavy prison sentences, *l'Humanité* declared that Czechoslovak authorities could "not count on" French Communists to countenance "a denial of justice whatever be the political positions taken by the condemned." The article elaborated this position in the following fashion: "No motive of state or of party, no false conception of international solidarity will make us accept such a caricature of justice which disfigures the face of socialism. We have to say it: what brings damage to the credit of the Czech state is less the dissemination abroad of the manifestoes of discontented intellectuals than the manner in which they have been treated in their own native country."[45] It then proceeded to take an indirect swipe at the Soviet Union: "We have not forgotten, as far as we are concerned, the lesson of the 20th Congress of the Communist Party of the Soviet

Union, and we will not agree to remain silent before injustice, arbitrariness, the violation of socialist legality."[46]

Just how far French Communists intend to go in their criticism of the standards of "socialist legality" in the USSR and Eastern Europe remains to be seen, but the party leadership does clearly appear to recognize now that its domestic credibility cannot be separated from events in the USSR and Eastern Europe. The more the PCF adopts a generalized stance on the rights of political dissidents, of course, the greater the likelihood it will find itself at odds with the Soviet and East European Communist parties over what constitutes the true obligations of "proletarian internationalism."

In sum, the PCF has adapted its revolutionary doctrine to the political realities of the French party system, and in the process of doing so, it has significantly adjusted its relationships with the Soviet and East European Communist parties. Despite its professions of commitment to democracy and notwithstanding its criticism of socialist legality in the USSR and Eastern Europe, however, its domestic outlook in the late 1970s is marked by basic continuities with its past. In the first place, the PCF retains a fundamental Marxist commitment to socialism as a necessary and higher stage of historical development. This commitment emerges clearly from its concept of the relationship between "advanced democracy" and "developed socialism" in France. In light of this commitment, it is important to underscore that orthodox Marxist doctrine does not envision that the "stages" of history can, or at least ever should, be reversed, for these stages reflect the logic of history itself, not merely fluctuating parliamentary majorities.

Second, the PCF, with the express purpose of moving history forward—i.e., of advancing France to socialism through the various phases of advanced democracy—continues to cling to the Leninist notion of the party as revolutionary vanguard and to Leninist principles of party organization. Whether this revolutionary vanguard role that the party assigns to itself is really compatible with the fundamental values of Western democracy, especially as these values bear upon the critical issue of *alternance*, remains open to real question.

Foreign Policy Perspectives

Although domestic issues dominated the discussions of the Communists and Socialists about a common program of government, foreign policy issues figured in them as well. The fundamental concern of the PCF in this realm was clearly articulated in the party's original draft for a common program. That draft document stated:

> Democratic France will itself sovereignly determine its institutions, its political and social life, its relations with other states.
> The effort of our people to advance the country toward economic and political democracy, then toward socialism, according to the ways and means that it will have itself chosen, cannot be undermined by any kind of foreign interference, pressure, and reprisal.[47]

Within this framework, the Communists supported a general arms reduction, beginning with the immediate renunciation of France's nuclear *force de frappe*, and called for the conclusion of an all-European collective security arrangement.[48] As regards the latter, the new government of the Left should take "measures designed to disengage France from the Atlantic Pact," which was a "political-military organization with aggressive ends, dominated by the United States."[49]

From the PCF standpoint, as the draft program attests, the prime threat to a government of advanced democracy would come from the United States and other members of the NATO alliance; but the Socialists saw the USSR as likely to present an equal, if not greater, problem. The French Communists, however, had for some time been asserting their right to chart their own course free of interference from Moscow, and they had on occasion, particularly during the Warsaw Pact invasion of Czechoslovakia in 1968, displayed their independence by criticizing Soviet policy. This history plus the language of the general declaration quoted above went a long way toward satisfying the Socialists' concerns. Consequently, the Common Program in large measure coincided with the Communist positions just outlined, with the notable difference that the Common Program made the dissolution of the Atlantic alliance dependent on the simultaneous dissolution of the Warsaw Pact.[50]

To the extent that the French Communists pushed for a diminished U.S. presence in Western Europe, it is important to note, the party's foreign policy squared well with Soviet strategic objectives. At the same time, the efforts of the French Communists to win political power create complications for the USSR in its superpower dealings with the United States.

If one keeps the latter point in mind, the report of Jean Kanapa, the Politburo member most identified with foreign policy formulation in the party, to the Central Committee in April 1975 becomes singularly instructive. Speaking on the theme of "peaceful coexistence and class struggle in 1975," Kanapa declared:

> The development of peaceful coexistence can reveal some real problems. We believe that the problems that result from it have to be resolved on each occasion on the basis of a principle that is common to all Communist parties. Their solidarity, their common action have to inseparably bear on one another. We could not, therefore, allow any démarche, whatever it might be, that in the name of peaceful coexistence among states would adversely affect the interests of the struggle we are leading against the power of big capital, for democracy and socialism.[51]

In even more pointed language, he asserted: "the antagonism that exists between socialism and capitalism as economic and social systems is an irreducible antagonism. It must inevitably end by the victory of one over the other, of socialism over capitalism. Peaceful coexistence by no means puts an end to this antagonism. It is simply the framework in which it unfolds."[52]

This report triggered an intensive campaign in the French Communist press to set the record straight about what détente, as delineated in the Final Act of Helsinki, did not mean to the PCF, and ought not mean to anyone else. In effect, the party sought to warn both the United States and the Soviet Union that French Communists were "extremely vigilant about not tolerating any truncated interpretation of peaceful coexistence that extended the territorial notion of the 'status quo' to the fundamental realities of the social and political struggle."[53]

As far as the West was concerned, the French Communist press repeatedly cited negative remarks by U.S. officials regarding participation of Communists in West European governments as violations of the principle of national self-determination, which the PCF maintained was vital to both détente and the Helsinki accords.[54] Parallel to this, the party launched a campaign against France's "sliding toward Atlanticism" (glissement vers l'atlantisme) under Valéry Giscard d'Estaing—as manifested in the country's increased political and military cooperation with NATO.[55] On the basis of U.S. officials' negativism about the participation of Communists in West European governments and France's alleged "sliding toward Atlanticism," the PCF charged that a "holy alliance," headed by the governments of the United States, West Germany, France, and Great Britain, had been refashioned within the framework of the Atlantic community.

The outcry against the four Western governments escalated significantly when it became known that their leaders had reached an agreement in a meeting in Puerto Rico on June 26-27, 1976, to withhold economic aid from Italy if the Communists there entered the government as a result of their showing in recent elections. As soon as news of the decision leaked out, the PCF Politburo issued the following statement:

> This decision constitutes an inadmissable interference in Italian internal affairs. It represents an attempt at intimidation of peoples, who, like the French people, aspire to democratically realize the social transformations that their interests and those of the nation require. It constitutes a new proof that the big bourgeoisie, rallied under the Atlantic aegis, mean to challenge the democratic choices formulated by peoples, to resist the verdict of universal suffrage, to make a mockery of national sovereignty.[56]

But if the PCF sought to discourage the United States and its three West European partners from banding together to protect the political status quo in Western Europe, it had a related message for Moscow. Kanapa's report clearly prodded the Soviet Union and the governments of Eastern Europe to look to their obligations of proletarian internationalism. It, in effect, argued that they should not allow the United States and its partners in the Atlantic community to assume that détente presupposed maintenance of the political, as well as the territorial, status quo in Western Europe.[57] To underscore this point, the PCF during this period gave strong backing to the Portuguese Communists, who had come under criticism from the Italian and Spanish Communists for efforts to pursue a hard-line revolutionary policy—even though the PCF leadership did not entirely agree with the Portuguese strategy.[58]

Kanapa sounded the theme once more in October 1975 at a preparatory meeting for the proposed conference of European Communist parties. He insisted that peaceful coexistence did not mean preservation of the domestic political status quo and that the current "crisis" in the capitalist nations of Western Europe "objectively places on the agenda the necessity of profound economic and social transformations opening the way to socialism." Moreover, he added that "social progress" along such lines could not be regarded as a "simple spin-off of the advance of détente and peaceful coexistence."[59]

French Communists did receive some satisfaction in the wording of the final document adopted at the Conference of European

Communist and Workers' Parties in East Berlin on June 29-30, 1976, particularly in the third paragraph of the preamble to the resolutions approved by the conference.[60] But that the party leadership remained as concerned as ever about the relationship between détente and the class struggle was obvious from Marchais's speech at the conference:

> The development of peaceful coexistence poses new problems in relations between parties of the socialist countries and parties of capitalist countries. The first share the correct idea that time works for socialism; the second do everything to put an end to monopoly capitalism as quickly as possible because it is of vital interest for the laborers. Some, by using for the most part the means of the state, carry on relations of cooperation (which is a considerable success) with the regimes that the others are struggling against by every means at their disposal. This is normal and there is no contradiction. We could not for all that allow any démarche whatever it might be, in the name of peaceful coexistence among states, to undermine the interests of the struggle that we are leading against the power of big capital for democracy and socialism. We are not aware of any higher duty than the one we have with regard to our working class, to our people.[61]

Concern that some foreign power or powers might take action against a government of the Left with Communist ministers led the PCF to reverse itself and, on May 11, 1977, endorse the *force de frappe*, deployed *tous azimuths*. According to Central Committee member Louis Baillot's elaboration, the party concluded that, given the existing state of France's conventional forces, *dissuasion globale* (all political and military support that a government of the Left would command at home and abroad) must for the present include the element of nuclear dissuasion in order to safeguard a Communist-Socialist government against outside action.[62] At the same time, the PCF supports a future defense policy based on universal nuclear disarmament.

At this juncture, one should note that the PCF leadership does not at all perceive the party's hard line on the relationship between peaceful coexistence and the class struggle, so noticeable in the French Communist press since 1975, as being at odds with the democratic image that it has assiduously labored to foster in recent years. Both notions figured in the "salutations" of the PCF that Gaston Plissonnier delivered at the 25th Congress of the Communist Party of the Soviet Union in February 1976.[63] The same was true with respect to Marchais's remarks at the Conference of European Communist and Workers' Parties in East Berlin. On the one hand, the

PCF leader made a special point to catalog the freedoms that socialism in France would respect, among them "universal suffrage with the possibility of the *alternance démocratique* that goes with it, of the right to the existence and activity of political parties, including parties of the opposition."[64] On the other hand, he emphatically contended:

> peaceful coexistence cannot in any fashion be identified with the social and political status quo in our country, with the partitioning of the world into spheres of influence dominated by the most powerful states. On the contrary, we call on the French laborers to find in the new relationship of forces existing in the world, in the détente that characterizes the situation in Europe, additional reasons for confidence in the outcome of their struggle for democratic change and socialism.[65]

Some observers may regard this state of affairs as an indication of ambivalence in French Communist policy deriving from competition between groups within the party leadership, but it more likely reflects the party's identification of two separate policy requirements of the same strategic goal: to reach power and then to wield it in order to advance the country along the road to socialism. Furthermore, the PCF appears to believe that Communist parties in other industrialized countries with democratic institutions confront similar policy requirements in responding to their objective situations. Insofar, for example, as the PCF leadership accepts the term *Eurocommunism* (the leadership claims that it is too limited since it does not expressly cover the Japan Communist Party), the leadership does so precisely because it perceives that the parties concerned have recognized the need to adopt similar approaches in dealing with the "crisis" of state monopoly capitalism that exists in their local contexts.[66]

The Impact of the Common Program

The PCF's long-range goal in signing the Common Program was to establish a concrete basis for at least sharing governmental power, but the document itself represented a statement of purpose designed to win additional support for the Left among French voters. In this regard, it appears to have had some effect. An exhaustive analysis of its impact on political dynamics in France would go considerably beyond the scope of this study; however, two observations are in order here.

First, the program's economic provisions of a more immediate and practical nature than the projected nationalizations had a particularly timely appeal from 1973 on, when inflation and unemployment became increasingly serious considerations for French voters. Several of the more important of these provisions deserve specific mention. As originally written, the Common Program called for a reduction of the forty-five-hour work week to forty hours without any loss of salary, and for a minimum monthly income of 1,000 francs.[67] (Six years later, the latter figure was raised to 2,400 francs.[68]) The program also proposed that the retirement age be lowered to sixty for men and fifty-five for women and that pensions be brought up to 75 percent of the highest ten-year average of salaried income.[69] According to the document, a shorter work week and earlier settlement—plus a new approach to economic development—would serve to stimulate employment, which it described as a "priority objective." In addition, the program promised legislation abolishing the discretionary right of layoffs and allowing the laborer recourse to the committee of enterprise.[70] Finally, the program declared that the "stabilization of prices" would constitute an "essential objective" of the union of the Left as the government of France, and it noted that the "nationalization of the key sectors of industry and the financial system" would play a "fundamental role in the struggle against inflation."[71]

The growing appeal of such measures to the French public was documented in several polls. For example, a survey conducted by SOFRES for *l'Express* in 1975 after a three-year period in which consumer prices had risen by roughly 33 percent showed that a significant majority of the public felt France was experiencing a "profound economic crisis" and that an even larger majority believed the crisis was far from over.[72] Although the poll indicated, curiously enough, that the public did not regard a Left government as a potential improvement over the Giscardian government, it did reveal a tendency on the part of the public to favor more active governmental efforts to deal with the economic situation. For instance, 77 percent of the respondents (as against 18 percent) held that lowering the retirement age would help to ameliorate the economic situation; 64 percent (as against 12 percent) felt the same way about a program of public works; 43 percent (as against 30 percent) believed that nationalization of the banks would help to better the economic situation; and 45 percent (as against 36 percent) supported nationalization of large enterprises for such a purpose.[73]

Second, voter support for the Left rose significantly after the signing of the Common Program, although the Socialist Party scored the great bulk of the gains. In the 1973 National Assembly elections, the Socialists claimed 19.2 percent of the vote, more than the

Federation of the Left, composed of the Socialists, Radical-Socialists, and the Convention of Republican Institutions, had won in 1967. The Communists, for their part, garnered 21.4 percent of the ballots. In the first-round returns of the cantonal elections of March 1976, however, the Socialist Party's share of the vote shot up to 26.5 percent. Moreover, these elections revealed a continuing tendency toward the "nationalization" of the Socialist vote—that is, toward a more balanced geographical distribution of Socialist voting support. Although the Communists did not register as spectacular an increase as the Socialists, the PCF did capture 22.8 percent of the ballots. *Le Monde* political analyst Raymond Barrillon, citing the statistics of the Ministry of the Interior, credited the entire Left with 56.5 percent of the vote in the cantonal elections.[74] Although the combined strength of the Left was not quite as impressive in the municipal elections of the following year, the Left still accounted for more than 51 percent of the vote. Communists and Socialists carried 57 new cities of more than 30,000 (22 for the Communists and 35 for the Socialists). In all, the opposition gained control of 159 of 221 urban centers of this size, with 153 going to the Communists and Socialists.[75]

Since the gains in voter support went largely to the Socialist Party, however, there remains a question as to whether they represented growing backing for the Left alliance as a whole or for just the Socialists. The answer to this question is of particular importance because it bears upon the capacity of the union of the Left to mobilize sufficient voter support to gain power.

A very intensive comparison of patterns of votes for the Left in the 1967 and 1973 legislative elections and the presidential election of 1974 has led two French analysts to conclude that there has been a gradual decline in what they term *social-centrism.*[76] By *social-centrism*, they mean the tendency of elements who vote for the Socialists and the moderate Center in the first round of balloting to back the Left in the second round only when they can thus check the political strength of the Gaullists and not aid the Communists. (Under the electoral law of the Fifth Republic, a candidate must receive an absolute majority of the vote on the first ballot to be elected automatically; otherwise, a second ballot is necessary. As a rule, a second round of voting takes place in 80 to 85 percent of the districts. It is the practice on this ballot to conclude electoral alliances. Parties with the closest political ties agree mutually to support those of their candidates who finished strongest in the first round vote and to withdraw all the rest. In its classical form, this practice leads to "second-ballot duels" between the Left and the Right. Such has been the case in France since 1962.) These voters in effect, then, serve as a kind of electoral "third force." According to the authors, the growing bipolarization of French politics has gradually been winnowing out such "social-centrist" elements from the backers of the Left, and the signing of the Common Program accentuated this trend in both the 1973 legislative elections and the presidential election of the following year. Therefore, they hold that the non-Communist vote in support of the union of the Left has been getting more homogeneous and stable.

This study was completed, however, before the Socialists registered rather spectacular new gains in voter strength in the 1976 cantonal elections, and there is evidence to suggest that these elections may have witnessed at least a slowdown, if not a reversal, of the trend noted in the study. A survey conducted by Makrotest for l'Express after the elections with the aim of analyzing the "new Socialist voters" is particularly instructive here. For example, it showed that of this group of voters—comprising about one-third of the total Socialist electorate and containing a majority of persons who had never before cast a ballot in an election—33 percent regretted the Socialist Party's alliance with the PCF, 46 percent approved the alliance, and 21 percent expressed no opinion. Perhaps more revealing, only 5 percent of such voters cited the Socialist Party's affiliation with the union of the Left as the chief reason for backing the party. The survey also indicated that some 29 percent of the new Socialist electorate constituted a soft vote that the Center-Right might attract away from the union of the Left without too much difficulty.[77]

A more recent poll conducted by IFOP for Paris Match from April 26 to May 3, 1977, offers some additional data of relevance to the issue. This survey attempted to probe the attitudes toward the Communist Party of backers of the parties that make up the political opposition. Even though it covered Communist as well as non-Communist voters, only 45 percent of the respondents thought that the recent positions adopted by the PCF (most particularly, its abandonment of the concept of the dictatorship of the proletariat and its criticisms of the Soviet government) marked a "profound change" in party doctrine. Of the rest of the respondents, 29 percent (including 33 percent of the Socialist voters) believed that the positions reflected "tactical and superficial changes," and 26 percent expressed no opinion.[78] On the other hand, 69 percent of the respondents favored allocation of some governmental ministries to the Communists; only 8 percent opposed such a course, and 23 percent were indifferent.[79]

Similarly, 61 percent of the respondents felt that the Communists and Socialists could form a durable government; 24 percent believed they could not, and 15 percent did not answer.[80] What one might conclude from this poll is that although a large segment of Socialist voters still viewed the Communist Party with suspicion, the majority were probably reconciled to the union of the Left.

The PCF and the 1978 Elections

As the 1978 National Assembly elections began to loom on the horizon, then, the political prospects of the union of the Left generally seemed bright in light of the showing of the Communists and the Socialists in the cantonal and municipal elections of 1976 and 1977. But a triumph of the Left in the 1978 elections depended upon the fulfillment of two interrelated conditions. First, the union of the Left had to hang on to the great bulk of the new Socialist voters, including the elements who displayed greater interest in the economic reforms that the Common Program promised than in the structural transformation of the French economy. Second, the union of the Left's potential supporters had to continue to see the alliance as the political nucleus of a stable government. Yet already in May 1977, when the Communists, Socialists, and Radicals of the Left opened talks to "update" the Common Program, there were ominous signs of growing problems that threatened to make both conditions unrealizable.

These problems stemmed, fundamentally, from the PCF's overall attitude toward the Left alliance. The party, as this study has attempted to show, had developed the notion of advanced democracy expressly to serve as a model of transition to socialism in a developed capitalist economy by parliamentary means. Since such a transition required a political alliance with the Socialists and a vast improvement in the Communists' public credibility, it led to a renunciation of the notion of the *parti unique* and eventually to a striking change in the party's public attitude with respect to France's existing democratic institutions. However, the PCF insisted more adamantly than ever that it must exercise the role of revolutionary vanguard and that "the possibility of constructing socialism in France is tied to the capacity of the Communist Party to exercise a directing influence [*influence dirigeante*] in the popular movement."[81]

This conception that the party must function as a "directing influence in the popular movement" has shaped the party's

approach to the other members of the "union of the Left." For
example, when Marchais first asked his Central Committee (in a
speech not published until 1975) to approve the original Common
Program, he observed that "the ideology that today animates the
Socialist Party is and remains absolutely reformist; fundamentally, it
is totally divorced from scientific socialism."[82] After the 1974
presidential elections, open references to reformist currents in the
Socialist Party began to appear in the Communist press. In
evaluating the prospects for the union of the Left in his report to the
22d Party Congress in 1976, Marchais again addressed this issue:

> The union of the Left is not in effect like a contract the simple signing
> of which would suffice to ensure its application; *it is a permanent
> struggle.* And this for two interrelated reasons. In the first place,
> because the bourgeoisie never reconcile themselves to the union of the
> workingman's and democratic forces and conduct an incessant struggle
> against it, with all the means at their disposal, in order to destroy it. In
> the second place, because this pressure does not go on without an echo
> within the Socialist Party.[83]

Subsequently, the slogan *l'union, c'est un combat* became a constant
refrain in Communist commentary about the alliance.

Behind such an approach, it is important to recognize, lay not
merely power considerations but also substantive concerns. The PCF
was keenly aware that its alliance partners did not share its views on
many matters. For example, the Socialist Party had evolved its own
principles of socialist economic planning, and these differed
substantially from Communist policy assumptions linked to the
theory of overaccumulation. Therefore, the Communists realized that
to the extent they felt it vital for their outlook to prevail in the
alliance, they would have to do battle with their partners to achieve
that end.

What produced difficulties in the period leading up to the 1978
National Assembly elections was primarily divergent Communist
and Socialist perspectives on the minimum number of nationalizations that a government of the Left must carry out initially to make
possible a transition to socialism. This issue had long been critical in
Communist-Socialist relations, far more so than most observers have
tended to appreciate. During the discussions in the early 1970s to
hammer out a common program of government, the two parties
struggled mightily over the question of nationalizations, although
they finally compromised on the nine concerns listed in the final
document (a much smaller number than the Communists had had in

mind).[84] Moreover, the PCF appears to have looked upon this question as the key test of the willingness of the Socialists to cooperate with it. Speaking to the Central Committee shortly after the signing of the original Common Program, Secretary General Marchais declared: "At the last minute, they [the discussions on nationalizations] even gave way to a genuine confrontation. This was no accident. It was a question in effect of a decisive issue, of the touchstone to judge the determination of proceeding to real changes, of breaking with the policy and the regime of big capital, of committing oneself to the path to socialism."[85]

In any case, the Communists began to assert as early as 1974 that the nationalization of the nine concerns listed in the Common Program was not sufficient to push the state sector over the minimum threshold that would guarantee the country's transition to socialism. They cited such factors as growing unemployment, a climb in the rate of inflation, and the energy crisis. Consequently, they called for an updating of the Common Program's nationalization provisions in preparation for the 1978 National Assembly elections. As the elections drew nearer, they became increasingly insistent on the subject.

With respect to updating these provisions of the Common Program, the PCF demanded the nationalization of not only four concerns that account for almost all of the steel and metallurgical production in France (Denain-Nord-Est-Longwy, Marine-Wendel, Empain-Schneider, and Chiers-Châtillon) but also Peugeot-Citroën and Compagnie Française des Pétroles-C.F.R.-Total.[86] The criteria set forth for nationalizations in the original Common Program afforded several possible justifications for the addition of these six concerns: they were "the principal centers of capitalist accumulation"; they were firms "surviving on public funds"; they were "enterprises that control branches essential to the national economic development."[87]

What the Communists were talking about was a package of nationalizations that would incorporate into the public sector of the economy 1,262,900 members of the industrial working population (15.6 percent of the total) and 324,000 employees from banking and finance. These nationalizations combined with those carried out earlier would produce a public sector comprising 32.8 percent of the industrial working population, accounting for half of national investment, and controlling at least 75 percent of the expenses for research.[88] But they would do so only if all fifteen of the concerns involved were treated as industrial "groups"—i.e., if nationalization applied to "branch enterprises" *(filiales)* in which the fifteen "mother concerns" *(sociétés mères)* owned 51 percent or more of the holdings.[89] Thus, the Communists wanted to nationalize some 1,450 separate enterprises that they claimed belonged to the mother fifteen. The Socialists refused to accept the Communist proposal. They would only consent to acquire state majority holdings in Peugeot-Citroën along with the steel and metallurgical industries. Furthermore, they insisted that the nationalization of branch enterprises be limited to those in which the mother concerns already possessed 98 percent of the holdings. On the basis of this principle, they eventually came up with a list of 227 branch enterprises to be nationalized. Such a figure fell far short of what the Communists would settle for, although the PCF did offer some concessions on the matter.[90]

By the summer of 1977, the talks to update the Common Program had reached a stalemate, and not even a September meeting "at the summit" could break the impasse. Although there were other disagreements involved in the collapse of the discussions, the Communists cited that over nationalizations as the critical one. Marchais set forth the Communist interpretation of events at a party rally in the wake of the successful summit meeting. After referring to the "minimum threshold of nationalizations" as being at "the root of the debate with the Socialist Party," he declared:

> One has to understand: when we say that by calculating at 729 the number of nationalizations that the Common Program foresees, we are making a maximum effort, it is not a question of amour-propre, obstinacy, or attachment to I do not know what dogma. No, it is indeed more simple: it is because below this threshold defined by the Common Program, the entire operation of the Common Program would be committed to failure in advance. Why? *Because it would allow big capital to get in like the wolf in the sheepfold.*
>
> Already, when we adopted the Common Program in 1972, we had to struggle on this point. In order to get an agreement we consented to reduce the number of industrial groups to be nationalized to nine. As we said together—I repeat—it was a question of a *minimum* threshold indispensable to guarantee the success of the social policy that you await. Moreover, it is why when we undertook this year to update the Common Program we also proposed to nationalize metallurgy, Compagnie Française des Pétroles, and Peugeot-Citroën, because of the new situation that has been created in these vital sectors.[91]

It was not just the merits of the nationalization issue, however, that caused the PCF to regard the dispute over it as so important, for the question of the minimum threshold had become linked to other political considerations in Communist thinking. The indications from opinion polls that the Socialist Party would record a spectacular rise in voting strength in the upcoming elections had given rise to increasing Communist concern. If the Socialists and the Radicals of the Left were to win nearly 30 percent of the vote as the polls suggested they would, the PCF would suffer a substantial defeat in its quest to be the dominant electoral force on the Left, for it could not hope to garner much more than 20 percent. Moreover, it would find itself in the position of a distinctly junior partner in any governing alliance.[92]

In signing the Common Program, to be sure, the Communists had realized that they were risking their relative political strength within the Left, and they had worried that the Socialists might score electoral gains at direct Communist expense.[93] At the same time, it seems likely that the PCF leadership believed an increase in the voting strength of the Socialist Party to be essential for the realization of a new majority of the Left. After all, the prospects of the PCF's winning 30 percent or more of the vote in the near future appeared dim, and if it managed to do so without a corresponding rise in the Socialist vote, the Socialist Party would probably abandon it. Even if the Socialist Party organization remained committed to the Left alliance, a large percentage of Socialist voters would almost certainly defect. What the Communist leadership very likely hoped would happen, therefore, is that both parties would register voter gains of relatively equal proportions.

When it began to look as if the PCF would in actuality find itself in a subordinate political position to the Socialist Party, the Communists followed a twofold course of action. First, they attempted to bargain for a larger share of the ministerial posts by arguing that these should be allocated on the basis of percentage of the popular vote, rather than on the traditional basis of number of deputies in the National Assembly. Second—and directly relevant to our analysis—they became more adamant than ever about their proposals for additional nationalizations. With the prospect of greater Socialist strength in a government of the union of the Left, the Communists felt it imperative to force a showdown with the Socialists on the question of nationalizations before the elections took place.

In his speech explaining the reasons for the breakdown of the talks to update the Common Program, Marchais said that the Communists remained committed to the union of the Left as the means of establishing a regime of advanced democracy that would in turn eventually lead to the realization of "socialism in the colors of

France." What was most instructive, however, was that he again sounded the theme that the union of the Left involved a "difficult struggle requiring perseverance."[94] In fact, the question of the minimum threshold remained unresolved as the first ballot of the National Assembly elections approached on March 12, 1978.

This situation left the political status of the union of the Left up in the air. One of the principal expectations of the parties in signing the Common Program had been that it would increase the vote for the Left by offering voters an alternative government based on an explicit legislative contract embodying both the principles of classical republicanism and a commitment to socialism. But without a definitive program for the union of the Left to stand on, there was even some question as to the precise meaning of second-round electoral alliances within the Left. (As we have already noted, the two-ballot French electoral system encourages electoral alliances in the second round of voting, and since the practice of making second-round electoral alliances is a general one, each party finds it essential to reach an understanding with some other party. Otherwise, a party would wind up exceedingly disadvantaged. From the outset, therefore, the Communists were certainly inclined to conclude a second-ballot voting alliance with the Socialists and the Radicals of the Left regardless of the status of the Common Program.)

The returns from the first round of voting on March 12 finally brought matters to a head. Instead of obtaining the 28 percent of the vote that the polls had indicated they would, the Socialists and the Radicals of the Left together garnered only 24.7 percent of the ballots (the Socialists captured 22.6 percent and the Radicals of the Left 2.1 percent).[95] The Communists, for their part, received 20.5 percent of the vote. Although the share of the ballots won by the Socialists and the Radicals of the Left did represent a substantial 4.1 percent increase over their combined total in 1973, it still did not give these two parties the superiority over the PCF that they had expected. Therefore, the Communists no longer saw themselves at nearly as great a disadvantage as they had thought they faced prior to the first-ballot returns, either in terms of the popular vote or the actual parliamentary representation they could anticipate receiving. Furthermore, the issue of whether there would be a governing majority for the Left was still undecided. Including the votes of the extreme Left and other diverse currents of opposition to the ruling majority, the Left went into the second ballot with 49.7 percent of the vote, as compared with 48.4 percent for the ruling majority.

The day after the first-ballot returns became known, the leaders of the Communists, Socialists, and Radicals of the Left again held a summit meeting. All three parties agreed that some evidence of formal accord on the final terms of the Common Program was necessary to persuade uncommitted voters that the union of the Left had enough cohesiveness to govern the nation effectively. The meeting produced a "common declaration," which stated:

> The parties of the Left solemnly affirm their desire to do everything to realize the establishment of a common majority on a common program for a common government of the Left.
>
> In this spirit, as soon as the country accords them its confidence, they will commit themselves to continue, starting from what has been achieved in the Common Program of 1972 and the proposals already approved during the course of the work carried on in 1977, negotiations aimed at clarifying the program that will become the legislative contract that the government of the union of the Left will be entrusted to implement.[96]

The declaration then went into some detail with regard to welfare measures upon which the union of the Left had already reached agreement. Some of these dated from the original Common Program, but others reflected the resolution of issues that had remained in dispute after the discussion of the previous summer to update the Common Program.[97] Although the declaration specified that the "composition [of a government of the union of the Left] will respect the will of universal suffrage," it was unclear as to exactly how great a concession this provision was to the Communist claim that ministerial posts ought to be apportioned according to the parties' respective shares of the popular vote. In an interview the next day, Marchais indicated that the Communists wished to use the first-ballot figures as the basis for determining the ministerial representation of the respective parties, but that François Mitterrand wanted to employ the second-ballot figures. The latter approach would presumably mean fewer cabinet posts for the Communists.[98]

Most important, however, the declaration gave no sign that the question of the minimum threshold had been resolved. It did commit the parties to resume serious discussion immediately after the second round of elections—provided, of course, that the union of the Left won a majority in the National Assembly—on the scope of nationalizations to be inscribed in the legislative contract. But Marchais made it clear that even though the PCF had agreed that further negotiations on the subject would have to wait until after the second-ballot returns were in, the party still attached critical importance to this issue.

Despite these maneuvers, the union of the Left failed to pick up any additional support on the second ballot. The ruling majority won 50.7 percent of the vote, and the parties of the opposition captured only 49.3 percent.[99] In the final distribution of seats—of which 423 out of the 491 were still contested on the second ballot—the ruling coalition received 290 to 200 for the union of the Left (Socialists, 104; Communists, 86; Radicals of the Left, 10). The figure for the opposition did represent a gain of 17 seats over its 1973 total, but the ruling coalition retained a comfortable majority.[100] In light of the expectations that the polls had generated, the outcome of the 1978 legislative elections represented a clear political setback for the union of the Left.

Prospects

What impact are the developments of 1977-1978 likely to have, then, on the role of the PCF in the French political system during the years immediately ahead? To a large extent, that will depend on their ultimate effect on the union of the Left, and this issue remains unresolved as of the spring of 1978.

Conceivably, assessments of the results of the 1978 elections by the Communists and Socialists could widen the recent estrangement of the two parties over the question of the minimum threshold of nationalizations to be inscribed in a common program of government. The Socialists, for their part, will have to weigh several possible drawbacks to continuation of the alliance. These relate mainly to the electoral situation.

To begin with, there has emerged a serious challenge to the Socialists from the Center. The precise reason for the failure of the Socialist Party to generate the voter support that the polls had predicted for it will undoubtedly be the subject of intensive analysis over the coming months, but it seems probable that "new Socialist voters," or their potential equivalents, made up the bulk of the soft Socialist vote that failed to materialize. These voters in all likelihood became upset at the political discord within the union of the Left; many may also have decided that their economic demands could be met by the present ruling majority.[101] The support of such elements almost certainly figured in a major way in the strong showing of the Union pour la démocratie française (UDF). As an electoral coalition of the Center (the Parti républicain, Giscardian republicans; the Centre des démocrates souciaux, the organization of Jean Lecanuet;

and the Parti radical, the regular Radical group headed by Jean-Jacques Servan-Schreiber), the UDF polled 21.4 percent of the vote, thus establishing itself as a political force on a par with the Gaullists, Socialists, and Communists. Because of this demonstrated strength, the UDF may now represent an attractive non-Gaullist alternative to the Socialist Party for wavering voters on the left who have misgivings about casting their ballots for an ally of the PCF.

In addition, the Socialists must reckon with the attitudes of the Radicals of the Left. After the second-ballot returns were in, Robert Fabre, the leader of the Radicals of the Left, announced that he considered himself "released" from the commitments to which he subscribed in signing the Common Program.[102] Whether he meant that he wished to abandon the alliance with the Communists is still unclear. If so, the Socialists would have to ponder that position carefully. However small the percentage of the vote that the Left Radicals control, that percentage is a significant element in the political strength of the non-Communist Left, for the Left Radicals have formed first-ballot alliances with the Socialists in preliminary electoral competition with the Communists.

As for the PCF, it has to take into account that the Socialist Party has for the present replaced it as the preeminent electoral force on the left. To be sure, Communist voting strength remained relatively intact in the 1978 elections, slipping only a percentage point from the 1973 level. But if the Communist leadership has been willing to concede a rough voting parity to the Socialists as a requirement for expanding the voting strength of the Left toward the center, its readiness to tolerate a situation in which the Communist vote remains static while the Socialist vote mounts is questionable. The PCF could therefore opt to concentrate on building up its electoral strength in order to reinforce its political weight on the left—even at the expense of exacerbating tensions between itself and the Socialist Party and causing a further deterioration of Communist-Socialist relations.

Dissolution of the alliance is by no means the only possibility, however. After considering the negative aspects of continued participation in the union of the Left, the Socialist leadership may still conclude that, on balance, Socialist electoral support will be greater if the party stays in the alliance than if it abandons the alliance. By the same token, the Communist leadership may decide that the PCF has no viable alternative to the union of the Left as a means of capturing at least a share of power and that this consideration should prevail, regardless of the disadvantages entailed.

Whatever courses the two parties elect to follow, it is important to bear in mind that they will probably make their choices in light of electoral concerns as well as policy objectives. This is especially true with respect to the Communists, for the voting strength that the PCF commands will directly affect its ability to function as "revolutionary vanguard" in any future discussions with the Socialist Party on the minimum threshold of nationalizations to be incorporated into a common program of government.

If the union of the Left holds together in some fashion, the PCF's role in the French political system will in all probability remain much the same as it has been during recent years. Should the alliance fall completely apart, however, the party could once again find itself acting as essentially an obstructionist force instead of as a significant catalyst for political change.

Notes

1. *L'Année politique, 1958* (Paris: Editions du Grand Siècle, 1959), p. 145. The impact of this revival of balloting procedures in force during most of the Third Republic becomes manifest when one looks at some additional statistics. In the second, or final, vote in the 1958 elections, the PCF received 20.5 percent of the total ballots cast. (Under the electoral law of the Fifth Republic, as we shall discuss in more detail later, only candidates who obtain an absolute majority of the votes in the initial round of balloting automatically win election; the rest must go through a second round of balloting, out of which a victor emerges regardless of whether he captures a majority of the votes or not.) For 20.5 percent of the ballots, however, the party garnered only 1.7 percent of the National Assembly seats. On the basis of the proportional representation system used under the Fourth Republic, the Communists would have received eighty-eight seats instead of ten. See J. M. Cotteret et al., *Lois électorales et inégalités de représentation en France 1936-1960* [Electoral laws and inequalities of representation in France 1936-1960] (Paris: Colin, 1960), p. 372, as cited in William Safran, *The French Polity* (New York: McKay, 1977), p. 111-112.

2. See "Déclaration commune du Parti communiste français et de la Fédération de la gauche démocrate et socialiste (24 février 1968)" [Common Declaration of the French Communist Party and the Federation of the Democratic and Socialist Left (February 24, 1968)],

Cahiers du Communisme (Paris), no. 3, March 1968, pp. 19-35. Although this document also reflected certain areas of disagreement between the two bodies, in its entirety it represented the basic foundation of constitutional reform that later got incorporated into the Common Program of Government of the Communist and Socialist parties in 1972. Among other things, it called for the abolition of Article 16 of the constitution, which gives the president the authority to assume emergency powers at his own discretion; for a form of governmental investiture by the National Assembly on the basis of a legislative contract; and for automatic dissolution of the National Assembly if the legislative contract could not be fulfilled because of a breakup of the coalition of parties comprising the government.

3. "Résolution du 16ᵉ congrès (Saint-Denis, 11-14 mai 1961)" [Resolution of the 16th Congress (Saint-Denis, May 11-14, 1961)] *Cahiers du Communisme*, nos. 6-7, June-July 1961, p. 575.

4. *L'Humanité* (Paris), December 6, 1962, p. 1.

5. Maurice Thorez, "Discours de clôture au Comité central (Ivry, 8-10 mai 1963)" [Speech of closure to the Central Committee session (Ivry, May 8-10, 1963)], *l'Humanité*, May 14, 1963, p. 5.

6. See French Communist Party, *Pour une démocratie avancée, pour une France socialiste; manifeste du Comité central à Champigny-sur-Marne 5 et 6 décembre 1968* [For an advanced democracy, for a socialist France: manifesto of the Central Committee at Champigny-sur-Marne, December 5 and 6, 1968] (Paris: Editions sociales, 1969).

7. Although the Communist and Socialist parties alone worked out the provisions of the Common Program, the Radicals of the Left also signed the document shortly after its formalization. This group split from the Radical-Socialist organization, then headed by Jean-Jacques Servan-Schreiber, over the question of the Common Program, i.e., whether the Radicals were to constitute part of the Left or should enter into a left-center coalition with the supporters of Jean Lecanuet. Robert Fabre emerged as the chief spokesman for the Radicals of the Left.

8. Paul Boccara, "Suraccumulation du capital et financement public de la production" [Overaccumulation of capital and public financing of production], in Paul Boccara, *Etudes sur le capitalisme monopoliste d'Etat, sa crise et son issue* [Studies on state monopoly capitalism, its crisis, and its end], 2d ed. (Paris: Editions sociales, 1974), pp. 41-69.

9. For Marx's own discussion of the issues dealt with here, see

Karl Marx, "Exposition of the Internal Contradictions of the Law," *Capital* (New York: International Publishers, 1976), vol. 3, pp. 247-253.

10. In the case of France, this public sector would consist of the public capital formed as a result of the programs of the Popular Front and the National Council of the Resistance.

11. French Communist Party (Economic Section), *Traité marxiste d'économie politique; le capitalisme monopoliste d'Etat* [Marxist treatise on political economy; state monopoly capitalism], 2d ed. (Paris: Editions sociales, 1976), vol. 1, pp. 40-41. One party study has attempted to show that in the year 1969 the public enterprises accounted for 20 percent of the total operating capital in France but received only 2.4 percent of the total profits. The study went on to contend that if these enterprises had gotten only the mean rate of profit claimed by other French enterprises, their profits would have amounted to 30 billion francs. The reader is then left to draw the conclusion that this sum was used to subsidize the profits of monopolies. See Henri Sèrge, et al., *Les entreprises publiques* [The public enterprises] (Paris: Editions sociales, 1975), p. 148.

12. See Paul Boccara, "Inflation accélérée, suraccumulation et politique des revenus" [Accelerated inflation, overaccumulation, and revenue policy], *Economie et Politique* (Paris), no. 262, May 1976, pp. 5-27.

13. French Communist Party, *Traité marxiste*, vol. 1, p. 420. See also Philippe Zarifian, *Inflation et crise monétaire* [Inflation and monetary crisis] (Paris: Editions sociales, 1975), pp. 162-169. For a party study on how inflation has affected workers' salaries, see Henri Nolleau, "De la misère moderne à la misère tout court" [From modern misery to just plain misery], *Economie et Politique*, nos. 251-253, June-August 1975, pp. 184-188.

14. See, for example, French Communist Party, *Traité marxiste*, vol. 1, pp. 131-142; and Patrice Grevet, "Besoins populaires et financement publique" [Popular needs and public financing], *Economie et Politique*, no. 258, January 1976, pp. 45-58.

15. Paul Boccara, "Quelques précisions sur la situation de la théorie de la suraccumulation-dévalorisation du capital dans le développement de la théorie marxiste et sur son application au C.M.E." [Some precise details on the state of the theory of overaccumulation-devaluation of capital in the development of Marxist theory and on its (the theory's) application to state monopoly capitalism], in Boccara, *Etudes sur le capitalisme monopoliste d'Etat*, pp. 313-314.

16. Paul Boccara, "Quelques perspectives de la crise du capitalisme monopoliste d'Etat et de l'instauration de la démocratie avancée" [Some perspectives on the crisis of state monopoly capitalism and the setting up of advanced democracy], in ibid., p. 327. Emphasis in original.

17. Marc Dupuis, *Nationaliser quels groupes? Pourquoi? Comment?* [To nationalize what groups? Why? How?] (Paris: Editions sociales, 1974), pp. 99-100.

18. See Paul Boccara, "Evolution et fonctionnement économiques dans la démocratie avancée, comme phase de transition révolutionnaire au socialisme" [Economic evolution and functioning in the advanced democracy as a phase of revolutionary transition to socialism], in Boccara, *Etudes sur le capitalisme monopoliste d'Etat*, pp. 359-389.

19. French Communist Party, *Traité marxiste*, vol. 1, pp. 185-190. For a party study of the technical economic considerations of this question, see Maurice Décaillot, *Le mode de production socialiste, essai théorique* [The mode of socialist production, a theoretical essay] (Paris: Editions sociales, 1973).

20. See Thesis 19 of "Thèses adoptées par le 19ᵉ congrès du Parti communiste français (Nanterre, 4-8 février 1970)" [Theses adopted by the 19th Congress of the French Communist Party (Nanterre, February 4-8, 1970)], *Cahiers du Communisme*, nos. 2-3, February-March 1970, p. 433.

21. French Communist Party, *Traité marxiste*, vol. 2, p. 415.

22. French Communist Party, *Programme commun de gouvernement du Parti communiste français et du Parti socialiste (27 juin 1972)* [Common Program of Government of the French Communist Party and Socialist Party (June 27, 1972)], introduction by Georges Marchais (Paris: Editions sociales, 1972), pp. 115-116.

23. Patrice Grevet, "Sur la démocratie avancée (intervention à la conférence fédérale de Paris)" [On advanced democracy (intervention at the Federal Conference of Paris)], *Economie et Politique*, no. 188, March 1970, p. 23.

24. Georges Marchais, "Rapport du Comité central au 19ᵉ congrès (Nanterre, 4-8 février 1970)" [Report of the Central Committee to the 19th Congress (Nanterre, February 4-8, 1970)], *Cahiers du Communisme*, nos. 2-3, February-March 1970, p. 61.

25. Georges Marchais, "Le socialisme pour la France" [Socialism for France], Report of the Central Committee to the 22d Party Congress, Saint-Denis, February 4-8, 1976, in *Cahiers du Communisme*, nos. 2-3, February-March 1976, pp. 31, 32.

26. Waldeck Rochet, *L'Avenir du P.C.F.* [The future of the P.C.F.] (Paris: Editions sociales, 1970), p. 123.

27. "Premier bilan des conversations engagées entre le Parti communiste français et le Parti socialiste sur les conditions fondamentales d'un accord politique" [First balance sheet of conversations between the French Communist Party and the Socialist Party on the fundamental conditions of a political accord], *Bulletin Socialiste* (new series of *Le Populaire de Paris*), no. 165, December 23, 1970, p. 4.

28. Ibid.

29. Week of Marxist Thought (April 22-29, 1971), *Problèmes de la révolution socialiste en France cent ans après la commune* [Problems of the socialist revolution in France 100 years after the Commune] (Paris: Editions sociales, 1971), p. 115.

30. Ibid., p. 126.

31. See "Motion adoptée par la majorité (Epinay-sur-Seine, 11-13 juin 1971)" [Motion adopted by the majority (Epinay-sur-Seine, June 11-13, 1971)], *Bulletin Socialiste*, no. 275, June 15, 1971, p. 1.

32. French Communist Party, *Programme commun*, p. 149.

33. Georges Marchais, *Le Défi démocratique* [The democratic challenge] (Paris: Grasset, 1973), pp. 116-117. Emphasis in original.

34. Ibid., pp. 129-130. Emphasis in original. See also "Déclaration commune des Parti communiste français et Parti communiste italien" [Common Declaration of the French Communist Party and Italian Communist Party], *l'Humanité*, November 18, 1975, pp. 1, 3.

35. "Ce que veulent les communistes pour la France" [What the Communists want for France], Political resolution adopted by the 22d Party Congress, Saint-Denis, February 4-8, 1976, *Cahiers du Communisme*, nos. 2-3, February-March 1976, p. 376.

36. For the full text, see Foreign Broadcast Information Service, *Daily Report: Western Europe* (Washington, D.C.), March 4, 1977, pp. N1-2. Emphasis added.

37. "Ce que veulent les communistes pour la France," p. 378. Emphasis added.

38. See Georges Marchais, "Le socialisme pour la France," pp. 44-51. Instead of using the term *dictatorship of the proletariat*, the political resolution of the congress employed the phrase *a political power representative of the laboring people.*

39. See French Communist Party, *Vivre libres; Projet de déclaration des libertés soumis à la discussion des Français* [To live free; a proposal for a declaration of liberties subject to discussion by the French people], introduction by Georges Marchais (Paris: Edition de

l'Humanité, 1975).

40. The complete text of Juquin's address is reproduced in *Cahiers du Communisme*, no. 11, November 1976, pp. 124-126.

41. See *Le Monde*, October 21-27, 1976, p. 5.

42. For its declaration, dated December 17, 1976, see *Cahiers du Communisme*, no. 1, January 1977, p. 124.

43. Charter 77 was a manifesto signed not only by a number of Czechoslovak intellectuals but also by elements from other social strata in the country demanding that the government respect political and civil rights as set forth both in the Czechoslovak constitution and in the Final Act of the Conference on Security and Cooperation in Europe in 1975.

44. *L'Humanité*, January 25, 1977, cited in *Cahiers du Communisme*, no. 3, March 1977, p. 120.

45. *L'Humanité*, October 19, 1977, p. 1.

46. Ibid.

47. French Communist Party, *Changer de cap; programme pour un gouvernement démocratique d'union populaire* [To change course; program for a democratic government of popular unity), introduction by Georges Marchais (Paris: Editions sociales, 1971), p. 220.

48. Ibid., pp. 221-223.

49. Ibid., p. 222.

50. See French Communist Party, *Programme commun*, p. 174.

51. Jean Kanapa, "Coexistence pacifique et lutte de classe en 1975 (Rapport au Comité central, Paris, 14-15 avril 1975)" [Peaceful coexistence and class struggle in 1975 (Report to the Central Committee, Paris, April 14-15, 1975)], cited in *Cahiers du Communisme* nos. 7-8, July-August 1975, p. 80.

52. Kanapa, "Coexistence pacifique et lutte de classe en 1975," cited in *Cahiers du Communisme*, no. 10, October 1975, p. 85.

53. See Jacques Denis, "Le succès de la conférence d'Helsinki; une étape et un tremplin pour l'action" [The success of the Helsinki conference; a stage and a springboard for action], *Cahiers du Communisme*, no. 10, October 1975, pp. 74-88. See also Martin Verlet, "Coexistence pacifique et lutte de classe aujourd'hui" [Peaceful coexistence and class struggle today], ibid., nos. 7-8, July-August 1975, pp. 71-85.

54. See, for example, Jacques Denis, "La doctrine Ford-Kissinger de souveraineté limitée" [The Ford-Kissinger doctrine of limited sovereignty], *France Nouvelle* (Paris), no. 1560, October 7, 1975, pp. 19-21.

55. See, for instance, Gérard Streiff, "La France et l'O.T.A.N.: une

réinsertion de fait" [France and NATO: a reinsertion in fact], *Cahiers du Communisme*, no. 4, April 1976, pp. 78-88.

56. "Déclaration du Bureau politique du Parti communiste français (Paris, 20 juillet 1976)" [Declaration of the Political Bureau of the French Communist Party (Paris, July 20, 1976)], *l'Humanité*, July 21, 1976, p. 1.

57. French Communists were particularly angry because the Soviet ambassador had visited the Elysée during the presidential elections of 1974. This visit the PCF leadership interpreted as a direct sign of Soviet support of the social and political status quo in France. The degree of offense that this episode caused can be gauged by the fact that some two years later Marchais brought it up again in an interview. See ibid., April 30, 1976, p. 8.

58. See, for example, the statement of a French delegation that had just returned from Lisbon in ibid., August 18, 1975, p. 2; and the comments of Marchais in *Le Monde*, August 20, 1975, p. 3.

59. "L'intervention de Jean Kanapa à la réunion de Berlin" [The intervention of Jean Kanapa at the Berlin meeting], *France Nouvelle*, no. 1562, October 20, 1975, p. 20.

60. See "Pour la paix, la sécurité, la coopération et le progrès social en Europe" (Document adopté par la conférence des Partis communistes et ouvriers d'Europe, Berlin, 29 et 30 juin 1976) [For peace, security, cooperation, and social progress in Europe (document adopted by the Conference of Communist and Workers' Parties of Europe, Berlin, June 29-30, 1976)], *l'Humanité*, July 3, 1976, pp. 4-5.

61. "Une période marquée par des évolutions profondes (Intervention de Georges Marchais à la conférence des P.C. d'Europe, Berlin, 30 juin 1976)" [A period marked by profound evolution (intervention of Georges Marchais at the Conference of Communist Parties of Europe, Berlin, June 30, 1976)], *l'Humanité*, July 1, 1976, p. 2.

62. See Louis Baillot, "Une politique pour la gauche au pouvoir" [A policy for the Left to power], *Cahiers du Communisme*, nos. 7-8, July-August 1977, pp. 14-23.

63. *Pravda* (Moscow), February 29, 1976, p. 8.

64. *L'Humanité*, July 1, 1976, p. 2.

65. Ibid.

66. See in this regard a statement by Jacques Denis upon his return from the East Berlin conference of European Communist parties, "Par la diversité des chemins" [By diversity of paths], *France Nouvelle*, no. 1600, July 12, 1976, p. 9.

67. French Communist Party, *Programme commun*, pp. 53, 55.

68. See the discussion in the next section.

69. French Communist Party, *Programme commun,* p. 55.

70. Ibid., p. 57.

71. Ibid., p. 133.

72. Sondage L'Express-Sofres in *l'Express* (Paris), no. 1260, September 1-7, 1975, pp. 38-39.

73. Ibid., p. 39.

74. *Le Monde,* March 4-10, 1976, p. 1.

75. Ibid., March 17-23, 1977, p. 1.

76. See Elizabeth Dupoirier and François Platone, "Une nouvelle étape dans le déclin du 'social-centrisme' " [A new stage in the decline of 'social centrism'], *Revue Française de Science Politique* (Paris), December 1974, pp. 1173-1204.

77. Sondage L'Express-Makrotest in *l'Express,* no. 1296, May 10-16, 1976, p. 31.

78. Sondage Match-IFOP in *Paris Match,* no. 1460, May 20, 1977, p. 68.

79. Ibid. When specific ministries were mentioned, however, there was a significant disparity in the levels of support for placing Communists in charge of them. Interestingly, the three ministries the respondents were least inclined to give the Communists were Interior, Foreign Affairs, and Defense. See ibid., p. 69.

80. Ibid.

81. See "Ce que veulent les communistes pour la France," pp. 384-385.

82. Georges Marchais, "Rapport au Comité central (Paris, 29 juin, 1972)" [Report to the Central Committee (Paris, June 29, 1972)], in *L'Union est un combat* [The union is a struggle], ed. Etienne Fajon (Paris: Editions sociales, 1975), p. 109.

83. "Le socialisme pour la France" [Socialism for France], report of Georges Marchais to the 22d Party Congress, Saint-Denis, February 4-8, 1976, in *Cahiers du Communisme,* nos. 2-3, February-March 1976, p. 57. Emphasis added.

84. According to Georges Marchais, the Socialists were initially prepared to nationalize only four of the nine firms. See his "Rapport au Comité central (Paris, 29 juin, 1972)," p. 104.

85. Ibid., p. 102.

86. In 1972, the Communists had sought to include all of these industries, plus a number of others, on the list for nationalization. For an enumeration of the concerns that the Communists had in mind then and a breakdown of their economic operations, see Alexis Cousin et al., "Données sur quelques grands groupes industriels

privés" [Data on some large private industrial groups], *Economie et Politique*, no. 215, June 1972, pp. 115-126.

87. See French Communist Party, *Programme commun*, p. 114. Actually, the Common Program had called for the state to purchase majority holdings in the steel and metallurgical industries, but the Communists had never felt that such an approach would give the state the type of control that it needed.

88. Roger Blin and Anicet Pors, "Les nationalisables" [The nationalizables], *Economie et Politique*, no. 274, May 1977, pp. 28-29.

89. For the original reference to the term *group*, see French Communist Party, *Programme commun*, p. 116.

90. They agreed to postpone the nationalization of Peugeot-Citroën and Compagnie Française des Pétroles-C.F.R.-Total and to exempt some 279 branch enterprises of the banking and financial industries from immediate nationalization. At the same time, they refused to abandon their basic notion of a minimum threshold. According to their calculations, the nationalization of just the 729 enterprises belonging to the nine original mother concerns, for example, would cover 500,000 workers and 5 percent of national industrial investment. See *l'Humanité*, September 27, 1977, p. 2.

91. Ibid., September 29, 1977, p. 4. Emphasis in original.

92. Because of the character of the impact of second-ballot voting alliances in the single-member districts of the French electoral system, the disparity in percentage of the popular vote between the Communists on the one hand and the Socialists and Radicals of the Left on the other would in all likelihood be greatly magnified in the distribution of seats in the National Assembly.

93. See Marchais, "Rapport au Comité central (29 juin 1972)," p. 118.

94. See *l'Humanité*, September 29, 1977, p. 4.

95. Voting statistics are those of the Ministry of the Interior as reported in *Le Monde*, March 15, 1978, p. 13. Prior to the first ballot, the Socialists and the Radicals of the Left had agreed to run only a single candidate from one party or the other. Only in this fashion could the Radicals of the Left, because of their very small percentage of the popular vote (less than 2 percent in 1973), ever hope to represent the Left on the second ballot in any districts and hence to gain representation in the National Assembly. In 1973, the two organizations had even run under a common label, the Union de la Gauche Socialiste et Démocrate, on the first ballot.

96. See ibid., p. 7.

97. In this part of the declaration, the Communist Party received major satisfaction on one particular point—the establishment of a minimum monthly wage of 2,400 francs.

98. See *Le Monde,* March 16, 1978, p. 8.

99. Voting statistics are those reported in ibid., March 21, 1978, p. 2.

100. Ibid., p. 1. The opposition included 201 deputies in all, with one deputy being unattached to the union of the Left.

101. On this point, one should recall the 1976 poll cited earlier, in which 29 percent of the new Socialist voters represented a soft vote that could conceivably be drawn away from the union of the Left.

102. *Le Monde,* March 21, 1978, p. 8.

3
Spain: The PCE and the Post-Franco Era

Eusebio M. Mujal-León

Spain has entered the post-Franco era. In June 1977, after forty years of authoritarian dictatorship, Spanish citizens voted in free elections. Those parliamentary elections, historic in so many ways, also marked the formal entry of the Partido Comunista de España (PCE) into the political arena.

Operating illegally since 1939 and for much of that time having more members outside Spain than within, the Spanish Communists had built a political base around the unofficial, parallel trade union movement known as the Comisiones Obreras (CC.OO.) and over the course of two decades prior to 1977 had developed into the most effective opposition force in the country.[1] This ability of the Communists to survive the rigors of clandestinity, coupled with their adaptive domestic policies and well-publicized efforts, particularly after the Czech invasion in August 1968, to cast a distance between themselves and the Soviet Union, seemed to suggest that the PCE would without great difficulty assume an important role in Spanish politics. However, the results of the June 1977 elections indicate that such an assessment was overdrawn. The Communists, it is true, did capture 9.2 percent of the national tally and received over 1.6 million votes (enough to make them the third largest electoral force in the country), but it was the Unión de Centro Democrático (UCD) led by incumbent premier Adolfo Suárez (34 percent) and the Partido Socialista Obrero Español (PSOE) headed by Felipe González (29 percent) that emerged as the clear victors in the contest. The performance of the Spanish Communists did not compare favorably with either that of the Italian Communists and French Communists

The author would like to express his appreciation to the Social Science Research Council for research support in the form of an International Doctoral Fellowship during 1977 and part of 1978.

139

throughout the post–World War II period or with the 15 percent that
the Portuguese Communists polled in April 1976. The PCE did not
win a deputy in either Galicia or in the conflict-ridden Basque
country, and had it not been for the remarkable performance of its
Catalan branch and of Communist candidates in Andalucía, it would
have made a truly dismal showing.[2]

There have been any number of explanations for the results. Some
observers would emphasize that the PCE, illegal until less than two
months before the elections, could not in the space of a few weeks
overcome the effects of forty years of hostile anticommunist
propaganda and its own ruthless tactics during the 1936-1939 civil
war. Moreover, there was the nature of the electoral law under which
the balloting took place. The Suárez government fashioned a law
that quite clearly discriminated against the Left. Although the law
purported to set up a system of proportional representation, it in fact
overrepresented the more conservative, agricultural parts of the
country.[3] The eleven provinces where 50 percent of the electorate
resided elected only 198 representatives to the Chamber of Deputies
and the Senate, but the remaining half of the eligible voters,
distributed in thirty-seven provinces, accounted for 359 seats. The
electoral law discriminated against the Left in other ways as well. It
not only kept the voting age limit at twenty-one years (thus
eliminating from the rolls some 2 million young people among
whom the opposition had gained quite an audience) but also placed
numerous obstacles in the way of the more than half a million
emigrant workers who theoretically could have participated in the
elections. In addition, the PCE's decision to direct the brunt of its
criticism during the electoral campaign not at Suárez but at the
collection of Francoist notables in Alianza Popular (AP) may have
backfired. This move certainly helped defeat the ultraconservative
AP, but it disenchanted many militants and sympathizers and
permitted the Socialists to profit by presenting themselves as
intransigent opponents of Francoism, opposed not only to the
Alianza but also to the more seductive, reformist image offered by
Suárez.

These explanations are correct as far as they go, but they are
insufficient to the degree that they do not explicitly recognize that
the poor Communist performance in June 1977 reflected the success
of King Juan Carlos and Premier Adolfo Suárez in keeping the
political initiative from the PCE in the year after Francisco Franco's
death. The Communists were unable to capitalize on their political
and organizational superiority because they could not galvanize the

forces necessary to impose a *ruptura* between the Francoist past and the democratic future. That role fell to Adolfo Suárez, whose *reforma* has been accomplished within the framework, if not the spirit, of the laws and institutions legated by Franco and who, in effect, consummated the *ruptura*.

This chapter will explore how such circumstances came about. It will focus on the interaction among the regime, the Communists, and the rest of the opposition during the transitional years of 1973-1977. For analytical purposes, we shall divide this critically important period into three distinct phases. The first—from December 1973 to November 1975—began with the assassination of Admiral Luis Carrero Blanco and ended with the death of Francisco Franco. During this phase, the Communists helped to forge an opposition front known as the *Junta Democrática* and predicted it would trigger the downfall of the regime. The gambit failed: the Junta did not encompass a sufficiently broad spectrum of the opposition, and perhaps more important, the Franco regime's position had not deteriorated sufficiently to make radical change a viable political alternative. The second stage lasted from November 1975 to July 1976. It coincided with the first government of the Juan Carlos monarchy and saw the success of Communist efforts to further unify the opposition. However, the new opposition coalition, Coordinación Democrática, included groups with rather different and contradictory views on how to deal with the government; as a result, it was generally incapable of decisive action. The third and final phase began with the designation of Adolfo Suárez as premier in July 1976 and concluded with the holding of the national elections. Suárez ably exacerbated the differences within the opposition and defeated the PCE's efforts to force a shift in the political balance of power. Under Suárez, the regime retreated, but it did so in orderly fashion.

The Prelude

The struggle for power in the post-Franco era began nearly two years before the death of the *caudillo* with the assassination of Admiral Luis Carrero Blanco in December 1973. That brutally efficient act of political violence, attributed to a branch of the Basque terrorist organization Euzkadi ta Askatasuna (ETA) was the death knell of the Francoist regime.

Although opposition organizations such as the Communist party had long been active in the struggle against the dictatorship, their predictions of its imminent downfall had taken on an air of unreality.

In the 1940s, the regime had defeated the opposition-sponsored guerrilla movement and had weathered the international isolation into which the defeat of the Axis powers in 1945 had thrust it. More recently, it had withstood the resurgence of powerful strike movements. In late 1973, it gave every indication of being able to assure its permanence.

Carrero Blanco's assassination changed all that. Not only was he the titular head of state and Franco's confidant, but the aging leader had charged him with insuring the continuity of the system. Carrero Blanco's physical disappearance thus meant the elimination of a key piece from the political chessboard. Many in the Spanish political elite understood as much, and in February 1974, even Carrero Blanco's extremely conservative successor, Carlos Arias Navarro, promised the establishment of "national political associations" and a general liberalization of the political system.

This speech raised the hopes of many moderate opponents of the regime, but it did not take long for disillusionment to set in. Government efforts to exile the bishop of Bilbao for including a call for Basque civil rights in a homily and the decision to execute anarchist Puig Antich in Barcelona came only a few weeks after Arias's speech. Such moves indicated that the new premier would have a difficult time shedding the habits and background he had acquired as minister of the interior.

A psychologically invigorated, albeit not very well organized, opposition confronted the Arias government in early 1974. Most of the as yet fledgling groups could be said to belong to one or another of four families.

Among the Socialists could be included the Felipe González–led PSOE, the Partido Socialista Popular (PSP), and a rapidly growing assortment of regional Socialist groups. The PSOE had been the premier organization on the Spanish left in the years preceding and during the civil war. For two decades after the end of that conflict, the PSOE endured the harsh repression unleashed by the regime (in that period the government arrested the members of no fewer than six National Committees, and in 1953 the secretary general of the party, Tomás Centeno Sierra, died mysteriously at the hands of the police).[4] By the early 1960s, however, it had lost much of its influence. Under the leadership of the exiled Rodolfo Llopis, the party increasingly lost touch with the changes taking place in Spain and proved progressively unable to rally new generations of Spaniards to the PSOE banner. One manifestation of this loss of influence was the growth of a variety of groups, each hoping to become the occupant of historic socialism's space on the Spanish political spectrum. This was the case, for example, of the Partido Socialista del Interior (later to become the PSP), headed by a prestigious university professor, Enrique Tierno Galván. Other Socialist groups developed, particularly in Cataluña, Galicia, the Basque country, Aragon, and Andalucia, but these had a markedly regional cast. We should also note here the presence of the Unión Social Demócrata Española (USDE), led by Dionisio Ridruejo and Antonio García López— which aimed at shifting the axis of Spanish socialism away from its Jacobin tradition and toward social democracy. The PSOE languished under the asphyxiating control of the Llopis exile leadership until its 12th Congress in October 1972, when militants from the interior (most notably, Pablo Castellanos, Felipe González, and Enrique Múgica) captured control of the party.[5] Llopis set up a rival faction and sought to gain exclusive recognition from the Socialist International for his group. His efforts (to which Tierno Galván rallied) failed, and in 1973 the International gave its blessing to the younger leaders associated with González. This decision was to have important longer-term consequences, for it insured West German and Swedish moral, organizational, and financial support for the PSOE.

Also in the opposition were various Christian Democratic groups. Potentially, the most important of these organizations were the Federación Popular Democrática (FPD) of José María Gil Robles and the Izquierda Democrática (ID) of Joaquín Ruiz Giménez. Regional Christian Democratic movements existed to one degree or another in Cataluña, Galicia, Valencia, and the Basque country, but it was only the pre–civil war Partido Nacionalista Vasco from the last region that had anything resembling a mass audience. Most of the Christian Democratic groups were what the Spanish call *grupos testimoniales* coalescing around individuals of great personal prestige but with little effective political organization. Their political future lay (despite Ruiz Giménez's proclivities for alliance with the Left) in the yet to be established Center, but whether they could come to occupy that part of the political spectrum depended not only on how the transformation of the regime came about but also on the decision of the Spanish episcopate to help actively in the organization of a mass Christian Democratic party.

So-called extreme Left groups made up a third sector of the opposition.[6] These organizations had proliferated during the 1960s in reaction to what they perceived as the PCE's abandonment of revolutionary principles. Some of the groups, such as the Partido

Comunista de España—Marxista-Leninista (PCE-ML) and the Partido del Trabajo (PT), were avowedly Maoist and had split off from the PCE in the wake of the Sino-Soviet rift. By contrast, others, such as the Organización Revolucionaria de Trabajadores (ORT) and Bandera Roja (BR), had eventually come to assume rigidly dogmatic Marxist-Leninist positions but had had their origins in the radicalization of the apostolic labor organizations in the early 1960s. All of these groups (and here we include some of the ETA factions) had well-defined, if rather narrow, bases among sectors of the working class in places such as the Basque country, Barcelona, Zaragoza, Madrid, and Navarre.

None of the various groups could match the strength of the PCE, the fourth component of the opposition. In 1974, the Spanish Communist Party was the only one of the organizations challenging the regime that, it may be said without great fear of contradiction, had a genuinely national—albeit thin—audience, that could be considered an authentic political party, and that could present a real, if not altogether attractive, alternative to the regime.

In the years after the civil war, the Spanish Communists had not only experienced harsh repression at the hands of the victorious Nationalists but had been ostracized by others on the left. Over the course of several decades and particularly after the emergence of Santiago Carrillo as the preeminent figure in the party after 1956, the PCE had worked to break out of this ghetto, abandoning its traditional anticlericalism and adopting a flexible stance toward new developments in the Spanish labor movement.[7]

In the late 1950s and early 1960s, the Communist leadership seized on the growth of worker and intellectual dissent in the country to predict the overthrow of the regime in the not-too-distant future and the creation of an "antimonopolist" *democracia política y social* in which the Left would play the leading role. When these predictions did not come true, the PCE had to reassess the Franco regime and to broaden its search for potential allies. The first steps in this direction came in *Nuevos Enfoques a Problemas de Hoy* (1967). There, Santiago Carrillo called attention to the emergence of an *evolucionista* current within the regime that opposed the more conservative sectors.[8] The *evolucionistas*, as he defined them, were the political representatives of the most advanced and dynamic sectors of Spanish neocapitalism. Carrillo did not argue for an outright alliance with this group—that would have been too daring a proposal in 1967 and would have posed serious problems within the party. He did suggest, however, that the "neocapitalists," whose own economic interests were being damaged by the regime, would be willing to sacrifice the existing authoritarian political structures in return for "social" peace. The PCE did not explicitly admit the necessity of cooperation with these elements for a few years, but when it did, it promised that in exchange for "neocapitalist" support of a *pacto para la libertad*, the change in political system would take place with a minimum of social violence and dislocation.[9] Since the late 1950s, it should be noted, the party had argued that the regime would fall by means of a largely peaceful *huelga nacional* ("national strike"), and as a consequence, it found no inconvenience in offering such a guarantee.

Already in the spring and summer of 1973, the PCE had entered into unofficial contacts with representatives of what it called the "neocapitalist" sector. Nonetheless, not until September of that year, after a government reshuffle made conditions more favorable, did the PCE Central Committee gave permission for party representatives to enter into formal negotiations.[10] The talks gathered momentum after Carrero Blanco's assassination in December and received a further impetus from the April 1974 revolution in Portugal.

By this time, the PCE had broadened its contacts to include Don Juan—son of Spain's last reigning monarch, Alfonso XIII, and father of Prince Juan Carlos, whom Franco had invested with the rights to the throne in 1969. The party suggested Don Juan could emerge as the arbiter of the post-Franco transition if he were to make an explicit condemnation of the regime and claim the succession rights for himself. So as to minimize the chances that a possible conflict with Juan Carlos might give Don Juan second thoughts, the PCE, without consulting with others in the opposition, generously declared that the *dauphin* could himself have a role in setting up "a provisional government of national reconciliation."[11] A key role in the negotiations with the exiled Count of Barcelona went to Rafael Calvo Serer, a former editor of the independent daily *Madrid* and once a close aide to Don Juan. He had likewise served as a point man in the Communist contacts with some "neocapitalists."

Thus, contacts and negotiations with Don Juan and with the PSOE, PSP, USDE, and various Christian Democratic organizations were all under way when news about Franco's illness broke in June 1974. The Communists, convinced that Franco would not physically last out the summer and that his regime would disintegrate rapidly after his death, insisted on the rapid creation of a unitary opposition front. Don Juan declined the Communist offer and adopted a wait-and-see attitude. So did most of the other groups with which the

Communists had been in touch, including the PSOE. The Socialists objected to the proposed alliance on the ground that only political parties and trade unions should be permitted to join. They rejected the Communist insistence on the participation of individual "personalities" such as Rafael Calvo Serer or Antonio García Trevijano and of *organizaciones de base* such as neighborhood and housewife associations. More important perhaps, the Socialists saw an undue haste in the project and felt, not unreasonably, that they were being asked to join in something that would help establish a Communist preponderance over the rest of the opposition.[12]

Convinced that the other groups were making a historic error from which they were unlikely to recover, the Communists went ahead with their plans and in late July 1974, just as Franco left the hospital, announced the creation of a Junta Democrática. The Junta was an unlikely coalition. Besides the Communists and the Comisiónes Obreras, it included groups such as the PSP, the Partido Carlista (supporters of the pretender to the throne, Carlos Hugo de Borbón Parma, and advocates of *autogestion*, or "workers' self-management"), the Alianza Socialista Andaluza, and independent personalities such as Calvo Serer, García Trevijano, and José Vidal Beneyto. All of them rallied around a twelve-point program (which was to last only until the convocation of elections to a constituent assembly) calling for the establishment of a provisional government, total amnesty, the legalization of all political parties, syndical liberties, separation of church and state, and eventual Spanish entry into the European Economic Community (EEC).

Special emphasis should be placed on the heterogeneity of the Junta and on the fact that it was in large measure a union of convenience. For the Communists, it represented a breakthrough in their efforts to get out of their post–civil war isolation and marked an important step in their efforts to assume a pivotal role on the left. For the PSP, in competition with the PSOE for international recognition, entry into the Junta established its credentials as something more than simply a university group united around the figure of Enrique Tierno Galván. Similar considerations must have entered the mind of Alejandro Rojas Marcos, who had pretensions that his ASA would become the principal Socialist group in Andalucía. Calvo Serer saw in the Junta the ideal vehicle to demonstrate the depth of his conversion from regime luminary to opposition stalwart. After all, what group could be considered more diametrically opposed to the Franco regime than the PCE?

Strictly speaking, the Junta did not represent much beyond the

PCE. Yet from a public relations point of view, it was an outstanding success. Impressive confirmation of this fact came with the revelation that in August 1974 Nicolás Franco, the nephew of the Generalísimo, traveled to Paris for a meeting with Carrillo and other representatives of the Junta. It benefited, moreover, from the enormous psychological advantage of being the only functioning opposition front for nearly a year. The other groups in the opposition sought to form a rival organization called the Congreso Democrático in September 1974, but this effort failed, largely because of divisions within the PSOE leadership, some of whom did not want their party to be directly identified with the creation of what was essentially an anti-PCE bloc. It was not until June 1975 that many of the groups outside the Junta, such as the PSOE, USDE, and various Christian Democratic groups, joined together and announced the formation of the Plataforma de Convergencia.

The Junta appeared on the Spanish political scene at a particularly fortuitous moment. One did not need to be an overly perceptive observer of Spanish politics to grasp that the country's political structures were slowly but surely losing their legitimacy. This is not the place for an extended discussion of the reasons for the shift in public opinion. Suffice it to point out that there was a growing awareness among Spaniards of all classes that the status quo could not long endure. Symptomatically, the changes taking place in Spanish society had begun to undermine the two fundamental pillars of the Franco regime—the Catholic church and the army—though the changes had affected the former much more than the latter.[13]

Government efforts to exile the bishop of Bilbao in February-March 1974 had brought relations with the Vatican and the Spanish Catholic hierarchy to the brink of a total rupture. Although in the end the regime backed down in order to avoid such a drastic step, relations did not really improve. Subsequently, in March 1975, the government prohibited an assembly sponsored by an auxiliary bishop of Madrid in the working-class district of Vallecas, and a month later the episcopate tacitly joined its voice to that of the opposition when it approved the official proclamation of an appeal for national reconciliation. All in all, however, it could be said that the hierarchy was simply moving toward a position of neutrality vis-à-vis the regime: the more serious discontent was visible among the lower clergy and among Catholic Action militants, who since the mid-1960s had increasingly adopted outright antiregime positions.

The armed forces were not immune to change either, although their greater discipline had kept things more under control. After

Carrero Blanco's assassination, it had become very clear that a generational cleavage existed in the military between those officers who had fought in the civil war and wanted the army to function as a partisan political instrument whose principal objective was to maintain the state's fidelity to the Francoist heritage, and other, younger officers who opposed such an orientation and wanted the professionalization of the military. For some time, the latter had an ally in the army chief of staff, Manuel Díez Alegría. His intervention against the most conservative sectors of the Spanish military in the aftermath of the Carrero Blanco assassination (Díez Alegría had personally dressed down and countermanded an order given by Iniesta Cano, the "ultra" head of the Civil Guard, to shoot demonstrators on sight) had earned him their enmity, and in June 1974 they were able to take advantage of some indirect contacts he had maintained with the Communists at the height of the December 1973 crisis to have him removed from his post. Some imagined Díez Alegría as the Spanish equivalent of General Antonio de Spínola in Portugal, but he was unwilling to assume that role. The Portuguese Movimento das Forças Armadas (MFA), on the other hand, did have a putative Spanish counterpart in the Unión Militar Democrática (UMD). The UMD advocated the democratization of the Spanish political system, but, in contrast to the MFA, most of the officers involved in the movement believed that change should be accomplished without the military's playing a major role. The government arrested eight officers affiliated with the UMD in June 1975; however, exact figures on the organization's strength were never revealed, and the extent of its influence can only be surmised.[14] Luckily for the regime, the Spanish army had not previously been involved in a disastrous colonial adventure, and when hard-line officers called for intervention in the Spanish Sahara in October 1975, the government decisively rejected that alternative.[15]

Hardly an issue of the PCE's biweekly *Mundo Obrero* went by in 1974 and 1975 that did not cite some new evidence of discontent within the regime or indicate that the end of Francoism was in sight. In retrospect, Communist assertions that the *huelga nacional* would take place under the direction of the Junta, that the Junta alone could unleash a strike movement powerful enough to neutralize the army and the 50,000-man Guardia Civil, appear far off the mark. In fact, a trial-run *acción nacional democrática* called by the Junta in June 1975 had little success. The Communists, as they had done on other occasions, not only overestimated their own strength and that of the opposition in general but also undervalued that of the regime.

With the wisdom of hindsight, we can see that the Junta did not bring together a sufficiently broad spectrum of the opposition to force a radicalization in the admittedly prerevolutionary situation developing in Spain after December 1973. A judgment as to whether responsibility for this fact should be assigned to the Communists for their obstinacy in insisting on a Junta including individuals and organizations to which the PSOE objected, or to the Socialists for making those objections, depends in large measure on one's ideological perspectives. Both sides bear responsibility in the matter—the Communists for their eagerness to ride roughshod over groups they felt had become politically irrelevant, and the Socialists for refusing to admit that the PCE might play a pivotal role in the democratization process.

Nonetheless, to focus extensively on the disunity of the opposition as the factor responsible for the failure of the efforts to bring Franco down would be incorrect. The other side of the coin was that few of the groups that had been economically or politically favored since 1939 were willing to break with the regime. Discontent was one thing; active opposition, quite another. Many incipient oppositionists still held out the hope that upon his accession to the throne Juan Carlos would move to force a real liberalization of the regime and thus pave the way for its economic and political integration into Western Europe. They had been deeply affected by the radicalization of the Portuguese revolution, and though they rejected *caetanismo* as a politically viable alternative, they also feared what would happen were the situation to get out of hand in Spain.

The PCE, in any case, was not as finely honed a political weapon as its leaders might have supposed or let on. Its organizational strength was impressive, if measured relative to that of other groups, but it was not exempt from problems. This was particularly true in Madrid, where it had suffered a heavy blow in early 1974 with the arrest of Executive Committee member Francisco Romero Marín. He had spent seventeen years in clandestinity directing the party in the capital, and his arrest brought with it the confiscation of an important part of the propaganda apparatus and forced the restructuring of the entire organization. This was difficult enough to do without having to prepare at the same time for an assault on the citadels of power.

Moreover, important sectors of the party (not just *gauchiste* intellectuals but working-class activists) were not enthusiastic about the idea of a *pacto para la libertad* insofar as it meant setting up an alliance, however temporary, with the representatives of "monopoly capital." Leftist dissidents in Madrid and Valencia had sought to draw these discontented elements from the party by forming an organization called the Oposición de Izquierda al Partido Comunista (OPI).[16] Besides criticizing the alliance policies followed by Santiago Carrillo, the OPI had demanded the right to function as an organized faction within the party.

In the labor sphere, too, the PCE had its share of problems. Through its influence in the Comisiones Obreras, it had developed into the preponderant force in the Spanish labor movement, but it is questionable whether this influence predominated other than at the top. In any case, although the CC.OO. had originally benefited from an ambiguous judicial status, by the late 1960s and early 1970s the regime had begun to crack down harshly on labor dissidence. One particularly successful raid in June 1972 netted Marcelino Camacho, Nicholás Sartorius, and a number of other top leaders of the movement during a meeting of the Coordinadora General. This blow and others like it effectively decapitated the Comisiones in Madrid and elsewhere. As a result, not only did control of the national movement pass to the Catalan branch (whose leader Cipriano García had not been in attendance at the ill-fated session), but when syndical elections in June 1975 showed that the regime had suffered a staggering defeat, with over 75 percent of the incumbent *enlaces* and *jurados* ("shop stewards") defeated in their bids for reelection, the PCE and its labor activists did not have the leadership available to capitalize on that turn of events and force through the *ruptura sindical*.[17]

Juan Carlos Takes Over

In November 1975, after a prolonged agony lasting well over a month and involving no fewer than six major operations, Francisco Franco died. Some had feared and others had hoped that his death would open the floodgates, but, ironically enough, the long death wait made the moment of his passing anticlimactic and probably contributed to a smooth transmission of power. In the end, despite the bravado of some in the opposition, the accession of Juan Carlos to the throne, forty-six years after the abdication of his grandfather, took place rather uneventfully.

The first government of the monarchy assumed office in December 1975. Those who had hoped for a rather clear break with the past were disappointed. Unsure of where real power lay within the regime and unwilling to test the extent of the powers Franco had legated to him,

Juan Carlos kept Carlos Arias Navarro on as premier. The cabinet, on the other hand, included a group of reformers—the most important of them José María Areilza and Manuel Fraga Iribarne, whom Arias appointed to the Ministry of Foreign Affairs and the Ministry of the Interior, respectively. Areilza, a former ambassador to the United States and France, had evolved by the late 1960s to a position in the moderate opposition, and during a 1970 state visit by West German President Walter Scheel, he and three other opposition figures had presented Scheel with a letter calling for German aid in forcing the democratization of Spanish political structures. From his post as foreign minister, Areilza was to present Europe with a more liberal side of the regime. Fraga Iribarne, the other great "reformist" figure in the cabinet, was a former minister of information who had voluntarily gone into political exile as ambassador to Great Britain in 1974 after refusing to participate in the "political associations" charade Arias had at that time sought to organize. He, like Areilza, must have received some assurances before entering the new government. Subsequent events were to reveal Fraga to have too authoritarian a personality to sustain his liberal reputation, but in late 1975 and early 1976 gestures such as having dinner with PSP leader Tierno Galván were still quite out of character for regime politicians.

Although Fraga and Areilza held strategically and symbolically important ministries, the government as a whole was only slightly more liberal than traditional Francoist governments. However, the entire period from November 1975 to July 1976 was characterized by a struggle between "reformers" and their opponents within the cabinet. The latter successfully weakened reform measures and drew support from "ultras" entrenched in the largely nonelected Cortes, in the state bureaucracy, and in the highest ranks of the military in their efforts to obstruct and delay. As before, Arias sought to convey the impression that he stood above the fray, but in fact the "bunker," as Santiago Carrillo pointedly referred to the Franco loyalists, knew very well that he was their ally.[18]

Although the Communists remained convinced that all efforts to reform the political system would fail, the entry of the "reformist" wing into the government in December 1975 visibly complicated the situation for the PCE. The Communists feared that other groups in the opposition, particularly the PSOE, would accept preferential treatment from the regime and perhaps even legalization in order to make their party of marginal significance. These circumstances made it imperative, from the Communist point of view, that a showdown with the regime come as quickly as possible.

Originally, the PCE had hoped to count on a united opposition front that could go on the offensive immediately after Franco's death. Soon after the constitution of the Plataforma in June 1975, the Junta had entered into conversations with the groups represented there with a view to bringing about the rapid unification of the two organizations. But the talks, although spurred by the proclamation in August of a decree law suspending habeas corpus for two years and the subsequent execution of several terrorists in September, had not progressed as the PCE had wished. The opposition faced the first government of the monarchy still divided.

The most important issues separating the Junta and the Plataforma had to do with the former's call for a provisional government and with the Communists' rejection of Juan Carlos as "a slightly disguised continuity."[19] The PCE, moreover, had been instrumental in having the Junta adopt as an article of faith the view, clearly expressed in the *Manifiesto de Reconciliación Nacional*, that "the dramatic evolution of the state by way of legal reforms [is] objectively and subjectively impossible."[20] It was not that the groups in the Plataforma opposed to such a stance were sure that the king would push for change, but they at least held open such a possibility, arguing that in any case to move frontally against the monarchy was impolitic and might precipitate a military putsch.

With a united opposition front impossible for the short term, the PCE chose to shift its emphasis to mass mobilization. This approach not only would channel growing popular discontent with the deteriorating economic situation (over 20 percent inflation and rising unemployment) against the regime but also, by helping to radicalize the political situation, would prevent any rapprochement between the government and the moderate opposition. The *jornadas de lucha* began in December 1975 with the party instructing its militants and sympathizers in the Comisiones Obreras and neighborhood and housewife associations to organize protests against the suspension of collective bargaining and against the wage freezes imposed by the government.

The movement got under way where the party was strongest, among transport, metallurgical, and construction workers and in the industrial belt around Madrid and Barcelona, but it soon spread. At its apogee in January and February, the strike movement involved more than 300,000 workers in the Spanish capital and virtually paralyzed Madrid and Barcelona.[21] In the former, the government had to order the militarization of the Metro and mail services; in the latter, of municipal employees.

The success of these strikes and the tragic deaths of five demonstrators during a peaceful march in favor of amnesty in the Basque city of Vitoria impelled the opposition toward a general agreement, and by early April 1976 the PCE could at last see its long-standing efforts bear some fruit. Representatives of the Junta and the Plataforma held a press conference at a prominent Madrid hotel and announced the fusion of the two organizations and the formation of Coordinación Democrática.

It was a pyrrhic victory. Although Coordinación brought together a multiplicity of opposition currents (from Maoist groups such as the ORT and PT to Ignacio Camuñas's liberal Partido Democrático Popular), the very extension of the coalition made concerted and decisive action difficult. The PCE could and did congratulate itself about outbidding the government for the temporary allegiance of the moderate groups, but in order for Coordinación to become a reality, the Communists had had to abandon some of their most cherished notions. The new coalition's declaration of principles issued no call for a provisional government (instead it talked about the need for a "constituent process") and made no reference to Juan Carlos or the monarchy.[22] Moreover, despite the relative success of the *jornadas*, few groups in the opposition saw mass mobilization as a way to change the political system. According to the majority viewpoint, *jornadas* might be useful as a way of showing the government that the opposition meant business, but under present circumstances they could not take the place of negotiations. Furthermore, it was not enough to be able to call strikes. The opposition needed to present a credible alternative.

The constitution of Coordinación and its acceptance of the need for a *ruptura pactada*, in effect, meant the defeat of the mass mobilization tactics supported by the Communists and the extreme Left and the victory of those groups that argued that the opposition should eschew confrontation. Ruiz Giménez's Izquierda Democrática had defended the latter position with particular vehemence, and ID had conditioned its entry into Coordinación on prior agreement that there would be no call for a provisional government and that the others in the opposition would consider the holding of free elections to be the equivalent of a *ruptura*.[23] The Communists had agreed to this condition, for they badly needed the presence of the Christian Democratic Izquierda Democrática not only to compensate for the absence of most liberal and social democratic groups but also to be able to point to the presence of the universally respected Ruiz Giménez in the coalition when the government attacked Coordinación and insisted that its victory would only bring revolution and chaos.

The governmental policy of selective toleration (so evident in the authorization of meetings of the Christian Democratic Equipo in January 1976 and of congresses such as those of the PSP, the PSOE-affiliated trade union movement known as the Unión General de Trabajadores, and the Federación de Partidos Socialistas in May and June and in the prohibition of events such as the provincial and regional assemblies of the Comisiones Obreras and of organizations affiliated with the PCE) increased the friction between the Communists and the moderate opposition groups. In fact, by late June, the PCE had to swallow without much comment the remarks of ID's Secretary General Jaime Cortezo to the effect that he saw no contradiction between having some parties in Coordinación opt for legalization while others remained illegal.[24]

Yet the government headed by Arias Navarro proved incapable of taking advantage of these divisions. Indeed, it was either unable or unwilling to crack the whip at a surprisingly defiant Cortes, which was threatening to emasculate what were little more than cosmetic, government-proposed revisions of the penal code and political associations law. Juan Carlos voiced his disappointment with the premier's performance (the king called him an "unmitigated disaster") in the course of an interview he granted a *Newsweek* correspondent in late April.[25] The debility of the Arias government threatened the future of the monarchy, and shortly after the king returned from an official visit to the United States, he finally acted, asking for and receiving Arias Navarro's resignation.

The Advent of Suárez

If Juan Carlos had held back in replacing Arias Navarro, it was primarily because he was unsure of who his new premier would be. The appointment of a new premier was no simple matter, for among the procedural obstacles Franco had placed in his successor's way, the most important was that he had given the Council of the Realm the power to select a *terna* of three candidates, from which the king could choose the new premier. Although the king could refuse to pick one of those chosen and instruct the council to give him a new selection, such an action could produce a constitutional crisis.

The *terna* presented to the king by the Council of the Realm in July

1976 included the names of former Foreign Minister Gregorio López Bravo, former Education Minister Federico Silva Muñoz, and Adolfo Suárez. In choosing the last of the three, the king appointed a relatively young man of forty-three who had previously been a secretary general of the Movimiento Nacional under Arias Navarro. Few people in Spain in July 1976 believed that this decision was a good one. The Communist economist Ramón Tamames called the appointment "a historic error,"[26] and *Mundo Obrero* referred to Suárez's first nationwide telecast as *reformismo puramente verbal.*[27] They were not alone. Only the more conservative elements applauded the choice, and, then, primarily because Suárez had made his career as an apparatchik in the Falange and seemed a fairly conservative sort. That Suárez would last out the summer, much less preside over an almost historically unprecedented transition from authoritarianism to democracy, was a thought that entered few minds.

And yet the new premier, young enough to have a political future still before him and not lacking opportunism, did just that. Suárez understood that decisive action by the government was a precondition for breaking the false unity of the opposition and imposing the "reformist" solution. Indeed, in retrospect, there appears to have been little that separated the Suárez reform plan from that of someone such as Fraga except that the new premier grasped the importance of style.

The Suárez cabinet was largely homogeneous. Although people such as Fraga and Areilza had been asked to join it, they had declined, and it contained no important political figures. The only major holdover was Fernando Santiago Díaz de Mendivil, minister of defense and first vice-premier under Arias, whom Suárez kept on as a gesture toward the military but quickly got rid of in early September after the minister had broken ranks and written a letter to a prominent "ultra" critic voicing his opposition to the Suárez reform plan.

Suárez presented his *reforma política* to the nation in September 1976. The program envisioned approval by the Cortes that autumn, approval by the electorate a few weeks later, and finally parliamentary elections by mid-1977. The *reforma* did not fail to find its critics on the Right and the Left. Suárez dealt with the former by threatening to have the king dissolve the Cortes if it did not approve the program. He handled the latter more circumspectly, showing a willingness to listen that his predecessors did not have. As some wags put it in explaining the differences between Arias and his successor: the former did not bother to listen; Suárez listened and then went his own way.

Suárez faced an opposition that at first glance appeared more united than ever. Indeed, in October 1976, a new opposition coalition named the Plataforma de Organizaciones Democráticas (POD) would appear on the political scene. It would include all of the groups in Coordinación as well as in the regional assemblies of Cataluña, Valencia, and Galicia, with only some Basque and Catalan nationalist groups conspicuously absent.

However, beneath the surface tranquillity, the opposition was in fact deeply split. The more moderate groups such as the Christian Democrats, the PSP, and the liberals saw Suárez's political reform program as insufficient in many aspects but thought it offered a solid basis for negotiation, particularly with respect to certain aspects of the electoral law.[28] The openness with which these groups received the government's proposals could not have surprised many people. Already at the time of the constitution of Coordinación, it will be remembered, Ruiz Giménez and his Izquierda Democrática had said they would consider the holding of free elections to be the political or moral equivalent of a *ruptura*. ID and others in the Christian Democratic Equipo entered into contacts with the Suárez government within weeks of its formation.

By contrast, the Communists (and others to their left) bluntly rejected the *reforma*.[29] The PCE Executive Committee in a September 1976 statement called it a "fraud" and "undemocratic."[30] As a precondition for any discussion about the electoral process, the Communists demanded the prior legalization of all political parties and the neutralization of the state apparatus. The PCE was instrumental in the drafting in late September of the so-called Valencia document, which also took a hard-line approach and called for the creation of a broad-based provisional government, the adoption of emergency economic measures, and the consummation of the *ruptura*.[31] This document drew instant criticism from the moderate opposition groups, and Coordinación shelved it.

Publicly, then, the PCE remained committed to a *ruptura*, but one wonders how much of the intransigence was simply posturing with a view to strengthening the party's hand in an eventual negotiation or to insuring its legalization at or about the same time as other opposition groups. In any case, the PCE could hardly keep repeating that things had not changed. They had, and substantially so. There was a de facto toleration of the party that could not have been imagined a year before. The unofficial headquarters of the PCE had been installed in downtown Madrid, less than a half-mile from the Dirección General de Seguridad, where Central Committee member Julián Grimau had died in 1964. The entire Madrid provincial committee had been presented at a public news conference in October. Police had been ordered not to go in and arrest members of the Executive Committee known to be meeting in the capital to decide their party's position with respect to an important strike that had been called in mid-November.

It should not surprise us that the rather rapid changes Spanish society experienced in the year after Franco's death had an impact on the PCE. After all, those changes were taking place along lines that were quite different from what the Spanish Communist leadership had predicted. A close reading of Communist documents from that period suggests the existence of a strong internal debate. Although the materials for an exhaustive analysis of trends within the party and the unraveling of the political and personal elements that helped create them are not available, it may be useful to focus on the different perceptions that manifested themselves in connection with the nationalities question and the labor movement.

The PCE had traditionally presented itself as the most vigorous proponent of autonomy and self-determination for the various regions, declaring its advocacy of federalism but calling for referenda in Cataluña, Galicia, and the Basque country to determine whether the local populations wanted outright independence or some form of association with the Spanish state.[32] There was little disagreement with these general propositions. The difficulties arose when one sector of the party (some Basques and representatives of the Valencian branch of the PCE, among others) demanded that in the program for the *ruptura* the leadership include a demand for self-government for *all* regions, not simply those mentioned above, and for the establishment of regional provisional governments the moment the Left consummated the *ruptura* at the national level.[33] This policy, in many ways consistent with traditional party demands, seemed dangerously utopian to a rival faction whose public voice was Executive Committee member Pilar Brabo. In a series of articles published in the summer of 1976,[34] Brabo argued against *rupturas parciales*. The call for regional provisional governments in the short term, she declared, would only serve to obstruct the drive for a national *ruptura* and would lend a certain credence to the views of those who said the Communists advocated the dismemberment of the national state. The PCE already had its hands full dealing with those such as Catalan politicians Josep Pallach and Josep Tarradellas, who advocated separate negotiations with Suárez, and it did not need a similar problem in every region. Although Brabo never explicitly said that the *ruptura nacional* was impossible, she did emphasize the difficulties the party would face in attempting its realization. In effect, she sided with those such as Manuel Azcárate, also of the Executive Committee and the party's principal theorist, who warned against too prolonged an insistence on the need for a *ruptura* lest we "lose the train of reality."[35]

Similar differences between maximalist and minimalist opinions developed in the labor movement. There the point at issue was whether to transform the Comisiones Obreras into a traditional labor union. Comisiones had emerged in the early 1960s as a movement based on factory assemblies whose militants took advantage of regime-sponsored syndical elections to infiltrate the official Organización Sindical (OS).[36] This mixture of legal and illegal work had helped the movement deal with the rigors of repression. By the latter part of the 1960s, it had become the principal labor organization in the country. Its success seemed to suggest that it would one day simply take over the OS. So long as the other groups in the labor movement were weak, the CC.OO. could eschew traditional labor union structures, with their bureaucracies and membership rolls, and maintain the fiction that it was a *movimiento socio-político* independent of all political parties. Basing himself on this notion, Marcelino Camacho in the winter of 1975 called for a *congreso obrero constituyente* and offered Comisiones as a vehicle within which other trade unions, such as the UGT and USO, could participate.[37] In a similar vein, in early 1976, the PCE's theoretical journal, *Nuestra Bandera*, stressed the continuing viability of Comisiones as a "trade union of a new type."[38] To convert CC.OO. into "an organization of militants and *afiliados*," the author declared, "would denude it of all its originality." This article appeared about the time of the massive January-February 1976 strike movement, when it still looked as if the *ruptura* might be realized. By the summer, the rapid growth of other labor organizations led to a reassessment of this strategy on the part of the Communist leadership and to instructions to Communist militants in the labor movement to push for the transformation of the Comisiones. Proposals along these lines were submitted and approved at a July 1976 General Assembly of the CC.OO.[39] But the move had its critics both within and outside the party, and some prominent party labor activists such as Nicolás Sartorius and Julián Ariza continued to talk about the need and possibility for a *ruptura* at both the political and syndical levels.[40] By the fall, it was clear that the success of the *reforma política* had eliminated any possibility of a *ruptura sindical* along the lines predicted by the PCE a year before. Symptomatically, *Mundo Obrero* published an editorial arguing that failure to transform the Comisiones would lead to its inevitable "gasification."[41]

By the time the government held its long-awaited referendum on the political reform program, the PCE had abandoned all hope it might be able to impose a *ruptura*. Although the party urged a negative vote in the referendum, this was more or less pro forma. The Executive Committee had already issued several statements indicating that the party had dropped its long list of demands and would participate "in a positive way" in the political process if there were democratic liberties. Now the focus of the PCE's efforts shifted to bringing about legal recognition of its presence in the country. One move to force the government's hand came several days before the referendum when Santiago Carrillo held a public news conference in the middle of Madrid. The uproar from the extreme Right was so great that the government had to respond. Within two weeks, Carrillo and seven other members of the Executive Committee had been arrested. His arrest triggered demonstrations in many Spanish cities, and overnight Madrid and Barcelona were painted and papered over with signs demanding his freedom. Offered safe passage out of Spanish territory, Carrillo refused; within a few days, nevertheless, he was granted provisional liberty and given free rein to carry on his political activities.

What remained was for the illegal, but no longer clandestine, PCE to become the target of the extreme Right. Isolated acts of violence against known party militants had already taken place, and the unofficial party bookstore in the university section of Madrid had been bombed. But none of those events compared to the cold-blooded murder of five people, including four Communist lawyers, at their offices in late January 1977. The assassination came the evening of the day an extreme leftist commando kidnapped the head of the Supreme Military Tribunal and demonstrated the degree to which the interests of the two extremes in Spanish politics coincided. Fortunately, a potentially disastrous military intervention did not materialize, and the crisis only drew opposition and government closer together. The Communists organized a mass funeral demonstration for their dead, with the participation of all major opposition figures. The PCE's first "great sally into the street" in the post-Franco era, as the Madrid daily *Informaciones* called it,[42] was an impressively disciplined outpouring of grief with a clear political dimension.

The legalization of the PCE and other political parties could not wait much longer. In mid-February, the Council of Ministers issued a decree law adopting a simple declaratory procedure that entailed notarized presentation of statutes for the legalization of political parties. Most groups, including the Communists, filed their papers. The government legalized a number of groups (including the PSOE) immediately, but declined to do so in the case of the Communists and the parties to their left. Suárez chose to send the matter to the Supreme Court for a judgment as to whether those parties fell afoul of prohibitions in the penal code against groups that obeyed an "international discipline" and whose activities aimed at the establishment of a "totalitarian" system. Overcoming the procedural obstacle appeared, at first, to be simply a formality, particularly in the Communist case, and a decision was expected within thirty days. However, the normally docile Supreme Court did not go along with the government on this occasion, and at one point some thought it might rule against the party. In the end, the court, after an emergency session with the minister of justice, declared itself incompetent to decide the issue and handed the case back to the government. Now, Suárez had little choice but to legalize the party outright. Announcement of his decision favorable to the PCE came on April 10, eight days before the thirty-eighth anniversary of Franco's victory in the civil war and shortly after the government decided to dismantle the moribund Movimiento Nacional.

News reports of this event and its aftermath fastened on military discontent about the move, and some observers even spoke of a potential coup attempt. Indeed, there was dissatisfaction with the decision (the minister of the navy, Pita da Veiga, and the minister of defense, Manuel Gutiérrez Mellado, had to cut short a visit to the Canary Islands to help smooth the problem). Nevertheless, it should be stressed that there was little chance of a successful takeover and that what really disturbed the high brass was the way the government had reached its decision. The issue of Communist legalization had been under discussion within the cabinet since January, but the final decision had apparently been taken in the absence of the three service branch ministers. As for the public at large, a poll published in the weekly newsmagazine Cambio 16 showed that 55 percent of those surveyed approved the legislation and that only 12 percent opposed it.[43]

We can perhaps speculate that though the delay in the legalization of the PCE may have been due in part to government fears of an adverse military reaction, this was not the whole story. By keeping the Communists in judicial limbo for several weeks, Suárez hoped to give himself and the various groups that might occupy the political Center an extra advantage. This was not an irrelevant consideration; though we have become accustomed in the wake of the June 1977 elections to speak of the inevitability of a Suárez triumph, it was not at all clear in February or March that he would be able to capitalize on his pivotal political role to the extent that he has.

Less than a week after the PCE's legalization, the party's Central Committee met in Madrid for the first time in nearly forty years. With only Dolores Ibárruri absent (she was still in Moscow but would return a short while later), the ranking leaders of Spanish communism met to prepare the strategy for the upcoming parliamentary elections. Santiago Carrillo's report to the session emphasized the need for the party to follow a moderate course, one designed not to provoke political destabilization.[44] He called for the establishment of a *pacto constitucional* among all the parties of the Center and Left and repeated the party's oft-stated position that the new Cortes should draft a new constitution to replace Franco's Fundamental Laws and then be dissolved. He indicated that the Communist leadership was open to the notion of forming a democratic electoral front with the PSOE and other forces of the Left, but he insinuated that such an alliance was unlikely, given what he called "the weight of Atlantic politics."[45]

The same Central Committee session approved the party's electoral program. It called for the constitution to make specific reference to the legalization of all political parties, to establish the supremacy of parliament over other branches of government, to set the vote at eighteen, to grant autonomy for nationalities and regions, and to enshrine the principle of church-state separation. In its economic aspects, the program called for fiscal amnesty and reform, the extension of unemployment insurance to those without jobs in the agricultural sector (a particularly serious problem in Extremadura and Andalucia), greater state participation in the social security system, and the creation of a *consejo económico y social* to function as the national planning board. The party did not advocate any major nationalizations, and on the whole, its short-term economic program was remarkably similar to that of the PSOE and the Unión de Centro Democrático.

Perhaps the most polemical aspects of the plenum were its decisions to shift the party's historical allegiance from the tricolor Republican flag to the traditional bicolor flag associated with the monarchy and reimposed by Franco after 1939, and to drop its insistence on a republican form of government. These decisions caused a commotion in some sectors of the party, and at the plenum eleven members of the Central Committee showed their opposition by abstaining. In fact, the shift on the monarchy issue had been under discussion in the Executive Committee for several months and had been prefigured by Santiago Carrillo's statement to an April 1976 press conference in Paris that his party would not be an obstacle if "through some miracle" the crown brought democracy.[46] The move, in any case, was not without its historical ironies. In December 1967, in one of the first public signs of disagreement with the Soviet Union, Carrillo had taken the Soviets to task for publishing an article in *Izvestiia* suggesting that a monarchy-led transition might be a viable path to the post-Franco era.[47] The PCE, then at the height of its insistence that the opposition could bring the regime down by means of a *huelga general*, vehemently rejected a stance that reality would force it to accept ten years later.

The campaign officially began three weeks before election day, but for the Communists, keenly aware that most polls gave the party only between 6 and 8 percent of the vote, it started immediately after the Central Committee meeting. The party's primary campaign objective was to minimize the electoral support of Alianza Popular. Fraga and his associates became a favorite target of Communist orators, who dubbed the group the *alianza impopular*, and, in fact, the only real flashes in an otherwise restrained campaign came when the two archrivals crossed verbal swords. At the same time, the Communists also directed much criticism at the PSOE. The PCE held several things against Felipe González and his party. In the first place, the PSOE preferred alliance with the Christian Democrats led by Ruiz Giménez and Gil Robles, rather than with the Communists, in the Senate races. A second, and perhaps more important, reason for Communist annoyance was that the PSOE, through a combination of skill and luck, seemed likely to reap many of the fruits of what the PCE considered to be its unique contributions to the democratization process. Sparring for hegemony on the left, each one accused the other of invading its political space. The critical remarks that the Communist leadership made about Felipe González on numerous occasions contrasted with its generally neutral or sometimes even favorable comments about Suárez. Only Ramón Tamames bluntly charged that the UCD was "nearly as Francoist and certainly as opportunistic" as the AP.[48]

Technically, the Communists ran a well-organized campaign, putting together the largest and most impressive rallies of any of the parties. In Madrid alone, they mobilized over 10,000 *interventores*, and within hours after the polls closed, the Communist leadership had a fairly accurate idea of the results in the province. A Communist-initiated recount in Madrid caused the UCD to lose a seat it had apparently won; moreover, most observers believe the party did not exaggerate when its lawyers claimed that they had proof that the

PSOE, not the Suárez-led Unión, had obtained a plurality of the ballots in Madrid. Nonetheless, the PCE, as indicated earlier, did not do well, receiving only 9.2 percent of the national vote.

The Post-Election Situation

The Spanish Communists emerged from the June 1977 elections clearly in a minority: they had only 20 seats in the Chamber of Deputies (the UCD had 165 and the PSOE 118), and their position was even more precarious in the Senate, where they held only 3 out of 248 seats. When the UCD and the PSOE came to agreement on a specific issue, as they did on several occasions in the first few months of the new Cortes's term, no one could stop them. Nevertheless, the Communists, though not particularly well situated to drive a hard bargain with either the Center or the Socialists (since their votes alone would never be decisive in passing or defeating a bill), were not entirely without bargaining power. This was particularly the case because of the influence they exerted in the labor movement through the Comisiones Obreras.

PCE leaders attributed the results of the elections primarily to the lingering effects of forty years of virulent, anticommunist propaganda, and Communist analyses in general sought to minimize the defeat suffered by the party. Moreover, they emphasized that the results clearly favored those forces interested in building a democratic political system in Spain and went against Alianza Popular and other, more overtly Francoist groups such as the Frente Nacional, which yearned for a return to the past.

In keeping with the latter theme, the thrust of Spanish Communist efforts after June 15 was to encourage the creation of a broad-based coalition government. Only such a government, the PCE declared again and again, could rally the popular support necessary to consolidate the nascent Spanish democracy. The Communists did not insist on their own participation in such a government: according to one formula they proposed, the UCD and the PSOE might form a coalition and then rely on the support of the PCE and other parties in the Cortes.

This proposal for a *gobierno de concentración nacional* did not elicit favorable responses from the Socialists, who saw in the suggestion a rather transparent attempt by the Communists to place the PSOE in a situation from which it could only emerge weakened. However, the idea of some sort of an emergency political and economic platform was not without its supporters. Indeed, in the months after the election there was a growing sense among politically aware Spaniards, even if they did not agree with the theses put forth by the PCE, that the country faced serious economic and social problems, problems that had been largely ignored during the transition to the post-Franco era.

Something certainly had to be done about the economy. It was in worse shape that it had been at any time in the previous two decades, with a rising rate of inflation (14 percent in 1975, 20 percent in 1976, and over 25 percent in 1977), a staggering balance-of-payments deficit (which had grown by one-fifth since 1976), and an unemployment rate that appeared destined to climb to more than 7 percent of the active population by the end of the year (which would mean that nearly a million people were unable to find jobs). In June and July 1977, the government announced a series of measures to deal with this crisis, but they were essentially piecemeal and represented a holding action more than anything else.

Insofar as any effort to right the Spanish economy meant putting a ceiling on wages, such a course could not be undertaken without the active acquiescence of the parties of the left and of the trade unions. By making some concessions, the Suárez government knew it could count on Communist support for certain initiatives. The Socialists, of course, were much less open to the idea of a *pacto social*. Flush from their electoral triumph, Socialist leaders were staking out a claim for themselves as *the* left alternative to the government. After June 15, they had begun to envision the emergence of an essentially two-party (PSOE-UCD or PSOE and whatever the center-right might come up with) system in Spain, with the Communists and Alianza Popular playing marginal roles in the new system. The PSOE confidently expected that after new general elections, probably to be held sometime in 1979, it would be able to form a government on its own terms.

Such ideas, it need hardly be stressed, did not sit well with the Communists. There had been constant sparring between the PCE and PSOE (and particularly between Santiago Carrillo and Felipe González) much before the June 1977 elections. In the months after the elections, the situation did not improve. González, for example, often reminded his audiences that there were three types of parties in Spain: parties in government, parties that stood ready to form a government, and, finally, parties that neither were in government nor had a chance of entering. The Communists, he inevitably concluded, were an example of the last type.

By late summer 1977 and particularly after the Socialists forced a motion of confidence vote (which they lost) in the Cortes in early September, the PCE and UCD were ready to draw together in an attempt to trim the Socialists' sails. The *Pacto de la Moncloa,* an economic and political agreement that all the major parties except the AP signed in late October and whose name comes from the prime minister's residence near the university in Madrid, was the most explicit manifestation of this confluence of interests between the Center and the Communists. There were others—especially in the labor movement, where the Suárez government tilted toward the Comisiones in their struggle with the UGT for labor hegemony. The Socialists bitterly criticized these moves and signed the *Pacto* only reluctantly.

Some observers saw the *Pacto* as the first step on the road to a Spanish version of the "historic compromise." Such an interpretation may yet prove correct, but so far the confluence of interests among the various parties seems to be more tactical than strategic. The UCD still looks on the PCE more as an instrument with which to increase its bargaining leverage vis-à-vis the PSOE than as a long-term partner. As far as the Socialists are concerned, they have little interest in a "historic compromise," and if their party consolidates its hegemony on the left, they will probably be in a position to frustrate efforts in that direction.[49] For their part, some Communist leaders, and particularly Santiago Carillo, may well be convinced of the viability and necessity of a "historic compromise" in Spain. At present, however, the primary Communist objective is to reduce the margin between the PCE and the PSOE. To this end, the PCE will pursue a two-pronged policy of, on the one hand, supporting Suárez—this will help, in the Communist view, to consolidate democratic institutions and to buttress the PCE's standing in the nation—while, on the other hand, keeping the door open to an alliance with the PSOE in the longer run. At some point, the Communists will have to make a choice, but there is no reason why they should not be able to use both levers simultaneously for some time to come.

Prospects

From this exploration of the role played by the Spanish Communists in recent Spanish politics, it should be clear why the PCE failed to assume a "hegemonic role in the process of change,"[50] which many party leaders still felt could be theirs in mid-1976. That failure lies at the root of the party's rather disappointing electoral showing. Had Spain experienced a rapid and revolutionary transition into the post-Franco era, the PCE would probably be in a very favorable position right now. Instead, the Spanish Communist leaders have found themselves in the rather uncomfortable predicament of having to explain away the magnitude of the Socialist victory and to reassure Communist militants and sympathizers that the situation is not irreversible.

Were the Spanish Communist Party a redoubt of conservative Stalinism, any optimism on the part of PCE leaders and followers about the reversibility of the situation would be ill founded. As it is, however, the PCE has undergone a dramatic transformation over the course of the last two decades, a transformation that may help the party in overcoming this initial disadvantage.

The Spanish Communists have ceased to function as an arm of Soviet foreign policy. Their evolution away from Moscow began in the early 1960s and deepened after the Warsaw Pact invasion of Czechoslovakia in August 1968. Led by Carrillo and international affairs expert Manuel Azcárate, the PCE became increasingly vocal in its criticism of the Soviet Union and in its rejection of the applicability of the Soviet model to Spain and, more generally, to Western Europe. On more than one occasion, the PCE publicly remonstrated against the suppression of fundamental political liberties and the repression of dissent in the Eastern bloc.[51] As a result, in early 1974 the Soviet journal *Partiinaia Zhizn'* declared that Manuel Azcárate had joined the side of "the declared enemies of socialism" in advocating the growth of an autonomous West European communist movement.[52] More recently, *New Times* accused the Spanish Communist leader of "bring[ing] grist to the mills of imperialism" by remarks he made to the West German weekly *Der Spiegel* and speeches he gave at Cologne and Lugano.[53] Certainly, the public airing of these differences is not likely to hurt the PCE in its quest for respectability, but the friction between the Spanish Communists and Moscow has truly reached significant proportions.

The PCE has evolved in other areas as well. In the ideological sphere, for instance, it has abandoned its traditional critique of "formal" bourgeois liberties and has apparently come around to the view that political, civil, and religious liberties are fundamental rights in any political system. Similarly, the Spanish Communists have made explicit their commitment to accept political pluralism and respect an opposition under socialism. Indeed, Santiago Carrillo has, on several occasions, embraced the principle of alternation in power and indicated his party's willingness always to abide by the electoral expression of the popular will. Although many Communist militants may interpret these innovations as tactical positions to be abandoned later, they may find these declarations of intent a corset out of which it may be difficult to wriggle.

Although the PCE has gone as far as any other West European Communist party in this process of adaptation—of Eurocommunization, if you will—it still has some important choices to make. This is true from the standpoint of international relations as well as in an organizational sense.

Relations between the PCE and the Communist Party of the Soviet Union reached a new low point in June 1977, two weeks after the Spanish elections, when the Soviet journal *New Times* launched a vitriolic attack on Santiago Carrillo as a consequence of his recently published book, *"Eurocomunismo" y Estado.*[54] The Soviets had good reason to react strongly; for in the book, which has since become an international best seller, Carrillo came very close to denying the socialist nature of the Soviet Union. The logic of his argument would have carried him in that direction easily enough, but he resisted the temptation to make a fundamental critique of the political and social systems now existent in the Eastern bloc. Whatever his reasons for avoiding that step, in the longer run the PCE will either have to back away from its challenge to Moscow or push ahead and break with the Soviet Union.

Organizationally as well, the Spanish Communist leadership will have to define its position more clearly. Specifically, it will have to respond to demands that it push the democratization of the party's structures and permit a full and uninhibited debate on all aspects of policy. Although some sectors of the PCE (in particular, the lawyers' *agrupación* and the group that has gathered around Manuel Sacristán at the journal *Materiales)* went on record early in this regard, it was not until the weeks and months immediately preceding the 9th PCE Congress in April 1978 that these ideas found a real echo throughout the party. The catalyst was the proposal the Central Committee made in early 1978 that the reference to Leninism be dropped from the party program. The proposal was, above all, a public relations gambit, but before having it approved by the congress, Carrillo and others in the Spanish Communist leadership had to endure a debate whose breadth and scope has had no equal among the other West European Communist parties. There has as yet been no abandonment of democratic centralism as an organizational principle. Nonetheless, the debate over the issue of Leninism has set in motion a process of democratization that the party apparatus will have a difficult time containing.

Communist efforts to expand their electoral and political audience, however, are not likely to bring immediate results. For the present, one reality the party has to accept is its numerical weakness in the Spanish parliament. Such a state of affairs will not change unless and until the Left is able to force "anticipated" elections before the expiration of the present legislature's term in 1981.

The convocation of "anticipated" elections should not be ruled out. It is conceivable that in the municipal elections scheduled for late 1978, the Left will emerge with a higher national percentage than the Center and Right. Neighborhood and housewife associations—there are more than 100 of the former in Madrid alone—have long been highly politicized, and the Left is influential there. With the turnout in the municipal elections likely to fall below the 80 percent mark registered for the parliamentary elections, a highly disciplined vote will have a much greater impact. Indeed, a preliminary assessment would lead one to expect municipal takeovers by the Left in some of Spain's largest cities. The uncertain economic climate will also play a role. Setbacks for the government in either or both of these spheres, then, could force Suárez to call new elections. At the same time, it should be stressed that Suárez will not necessarily be a passive actor in the situation. Depending on what the mood of the country is in the wake of the anticipated favorable vote in the referendum on the new constitution, he could decide to seek early national elections for his own benefit.

Certainly, it is too early to tell what the prospects for a shift in the "correlation of forces" within the Left are in the short to medium term. Much will depend on whether the Socialists can consolidate their national electoral triumph with a similar performance in the municipal elections and can also develop an edge in the labor movement. In this latter respect, it is worth noting that although the Socialists have made great strides in overcoming the initial advantage of the Comisiones, the Comisiones have come out ahead in the syndical elections held in early 1978. The struggle for hegemony on the Left will for some time center in the labor movement. If the Socialists can maintain and expand their influence there, the PSOE will have an advantage in its dealings with the Communists that few Latin European Socialist parties have had.

Competition between the PCE and the PSOE will likely be a fixture of the Spanish political scene for some time to come, but we should not lose sight of the fact that, even now and however reluctantly, each side perceives the other to be a natural ally on the road to socialism. In contrast to the Social Democratic parties of Northern Europe, the PSOE considers itself a revolutionary, Marxist organization, and it is not inalterably opposed to reaching an understanding with the Communists. Certainly, the Socialists would like to gain power alone, but if they fail in this effort, it will probably be only a matter of time before the two parties work out some sort of common platform or program. The principal obstacles to such a development up to now—the fact that an entente, by conjuring up visions of a "popular front," would encourage the extreme Right, and the Socialist desire to attain power without the Communists and, otherwise, to delineate with some precision the areas and limits of Communist influence—are conjunctural in nature and will tend to diminish as time passes.

Any assessment of Communist prospects for the longer term must emphasize, however, the improbability of the PCE's acquiring a role on the Spanish left comparable, for example, to that of the PCI in Italian politics. At the same time, and precisely because of Communist efforts to reach parity with the PSOE, we can expect a deepening of the evolutionary process (which, it should be stressed, is not necessarily equivalent to "social-democratization") already under way in Spanish communism. We should be wary of suggesting the inevitability of further changes or of minimizing the obstacles in their way, but we must not forget that at least the peculiar constellation of the Spanish Left today does favor such an evolution.

Notes

1. Due to the paucity of data, it is impossible to present a detailed picture of the strength and regional distribution of PCE membership. At a Central Committee meeting in July 1976, the Communist leadership set a target figure of 300,000 members by the end of the year, but it is very unlikely that this total had been reached even by the end of 1977. In a November 1976 interview with the party newspaper *Mundo Obrero* (published in Paris until the PCE's legalization in April 1977, and thereafter in Madrid), the Executive Committee member responsible for the Madrid party organization, Victor Díaz Cardiel, claimed 10,000 members in the province. At the conclusion of a Madrid provincial party conference in April 1977, the claim was that the party had 18,000 members. This, it now appears, was an inflated figure. A report to the Second Conference of the Barcelona organization in March 1977 (*Segunda Conferencia de Barcelona* [Second Conference of Barcelona], n.p., n.d., p. 22) indicated that the Partit Socialista Unificat de Catalunya (PSUC—the formally

autonomous Catalan Communist body) had less than 3,000 members
at the end of November 1976, 4,600 in February 1977, and about 5,500
in early March. What information is available in early 1978 suggests
that the Spanish party has somewhere in the neighborhood of 200,000
members, and a regional breakdown shows the PCE to have some
40,000 members in the Catalan provinces and in Andalucía, slightly
over 30,000 in Madrid, and 10,000 in Asturias and Zaragoza. See
Diario 16 (Madrid), April 21, 1978.

Little is known, at this writing, about the social composition of the
current membership, for the party has not as yet released a general
breakdown. When we look at the social background of the delegates
to the Ninth PCE Congress, an admittedly uncertain barometer, we
see that 53.8 percent of the delegates were workers and employees, 31.7
percent were professionals and others considered part of the *fuerzas de
la cultura*, and the rest about evenly distributed between peasants,
self-employed workers, and entrepreneurs. See *El País* (Madrid),
April 23, 1978.

2. For details, see my "Analyses of the Communist Performance
in the 1977 Spanish Election," in *Spain at the Polls*, ed. Howard
Penniman (Washington, D.C.: American Enterprise Institute, 1978).

3. For exact figures, see Enrique Curiel and Javier García
Fernández, "Territorial Representation," *Triunfo* (Madrid), June 4,
1977.

4. Xavier Tusell, *La Oposición Democrática al Franquismo* [The
democratic opposition to Francoism] (Barcelona: Editorial Planeta,
1977), p. 263.

5. Ramon Chao, *Después de Franco, España* [After Franco,
Spain] (Madrid: Ediciones Felmar, 1976), pp. 215-217. For the
international aspects of the struggle, see the section entitled
"International Relations" in the report of the Executive Committee
to the delegates at the 13th PSOE Congress in 1974. PSOE, *XIII
Memoria de la Gestión que Presenta la Comisión Ejecutiva*
[Thirteenth report of work presented by the Executive Committee],
October 1974, pp. 4-9.

6. For a useful overview of these groups, see Xavier Raufer's
article in *Est et Ouest* (Paris), March 16-31, 1976, pp. 12-20.

· 7. Those interested in a more thorough discussion of these
policies from a historical point of view should consult either Guy
Hermet's *Los Comunistas en España* [The Communists in Spain]
(Paris: Ruedo Ibérico, 1971); or this author's chapter on "The
Domestic and International Evolution of the Spanish Communist
Party," in *Eurocommunism and Détente*, ed. Rudolf L. Tökés
(New York: New York University Press, 1978).

8. Santiago Carrillo, *Nuevos Enfoques a Problemas de Hoy* [New approaches to problems of today] (Paris: Editions Sociales, 1967), pp. 25-32, 95-101, and 111-116.

9. See Santiago Carrillo's report to the Central Committee in *VIII Congreso del PCE* [Eighth Congress of the PCE] (Bucharest, 1972), pp. 21-31.

10. *Mundo Obrero*, September 5, 1973.

11. Ibid., May 8, 1974.

12. The PSOE had some difficulty enforcing its decision. In places such as the Canary Islands, the party federation initially joined the Junta and left only after intense pressure from the national organization.

13. The evolving role of Spanish Catholicism is analyzed thoroughly in Rafael Belda et al., *Iglesia y Sociedad en España, 1939-1975* [The church and society in Spain, 1939-1975] (Madrid: Editorial Popular, 1977); and in José Chao Rego, *La Iglesia en al Franquismo* [The church under Francoism] (Madrid: Ediciones Felmar, 1976). Not surprisingly, less has been written about the changes taking place in the military. A seminal analysis, which focuses on changes in military recruitment patterns after Franco's victory, has been written by Julio Busquets, who in June 1977 was elected to the Cortes on the Catalan Socialist ticket. His book *El Militar de Carrera en España: Estudio de Sociología* [The career military man in Spain: a sociological study] (Barcelona: Ediciones Ariel, 1967), is still must reading. Also of interest is Manuel Díez Alegría's *Ejercito y Sociedad* [Army and society] (Madrid: Alianza Editorial, 1972), which presents a "professional" view of the relation between civil power and the armed forces.

14. The British Communist newspaper, *Morning Star* (London), March 24, 1976, cited unofficial sources to the effect that the UMD had a membership that included 461 captains, 11 majors, 54 lieutenant colonels, 21 colonels, and 5 general officers.

15. The Communists recognized this difference in the Portuguese and Spanish situations early on, and they wanted the Spanish armed forces to remain neutral and not become actively involved in politics. See the Santiago Alvarez statement in *Nuestra Bandera* (Paris), no. 75, May-June 1974, p. 33.

16. The text of their manifesto was published in the *Mundo Obrero* put out by the pro-Soviet faction then challenging Carrillo. See the issue of June 15-30, 1973.

17. A heated debate over the strategy to be followed in the labor movement took place at the PCE's 2d National Conference in September 1975. See a partial transcript of these debates in the

172	*Eusebio M. Mujal-León*

theoretical journal of the PCE, *Nuestra Bandera*, no. 81, October 1975.

18. The phrase appears in Santiago Carrillo's report at the Eighth Congress in *VIII Congresso del PCE*, p. 7.

19. Interview with Carrillo, *l'Humanité* (Paris), October 25, 1976.

20. *Mundo Obrero*, 3rd week of April, 1975.

21. See Victor Díaz Cardiel et al., *Madrid en Huelga, Enero 1976* [Madrid on strike: January 1976] (Madrid, Editorial Ayuso, 1976).

22. *Mundo Obrero*, April 9, 1976.

23. See "La Democracia Cristiana Afronta el Futuro" [Christian Democracy faces the future] (Report presented to the first ID Congress in early April 1976, mimeograph), pp. 5-8.

24. *El Europeo* (Madrid), June 19, 1976, p. 17.

25. *Newsweek*, April 26, 1976.

26. *Cuadernos para el Diálogo* (Madrid), July 10, 1976, p. 24.

27. *Mundo Obrero*, July 14, 1976.

28. See Eugenio Nasarre's "Ponencia Sobre Estrategia Política" [Report on political strategy], October 12, 1976 (mimeograph). Delivered at a meeting of the top Christian Democratic leadership at Miraflores.

29. Earlier, at a PCE Central Committee meeting in Rome in late July 1976, the party had demanded that Suárez (1) grant a complete and general amnesty for all political crimes; (2) declare inoperable the law on political associations submitted by Arias; (3) resign and submit to the formation of a provisional government; (4) accept quick elections to a constituent assembly; and (5) grant full autonomy to the Catalan, Basque, and Galician regions. See Santiago Carrillo's report to the plenum, *De la Clandestinidad a la Legalidad* [From clandestinity to legality], July 1976, pp. 9-11.

30. *Mundo Obrero*, September 15, 1976.

31. Ibid., October 27, 1976, carried the text.

32. General statements of the party's position may be found in Dolores Ibárruri, *España, Estado Multinacional* [Spain, multinational state] (Paris: Editions Sociales, 1971); and in Santiago Alvarez, "Notes on the National Problem in Spain," *Nuestra Bandera* no. 84, March-April 1976, pp. 13-25.

33. *Mundo Obrero*, July 7, 1976, carried an article by Ernest Marti making this point.

34. Ibid., June 11 and July 26, 1976.

35. Manuel Azcárate, "*Nuestra Bandera*, Today," *Nuestra Bandera*, no. 85 (n.d.), p. 3.

36. For an exhaustive analysis of the evolution of the labor movement in Spain, see Jon Amsden, *Collective Bargaining and Class Struggle in Spain* (London: Weidenfeld and Nicholson, 1972).

37. *Cuadernos para el Diálogo*, June 19, 1976, pp. 49-50. The *Manifiesto de la Unidad Sindical* issued in January 1976 can be found in *CC.OO. en Sus Documentos, 1958-1976* [The CC.OO. in its documents] (Madrid: Ediciones HOAC, 1977), Appendix, pp. 5-30.

38. Carlos Elvira, "From the Democratic Rupture to Unitary Sindicalism," *Nuestra Bandera*, no. 83, January-February 1976, pp. 26-30.

39. See the documents in *Asamblea General de CC.OO.* [General assembly of CC.OO.] (Barcelona: Editorial Laia, 1976).

40. Ibid., p. 35.

41. See *Mundo Obrero*, October 6, 1976.

42. *Informaciones*, January 27, 1977.

43. *Cambio 16* (Madrid), May 1, 1977. At the same time, it is interesting to note that a poll conducted for the newspaper *El País* (Madrid) and reported in that source on May 24, 1977, found Carrillo to have the second highest "negative" rating of any Spanish politician. He was only outdone by Fraga Iribarne.

44. Santiago Carrillo, "Informe Presentado al CC" [Report presented to the Central Committee] (April 1977 mimeograph).

45. Carrillo was, at least in part, trying to gain some political capital here, for several weeks earlier he had expressed opposition to an electoral front with the Socialists because it might polarize the country and thus "put in great jeopardy the democratic process." *Informaciones*, March 14, 1977.

46. *Mundo Obrero*, April 16, 1976.

47. Ibid., December 31, 1967.

48. *Diario 16* (Madrid), April 25, 1977.

49. The PSOE, at the same time, has not hesitated to side first with one and then the other rival in an effort to enhance its own bargaining power and to facilitate its accession to government. Discussions over the municipal elections are instructive on this point. The Socialist leaders entered into negotiations with the Communists in December 1977 on possible joint lists for the elections. Whether or not the PSOE ever had any intention of forming such an alliance with the PCE, the fact is that by mid-March 1978 the Socialists and Suárez came to terms on a municipal electoral law that worked to their advantage and against all the other political forces in the country.

50. The phrase was used in the principal report approved at the 3rd

Conference of the Madrid Provincial Committee in April 1976 (mimeograph), p. 18.

51. *Nuestra Bandera*, no. 90, pp. 51-54, reprinted some of the documents contained in the Czechoslovak White Book about discrimination directed at the signatories of Charter 77 by the authorities in Czechoslovakia.

52. For sources and more detailed discussion, see this author's "Spanish Communism in the 1970's," *Problems of Communism*, March-April 1975, pp. 43-52; and idem, "The Domestic and International Evolution of the Spanish Communist Party."

53. *New Times* (Moscow), January 1978, no. 3, p. 14.

54. For the volume itself, see *"Eurocomunismo" y Estado* [Eurocommunism and the state] (Barcelona: Editorial Grijalbo, 1977). The Soviet attack appeared in *New Times*, June 1977, no. 26, pp. 9-13.

4
Portugal: The PCP and the Portuguese Revolution

Eusebio M. Mujal-León

On April 25, 1974, following the military coup d'état that overthrew the regime of Marcello Caetano, the Portuguese Communist Party (Partido Comunista Português, or PCP) emerged from nearly fifty years of clandestinity. For almost two years thereafter, the PCP and its allies, operating with a strategy premised on the viability of revolutionary Leninist politics, were near the fulcrum of power. Since the failure of a leftist coup attempt in November 1975, however, the party's fortunes have been in decline—the election of António Ramalho Eanes as president of the second Portuguese republic in June 1976 and his subsequent designation of Socialist Party Secretary-General Mário Soares to head the first constitutional government being the latest major defeats the PCP has suffered. With the prospects for the flourishing of West European–style parliamentary democracy in Portugal clearly better than at any time in recent years, it is an appropriate moment to stand back and assess the recent course of Portuguese communism and to discuss its possible future direction.[1]

Accordingly, this essay will explore in some detail how the Portuguese Communists adapted to the political and social reality that they encountered after April 1974. A concluding section will look at possible future patterns of PCP participation in Portugal's political process and consider what the prospects are for a shift in the party's orientation, away from the avowedly Leninist approach to politics that the party has followed so far and toward the more accommodating, pluralistic, and consensual stance that other major West European Communist parties have adopted.

The Legacy of Clandestinity

The PCP entered the post-April 1974 period with a long history of underground activity, having experienced harsh repression at the

175

hands of Portuguese authorities. Nearly fifty years of internal exile
(the PCP was legal only five years, from its founding in 1921 until
1926) had a profound impact on the Portuguese Communists and
their attitudes. This comes through vividly in an article entitled "The
Moral Superiority of Communists," which PCP Secretary-General
Alvaro Cunhal published in early 1974.[2] Cunhal's repeated references
to "moral strength" and his exhortations to "moral endurance"
reveal the almost religious intensity with which he (and we may
presume his party) held it the Communists' duty to be not only "the
revolutionary political vanguard of the proletariat" but also its
"moral vanguard." Even the slightest deviation from the classical
Leninist code, Cunhal stressed, would have a "demoralizing" effect
on all aspects of the party's work and would therefore be an obstacle to
the fulfillment of its historical mission.

This perspective affected the PCP's relations with other organizations and the types of alliances into which it was willing to enter and
indeed had a greater influence on how the Communists viewed others
on the Portuguese political scene than did the party's "Soviet
connection." In this regard, it should be stressed that the generally
accepted interpretation of the relationship between the PCP and the
Communist Party of the Soviet Union (CPSU)—which emphasizes
the latter's role in determining the radical cast of Portuguese
Communist policies after April 1974 and particularly in the summer
of 1975—is incorrect on both factual and interpretative grounds. To
begin with, the Soviet Union seems never to have developed a
cohesive and unified policy toward Portugal.[3] Events in Portugal
sparked lengthy and complex debates not only within the Soviet
foreign policy establishment (about the compatibility of encouraging
structural change in Europe and maintaining détente with the
United States) but also between the CPSU and most West European
Communist parties (about the continued viability of Leninist
methods of reaching power). These debates could only have
constrained whatever efforts the Soviets might have wanted to make
to influence the Portuguese Communists.[4] More important from our
point of view, seeing the PCP as essentially a tool of the Kremlin
ignores a more significant dimension of the situation; that
unswerving fidelity to the Soviet Union was the foreign policy
expression of the tough, sectarian outlook on politics that the PCP
had developed during the clandestine period. In the minds of the
Portuguese Communist leadership, the domestic and foreign policy
components of its strategy became inextricably linked. Arguably,
then, there has been a domestic imperative governing the relationship

with the CPSU, and the PCP's policies, present and future, can best be examined by focusing not on that relationship but on the party's response to its domestic environment.

Some observers of the Portuguese political scene—after seeing the PCP's overt Leninism, aggressive drive for power, sectarian posture, and disdain for bourgeois political parties and institutions in the months after April 1974—wasted little time in concluding that the Portuguese Communists were not only out of touch with Portuguese reality, but also had moved to seize power because of Soviet directives. But was a strategy predicated on a forceful seizure of power in fact an outlandish and unreasonable option after the overthrow of Marcello Caetano? Not at all. First, the overthrow of Caetano's regime was the work not of political parties, but of a small number of Portuguese military officers—some generals such as António de Spínola and Francisco da Costa Gomes and some younger majors and captains who had organized themselves into the Armed Forces Movement (Movimento das Fôrças Armadas, or MFA).[5] The latter had been profoundly affected by the disastrous experience of fighting to uphold the Salazarian dreams of Lusitanian empire, and in the months after the takeover, they came to look on the MFA as a sort of movement for national liberation whose principal task was to play a vanguard role in the promotion of social change. Moreover, they assumed a preponderant role in the affairs of the country and wasted little time in evidencing a profound distrust of traditional electoral parties.

Second, the political and social Center, which constituted the logical constituency base for the traditional electoral parties, was weak, ineffective, and demoralized. A noted student of authoritarian regimes has observed that such regimes characteristically produce weak moderate and liberal elements.[6] By discouraging political mobilization and involvement and by periodically undertaking feeble efforts at internal liberalization and reform, the Portuguese regime had managed in fact to neutralize or co-opt most oppositionists. Opposition, clandestine by force of circumstance, could easily come under the influence of the most radical and well-organized group, the Communists.

When the revolution took place, the Portuguese Communists emerged from clandestinity with not only the aura of the resistance but also a solid organization and the strongest influence among the most combative sectors of the society—the industrial workers in the Lisbon-Setúbal region and the agricultural laborers of the Alentejo. During the political instability (at times bordering on anarchy) that confronted the PCP in the aftermath of the coup, its continued reliance on the Leninist political style that it had developed during the clandestine period was indeed a viable choice.

How this style was reflected in practice after April 1974 can best be analyzed by distinguishing four phases: from April 1974 to March 1975, from March to August 1975, from August to November 1975, and from November 1975 to the present. In what follows, we shall examine in some detail how the Communist leadership perceived the political situation in each of these periods and how they shaped their party's policies as a result of these perceptions.

A Period of Caution

For almost a year after the overthrow of Marcello Caetano, that is, until the March 1975 flight of General Spínola, the PCP acted as a force for order and moderation. Unsure of the configuration of power in Portugal, the Communists were cautious in their commitments, whether to the MFA or other political parties. Although the threat from the Right seemed eased by the resignation of Spínola from the leadership of the supreme revolutionary authority, the Junta of National Salvation (Junta de Salvação Nacional, or JSN), in September 1974, it was only his final departure from the scene in March 1975 that convinced the PCP that the time was ripe for a more aggressive tack.

A wariness of Portugal's new military rulers and an uncertainty as to whether the PCP would be accorded immediate legal recognition served to temper the exuberance with which the Communists greeted the overthrow of Marcello Caetano. The day after the coup, the party's Central Committee warned that "the legalization of the PCP will be the criterion for assessing whether democratic liberties have been instituted in Portugal."[7] As the only opposition group to have previously devoted much attention to organizing in the armed forces, the Communists may quite possibly have known that a coup was imminent. But, though they were certainly aware that anti-Caetano feeling was on the rise in the military, there is little evidence that the PCP was closer to or exercised greater influence on the MFA conspirators than other political groups. For that matter, many in the MFA seemed rather vague as to the role they expected the Communists to play in the revolution. In fact, when General Spínola (in his capacity as head of the JSN) extended to the Communists an invitation to join the first provisional government, offering PCP Secretary-General Cunhal a seat as minister without portfolio and another leading Communist, Avelino Gonçalves, the sensitive post of labor minister, the action, if we are to believe the testimony of Otelo Saraiva de Carvalho, surprised many in the MFA.[8]

Spínola evidently expected that Communist entry into the government not only would significantly lessen the party's ability to maneuver but also would give the government leverage (through the PCP) on the increasingly restive labor movement. The Communists, for their part, were keenly aware of the dangers involved, particularly as the decision would leave the party open to sniping from the Left, but they apparently felt that the recognition and legitimacy afforded them was well worth the risk. Certainly, the PCP leadership had never entertained any illusions about Spínola and his attitudes. For example, when his book *Portugal e o futuro* ("Portugal and the Future") first appeared in February 1974, advocating a federative solution to Portugal's colonial problems, the Communists warned that the Caetano regime's "second line of defense was being prepared."[9] But so long as Spínola appeared able to put off a final break with the MFA, the PCP leadership refrained from openly attacking him. The MFA had not yet attained a preponderant influence within the armed forces, and bodies such as the JSN and the provisional government still were potential rival centers of power.

In such a setting, the Communists pursued a dual strategy—on the one hand, reinforcing their ties with the MFA; on the other, vehemently insisting on the importance of unity with other parties and groups. Of course, the PCP has always insisted on the need for unity, but here one should distinguish between the offensive and defensive uses of the threat of fascism and reaction. In this first stage, in contrast to what became the case after March 1975, the party used appeals for unity against the threat of reaction for essentially defensive purposes. Thus, it adopted an entirely moderate and accommodating stance toward parties such as the Socialist Party (Partido Socialista, or PS) and the Popular Democratic Party (Partido Popular Democrático, or PPD): the PCP's Cunhal could call such parties "partners in the struggle" *(companheros de luta)*.[10] In the realm of social policy, the party urged restraint, arguing not only that profound reform of social and economic structures was outside the scope of the MFA program, but also that the key to holding back the "reactionary offensive" was to avoid the intensification of social conflict.[11]

Despite this moderate line, the PCP moved deftly to consolidate its own positions. For example, it used its control of the Labor Ministry (although Avelino Gonçalves resigned in July 1974, his successor as

minister, José Inacio da Costa Martins of the MFA, was close to the
Communists, and they retained and expanded their influence—
particularly at the subsecretary level) to assure its control over the
fledgling labor movement and the trade union vehicle known as
Intersindical. It also worked through the unity opposition coalition
known as the Portuguese Democratic Movement/Democratic Electoral Commission (Movimento Democrático Português/Commissão
Democrática Eleitoral, or MDP/CDE). During this phase, the
MDP/CDE proved a particularly useful instrument not only for
insuring Communist influence at the municipal and provincial
administration level but also (especially as long as the fiction of the
MDP/CDE's independence could be maintained) as an instrument
for mobilizing sectors of the Portuguese population that were "more
difficult to reach through socially and politically advanced
slogans."[12]

Part of the reason for the Communists' restraint disappeared in
September 1974, when the simmering conflict between Spínola and
the MFA finally reached crisis proportions. After granting permission for a "silent majority" march on Lisbon, Spínola found himself
obliged on September 28 to step down as head of the JSN. Moreover,
in the aftermath of his resignation, it became particularly evident that
if the Armed Forces Movement had ever had any intention of
returning to the barracks and turning power over to the civilians, this
was growing to be less and less the case. Increasingly attracted to the
Peruvian and Algerian models of military intervention in the
developmental process, the most radical in the MFA began to
envision their organization playing a role quite similar to that of the
national liberation fronts against which they had fought in Africa
and to see it their duty to liberate the Portuguese people. "We go to
the people," said one young officer when asked the purpose of the
cultural dynamization campaign initiated by the MFA after
September 1974, "to help them escape from the long night of
ignorance."[13]

The implications of these developments were not lost on the
Communists. For one, the PCP sensed the possibilities for an even
greater leftward shift in the not-too-distant future. This was apparent
at the Seventh PCP Congress in late October. To be sure, press
coverage of the one-day extraordinary session tended to emphasize the
approval of a generally moderate Emergency Platform and revisions
of the 1965 party program that muted criticism of Portuguese
participation in the NATO alliance and eliminated the phrase *the
dictatorship of the proletariat* from the Portuguese Communist

lexicon.[14] *The Guardian* (Manchester), to cite but one prominent example, declared that the results of the Congress should "allay fears in Washington and Europe about a 'Red Menace' in Portugal."[15] Although the Congress indeed revealed the party's ambivalence as to the course to follow in the months ahead, the broader significance of Alvaro Cunhal's principal report to the delegates lay in its indication that the party leadership had begun to consider seriously the medium-term prospects for radicalization.[16]

Cunhal's assessment of the September events was highly positive:

> It will remain a date of transcendent importance in the history of Portugal's democratic revolution. Since then political power has gained a greater homogeneity and a greater capacity to act; the state apparatus has consolidated; the MFA and the democratic forces have become strengthened: the alliance between the popular movement and the military has been confirmed as the political axis around which the democratic changes revolve. It is still too early to measure the full import of the counterrevolution's defeat at the end of September. If the progressive forces prove capable of adopting adequate measures for exploiting their victory in depth, it may then be claimed that the construction of democracy in Portugal is an irreversible process.

The irreversibility of the revolution, he went on to argue, depended on resolving the split between economic and political power that had existed in Portugal after the 25th of April. "Political power" had been in the hands of "democratic forces" since that date, but "economic power remained in the hands of the monopolists and latifundists." That situation, he continued, could not go on much longer: "Either the monopolies and the latifundia take over political power, installing a new dictatorship, or the democratic forces—in order to construct a new Portugal—put an end to [the former's] economic power." Before September 1974, the PCP had repeatedly stressed that the MFA program—notable in any case for its vagueness and variety of possible readings—did not foresee any radical economic changes, and up to then the party had raised the possibility of nationalization and expropriation only in the case of enterprises guilty of economic sabotage. Now Cunhal emphasized the need for antimonopoly measures in the near future. His analysis implicitly presented stark alternatives. There was to be no place for a West European–style political system in Portugal; the country's social structure could not support capitalistic economic concentration and broad political democracy at the same time, for the Portuguese bourgeoisie, in the Communist view, was not strong enough to ensure its domination without resorting to violence and the establishment of a new fascist dictatorship.

Posing the alternatives so harshly would eventually dramatically narrow the options open to the PCP and make it more responsive to radicals within and outside the military. For the moment, however, the Communists were hesitant to commit themselves irrevocably to a fight they were still not confident they could win. They therefore continued to foster ties with the broad spectrum of moderates and leftists within the MFA and Provisional Government by harping on the specter of a right-wing coup.

In order to counter this putative threat, the Communist leadership throughout the period attempted to forge a broad alliance of social forces based on the working class and embracing the peasants, intellectuals, and sectors of the middle class—all of whom were or "objectively" should have been interested in supporting the revolution. It should be understood, however, that the Communists had difficulty in garnering support for their notions of agrarian reform in the area north of the Tagus River, where small landholdings predominated and reform meant expropriation. The PCP's *ouvrièriste* approach to the problem of political power only reinforced the antagonism. Moreover, during this phase (and subsequently), the party made little effort to disguise its view that the political parties of the bourgeoisie were rapidly becoming obsolete. This approach was doubtless influenced by the legacy of clandestinity—which led the PCP to expect that the other parties on the Portuguese scene would soon enough demonstrate their instrinsic weakness—but the months after September 1974 reinforced the party's perspective.

Given the special conditions existing in Portugal after September, it was the MFA (not the political parties) that had emerged as the principal actor, and it was therefore the MFA that constituted the logical axis upon which the party might rest its political alliances. In the PCP's view, the MFA had become "the guarantor of the democratic process"; hence, partnership with it was the imperative of the moment. The Socialists and the Popular Democrats would have to face that reality and respond as they saw fit.[17]

Yet for all its latent hostility toward other political parties, the PCP still insisted that they had a role to play, if only they would change their orientation and look left instead of to the right. There were two reasons for this attitude. First, it would have been impolitic and have unnecessarily aggravated matters in the international sphere to break openly with ruling members of the coalition, particularly since the

Socialists had excellent relations with Social Democrats who controlled governments in several European countries. More important to the Communists, the elimination of the Socialists could have backfired at home, since some sectors of the "radical military"[18] saw *all* political parties as an obstacle to the construction of a socialist society and, egged on by ultraleftists, would presumably have had no compunction in turning against the PCP after first eliminating the Socialists. Thus, the Communist leadership had to engage in a careful balancing act—seeking to weaken the other parties and minimize their role in the revolution without undercutting the PCP's own relationship with the MFA.

It was not surprising that the radical audience in the MFA to which the PCP directed its attention did not believe it could depend on most of the many political parties that had surfaced in post-April Portugal—by one count they numbered at least four dozen[19]—to accomplish the transformation of Portuguese society. Not only had these parties (if they had even existed) failed to overthrow the *Estado Novo* and had the MFA to thank for the fact that Caetano was no longer around, but their commitment to what the radicals came to consider the aims of the revolution was open to question. Against this generally bleak picture, the PCP stood out in striking contrast. The Communists, though not altogether to be trusted, voiced whole-hearted support for any and all MFA initiatives and were almost alone in arguing the absolute necessity of the MFA's presence in the Constituent Assembly scheduled to be elected in April 1975—and beyond, for that matter—in order to guarantee the continued success of the revolution. Moreover, the politically inexperienced and somewhat unsophisticated officers of the MFA left wing found the political analyses of the PCP compelling, especially when, as in the case of Communist insistence that the alternative to the MFA was fascist rule, the arguments gave an ideological justification for the MFA to continue to run the country. Add to that the organizational and mobilizational talents the party could put at the MFA's disposal in the larger cities and in the South, and one can readily understand why the military radicals, although certainly wary of the Communists, at least did not regard the PCP with the disdain they reserved for the other parties.

Eager to strengthen the hand of the military radicals, the PCP and groups to its left had, in the aftermath of the "silent majority" demonstration, called for a purge of the still considerable number of conservative officers who remained in the Portuguese armed forces, but this had not happened. The results of the elections to the individual MFA branch assemblies in early 1975, in which prominent radicals such as Otelo Saraiva de Carvalho were defeated,[20] demonstrated the continued strength of the conservative elements and suggested that the radicals' power reflected more the influence they exerted over the "commanding heights" of the military establishment than the support they had at the unit level (we must exclude here most of the units composing the elite security force known as COPCON, short for Comando Operacional do Continente, or the Continental Operations Command). In fact, with the change in the composition of the MFA General Assembly wrought by the service-branch elections, the prospects were good for defeating the radicals' bid for control of that body at a plenary session scheduled for early March.

This being the case, it is difficult to understand what the conservatives hoped to gain from the March 11 coup attempt. Nevertheless, on that date, there was an aerial attack on RAL-1, a unit known for its leftist sympathies. The rebels apparently expected their action to trigger a broader-based response, but when other units refused to join, the coup collapsed. Even now a debate rages as to the motives for the affair—there is a variety of plot and counterplot explanations. But whatever the answer, one thing is sure; the coup, as poorly executed as it was conceived, gave the radicals in the MFA an unprecedented opportunity to deal a crushing (and nearly fatal) blow to political and military moderates.

Radicalizing the Revolution

In the wake of the coup attempt, the victorious left wing of the MFA pressed forward with economic and political measures designed to take advantage of the new situation. Among its first moves was the creation of a twenty-five-man (later expanded to a twenty-eight-member) Council of the Revolution (CR) with full executive and legislative powers and the dissolution of the recently elected MFA General Assembly, where the radicals had suffered significant reverses. The CR, vested with supreme political authority, wasted no time in issuing a series of nationalization decrees (which marked a clear break with the transitional plan put forward by Ernesto Augusto de Melo Antunes) and in establishing a powerful Ministry of Economic Planning and Coordination to direct the government's "antimonopolistic" economic policies. To head that ministry, the MFA named Mario Murteria, a prominent economist with close ties to the MDP/CDE. His appointment and the designation of additional members of the MDP to other ministerial posts came over the objections of the PS and PPD, which also voiced disapproval of a decree suspending three parties (the Partido Democráta Cristão, headed by former Major Sanches Osorio, and two Maoist groups, the Movimento Reorganizativo do Partido do Proletariado and the Aliança Operaria e Camponesa) and barring them from participation in the Constituent Assembly elections to be held a month later. Reflective of the new balance of power in the country was the agreement signed in early April between the MFA and all the major political parties guaranteeing the "institutionalization" of the MFA.[21] The *acordo constitucional* gave the Council of the Revolution the power to make the principal domestic and foreign policy decisions during a period of three to five years and included a provision setting aside 240 places in the still-to-be-elected parliament for the MFA representatives. The Movimento explained the move by declaring that under these conditions the revolution could develop in "an atmosphere of freedom but free of sterile and divisive political party strife"; however, of the parties signing the accord, only the PCP and the MDP did so with any enthusiasm.

For the Communists, the defeat of the rightist coup attempt and the prompt announcement of measures to assure dominance of leftist elements within the MFA seemed to set the structural conditions for finally resolving the dichotomy between political and economic power that had existed since April 1974. Given the Portuguese domestic situation in the period from March through August 1975— and the perspective from which the PCP approached that reality— any decision other than to have opted for a continued and rapid radicalization of the revolution would have been unthinkable. The results of the April 1975 Constituent Assembly elections—which showed the Socialists with a comfortable plurality of nearly 38 percent of the vote, the Popular Democrats with something over 26 percent, and the Communists trailing with under 13 percent[22]—could only have underscored for the PCP leadership the correctness of its decision. If the moderate parties of the Center and Left were to succeed in establishing a parliamentary democracy in Portugal, the Communists could expect to play little more than a secondary role in the country's evolving political process.

Once having forsaken democratic parliamentary politics, the Communists found the range of possible political alliances open to them dramatically narrowed. Their choice was to work with the leftist provisional government of Prime Minister Vasco Gonçalves and the radical elements within the MFA. Although in the months that followed, the PCP was to grow increasingly concerned over the widening rift between the military populists and the pro-Communist officers coalescing around Gonçalves, for the moment the party leadership was confident that the MFA radicals could not afford to embark on a policy of profound structural changes in Portuguese society without the PCP.

For the PCP, collaboration with the MFA meant in effect the jettisoning of the Socialists as possible allies. Of course, the Communists still went through the motions and called for unity of the Left—including the Socialists—but they did so with increasingly restrained enthusiasm. And by the end of July, after the PS had withdrawn from the coalition government of Vasco Gonçalves, the PCP's leadership was ready to attack Socialist policies as "the axis of reactionary activities" and accuse the PS leadership of allying itself with "reactionary and conservative forces and against those of progress and revolution."[23]

One other consequence of the shift in PCP policy was that the party now turned its attention to cultivating alliances with groups to its left. Earlier, the party could afford to ignore the existence of the ultra-Left *groupuscules*[24] as a rhinocerous might a mosquito, but once having rejected "electoral politics and electoralism" in favor of "the dynamics of force," as Cunhal called it,[25] it had to deal with these groups and to contend with their influence in the PCP as well as in the mass organizations. Internally, the problem was how to cope with the thousands of new members who had entered the party since April 1974. In little more than a year, the party had gone from an organization of 2,000 to 3,000 members to one with more than 100,000 members.[26] Not surprisingly, some in this new and untried following, expecting an uninterrupted advance to the new society, tended to be disenchanted by the inevitable twists and turns and the tactical retreats and readjustments ordered by the party leadership. Likewise, in the labor movement and among sectors of the population where Communist influence had traditionally been strong, the party now found itself having to respond much more urgently than before to the challenges from the groups of the extreme Left. The numerical and organizational weight of the latter was nowhere near that of the PCP, but their criticism of Communist *dirigisme* and their calls for "direct democracy" outside traditional party structures struck a responsive chord among the populist elements of the MFA, with whom these groups effected a tacit alliance.

Regardless of Communist perceptions and commitments, when it came to the implementation of policies, the PCP found itself during this phase by no means the master of the situation, reacting as often as not to others' initiatives. In no position to dictate strategy to the MFA radicals, the party had to endure their endless debates and resolutions on how to structure the organs of power for the transition to socialism. With regard to one such resolution, which called for the establishment of neighborhood and workers' councils, the Communists could try to reassure themselves that the "more direct participation of the MFA in the process did not dispense or annul, but on the contrary reaffirmed, the vanguard action of the party of the Portuguese working class."[27] However, it is clear that by this time many officers in the MFA had come to believe that the military—as an *independent* organization above political parties—should play the leading role in the construction of socialism. Even those whom we have chosen to call the pro-Communist officers in the MFA, though frequently adopting positions that were close to that of the Communists, were not pliant tools of the PCP. They had their own inchoate vision of the nature of the MFA-PCP alliance, and we can be sure that if they had succeeded in their revolutionary venture, they had no intention of simply handing power over to Cunhal and his associates.

But these were the tribulations of a party whose star appeared to be on the rise. The declining fortunes of the Socialists in the spring of 1975 offered a vivid contrast. Because the PS had made no effort to disguise its belief that the military should retire from an active role in politics as soon as possible, its relations with the MFA had been strained for quite some time. After the Socialist victory in the Constituent Assembly elections, these relations grew worse as the MFA first refused Socialist demands for immediate local and provincial elections and then officially recognized the Communist-controlled Intersindical as *the* national organization of trade unions, thereby undermining the position of Socialist and other union elements. Not surprisingly, the Socialists concluded that there was little place in the radicals' plan for the PS, and they began to cast about for an issue on which to challenge the MFA. The occupation of the plant of the Lisbon newspaper *Republica* by striking typographical workers in late May 1975 gave the PS its opportunity.[28] When the MFA failed to comply with repeated Socialist demands that the workers who had taken over the premises be evicted, the PS finally withdrew its members from the cabinet, on July 11.

Despite their apparent weakness, the Socialists picked a good time to challenge Prime Minister Vasco Gonçalves, the MFA radicals, and the PCP. In midsummer 1975, for the first time since the overthrow of

Marcello Caetano, the MFA could not count on the enthusiastic and automatic support of a large part of the Portuguese people. The interminable debates over subtle ideological nuances—which took up so much of the Council of the Revolution's time—seemed increasingly irrelevant and contributed to a growing sense of popular alienation over decisions being taken (and, as often as not, being disregarded) in the heady and intoxicating Lisbon atmosphere. The rise of separatist sentiment in the Azores and the utter failure of the Portuguese decolonization scheme in Angola only added to the general tension. On the economic front, too, the government was beset with difficulties: it had a stagnating economy with rising unemployment (250,000 according to official figures, but with the prospect that the number could easily double as a result of the anticipated return of thousands of settlers from the former colonies), and a climbing balance-of-payments deficit brought on by the need to import more and more agricultural products. These economic problems could be alleviated only through the imposition of austerity measures, yet, unfortunately for Gonçalves and the radicals in the MFA, such a strategy required a not inconsiderable amount of political capital—something the beleaguered prime minister did not have.

Within the MFA, too, Gonçalves had increasingly come under fire not only from the military populists but also from a small nucleus of "moderate" leftists who still remained in the Council of the Revolution. If Gonçalves was able to survive their uncoordinated efforts to remove him as prime minister during July and part of August, it was primarily due to the MFA's almost instinctive reaction to rally around him in the face of the simultaneous Socialist attack. In early August, however, Ernesto Augusto de Melo Antunes and eight other officers of the Council of the Revolution finally issued a public statement, the "Document of the Nine" *(Documento dos Nove),* bitterly criticizing incumbent Prime Minister Gonçalves for leading Portugal toward an East European–style totalitarian regime, for trying to impose "political dogma in a sectarian and violent fashion."[29] The alternative strategy proposed by "the Nine" was to work toward the creation of a broadly inclusive bloc, composed of urban and rural workers and most sectors of the middle class, a bloc that would be capable of ensuring Portugal's peaceful long-term movement toward socialism. Although the signatories of the document saw themselves as the true heirs to the April 1974 revolution and their proposal as the only viable *alternative de gauche* open to the MFA, it was really their critique of Gonçalves that struck the most responsive chord among wide segments of the armed forces. But it is highly improbable that the dissident "moderates" on the CR could have pressed forward and forced Gonçalves's eventual ouster in early September had they not been able to secure the temporary support of Saraiva de Carvalho, the ambitious and mercurial commander of COPCON forces.[30]

Without underestimating what the Communists had to gain from the final elimination of all resistance to the radicals within the MFA and without slighting the PCP's ability to coordinate demonstrations and strikes in favor of Gonçalves, one should point out that the party was essentially a marginal spectator to the drama being played out in the MFA General Assembly and the Council of the Revolution in late July and early August. It could do little about the progressive disintegration of the MFA except to continue, as it had done so often in the past, to urge the radicals to put aside their differences with one another and the PCP.

In an attempt to gain some political leverage, the PCP leadership in this period tried to cultivate and perhaps split off from the Socialist Party left-wing elements possibly disaffected by the PS leadership's decision to effect a tacit alliance with more conservative, and in some cases openly reactionary, forces only then publicly reemerging in the country. However, these Communist efforts (which included instigating invitations to such prominent PS left-wingers as António Reis and António Lopes Cardoso to enter Gonçalves's new Provisional Government, i.e., the one formed after the Socialists had withdrawn) had only the opposite result, serving—at least for the time being—merely to rally the Socialist leadership around Mário Soares and his decision to break with the MFA.

The unexpected strong support the *Documento dos Nove* elicited in the armed forces as well as the decision by Saraiva de Carvalho to oppose Gonçalves forced the PCP temporarily to adopt a more conciliatory stance than it had in early July, when it had called for rapid constitution of "homogeneous revolutionary power" *(poder revolucionário homogeneo)* in response to the Socialists' decision to withdraw from Portugal's coalition government.[31] This tactical retreat was signaled at a Central Committee meeting on August 10, where Cunhal argued against "a hardening of positions" and against "a rigid demarcation line of those for and against the revolution," and urged once again a defensive "unification of all forces concerned with the process" of combating "fascist and reactionary forces."[32] But in mid-August, as the military populist faction of the MFA turned from Carvalho and for the main part moved back to Goncalves, the

PCP abandoned its conciliatory stance and effected a rapprochement, under the auspices of the COPCON military populists and Fifth Division officers close to the PCP, with the parties of the ultra-Left.[33] Fueled by a mutually held contempt for the Socialists and by the apparent belief that the choices had by this time narrowed to either revolutionary socialism or fascism, these parties combined to form a United Revolutionary Front (Frente Unitário Revolucionário, or FUR) and adopted a joint platform calling for "a powerful offensive of the masses against fascism, social democracy and imperialism, and the advancement of the revolutionary process."[34] For a few days in August, it seemed the PCP (in "unholy alliance" with the ultra-Left, or so Soares described the entente) was ready to reenact the assault on the Winter Palace.

The alliance, however, proved to be short-lived, and there was no climactic storming of the citadels of power. At the last moment, realizing the fundamental weakness of its position and the fact that the radicals within the MFA had lost their initiative, the PCP pulled back, deciding to accept Gonçalves's ouster and proposing talks with the Socialist leadership. These steps signaled a new stage in Communist policy.

In the next stage, which was to last until the abortive leftist coup of mid-November, the PCP found itself in a political situation that—though deteriorating—was not totally devoid of opportunities. Its decision to abandon Gonçalves and to enter the sixth provisional government under Admiral José Pinheiro de Azevedo (albeit with only one minor portfolio—public works) reflected a sober assessment of the significant shift that had occurred in the balance of forces in the country.

Battling Worsened Odds

The PCP would clearly have preferred that Gonçalves remain in power as head of a left-leaning government and certainly did not relish the almost certain efforts of the Socialists to deprive the party of the positions it had so laboriously acquired in the various ministries and in the media. Yet the change of government was not entirely disadvantageous either to the PCP or, more generally, to all those forces still interested in a radical political solution.

In the first place, a new government, especially one tilting to the right, the Communists reasoned, would have to carry primary responsibility for stabilizing not only the political situation (in both the military and civilian spheres) but also the economic situation. This task seemed beyond the capability of the PS. Moreover, "Socialist hegemony" in the cabinet, as the Communist leadership called it, might have an unsettling effect on the PS itself, exacerbating tensions within and perhaps ultimately splitting that party.

Although the Communists defined the new phase as one in which "the forces of the Left had receded," they still insisted that the situation in Portugal had significant "socialist and revolutionary" potential.[35] That perspective, publicly noted for the first time by the PCP in October 1974, was what, in their minds, made Portugal unique in Europe. Bourgeois democracy, they were convinced, could not work. Because of the low level of industrial and agricultural development in Portugal, Cunhal continued to insist, the triumph of Socialist positions would bring with them the restoration of capitalism and "such a degree of exploitation that only a repressive apparatus could impose it."[36] As the Communists would claim in November, the "national democratic" revolution had gone too far to be reversed without "the destruction of liberties and the implantation of a new dictatorship."[37]

Once again, the principal enemy was "fascism." At one level, the raising of this specter harked back to the earlier stages of the Portuguese revolution, when the party had in mind primarily its defensive connotations. However, an offensive dimension also lurked closely in the background. The Communists saw the present political preponderance of the Socialists less as a function of PS strength than as the product of the division of the revolutionary forces, particularly of the MFA. The struggle against "reaction" during this stage would serve a dual purpose: on the one hand, it would bind the MFA together and reunite the military populists, pro-Communist officers, and supporters of "the Nine"; on the other hand, it would force the Socialists to choose either continued alliance with the Popular Democratic Party (which the Communists now openly described as a party of reaction) or alliance with the PCP and some parties of the ultra-Left.

Only marginally committed to the latest provisional government, the PCP could now take "leftist" positions with relative impunity. It no longer had to defend official policies and was thus much more able to compete with the *gauchistes*, preempting the appeals these groups could make to the agricultural laborers of the Alentejo and to the industrial working class. Workers under Communist control—e.g., those in construction and metallurgical unions—could now make outlandish wage demands, forcing the Socialists, who currently bore the largest share of responsibility for economic policy by virtue of their control of the Ministry of Finance, into the position of urging restraint. Consequently, the Communists had an easier time than before in blunting Socialist efforts to win control of key unions in Intersindical.

The PCP was also in a comfortable position with regard to the agrarian reform program. Although Agriculture Minister António Lopes Cardoso was a Socialist, Vitor Louro, a Communist, served in the critically important post of secretary of state for agrarian structure and as often as not worked at cross-purposes with the minister. In the regional Agrarian Reform Centers (Conselhos Regionais da Reforma Agraria, or CRRAs), Communist directors held over from the Gonçalves government could disregard the directives emanating from Lisbon and rule their jurisdictions as largely autonomous fiefdoms, in some cases encouraging land-hungry laborers to occupy land illegally. The party could then claim credit for advancing agrarian reform, and it was the Socialists who had to remove the illegal occupants.

Ironically, the ouster of Gonçalves and the attendant rise in the influence of conservative elements in the ruling Armed Forces Movement worked to improve the opportunities for the Communists to carry on organizational work in the MFA aimed at strengthening the hand of its leftist elements. Without understanding the extent of such work carried on by the PCP before August 1975, it is clear the party had felt constrained in that earlier stage to act with great restraint in its dealings with the military lest too open an intervention in MFA affairs antagonize some group among the military radicals. Now, however, the Communists found themselves no longer the weaker element in the alliance with the Movimento and, conscious of the leverage to be gained, played a significant role in fomenting indiscipline in military units. Thus, the PCP was at least partly responsible—along with the ultra-Left—for organizing a loosely structured soldiers' union, Soldiers United We Shall Overcome (Soldados Unidos Vencerão, or SUV), and for the disappearance of weapons from military arsenals throughout the country. The only way the government could stop the growing disorder within the military, Cunhal warned in one speech, was "to stop the purges of leftist elements" and "to reinforce the positions of the revolutionary Left in the military and the government."[38] (Unrest in the army—especially among units in the Lisbon and Oporto military regions—was indeed becoming a serious problem for the government: by early November matters were so grave that security forces refused to intervene when a construction workers' demonstration besieged the national government palace in São Bento.)

Already by mid-October, perhaps a bit earlier than the Communist leadership had anticipated, the tide had appeared to shift against the Pinheiro de Azevedo government and moderate forces within it. Sensing this and arguing that now "the danger of a right-wing reorganization had been overcome," the Communists began to issue strident calls for the restructuring of the cabinet and of the Council of the Revolution.[39]

Matters reached crisis proportions in mid-November, when amid rumors of coups and countercoups, Intersindical organized a massive rally in Lisbon to demand Pinheiro de Azevedo's dismissal and the return of Vasco Gonçalves. To this challenge, the cabinet responded by suspending its own activities and refusing to resume operation until the Council of the Revolution gave it a vote of confidence. With the situation at an impasse and with the prospect of a purge of remaining left-wing elements in the Council of the Revolution imminent, some army units staged a leftist version of the March 1975 Spínola comic opera coup attempt.

This is not the place to undertake a detailed consideration of the rebellion, or to try to pinpoint the degree of Communist involvement—which has not been, and may never be, conclusively established.[40] In a series of speeches after the coup,[41] the PCP's leadership noted that the party had never come out openly in favor of confrontation and had always urged a political solution to the crisis (to be sure, the PCP would have preferred to pursue its objectives without having to resort to a coup). But such subtle and legalistic distinctions do not conceal the fact that Communists, along with representatives of various ultra-Left groups such as the PRP-BR and the Popular Socialist Front (Frente Socialista Popular, or FSP), were prominently and heavily involved in the coup at the level of neighborhood and workers' commissions and in the activities of the Intersindical unions mobilized in and around Lisbon on the night of the coup, November 25-26. The PCP leaders presumably held back until they could see which way the tide was running, and chose not to commit themselves when they saw the ease with which the revolt was being put down.

Thus, the Communists, who for several months had openly challenged the legitimacy of the sixth provisional government, for a second time pulled back from a decisive test of strength. It remained for the PCP to beat an orderly retreat and attempt to minimize the enormous defeat dealt to itself and the ultra-Left.

Reaction to Defeat

Although the Communists could have rationalized their acquiescence to Vasco Gonçalves's ouster in late August as a temporary and tactical retreat, confidently expecting that they would in the near future recover the offensive, the implications for Communist policy of the defeat inflicted on November 25 were of a different order. Although, in the period since that disaster, the party could retain its faith that matters had not completely gotten out of hand, its hopes for a rapid advance of the revolutionary process were dashed.

PCP could insist on the necessity for continued intervention by the military in political life and on the absolute need for an alliance between the armed forces and the "popular movement," but it was for the most part swimming against the tide of events. In the aftermath of the November coup attempt, over 150 leftist officers were arrested, COPCON was disbanded, and Carvalho, Rosa Coutinho, and Army Chief of Staff Carlos Soares Fabião (among others) were ousted from the Council of the Revolution. Melo Antunes's "Group of Nine" *(Grupo dos Nove)* found itself at the left end of the political spectrum in the council, arguing for continued MFA leadership of Portugal's march toward socialism and for the "indispensability" of Communist participation in the process. But these were not the priorities of those career military officers of the permanent staff *(quadro permanente)*—men such as new Army Chief of Staff Ramalho Eanes and former Interior Minister Mário Firminio Miguel—who had been instrumental in putting down the rebellion and now emerged as power brokers. Opposed to continued military involvement in politics, these officers pushed forward with plans to restructure and streamline the military so that they could turn full political power over to civilians and return to the barracks as quickly as possible. To this end, they demanded a revision of the constitutional pact that had been signed between the MFA and the political parties in April 1975. The new version, signed by the PCP and other major parties in late February 1976, reflected the changed situation. It contained no reference to the MFA, the MFA's General Assembly, or the military's leading role in the Portuguese revolution and sought as well to relegate the Council of the Revolution to a primarily advisory capacity.[42]

Even though in their rhetoric the Communists clung to their theoretical judgments concerning the unviability of bourgeois democracy in Portugal's political future and the need to defend and consolidate such revolutionary gains as agrarian reform and nationalization, they recognized that the new situation demanded moderation of actual party policy at all levels, particularly at the level of political and social alliances.[43] The PCP now dropped the aggressive, leftist-oriented stance of the previous phase. In fact, it excoriated the extreme Left for "goading the enemy and provoking his attack when you are not in a position to withstand or defeat him."[44]

Circumstances called for the Communists to conclude an alliance with the Socialists, but this was no easy matter. The Socialist leadership, for its part, had no intention of accepting the repeated Communist proposals for the elaboration of a common platform, preferring to steer clear of any entanglement with the PCP (or for that matter with the PPD, which called for the ouster of the Communists from the Provisional Government) which might cost it support among members of some class or in some section of the country. Faced with the categorical unwillingness of the Socialists to join with them, the Communists sought to foster contacts between the two parties at the base level through such social organizations as trade union commissions and neighborhood and workers' commissions and at the same time to prepare for the parliamentary elections in April 1976 with the hope of forestalling a coalition government formed by the right-of-center Social Democratic Center (Centro Democrático Social, or CDS) and the PPD and of making a PCP/PS coalition at least an arithmetical possibility. This strategy could have the additional advantage of expanding the party's audience among the middle classes and might thereby help coalesce a broad alliance of those social sectors that were objectively interested in the revolution at this stage but were hesitant to join with the Left and, in particular, with the PCP.

The new approach was particularly evident in the tone of the mass demonstrations the Communists sponsored during this phase to protest various government decrees increasing the cost of food staples, energy, and transportation as well as decree suspending collective bargaining, which in effect froze wages for more than 750,000 workers. These demonstrations lacked the offensive thrust of the marches and rallies organized the previous fall and were primarily vehicles for developing what the Communists call "unity of action" on "bread-and-butter" economic issues. Symptomatic of the change, too, were passages in official party documents criticizing the trade union leaderships for excessive politicization of their organizations and their "bureaucratic" methods of leadership,[45] behavior that was not conducive to the lowering of tensions within a given mass organization or to the reconciling of differences between Communist and Socialist workers.

These efforts assume particular importance when viewed in the context of the party's preparations for the 1976 parliamentary elections. That the PCP should be insisting on the importance of those elections as an instrument for forcing an eventual understanding between itself and the Socialist Party was not without its ironies. However, it was consistent with the party view that the time for the "dynamics of force" had temporarily passed. The organization for the campaign began in early January and included the formation of national, regional, and district electoral commissions, which—in coordination with a special task force headquartered in Lisbon— were to make empirical analyses of voting patterns and recommend to party leaders at various levels what issues should be raised in a given zone or what sectors of the population it might be useful to cultivate in a given area.[46] In its campaign propaganda, the PCP sought to tone down its *ouvrièriste* image and to cultivate the broadest possible social base by referring to itself as "the party of the workers" rather than as "the party of the working class and all workers" and by arguing that a vote for the Communists was "a vote for antifascist and democratic unity."[47]

The outcome of the parliamentary elections indicated that the Communist strategy had been at least partially successful.[48] The Socialists' share of the vote declined nearly 3 percent from their 37.9 percent showing of the previous year, and the number of PS seats in the assembly dropped from 116 to 107. Similarly, the PPD's share went from 26.4 to 24 percent, and the party lost 9 seats, leaving it a total of 71. On the other hand, the CDS increased its relative share, from somewhat more than 7.5 percent to nearly 16 percent, and more than doubled its previous holding of 16 seats, capturing 41. The PCP also increased its percentage of the vote (by more than 2 percent), winning 14.6 percent of the overall figure, and it bolstered its representation in the assembly by 10 seats, giving it a total of 40. With only 112 out of 263 seats, the PPD and CDS could not form a government, but a majority Socialist-Communist coalition government had, at least numerically, become possible.

Beyond these global details, several additional comments about the Communist showing are in order. The PCP scored significant gains in its traditional strongholds—the industrial cities and the South— becoming the leading vote-getter in Beja, Evora, and Setúbal; and it registered only slight losses (or in some cases, even minimal gains) in the North. In achieving these results, it picked up some votes from the

Portuguese Democratic Movement (MDP), which had come to be viewed almost universally as little more than a front for the PCP and which did not field candidates in this election. This gain was most pronounced in the South, for the MDP's former supporters in the North apparently chose in large part to vote Socialist. On the negative side, the voting results demonstrated the markedly regional nature of the PCP's constituency and the apparent failure of Communist efforts to expand from that base and win new support among employees of the tertiary sector, medium and small farmers, and elements of the middle class.

The alignment of parliamentary seats made a Socialist-Communist alliance at the national level possible, and the Communist leadership ceaselessly predicted the Socialists' inability to govern alone; but the PCP still lacked the leverage to impose its will. If the Communists abstained on votes dealing with legislation they considered vital, a PPD/CDS bloc vote could defeat those measures. Moreover, the procedural rules adopted in the Constituent Assembly made it possible for a government to rule without a working majority. On motions of no-confidence in the government, there had to be an absolute majority in favor for the government to fall. However, the Communists would not likely vote with the PPD and CDS or vice versa, and to abstain would in effect cause defeat of the motion. Thus, there was a likelihood that the Socialists could form a government on their own with less than a majority of the seats and without having to deal with the PCP.

Faced with this frustrating prospect, the Communists decided to field their own candidate in the June 1976 presidential elections, in the hope of gaining more leverage on the future government. This decision was taken despite the PCP's long insistence on the preferability of having a military man as president of the Republic. The party had hoped that, given the broad executive powers granted the president by the February 1976 constitutional accord, the Council of the Revolution would designate a consensus candidate. But the CR proved unable to agree on a candidate, and two members of that body—Prime Minister Pinheiro de Azevedo and Army Chief of Staff Ramalho Eanes—announced their candidacies. Although Pinheiro de Azevedo ran as an independent, Eanes quickly received the support of the three largest parties—the CDS, the PPD, and the PS—which together had collected nearly 75 percent of the vote in the recent parliamentary elections. By putting forth their own candidate, Central Committee member Octavio Pato, the Communists initially hoped to deprive any one candidate of an absolute majority in the first

round, thereby forcing a second vote, prior to which the PCP might
extract some significant concessions. If things did not seem to be
going well, the party could withdraw even before the first round.
However, this option was foreclosed when Otelo Saraiva de Carvalho
entered the contest as the candidate of a loose coalition of the ultra-
Left. Carvalho's presence made it absolutely imperative that Pato
continue in the race, lest Carvalho preempt the role of spokesman for
the Left.

The results were, from the Communist point of view, disastrous.[49]
Carvalho, in finishing second to Eanes, received over 17 percent of the
vote (more than double Pato's total), handily outdistancing the
Communist candidate in PCP strongholds in the South and draining
away more than 400,000 of the votes the party had won in April 1976.
Whatever chance the Communists might have had of preventing the
Socialists from forming a minority government in the wake of the
parliamentary elections evaporated after the presidential contest. As
anticipated, Eanes called upon Soares to head the new government,
and in midsummer the Socialist leader presented his cabinet and
government reform program to the assembly.

The PCP candidly admitted that it had lost ground in the
presidential election, but it tried to take some solace from the fact that
the combined totals for Carvalho and Pato gave the revolutionary
Left a 24 percent share of the vote—some 200,000 more votes than the
groups supporting the two candidates had received in the April
election. This was seen as an indication of a still substantial reservoir
of support for more radical options, although the Communist
leadership warned against any illusions that the Left could, in the
near term, return to the use of "superior forms of struggle." In
particular, the PCP rejected the call of the ultra-Left for the formation
of a revolutionary front and the return to mass-demonstration
politics. It should be noted that this moderation was still only a
tactical maneuver: the PCP predicted that the program of the new
government concealed "the intentions of a rightist, social democratic
policy, full of dangers for Portuguese democracy," and it still
maintained that bourgeois democracy was unviable in Portugal. It
declared its opposition to any measures seeking to shift the burden of
economic stabilization onto the working class.[50]

Despite harsh criticism of the Socialist government, however, the
Communists did not present any formal motion of censure in the
National Assembly during the rest of 1976. Instead, they redoubled
efforts to have the PS invite them into a coalition government. These
overtures were rejected, as was a Communist appeal to the Socialists

to agree to joint PS-PCP candidate lists in the December 1976 municipal elections. Frustrated in the latter attempt but determined to overcome its poor showing in the June presidential election, the PCP formed its own electoral front—the United People's Electoral Front (Frente Eleitoral Povo Unido, or FEPU)—with the MDP and leftist independents.

In the elections, the Socialists and the PPD (or Social Democratic Party—Partido Social Democrático, or PSD—as it had renamed itself at its congress in late October 1976) each polled over a million votes, but the FEPU polled nearly 740,000 votes and, benefiting from a light voter turnout, gained control of more than 250 municipal assemblies. The Socialists, by more or less holding their own in the municipal elections, avoided having to accept coalition with either the Right or the Left. The Communists, for their part, demonstrated that they remained a force to be reckoned with, particularly since by early 1977, at the Intersindical congress, the PCP had once again consolidated its control over labor. Socialist efforts to break that monopoly not only ran aground but in some cases even backfired, as the PS lost control in some unions (such as the banking employees in the South) that it had heretofore dominated. What was more, after announcing in mid-March 1977 a decision to devaluate the escudo by 15 percent, to authorize price rises for some foodstuffs, and to order the return of some nationalized properties to their previous owners, the Socialists could hardly expect things to brighten up for them in the labor movement.

The PS has also been beset with internal difficulties. At the 2d PS Congress in early November 1976, a rival leadership list presented by the Socialist left wing succeeded in winning 25 percent of the delegates' votes, and a few days later the visible head of that faction resigned as minister of agriculture in opposition to his party's moderate agrarian policies. The factional strife did not subside through 1977, and late that year Lopes Cardoso (the former minister of agriculture) and two other Socialist deputies announced that they were leaving the Socialist parliamentary group and would vote as independents.

The Communists have not tired of condemning the economic policies of the Soares government and have not hidden their belief that the PS will eventually have to come to terms with them and make significant concessions in exchange for Communist parliamentary support. Such an outcome cannot be entirely ruled out, but Soares still has substantial room for maneuver. He demonstrated this fact by managing to negotiate a formal partnership with the CDS after his government lost a vote of confidence in December 1977. How long this entente will last, of course, is still an open question. At least it weathered separate PSD and PCP challenges in the assembly in February 1978.

The PCP's Future Course

It has been suggested in the preceding pages that the radical and revolutionary cast of Portuguese Communist policy since April 1974 can best be understood when it is viewed as a response to the highly unstable political situation that the PCP encountered after the overthrow of Marcello Caetano. Moreover, it should be recognized that the Portuguese Communists have been operating in a situation qualitatively different from those that the French and Italian Communists encountered after World War II: (1) there was no allied army of occupation in Portugal in 1974 (in fact, the country's armed forces were among the most radicalized sectors of the society), and (2) in light of the international situation, direct United States or West European intervention in Portuguese events seemed unlikely. Under these circumstances, it is not surprising that the Communist leadership, steeled by a lengthy clandestine experience, chose a radical course.

Subsequent events, particularly the election of Ramalho Eanes as president and the designation of Mário Soares as prime minister, suggest that the PCP may have lost its gamble; nevertheless, the outcome is still unclear. If Portugal fails to institutionalize a West European-style parliamentary democracy, that would certainly tend to reinforce the conviction of the Communists that their disdain for and opposition to bourgeois democracy and parliamentary politics have been well founded.

But even a continued evolution toward a parliamentary system of government does not automatically ensure a change in Communist perspectives. Under what circumstances and how soon might the PCP abandon its Leninist outlook and adopt the pluralistic and consensual stance that has become an increasingly important part of the ideological baggage of the other major West European Communist parties? It is these questions that we address in the concluding remarks below.

Before embarking upon an examination of possible Communist policy under a parliamentary democracy, however, let us briefly turn to a description of the problems—political and economic—whose solution is a precondition for the achievement of democratic stability in Portugal. In a broad political sense, Soares and the moderate elements in Portugal need to forge a national consensus not only on the accomplishments of the April 1974 revolution but also on the institutionalization of a parliamentary system as the best guarantee for preserving those gains. Opposition to the attainment of that consensus has and will continue to come from the extremist movements of both the Right and the Left—the first of these denying the legitimacy of the April revolution, the second rejecting the principles of parliamentary democracy as a vehicle for defending those gains and expanding them. It is the social groups on which these movements are based (the small-scale and medium-scale farmers of the North and the *retornados* from the former colonies settled in the large urban centers, on the one hand, and the industrial working class and the agricultural proletariat of the South, on the other hand) whose political and social integration the regime must foster in the months ahead.

That is only the political side of the equation. The success of the venture is also conditioned by, and intimately linked to, the revitalization of the Portuguese economy, which has to recover from a political and social revolution that generated a climate of deep insecurity. The decolonization scheme to which the MFA committed itself after it assumed control of the government resulted in a radical restructuring of trade patterns, the elimination of the sizable profits derived from the exploitation of precious metals and other resources of the former colonies, and a mass exodus of white settlers, whose numbers swelled the unemployment rolls in the metropolis. Moreover, sources of investment capital, foreign and domestic, dried up because of the manner in which the nationalization and agrarian reforms were carried out. In addition, there have been a decline in the remittances of emigrants (a source of substantial income for the country) and a loss of tourist revenues—both of which not only have made it difficult for the government to cover Portugal's traditional agricultural deficiency with food imports but also have contributed to a growing balance-of-payments deficit. To turn the situation around, while making good on the promise to achieve a more equitable distribution of income, will require great political dexterity.

The success of Soares and those who follow him in coping with these problems is obviously by no means assured. But let us assume—for the sake of argument and because the record so far has not been altogether poor—that they are at least partially successful. What then can we expect of the PCP?

With the progressive consolidation of a parliamentary democracy in Portugal, the Communists will have either to maintain their commitment to the "dynamics of force" and run the risk of becoming a marginal force influential in but a relatively narrow sector of society or else to change their party's stance and, like their counterparts elsewhere in Western Europe, direct their energies toward reassuring and gaining the support of the domestic middle classes. As the experience of other Communist parties suggests, however, the process of adaptation and change is likely to be slow, with changes of profound strategic significance appearing at least initially to be simply tactical readjustments. Therefore, it may be quite some time before the PCP comes to share the view of other West European Communist parties that profound structural changes in their respective societies must be fostered and promoted (although not necessarily concluded) within the parameters of the institutions of a parliamentary democracy. In this regard, one should pay careful attention to changes in the PCP's attitude toward its social and political alliance partners, to changes in its international relationships, and to changes in its ideology and organization; for, as research on other Communist parties has suggested,[51] the beginnings of the deradicalization of the PCP will be reflected in those spheres.

What are the prospects for change in the short to medium term? To a large extent these depend on a change either in attitude of the Communist leadership or, more radically, in the composition of that leadership. The likelihood that the present leadership would make such a shift is very slight—*Avante!* has dismissed the possibility of the "domestication" of the PCP as the "dream of national and international social democracy."[52] Secretary-General Cunhal has been the architect of and guiding spirit behind the radical policies followed by the PCP, and his highly moralistic and sectarian view of politics makes any prediction of such a change in his orientation rather farfetched. There is, moreover, no reason to believe that he is not the dominant force within the Central Committee of the PCP. And although we have no reason to think that any other member of the leadership has mounted a challenge to Cunhal's leadership (say at the Eighth Congress of the party in 1976), it is important to remember that any such move, had it occurred, would as likely have been grounded in a criticism not of the radical orientation of Cunhal's policies, but of perceived irresoluteness in his revolutionary leadership.

Let us examine briefly why this would probably be the case. First, it is clear that the Communists look to the Portuguese working class for much of their organizational strength and electoral support. However, in contrast to the situation in many other European countries, in Portugal a sizable segment of the working class is susceptible to radical rhetoric, a phenomenon that perhaps reflects the latent influence of anarchosyndicalist traditions and ideas. Consequently, as the strong showing of Carvalho in the presidential elections demonstrated, the PCP cannot consider Portugal's industrial and agricultural proletariat an exclusive fief; in drafting party policies, the PCP's leaders must constantly compete with the utopian and demagogic line of the ultra-Left. Thus, there is little chance that a move within the PCP to blunt its radical perspective would find much support in the social base of the party in the near future, particularly since the inevitable government measures to enforce wage controls and reassert industrial discipline will presumably only increase the restiveness of workers. To the degree that those measures will exacerbate (at least in the short run) divisions along class lines in the country, they are unlikely to lead to changes either in the PCP's organizational style or in its ideology.

The short-term and medium-term prospects for an evolution of Portuguese communism also depend on the future role of the military in the country's politics. It seems that the military will play an increasingly important political role, especially since it is to them—as the effective wielders of power—that the government inevitably has to turn for backing in the austerity period the Portuguese economy is now entering. The Communists will support the remaining leftist elements in the military in whatever way they can. They will do this not because Melo Antunes, Vasco Lourenço, and others directly support the Communists or share their views (as we have seen, "the Nine" played a critical role in preventing a Communist seizure of power), but because in continuing to insist on safeguarding and expanding the socialist accomplishments of the Portuguese revolution, on the necessity that the PCP play a role in that enterprise, and on the need for the military Left to function as a catalyst therein, the latter are allies (albeit "objective" ones only) in the Communists' struggle to regain—if not necessarily the initiative—at least some of their lost influence.

How the military Left perceives its future role was suggested in August 1976, when the leftists on the Council of the Revolution, faced with a choice between retaining what operational commands they held and continuing to be members of the CR, chose the latter course. This supreme military organ may well have been reorganized to weaken leftist control of military units, but the decision has in fact also served to make the CR a last redoubt of leftist influence. Moreover, in the spring of 1977, after long silence dating back to before the presidential elections, Antunes began once again to make public declarations, urging that the Council of the Revolution and also the special Constitutional Commission (a type of constitutional tribunal with the power to declare laws unconstitutional) play a more active role. He saw both as functioning as centers of power, parallel to the National Assembly and the cabinet.[53] More recently, Antunes gave the Spanish magazine *Cuadernos para el Diálogo* an interview in which he decried the general trend to the right in Portuguese politics.[54] It is impossible to foretell how long the equilibrium between right and left factions in the military will last (although events in early 1978, such as the ouster of Vasco Lorenço from his post as commander of the Lisbon military region, suggest that the latter is rapidly losing influence) and what role Eanes will play in the resolution of a possible conflict. But one can assert without great fear of contradiction that while the PCP views the situation with concern and fears his rise as a Lusitanian de Gaulle, it also sees Eanes as a possible ally in the struggle against more conservative elements.

For the present, there is little chance that the PCP will change: the situation does not now and may not for some time require it. The leadership still believes that despite "tactical" failures, the political line articulated over the last three or four years was the best possible one and remains so (there has, after all, not been a decisive defeat). As Cunhal said in an interview with *Expresso,* "In its essential aspects the PCP's strategic line has been confirmed by life."[55]

There was some speculation that this perspective might be moderated by the expansion of the PCP Central Committee from 36 to 90 full and candidate members at the party's Eighth Congress in November 1976, for some of the new cadres are persons who had joined the PCP after April 1974 and whose outlooks have therefore not been shaped by the clandestine experience.[56] However, it should be emphasized that although this development may have long-term implications, its immediate importance seems limited. The composition of the party's supreme organ—the Political Commission—continues unchanged, and most of those who entered the enlarged CC with *full* voting rights had been active in the PCP apparat before 1974. Change in the PCP's perspective will probably come only with the rise to power within the party of another generation of Portuguese Communists—cadres who neither experienced the era of clandestinity nor played any leading role in the PCP's actions during the heady months following the April 1974 coup.

Notes

1. For an earlier assessment of the PCP, see Arnold Hottinger, "The Rise of Portugal's Communists," *Problems of Communism*, July-August 1975, pp. 1-17. See also George W. Grayson, "Portugal and the Armed Forces Movement," *Orbis*, Summer 1975, pp. 335-378; and Kenneth Maxwell, "The Thorns of the Portuguese Revolution," *Foreign Affairs*, January 1976, pp. 350-370.

2. The title was translated from the Portuguese text, which was published in Lisbon by Ediçoes Avante, 1975. When published in *World Marxist Review* (Toronto), January 1974, pp. 25-35, the article bore the more neutral title "Communist Ethics." All quotes are from the latter version.

3. On this point, see Joan Barth Urban's "Contemporary Soviet Perspectives on Revolution in the West," *Orbis*, Winter 1976, pp. 1359-1402.

4. The PCP, it should be noted, enjoyed a considerable latitude for action because it served as a bridge between Moscow and the various national liberation movements in southern Africa. To the latter, the Portuguese Communists' revolutionary intransigence was quite appealing.

5. The best historical account of the events leading to the April 1974 coup is in Avelino Rodrigues, Cesário Borga, and Mário Cardoso, *O movimento dos capitães e o 25 de abril* [The captains' movement and April 25] (Lisbon: Moraes Editores, 1974).

6. See Juan Linz, "Opposition in and under an Authoritarian Regime: The Case of Spain," in *Regimes and Oppositions*, ed. Robert A. Dahl (New Haven, Conn., and London: Yale University Press, 1973), pp. 188 ff. See also Juan Linz, "The Sources of Radicalism in the Iberian Peninsula" (Mimeograph, February 1975).

7. See *Comunicados do CC de PCP* [Communiqués of the PCP CC] (Lisbon: Ediçoes Avante, 1975), p. 19.

8. Otelo Saraiva de Carvalho, *Cinco meses mudaram Portugal* [Five months that changed Portugal] (Lisbon: Portugalia Editore, 1975), p. 17.

9. See the broadcast by Radio Free Portugal, the PCP's transmitting station, on March 2, 1974, as translated in Foreign Broadcast Information Service, *Daily Report: Western Europe*, March 6, 1974, p. X1-X2.

10. Alvaro Cunhal, *Discursos Políticos* [Political discourses] (Lisbon: Ediçoes Avante, 1975), p. 79.

11. Ibid., pp. 53-59.

12. See the interview with PCP Central Committee member Aldo Noguiera, *Rinascita* (Rome), December 13, 1974.

13. See *l'Express* (Paris), February 10-16, 1975, p. 40.

14. The Emergency Platform, it is true, did refrain from advocating radical measures such as nationalization of major enterprises and banks. At the same time, it urged "the strengthening of the democratic state" through a purge of the governmental bureaucracy and a reorganization of the paramilitary forces. The platform and the 1974 party program can be found in *VII Congresso (Extraordinário) de PCP* [The Seventh Congress (Extraordinary) of the PCP] (Lisbon: Ediçoes Avante, 1974). The program approved in 1965 at the Sixth PCP Congress was republished in a third edition in the spring of 1974 by Ediçoes Avante.

15. *The Guardian* (Manchester), October 28, 1974.

16. See Cunhal's address to the Congress in *VII Congresso*, pp. 21-48. All quotes in the following paragraph are from that speech.

17. According to the PCP, however, there was still time for a Communist-Socialist entente to play "a highly positive role" despite the fact that the Socialist Party had undertaken a "shift to the right," which brought it "nearer to and in certain respects in identification with the most conservative forces." *Avante!* (Lisbon), January 29, 1975. Cunhal was less optimistic about the Popular Democratic Party, which was "born from the womb of the fascist dictatorship and suckled from the breast of fascism [its] first political milk." Ibid., February 27, 1975.

18. The term *military radical* describes members of a loose coalition grouping two more or less distinct factions within the MFA, factions whose submerged political and personal differences came to the fore after March 1975 but who, until then, assumed more or less similar stances on the need to insure continued MFA participation in the political process, the MFA's formal institutionalization, and the apportionment of seats for its representatives in the Constituent Assembly. There were, on the one hand, officers close to Prime Minister Vasco dos Santos Gonçalves; they looked for the Communists to be the political axis upon which a united front of the Left could be formed. Few among them were outright members of the PCP, and their alignment with the Communists reflected, more than anything else, a distrust of and aversion to spontaneous popular mobilization. On the other hand, there were those members of the MFA radical wing who rallied around Otelo Saraiva de Carvalho and, to a lesser degree, Navy Admiral António Rosa Coutinho. For these

officers, who might be loosely described as military populists and who were to develop (especially in Carvalho's case) close ties with such extreme Left groups as the Revolutionary Party of the Proletariat-Revolutionary Brigades (Partido Revolucionário do Proletariado-Brigadas Revolucionárias, or PRP-BR) and the Popular Democratic Union (União Democrática Popular, or UDP), the Portuguese revolution could be further advanced only by discarding traditional political organizations and establishing direct links between the MFA and the people *(povo)* through workers' and soldiers' councils.

19. A useful compendium of information about the diverse parties is *Partidos e Movimentos em Portugal* [Parties and political movements in Portugal] (Lisbon: SOAPLI, 1975).

20. *Expresso* (Lisbon), February 8, 1975.

21. The text of the *acordo* is in the *Boletim das MFA* (Lisbon), April 22, 1975.

22. For the complete election results, see *Expresso*, April 30, 1975.

23. *Avante!*, July 24, 1975.

24. A good description of the small groups operating on the extreme Left in Portugal can be found in Xavier Raufer, "Movements of the Extreme Left in Portugal," *Est et Ouest* (Paris), June 1975, pp. 269-280.

25. See his speech in *Avante!*, June 26, 1975. An even blunter expression of Cunhal's views came in his celebrated interview with Oriana Fallaci in *L'Europeo* (Milan), June 15, 1975. Asked whether the PCP's strategy was not playing into the hands of the European Right and embarrassing other European Communists, Cunhal replied: "How I am grieved, torn to pieces, distressed! I am distressed! Truly distressed! Poor Italian Communists! I shed tears for the Italian Communists! For all the Communists in Europe, I shed tears, I curse myself, I suffer! Of course, I know their laments. Those are the ones they repeat to me when they come here.... Faced with the laments of West European Communists, I have but one answer: we, we do not await election results to change structures and to destroy the past. We accomplish the revolution, and this revolution has nothing to do with all your systems."

26. See *Avante!*, July 17, 1975. For details on the organizational structure of the expanding PCP, see the party's organizational bulletin, *O Militante* (Lisbon), June 1975.

27. See *Avante!*, June 5, 1975.

28. In laying down this challenge to the MFA radicals, the

Socialists were aware that to phrase their dispute with the military in terms of struggle over freedom of the press was a tactically shrewd move, made all the more dramatic because it coincided with the occupation a few days later of the Catholic hierarchy's transmitter at Radio Renascença. The Socialist decision was sure to strike a responsive chord—despite the fact the PCP participation in and responsibility for the occupation of *República* was at best indirect and may have been largely a response to the militancy of workers associated with the Maoist-inspired UDP—not only domestically but (perhaps more important) among Europeans and North Americans who viewed developments in Portugal, and the growing Communist influence in particular, with a great deal of concern.

29. This statement was published in *O Jornal* (Lisbon), August 8, 1975.

30. Carvalho's personal rapprochement with "the Nine" came as something of a surprise. Nevertheless, it was the logical outcome of his always wary approach to the Communists—an intuitive mistrust he felt confirmed in early August when unidentified leftist officers (no one publicly accused them of being Communists or of having the backing of the PCP, but Carvalho obviously came to believe the party was responsible) led a mutiny in an elite commando regiment that formed part of the COPCON command structure. *O Jornal* of August 8, 1975, analyzes the "Neves affair." The COPCON officers also drafted their own document at this time, criticizing Communists, Socialists, and moderates within the military. See *Expresso*, August 15, 1975.

31. *Avante!*, July 10, 1975.

32. See the text of Cunhal's address to the CC in ibid., August 11, 1975.

33. An article in *Expresso* of August 30, 1975, summarizes the twists and turns of Communist policy during this critical month.

34. For the text of their communiqué, see Foreign Broadcast Information Service, *Daily Report: Western Europe*, August 26, 1975, p. M4.

35. *Avante!*, September 18, 1975.

36. See, for example, ibid., October 9, 1975.

37. Ibid., November 13, 1975.

38. Ibid., October 23, 1975.

39. Cunhal took this stand at a rally in Torres Novas. It was time, he went on to say, for the MFA "to resume its dynamic participation in Portuguese politics in alliance with the progressive political forces

and the popular movement." See *Diário de Noticias* (Lisbon), October 20, 1975.

40. For the official version of the events, see *Relatório da Comissão de Inquérito as Acontecimentos do 25 de Novembro* [Preliminary report of the commission of inquiry into the events of November 25] (Lisbon, 1976). The PCP admitted that there was evidence that individual Communists had participated in the coup attempt, but it insisted that there was no evidence of direct involvement on the part of the leadership. *Avante!*, January 22, 1976.

41. See speeches published in *Avante!* in early December 1975.

42. *Expresso*, February 26, 1976.

43. See PCP Secretary General Cunhal's statement in *Avante!*, December 12, 1975.

44. *Diário de Noticias*, January 16, 1976.

45. See, for example, the Central Committee statement in *Avante!*, December 16, 1975.

46. Ibid., March 16, 1975.

47. Ibid. This whole issue of *Avante!* is devoted to the party's National Conference. According to this account, some cadres openly objected to the adoption of the language *party of the workers*.

48. See *Expresso*, April 30, 1976.

49. See, e.g., the PCP's commentary in *Avante!*, July 1, 1976.

50. See, for example, ibid., July 29, 1976.

51. See, for example, a number of the essays in Donald L. M. Blackmer and Sidney Tarrow, eds., *Communism in France and Italy* (Princeton, N.J.: Princeton University Press, 1976).

52. *Avante!*, December 4, 1975.

53. *Expresso*, November 5, 1976.

54. *Cuadernos para el Diálogo* (Madrid), February 26, 1977.

55. *Expresso*, November 19, 1976.

56. See *Avante!*, November 18, 1976.

5
Greece: Communism in a Non-Western Setting

Dimitri Kitsikis

When the Communist Party of Greece emerged in the summer of 1974 from nearly a generation of illegality, it confronted a Greek political scene vastly different from that in which it had last functioned openly twenty-seven years before. The party had been outlawed in November 1947, at a moment of civil war when the Communists, relying on guerrilla tactics and on supplies smuggled into Greece from Yugoslavia, Bulgaria, and Albania, seemed to have very serious prospects of taking power in Greece by force. At that time, all anticommunist elements in the country, united in a common front under the direction of a broad coalition government headed by the eighty-seven-year-old Liberal Themistocles Sofoulis, supported the ban imposed against the insurgents.

In contrast, by 1974 the Communists, who had been responsible for the long-ended "guerrilla war" *(andartopolemos)* of 1946-1949, no longer were the main focus of hostility for Greece's traditional political elite; that role now fell to the vehemently anticommunist elements responsible for the Georgios Papadopoulos-Dimitrios Ioannidis military dictatorship of 1967-1974. On April 21, 1967, army officers of peasant and petit-bourgeois extraction who had fought communism in the mountains of Greece for the sake of the politicians of Athens during the late 1940s staged a coup d'état against the same elite they had earlier served. Laying sole claim to the anticommunist banner, but at the same time claiming to represent an ill-defined ideology aimed at social justice for all Greeks in the face of inequities created by the country's wealthy urban political oligarchy, the officers—both Papadopoulos and Ioannidis were colonels—toppled their masters and imprisoned many of them. Political activity was suspended; dissenting opinion was severely repressed; and a military-authoritarian rule destined to last seven years was introduced.

The military regime was finally brought down—by increased

restiveness at home following the replacement of Papadopoulos by the more rigid Ioannides, by worsening inflation and deepening economic trouble, and, most immediately, by its gross mishandling of the Cyprus crisis of 1974. But the trauma the military rulers had created for the Greek aristocracy was such that the pre-1967 oligarchic elite that returned to power did so with a much more tolerant attitude toward communism, the junta's professed bogeyman. On July 23, 1974, Konstantinos Karamanlis was recalled from France, where he had lived in voluntary exile since resigning as prime minister of Greece in 1963, to form a coalition government preparatory to the holding of new elections and the full restoration of parliamentary rule. Prime minister from 1955 to 1963, he had been accused by all opposition parties of rigging the parliamentary elections of 1961 and of moral responsibility for the death of United Democratic Left deputy Grigorios Lambrakis in 1963.[1] Sensitive to the scars left by seven years of dictatorship, Karamanlis's immediate concern upon returning home was to demonstrate to his countrymen that accusations of authoritarian tendencies made against him in the past had been false and that he was, in fact, Greece's best democrat. His behavior since 1974 has clearly been designed to secure his own place in history—that is, less toward coping with communism than toward making clear to his compatriots that he is the country's best hope for averting events of either the 1946-1949 or 1967-1974 varieties.

Thus, the return to power of Karamanlis and the pre-1967 sociopolitical elite he represents has resulted in an unexpected opportunity for the rebirth of Greek Communist strength. Whether the Communists will be able to take advantage of this opportunity to improve their standing in the political arena still remains an open question. As of early 1978, their record of achievement in this regard has been spotty at best. In the long run, of course, their fortunes will depend (1) on whether they succeed in avoiding the errors they committed in the past (i.e., unconditional obedience to Moscow and hostility toward the peasantry), and (2) on whether they manage to formulate a political strategy acceptable to all factions of the communist movement and compatible with the realities of Greece "after the colonels."

The present chapter will attempt to summarize the development of communism in Greece—its strengths, weaknesses, and electoral record—from its origins just after the Russian Revolution in 1918-1920 to its reappearance as a legally active movement contesting the parliamentary elections of 1974. Then, after examining the relationship between communist ideology and Greek socioeconomic realities, it will discuss what the Greek Communists have been doing to try to exploit the opportunity that has presented itself and what their prospects for success are.

Communism in Greece to 1974

The Greek workers' movement began to develop in the 1870s, but it was not until November 17, 1918, that the Workers' Socialist Party of Greece was established, during a Panhellenic Socialist Congress in Piraeus. The party grew out of the fusion of diverse, small socialist groups that had emerged before or during World War I. At the party's 2d Congress, held in Athens between April 18 and 26, 1920, supporters of the Third (Communist) International, founded in Moscow in March 1919, asserted control and added the word *Communist*, in parenthesis, to the party's title. The party adopted the hammer and sickle as its emblem and formally entered the Comintern; however, the title of the party daily, *Rizospastês* ("Radical"), which had commenced publication in 1917 before the Piraeus congress, remained unchanged.[2]

One of the problems the new Communist party had to face was the very limited scale of heavy industry in Greece during the first half of the twentieth century. The absence of an industrial working-class base was bound to hinder the electoral performance of a proletarian party. This clearly explains why Greece failed to develop a social democratic or reformist-internationalist party of the working class as most countries of Western Europe did during this period. The names of certain left-of-center parties that did develop were misleading. For example, Alexandros Papanastasiou's Agrarian and Workers' Party, which was active between the two world wars, and the Socialist Democratic Party, with which Georgios Papandreou contested the 1946 elections,[3] though based on Western ideas, were certainly not working-class Socialist parties. In fact, the only serious attempt to create a non-Communist workers' party was that of Elias Tsirimokos and Professor Alexandros Svolos, who founded the Union of People's Democracy (Enosê Laïkïs Dêmokratias, or ELD) during the German occupation of Greece and fought the Germans as part of the National Liberation Front (Ethniko Apeleutherôstiko Metôpo, or EAM). The ELD, however, received just 3,912 votes in the 1951 parliamentary elections—the only elections in which it ran alone—and then disappeared. The United Democratic Left (Eniaia Dêmokratikê Aristera, or EDA), established to fill the gap left by the outlawing of the Communist Party in 1947, was the spiritual heir of the

EAM, not of the ELD.

In the first national election it contested, the Workers' Socialist Party (Communist) received fewer than 20,000 votes, and each of the party's candidates was defeated in the electoral district where he ran. By the elections of November 7, 1926, the Communists had officially changed the name of their party to the Greek Communist Party (Kommounistiko Komma Elladas, KKE), but they campaigned as the United Electoral Front of Workers, Peasants, and Refugees in an attempt to attract the votes of the uprooted Greeks repatriated from Asia Minor under terms of the 1923 Greek-Turkish Treaty of Lausanne. The KKE received 41,982 votes, or 4.4 percent of those cast. Owing to the proportional electoral system used for the first time in these elections, this performance secured the Communists 10 seats out of 279 in parliament.

During the rest of the interwar period, the Communists' electoral fortunes varied from election to election, but they never received more than 10 percent of the votes cast. They won parliamentary seats only when the proportional electoral system was used (1926, 1932, 1936), never when the majority candidate in each district automatically won the seat contested (1923, 1928, 1933, 1935).

In the elections of August 19, 1928, the Communists' vote total fell to 14,325, only 1.4 percent of those cast, and not one of their candidates was elected. But after the world economic crisis, their performance improved. The elections of September 25, 1932, gave them 58,223 votes (5 percent) and 10 deputies. The figures remained approximately the same in the elections of March 5, 1933, with the KKE getting 52,958 votes (4.6 percent)—though no parliamentary seats—and then increased considerably in the elections of June 9, 1935. Profiting from the abstention of all parties of the Center and of the non-Communist Left (some of whose supporters voted for the Communists rather than abstain), the KKE amassed 98,699 votes, an interwar high of 9.6 percent of the total, even though the majority electoral system in force still kept them out of parliament. Because of the reintroduction of the proportional electoral system, 15 parliamentary seats out of a total of 300 went to Communists in the elections of January 6, 1936, but the total vote received by the party fell to 73,411, or 5.8 percent of those cast.[4]

Clearly, the Communists still represented a small minority in the country. The absence of heavy industry in Greece, which might have supplied a working-class base of support, was reflected in the social origins of the members of the Communist parliamentary group of 1936: some workers in the tobacco industry, a hairdresser, a streetcar employee, a barrister, and a high school principal.[5] Total party membership in 1936 was only 14,000.

During the dictatorship of General Ioannis Metaxas from 1936 to 1941—as during the 1967-1974 military dictatorship—the KKE was particularly weak, corroded by internal strife. From 1936 to 1941, it was split into three groups. At the head of two of these groups—called the Former Central Committee and the Provisional Leadership—Metaxas's police put its own agents. The third group took shape in the country's prisons, especially in the prison of Akronafplia Fortress in the Peloponnesos. One of the members of this last group, Pavlos Nefeloudis, who is still a Communist today, wrote in his memoirs, published in Athens in 1974, that at the time of the establishment of the Metaxas dictatorship "there was no contact of the party with the rank and file."[6] The KKE had done nothing to prepare itself for the eventuality of a coup, even though it suspected that one was in preparation. As a result, as in 1967, many of the Communist Party's leaders were arrested in their beds on the night of the coup.

Metaxas's death on January 29, 1941, cut off George II, Greece's "English" king (so called because of his pro-British sympathies and because of his twelve-year exile in Great Britain prior to his restoration in 1935), from the Greek masses, after he had already been cut off from the bourgeoisie by the general's 1936 coup. In May, the king departed his country once more, abandoning Greece to any movement that would support parliamentary democracy to please the middle class and set up national resistance to the Axis invaders and promote social justice to please the masses. Here was an unprecedented opportunity for the Communist Party to exploit, if only it would dress in the democratic mantle. And on September 27, 1941, the Communists responded by founding in Athens, in an atmosphere of social leveling due to hunger, the National Liberation Front (EAM).[7]

There is no doubt whatever that the EAM, the most important organization of Greek resistance to the Axis occupation, was at the beginning the Communist Party itself. This is openly acknowledged in the memoirs of Communist EAM leader Petros Rousos, which were published in Bucharest in 1966 by the party's press in exile, the *Politikes kai Logotehnikes Ekdoseis* ("Political and Literary Press").[8] Rousos describes with pride the extraordinary transformation of the Greek Communist Party, through the EAM, from an extremely weak and divided entity in May 1941 into the dominant political force in Greece at the end of the Axis occupation. According to Rousos, the social leveling produced by the occupation made the EAM an enormous fraternity of more than one and a half million members—out of a total population at the time of 7,350,000—united by the most benign sentiments of solidarity and sacrifice. The organization's ranks included six bishops, hundreds of priests, and great numbers of Greek patriots who fought the Germans as members of EAM while remaining totally unaware of the KKE's unconditional subservience to the Soviet Union.

Communists often equate foreign occupation with a dictatorial regime that is not favorable to them. Indeed, the Greek Communists have frequently compared the military regime installed on April 21, 1967, to the German wartime occupation.[9] But the comparison hardly seems convincing. It does not explain why the strength of the Communists went up tremendously during the German-Italian-Bulgarian occupation of 1941-1944, whereas during the 1936-1941 and 1967-1974 dictatorships, when they had to suffer less repression, they had no success at all.

The KKE temporarily increased its membership from 14,000 in 1936, when Metaxas outlawed the party, to 350,000 in 1944, when the German occupation ended, by exploiting Greek national sentiment. Yet within three years the Communists' utter disregard of national sentiment and Greek values, vividly demonstrated by the way they waged the 1946-1949 guerrilla war, sent them down to defeat—disgraced and outlawed politically in 1947 and finally beaten militarily in 1949.

They reappeared in disguise on the Greek political scene as early as 1951, when the Communist-dominated party called the United Democratic Left (EDA) was founded. But the Communists, before the war always a small minority of under 10 percent of the electorate, could hardly expect to do much better after the disastrous outcome of the civil war. The EDA received 24.3 percent of the vote in 1958, but most of these were protest votes by left-of-center non-Communists against the three-year-old Karamanlis government, which they considered much too conservative socially. More typical of the Communists' postwar performance were the elections of February 16, 1964 (the last before the coup d'etat of April 21, 1967), when the EDA garnered only 11.8 percent of the votes cast.

In 1967, as in 1936, the Communists were caught unawares by the military coup d'etat. They put up no resistance whatsoever, and Greek communism appeared to be on the verge of collapsing completely. The inevitable result soon followed. Differences broke out openly between the leadership of the Communist Party situated "in the exterior," i.e., in the Communist countries of Eastern Europe, and the leadership of EDA, representing communism "in the interior," or within Greece.

Long before 1967, EDA had complained of being obliged to follow the directives of Communist leaders settled outside of the country since 1949, who had—in the opinion of the militants of the interior—lost contact with Greek reality.[10] Moreover, the exiled Greek Communist Party, EDA leaders maintained, had had a very turbulent and disgraceful history abroad, with internal disputes so violent that many had lost faith in it. Such was the case with Dimitris Vlantas, KKE Politburo member from 1947 to 1956 and minister of defense of the Communist guerrilla government from 1948 to 1949. The experiences that had destroyed his belief in the party are worth recounting in some detail.

Vlantas had been a member of the Greek Communist Party since 1924. In 1943, during the Axis occupation, he founded and led the Communist-inspired United Panhellenic Youth Organization (Eniaia Panellênia Organose Neôn, or EPON). During the civil war, he was the Communists' minister of agriculture, then minister of defense. But in March 1956 he was excluded from the party as a member of the overthrown Stalinist leadership of the KKE headed by Nikos Zahariadis. He was exiled, by decision of his party and the Soviets, for eleven years in the Carpathian Mountains of Romania, where he lived under extremely harsh conditions. Finally, in October 1967, he managed to find refuge in Paris, where he still lives today. Even though he still considered himself a Marxist (though no longer a Leninist), leftist French journalists such as Eric Rouleau of *Le Monde* refused to help him publish his memoirs. Instead, he was obliged to give part of them to the rightist Athenian newspaper *Akropolis*, which published them, in the form of an interview, in a series of four articles, which appeared between April 1 and 5, 1973.[11]

In his recollections, Vlantas makes a disclosure that adds a new element to the explanations given by others who have written on the period—for example, Evanghelos Averoff-Tossizza and Dominique Eudes—of the decisive rift during the civil war between the secretary general of the KKE, Nikos Zahariadis, and the head of the Communist government and army, Markos Vafiadis.[12] Vlantas says that the Soviets told Zahariadis that in 1948 they had received a letter from Zafiadis (or Markos, as he was generally known) addressed to the Central Committee of the Communist Party of the Soviet Union (CPSU), accusing Zahariadis of being a traitor. Vlantas seems to believe that the letter really existed, but he himself did not see it—which of course leaves open the possibility that Stalin had forged the accusation to widen the rift already separating the two leaders.

Another of his recollections concerns a serious incident that occurred in 1955 in Tashkent, Uzbekistan, between rival groups of Greek Communist refugees in the USSR. In 1955, Vlantas was in Moscow, a KKE Politburo member. The party asked him to go to Tashkent to cope with a factional group that had developed among the 12,000 former Greek Communist *guerrilleros* living there. The disruptive faction was headed by Communists opposed to the Zahariadis leadership, with the well-known Markos Vafiadis, Dimitris Partsalidis, Leonidas Stringos, Kostas Kolliyannis, and Takis Dimitriou prominent among them. As Vlantas tells it, however, the factional group had in fact been organized by the Soviet authorities, who had themselves decided to oust Zahariadis.[13]

When Vlantas arrived in Tashkent, a CPSU representative asked him to help the factional group rather than destroy it and to become its leader with Soviet backing. Vlantas refused. In retaliation, on August 18, 1955, when Zahariadis himself arrived in Tashkent, the Soviet Security Police armed about 500 Greek Communists with knives in order to try to murder Vlantas. Vlantas suggested to Zahariadis that they both go back to Bucharest, Romania, where the headquarters of the Central Committee of the Greek Communist Party was located, and attempt from there to quell the factional group. But the appeal was in vain, and Vlantas remained in Tashkent. On September 10, 1955, 500 armed factionalists attacked the party's offices in Tashkent under the direction of Soviet security agents. Vlantas and thirty-five of his men barricaded themselves inside, using furniture to block the doors. The battle lasted nearly two hours, with the assailants shouting "Death to Vlantas." Finally, 3,000 former *guerrilleros* came to Vlantas's aid from different parts of the city and succeeded in liberating him. He returned to Bucharest.

In October 1956, Vlantas was arrested in Bucharest and, as has already been mentioned, sentenced to internal exile within Romania. (After the former party began legal activities in Greece in the mid-1970s, it insisted on being called simply the KKE. However, to distinguish it from both its unified predecessor and its current "interior" competitor, we shall refer to it hereafter as the KKE-Exterior.)

Although the 1967 coup in Athens precipitated the crisis between Greek Communists abroad and those at home, a formal split did not take place until February 1968, at the 12th Plenum of the party's Central Committee. There then emerged a Greek Communist Party "of the exterior" and a Greek Communist Party "of the interior." The EDA, although no longer allowed to operate in the open as the

Communists' legal façade because the regime of the colonels had outlawed all political parties, leaned heavily toward the Communist Party "of the interior," whose viewpoints it by and large shared.

It should be noted, however, that this split did not represent the only factionalization of the Greek Communist movement during the 1960s, even if it was the most serious one. In 1964, a Maoist group had broken away from the EDA. Led by Iannis Hotzeas and Isaak Iordanidis, it issued a monthly review called *Anagennêsê* ("Rennaissance") up to the time of the military coup in 1967.

The End of Illegality

All these various Communist elements survived the hardships of the years of the Papadopoulos-Ioannides dictatorship and entered the overt political arena in the summer of 1974 after the restoration of parliamentarism in Greece. They tried to increase their constituencies in the country by putting pressure on the Karamanlis government to allow the repatriation en masse of all Greek refugees who had lived in Eastern Europe and the Soviet Union since 1949.

The Greek parliament opened a debate on the matter on February 20, 1975. Konstantinos Stefanopoulos, minister of the interior, said that the number of refugees involved was approximately 100,000, and that although the government could not permit so many people to come back at the same time, it would permit individual repatriation. Each refugee would merely have to fill out an application for repatriation. The minister added that in fact repatriation was very easy, and that the government was no longer asking applicants for a declaration of political beliefs.[14]

In practice, the procedure has not proved quite as simple as Stefanopoulos suggested it would be. For example, the Ministry of Public Order did refuse to repatriate Markos Vafiadis from the USSR, even though Vafiadis made an official application on July 25, 1976.[15] Nevertheless, many refugees have returned to Greece since 1974. For instance, seventy-one Greek Communist refugees arrived in Piraeus by boat from Tashkent on October 4, 1976, and were received in the harbor by a great number of their comrades.[16] This sort of reunion has been a source of great concern to anticommunist circles in the country, who fear that at least some of those repatriated have been trained abroad for guerrilla warfare and are secretly bringing weapons into the country with them.

Despite the new political atmosphere favoring them, the Commu-

Table 1: Results of Greek Parliamentary Elections of November 17, 1974

Parties and Electoral Alliances	Votes cast	Percent of total vote	Number of seats	Percent of total seats
Conservative New Democracy (ND[a])	2,670,804	54.37	220	73.33
Center Center Union -- New Forces (electoral coalition of EK and NPD[b])	1,002,908	20.42	60	20.00
Non-Communist Left Panhellenic Socialist Movement (PASOK[c])	666,806	13.58	12	4.00
Communist United Left (electoral coalition of EDA, KKE-Interior, and KKE-Exterior[d])	464,331	9.45	8[e]	2.67
Other[f]	107,507	2.18	0	0
TOTAL	4,912,456	100.00	300	100.00

Table 1 (cont.)

[a] *Nea Demokratia.*

[b] *Enose Kentrou - Nees Dynameis.*

[c] *Panellenio Sosialistiko Kinema.*

[d] *Eniaia Demokratike Aristera, Kommounistiko Komma Elladas-esoterikou,* and *Kommounistiko Komma Elladas.*

[e] Of which the EDA got 1, the KKE-Interior got 2, and the KKE-Exterior got 5.

[f] This category, embracing a variety of small parties and splinter groups, includes the Maoist Revolutionary Communist Movement of Greece (*Epanastatiko Kommounistiko Kinema Elladas* -- EKKE), which received 1,013 votes, or 0.02 percent of the total vote cast.

SOURCE: Richard F. Starr, Ed., *Yearbook on International Communist Affairs 1975,* Stanford, Cal., Hoover Institution Press, 1975, p. 202.

nists did not do spectacularly well in the general elections held under Karamanlis on November 17, 1974. A Communist electoral front called the United Left (Eniaia Aristera, or EA) garnered 464,331 votes—9.45 percent of the total—and 8 of 300 parliamentary seats (see Table 1). The electoral coalition joined three Communist parties: the EDA, led by Elias Iliou; the Communist Party "of the interior" (Kommounistiko Komma Elladas—esoterikou, or KKE-Interior), headed by Secretary General Haralambos (Babis) Drakopoulos and Leonidas Kyrkos; and the Communist Party "of the exterior" (Kommounistiko Komma Elladas, or KKE-Exterior), led by Harilaos Florakis (Yotis). The eight people who won election to parliament on the United Left slate included Elias Iliou of EDA; Babis Drako-poulos and Leonidas Kyrkos of KKE-Interior; and Harilaos Florakis (Giotis), Grigorios Farakos, Mrs. Mina Yannou, Konstantinos Kappos, and Dimitris Gontikas of KKE-Exterior.

Five out of the eight deputies, it should be underscored, belonged to the orthodox, pro-Soviet KKE-Exterior. That this share of the seats reflected the party's relative popular strength was attested by the sales of its Athenian daily, *Rizospastês*, which sold nearly twice as many copies as did *Ê Avghê*, the daily of the KKE-Interior and EDA. During the week of July 26-August 1, 1976, for example, *Rizospastês's* sales averaged 13,904 copies a day, or 2.8 percent of the total sales of the thirteen dailies in the Athens-Piraeus area (see Table 2). This figure ranked it eighth on the list of thirteen papers. *Ê Avghê's* sales, in contrast, averaged 7,312 copies a day, or 1.5 percent of the total sales. This figure put it at the very bottom of the list of papers.

The Maoist Revolutionary Communist Movement of Greece (Epanastatiko Kommounistiko Kinêma Ellades, or EKKE) ran a separate slate in the 1974 elections. It got only 1,013 votes, or 0.02 percent of the total. (It should be noted here that the Revolutionary Communist Movement of Greece does not enjoy a monopoly on the Maoist label. Indeed, there are now more than twenty ultra-Left splinter organizations in Greece, the most "Maoist" of them being the Organization of the Marxist-Leninists of Greece—Organôsê Marxis-tôn Leninstôn Elladas, or OMLE.)

From the 1974 election figures, then, it was clear that neither the prolonged clandestine existence of the KKE since 1947 nor seven years of antiparliamentary military dictatorship had diminished the Communists' strength in Greece. When Communist forces were allowed to reappear lawfully and contest elections in 1974, they obtained the roughly 10 percent of the vote that they had traditionally captured. Non-Communist left-of-center voters who had at times pushed EDA figures above this level in earlier years—to as high as 24

Table 2: Average Daily Sales of Newspapers
in the Athens-Piraeus Area

(Week of July 26 – August 1, 1976)

Papers, ranked by sales	Number of copies sold	Percent of total sales
1. *Ta Nea*	137,775	28.2
2. *Apoghevmatinē*	80,668	16.5
3. *Eleutherotypia*	75,590	15.5
4. *Vradynē*	49,514	10.1
5. *Akropolis*	33,295	6.8
6. *To Vēma*	28,444	5.8
7. *Ē Kathēmerinē*	22,026	4.5
8. *Rizospastēs*	13,904	2.8
9. *Eleutheros Kosmos*	13,644	2.8
10. *Athēnaïkē*	11,515	2.4
11. *Estia*	7,398	1.6
12. *Ethnikos Kēryx*	7,330	1.5
13. *Ē Avghē*	7,312	1.5
TOTAL	488,415	100.0

SOURCE: *O Tahydromos* (Athens), August 5, 1976.

percent in 1958—this time channeled their support elsewhere, most notably to Andreas Papandreou's Panhellenic Socialist Movement (Panellênio Sosialistiko Kinêma, or PASOK).

In these circumstances, several questions about the future of communism in Greece arose. Would the Communists find new bases of support in the Greek populace, which had remained unresponsive for so long to Communist appeals? Would the Communists, so badly defeated in 1949 after the collapse of their armed rebellion, be able to avoid past errors such as unconditional submission to the will of a foreign power (i.e., the Soviet Union) and inability to adapt to peasant realities? And would they adopt political tactics conducive to furthering a modus vivendi with the Karamanlis government and not destroy this new opportunity for greater Communist influence in Greek political life? The years since the 1974 elections have shed some fresh light on these matters, but the questions themselves have lost none of their pertinency. Therefore, it is appropriate to look at what the Communists have been doing and what their prospects are within the framework of an exploration of this set of issues.

Communism and Greek Reality

Despite much economic progress over the last twenty years, Greece is still in essence an underdeveloped country. The numerically predominant elements in Greek society are the peasantry and the lower middle classes. The country has few large industries under local ownership. The ruling middle class stems largely from comprador ranks—those who work for or have business ties with foreign firms. Industrial workers are limited in number. All this is bound to affect the fortunes and stifle the appeals of a proletarian movement.

The adherence to traditional values, which is normal for a peasant and petit bourgeois population, is accentuated in Greece by the fact that the country's population is, demographically, one of the world's oldest. Not only is the Greek birthrate very low—0.5 percent a year—but emigration over a long period from rural villages directly to foreign countries has also left the countryside peopled predominantly with old folk. This state of affairs is in absolute contrast with that in Turkey, for example, which has—despite emigration—a very young population and an annual population increase of 2.5 percent.

An additional factor affecting the Communists' situation is that traditional Greek values are non-Western. Despite the long-standing myth—fostered by a West eager to discover noble ancestors in its genealogy—that Greek culture is Western, it is not and never has been. There exists—according to a long line of thought represented by the greatest spiritual figure of Eastern Orthodoxy, Saint Grigorios Palamas, and the famous fifteenth-century Greek philosopher Georgios O Trapezountios—a traditional Russian-Greek-Turkish-Persian-Arab civilization, in which Greek Orthodoxy and Islam are not contradictory but rather two aspects of the same reality.[17] Western penetration into the area of this civilization beginning with the crusades of the eleventh century led in Greece to the development of a pro-Western political trend—or "Western party"—and to an anti-Western traditional political trend, or "Eastern party." The overwhelming power of nineteenth-century Western Europe succeeded in imposing on Greece in 1821 a Westernist revolution and a West-inspired political and cultural elite—the liberals[18]—who remain today the most enthusiastic supporters of the assimilation of Greece into the European Common Market. A typical expression of the Western-liberal perspective can be found in a 1977 article on the Greek-Turkish crisis by an Athenian lawyer, who argued that the Greeks ought to rejoice if Turkey slipped into the Soviet orbit because Greece would then become the West's only "darling" in the region![19] The Eastern party, which lost out in 1821 but which continued to reflect most accurately Greek values, has taken refuge today in the Orthodox monasteries spread throughout the country and, in the form of a trend that could be labeled "Eastern modernist," in the Greek army. Both the monasteries and the military, populated by peasant children of the Greek countryside, get strong support from Greek society's most numerous elements.

Communism, which is, like liberalism, a Western ideology imported into Greece, has not yet succeeded in developing there a real agrarian variant that would—in fact if not in theory—give precedence to the peasant and the countryside over the industrial worker and the city. The "Maoists" of Greece are no different from those of the West. They are essentially confined to the cities and know nothing about the countryside. And their weekly Athenian newspapers—*Laïkos Dromos* ("The Road of the People") of OMLE and *Laïkoi Agônes* ("People's Struggles") of EKKE—are more concerned with the presentation of China's and Albania's views and activities and with anti-Soviet attacks than with promoting the views of the Greek peasantry. *(Laïkos Dromos* gets official support from China, and Peking's New China News Agency on occasion quotes it.)[20]

Only during World War II did agrarian communism in Greece have a genuine supporter, Aris Velouhiotis, the founder and head of the Communist guerrilla National Popular Liberation Army

(Ethnikos Laïkos Apeleutherôtikos Stratos, or ELAS), which was mainly a peasant army. At the end of the war, however, in June 1945, Aris was condemned as an adventurist by the KKE leadership and killed. All Greek Communist parties today praise his example with endless eulogies and blame others for his death. But no party has adopted his ideas.

As a result, Greek communism has not the slightest originality and has no mass base of support. All variants of communism that exist in the West are present in Greece, but only as imported, alien phenomena. Even the Greek slogan "socialism with national colors" gets articulated in a strictly Western framework and has little meaning for nonindustrialized Greece. It is a slogan for Italian and French Communists, not for their Greek counterparts. One might argue, in fact, that "Greek communism" does not exist, only "communism in Greece." This point of view is confirmed by study of the political activity of Mikis Theodorakis.[21]

Mikis Theodorakis

Mikis Theodorakis, Greece's best-known contemporary composer, was born in 1925 and studied music in Athens from 1943 to 1950. But he completed his studies in Paris from 1954 to 1960, and his music, as he himself, became Westernized Greek. He maintains close contact with Paris and, like Karamanlis, has been influenced by French politics.

From the age of seventeen, Theodorakis has been a Communist. Before 1967 he was an EDA leader and member of parliament, and when the Democratic Youth Lambrakis movement was founded in 1963, he assumed its directorship. After the KKE split of 1968, he became a Politburo member of the KKE-Interior, but he left the party in 1972 for reasons we will examine below. In 1974, when EDA was re-constituted, he once again assumed a leadership post in it as a member of the party's Executive Committee. Finally, after the dismal showing of the EDA and KKE-Interior in the November 1977 elections, he opted, in a typically abrupt volte face, to pursue his purposes through cooperation with the KKE-Exterior.

Theodorakis had always used the enormous prestige he enjoyed as a composer for political purposes, and his post-1974 public declarations showed no change in this respect. His avowed intention was to become the Communist counterpart of Andreas Papandreou and to regroup all Greek Communists under his leadership. He had even set forth how he proposed to do this.

In a twenty-five-page memorandum dated April 1972, Theodorakis explained to his former comrades the reasons for his resignation that year from the KKE-Interior. Citing the abortive Czechoslovak experience under Alexander Dubček in 1968 and the government of Salvador Allende then in power in Chile to support his views, Theodorakis wrote:

> The experience I got from my participation in the leadership of the Greek Communist Party-Interior over the last two years, has revealed to me that the international Communist movement has ceased to represent revolutionary change. . . . Such revolutionary change is not admissable within the framework of military confrontation between the two superpowers. Therefore revolutionary change in Greece is connected with the full independence of revolutionary forces. . . . This certainly does not mean that an independent people's movement will not be faced with the furious reaction of imperialism. . . . Nor does it mean that in the [resultant] clash the natural allies of the movement will not be the Soviet Union, the socialist camp and the Communist parties of the world.[22]

Theodorakis continued his argument by calling for the dismantling of all existing Greek Communist organizations and the regrouping of all their members in a new independent people's movement. He did not specifically name a leader for the proposed movement, but the tone of his memorandum left little doubt that he envisioned himself in the role. As for the cultural context of the movement, he clearly grounded it in Western civilization by proclaiming, "I staunchly believe that the twentieth century is the century of liberty, the century of the triumph of a universal civilization."[23]

Theodorakis, who had been imprisoned by the colonels' regime for a time and had then spent four years in exile in Paris, returned to Greece in July 1974—two years after writing this memorandum— when Karamanlis made all political parties legal. Recordings of the controversial composer's music, banned during the 1967-1974 military dictatorship because of their use for political purposes (most notably in the film *Z*), began to sell in huge numbers. Yet, despite his popularity as a composer and his previous election as an EDA member of parliament in the 1964 elections, Theodorakis failed to win a parliamentary seat in November 1974, when he ran as a candidate of the Communists' United Left (EA). This was not an unwelcome development for the orthodox Greek Communist apparatus, whose members worried about the composer's disobedient mind. But it assured that Theodorakis would continue in Greece the "independent" tactics and quest for an independent people's movement which he had begun abroad. For the time being, Theodorakis would act from within the ranks of the EDA, a party well suited to his needs. As he declared to the non-Communist, Center daily *To Vêma* in the late summer of 1976: "I belong to EDA. They are old Communists with all the wisdom and experience of a life filled with anguish, thought, and action. They do not have blinders. They are totally free."[24]

Nevertheless, Theodorakis used the non-Communist press of Athens much more than *Ê Avghê*, the joint daily of the EDA and the KKE-Interior, to present his views to the Greek people. In August 1976, for example, he published in the right-wing mass-circulation daily *Apoghevmatinê* two articles under the imposing title, "The Only Way Out of the Pincers of the Two Blocs: National Unity behind Karamanlis."[25] In both articles, he strongly criticized Andreas Papandreou's uncompromising opposition to the Karamanlis government and repeated his already well-known conviction— publicized with the slogan "Either Karamanlis or the tanks!"—that Karamanlis represented the country's only defense against the military's return to power and therefore deserved the full support of all Greeks.[26]

Then, on September 6, 1976, the same rightist newspaper began publishing a fifty-page report, entitled "Let Us Build up a New Left with Greek Colors," which Theodorakis—clearly borrowing from the French Communist slogan, "Socialism with the colors of France"—had presented two months earlier to the Steering Committee of EDA. In this report, Theodorakis had stated in the clearest terms yet the independent attitude he would have the Communists of Greece adopt.[27] In essence, his point of view was that Greek Communists, whatever the reaction of international communism (i.e., Moscow, primarily), had to propose a "national compromise" to the governing Right, a compromise comparable to the "historic compromise" that Italian Communist leader Enrico Berlinguer had proposed to the ruling Italian Christian Democrats.[28] Greek Communists had to collaborate with the Karamanlis government, he said, in order to prevent an authoritarian comeback.

Theodorakis justified his call for the assertion of Greek Communist independence and the rejection of submission to policy directives from abroad in the following way:

> I believe that orthodox Communists very rightly accuse [nonruling] European Communist parties [the Eurocommunists] of in fact abandoning communism. This is a game of words. For what, after all, is communism? It is no longer possible to define it in a purely theoretical way. It is neither pure Marxism nor classical Leninism.

More than fifty years of practical application have given the word communism a clear historical and substantive meaning. Communism is Soviet Stalinism with the improvements and variations which have been incorporated after the 20th Congress [of the Communist Party of the Soviet Union]. Consequently, accusations made by the supporters of Soviet communism, to the effect that the [nonruling] Communist parties of Europe have given up the basic principles and main characteristics of what is commonly called communism, can be said to be correct. . . . I tend to believe that for those Europeans, including myself, to whom thousands of signs indicate that the time for European socialism is upon us, one of the most serious obstacles on the path to socialism is Stalinist communism, distorted and frozen Marxism. . . . The new policy [which I suggest] is socialism with national colors. EDA has proclaimed in favor of it courageously, plainly, and clearly. The KKE-Interior, however, is hesitating.

The dramatic way in which Theodorakis's unorthodox views were publicized—by appearance in a right-wing mass-circulation newspaper—led many to believe that a rift had developed between the composer and his party and that the ideas expressed in *Apoghevmatinê* were Theodorakis's alone. But Theodorakis stated in his published text that the EDA supported his views, and what we know of EDA chairman Elias Iliou lends credence to Theodorakis's assertion—at least as far as Iliou himself is concerned. Why, then, did Theodorakis publish his report in *Apoghevmatinê?* The answer lies, it would seem, in the relationship between EDA and the KKE-Interior. The two parties collaborated, but there were members of both, and especially of the KKE-Interior, who felt that Theodorakis and Iliou were moving too far too fast. They were "hesitating," as Theodorakis stated in his report. The joint press organ of the EDA and KKE-Interior, *Ê Avghê*, which was edited by the number-two man in the KKE-Interior, Leonidas Kyrkos, was in fact entirely controlled by the KKE-Interior. As a result, when the EDA and KKE-Interior disagreed, the EDA was left without a party daily newspaper in which to express itself. Under such circumstances, the EDA, and in this case Theodorakis, were obliged to use the non-Communist press to make their views known.

Of course, Iliou was old and ailing, and Theodorakis might have been the new and dynamic leader who could unite the two parties and give them a broader base of popular support. He was interested, with Iliou's connivance, in using his personal prestige and the support of public opinion to impose his views on both the EDA and the more recalcitrant KKE-Interior. The publication of his program in

Apoghevmatinê, which sold approximately ten times as many copies as *Ê Avghê*, may not have been ill conceived as a means of stimulating developments in this direction.

The KKE-Exterior's reactions to Theodorakis's attempt to use public opinion to bolster his position within the Communist movement were, predictably, quite hostile. But even among moderate Communists it failed to elicit universal approval. Indeed, it caused a widening of differences between EDA leader Iliou and KKE-Interior leader Drakopoulos. Iliou urged the militants of the KKE-Interior to abandon the Communist label and join the ranks of EDA: "My KKE-Interior friends insist on calling themselves a Communist party. . . . They do not realize that the Soviet Union has the copyright on such a title and that it has conceded this to Florakis. Whatever they say, declaring themselves Communists, they are considered apostates. I am telling them: the right thing to do is to come back to EDA."[29] Drakapoulos's response to this suggestion was a very clear "no."[30] Basically, of course, his unwillingness to unite behind Theodorakis reflected personality issues, for both the EDA and KKE-Interior have the same Eurocommunist orientation.

Reaction of the Right

The reaction of the Right and of the Karamanlis government to the composer's proposals for collaboration, on the other hand, was quick and very favorable, indicating not only a readiness to collaborate but also a desire to see Theodorakis's aspirations within the Communist movement fulfilled. Indeed, an atmosphere favorable to the promotion of the idea of a national (or "historic") compromise between moderate Communists and the Karamanlis Right had been developing almost since the fall of the military dictatorship, and certainly since the elections of November 1974. At times this had led to exercises in mutual flattery. Georgios Rallis, for instance, leader of Karamanlis's New Democracy party (Nea Dêmokratia, or ND) and one of the pillars of his government, made the following comments about the EDA's Elias Iliou in March 1975:

> The man who gave me the key to the Greek political situation was Elias Iliou. This leader of the Left, a humanist respected by all, even by his most staunch opponents, has had an inhuman fate. At the time of the civil war, he was deported for five years, from 1946 to 1951, and subjected to continuous torture during two of them. Then came his difficult and dangerous experience in semiclandestinity. In 1967, the

coup d'etat took place, and the venerable leader, whose health had been compromised by so many hardships, was again deported, to Yaros, and tortured, before being transferred as a prisoner to the military hospital of Athens, where he stayed during four trying years. But nothing succeeded in making him submit. He has always spoken without fear. And now he still speaks without hate.[31]

And Iliou reciprocated as follows:

Take Rallis's case: he was imprisoned by the military on the basis of laws he had himself issued against us. The colonels did not need to resort to exceptional measures. The traditional Right fell victim to the arsenal it had built up to muzzle the Left. This made it think. From now on, we are trying on both sides for mutual understanding.[32]

Now, however, Theodorakis had broached the subject of cooperation publicly and had received a public response.

Since Iliou's Communists were far weaker than Berlinguer's Italian Communists, Karamanlis did not feel that he need fear—as Italian Christian Democracy may have to—being used by the Left in any compromise arrangement that is reached. He endorsed collaboration with the EDA/KKE-Interior and hoped to exploit it to increase his own popularity—though, as we have seen, the Communists, like Karamanlis himself, lacked firm ties to the peasantry and lower middle classes. He may also have seen the promotion of Theodorakis's "independent Left" and "national compromise" ideas as a means of preserving disunity in Communist ranks. Certainly, the tone of the Right's praise of Theodorakis invited this interpretation. In September 1976, for example, *Apoghevmatinê* observed:

Apoghevmatinê has lately extended its hospitality to two articles by Mikis Theodorakis, related to the Aegean crisis. They made a great and profound impression, mainly among the broad masses of the Greek people. The government itself took a stand on them through a government statement emphasizing the patriotic character of Theodorakis's views. Nearly all of the Athenian press commented on them. . . . In fact, with his articles, Theodorakis has definitely laid the basis for a *New Greek Left*, which, with courage and responsibility, slashes the ties with all the sins and faults of the past.[33]

And the general reaction of the KKE-Exterior to the "new Left" and "national compromise" ideas was accommodatingly violent and uncompromising. Harilaos Florakis had definitely stated his party's view of what was happening in Greece on March 19, 1975, at the 11th Congress of the Hungarian Socialist Workers' Party:

> On its road, the Communist Party [of Greece] has to face not only the militarist movements inspired by the United States and the conservative politics of the government, but also the obstacles put up by the revisionist group of the Right which has detached itself from the Party, presents itself under the name of "Communist Party of the interior," and today works inside the workers' movement in collaboration with the ruling class.[34]

The November 1977 Elections

New parliamentary elections in November 1977 dealt a blow to both the moderate Communists and the Karamanlis forces, thus rendering a "national compromise" between the Communist Left and the Karamanlis Right even more problematic than it had been previously. Before the elections, Theodorakis, piqued by the KKE-Exterior's attacks on him and by his failure to unite even the EDA and KKE-Interior under his leadership, left the country, but the EDA and KKE-Interior joined with two small social democratic groups and one from the national-socialist ranks of the Right to form the Alliance of Progressive and Leftist Forces (Symmahia Proodeutikôn kai Aristerôn Dynameôn) to wage the campaign. This coalition, as Table 3 indicates, fared poorly. It garnered less than 3 percent of the total vote, and it won only two seats in parliament. These went to Elias Iliou of EDA and Leonidas Kyrkos of the KKE-Interior. (Apparently, the dismal showing of the EDA and KKE-Interior made an impact on Theodorakis. He returned to Greece and decided to cooperate with the KKE-Exterior.) Karamanlis's party captured less than 42 percent of the vote, as compared with 54 percent in 1974. In doing so, it lost the support of an important segment of the traditional voters of the Right, especially among the peasants in the countryside.

Although the proliferation of new parties complicated the picture somewhat, Andreas Papandreou's PASOK plainly registered the biggest gains, boosting its share of the ballots from 14 percent in 1974 to 25 percent in 1977. At the same time, the orthodox Communist forces, the KKE-Exterior, did well too. This party alone garnered about the same percentage of votes that the United Left coalition had obtained in 1974. In doing so, it apparently won over the greatest part of the electorate that had supported the Eurocommunist parties in 1974.[35] It is also worth noting that the "Maoists," though still a minute minority, bettered their 1974 showing considerably, raising their share of the total vote from 0.02 percent to 0.41 percent and for the first time making their presence felt in the countryside.[36]

These results carried several implications of significance for the present discussion. First, they demonstrated conclusively that Greece is not only an economically and socially underdeveloped country but a non-Western one in cultural terms as well. All the main losers fall into the category of pro-Western intellectuals. Karamanlis is the *arhontohoriatis* ("the peasant who dreamed of becoming a gentleman") and calls to mind Molière's bourgeois-gentilhomme by his championing of "European enlightenment" and vaguely social democratic values. Similarly, the elements in the Union of the Democratic Center and most of those involved in the Alliance of Progressive and Leftist Forces derive their inspiration from European ideas, whether social democratic or Eurocommunist in nature. In contrast, the chief winner, Andreas Papandreou and his PASOK, has more and more openly espoused a Third World national-socialist ideology—at least in words—and sought the support of small peasant owners and petit bourgeois city dwellers. It was from these segments of society, especially the peasants, that much of the party's new strength came.

Second, the results showed that the orthodox, pro-Soviet KKE-Exterior had profitably exploited the freedom to organize and the absence of anticommunist propaganda during the previous three years. Not only did it retain the hard core of its 1974 backers, but it, in effect, managed to rally most of the supporters of the Communist movement behind its banner.

Third, the results indicated that the Euromania of Greek intellectuals (including Eurocommunists, Eurocentrists, and Euro-Karamanlists) had pushed an important section of the Greek people into the arms of PASOK. This development greatly enhances the chances for communism to prosper in the country. Papandreou's party is certainly not a Communist party. But its virulently anti-American and anti-NATO stand, its disinclination to offer any public criticism of communism, its avowed ambition to regroup the EAM forces of 1941-1944 under its leadership, and the KKE-Exterior's silence with regard to Papandreou's positions and actions—all create an environment in which the spread of Communist ideas among the most traditional circles of the Greek countryside becomes easier. Furthermore, Papandreou's anti-Turkish feelings, not unlike those that General Dimitrios Ioannidis displayed in 1974, can only perpetuate the Greek-Turkish conflict, widen the existing gap in the Greek-Turkish world, and thus benefit the Soviet Union.

Table 3: Results of the Greek Parliamentary Elections of November 20, 1977

Parties and Electoral Alliances	Votes cast	Percent of total vote	Number of seats
Conservative			
National Party (EP[a])	349,851	6.82	5
New Democracy (ND[b])	2,146,687	41.85	172
Center			
Party of New Liberals (NF[c])	55,560	1.08	2
Union of Democratic Center (EDIK[d])	613,113	11.95	15
Non-Communist Left			
Panhellenic Socialist Movement (PASOK[e])	1,299,196	25.33	93
Socialist and Eurocommunist			
Alliance of Progressive and Leftist Forces (electoral coalition of EDA, KKE-Interior, the Party of Socialist Initiative, the Movement of the Socialist Way, Christian Democracy[f])	139,762	2.72	2
Communist			
KKE[g]	480,188	9.36	11
"Maoist"			
EKKE[h]	11,962	0.23	0
LDE[i]	9,500	0.18	0
Other	24,691	0.48	0
TOTAL	5,130,510	100.00	300

a Ethnikē Parataxis of Stefanos Stefanopoulos and Spyros Theotokis. This is a new party.

b Nea Demokratia of Konstantinos Karamanlis.

c Komma Neofileleutherōn of Konstantinos Mitsotakis. This is a new party.

d Enōsē Dēmokratikou Kentrou of Georgios Mavros. In 1974, this party was known as Center Union-New Forces.

e Panellēnio Sosialistiko Kinēma of Andreas Papandreou.

f Symmahia Proodeutikōn kai Aristerōn Dynameōn. This coalition, under the presidency of EDA leader Elias Iliou, includes Eniaia Dēmokratikē Aristera, Kommounistiko Komma Elladas Esōterikou, Komma Sosialistikēs Prōtovoulias, Kinēsē Sosialistikē Poreia, and Hristianikē Dēmokratia. The third and fourth parties of the coalition were founded after the 1974 elections -- the former by people who left the Center Union-New Forces and the latter by people who left PASOK. Hristianikē Dēmokratia is headed by N. Psaroudakis, who came from the national-socialist ranks of the Right and had in the past violently attacked Communists, Jews, and Freemasons.

g Kommounistiko Komma Elladas. Although unofficially known as the Communist Party of Greece--Exterior, the party rejects the "Exterior" label, for it considers itself the only real Communist Party of Greece.

h Epanastatiko Kommounistiko Kinēma Elladas. Even though the EKKE expresses support of China, it does not have the official backing of Peking.

i Laikē Dēmokratikē Enotēta. This party, which publishes the weekly Proletariakē Sēmaia (Athens), calls itself Maoist but adheres to the Albanian line, not that espoused by the post-Mao leadership in China. Headed by Iannis Hotzeas, it came into being in 1976 as a splinter group from a pro-Chinese party, Organōsē Marxistōn Leninistōn Elladas (OMLE), which now goes under the name of Marxistiko Leninistiko Kommounistiko Komma Elladas (M-L KKE). The latter party--led by Isaak Iordanidis, whom the Chinese leadership in Peking has received officially -- did not participate in either the 1974 or 1977 elections. However, it contines to publish Laïkos Dromos (Athens).

SOURCES: To Vema (Athens), November 22, 1977, and Ē Kathēmerinē (Athens), November 24, 1977. The author, who was in Athens at the time of the elections, has made corrections and added explanatory details. It should be noted that the official figures to be published in the govermental series in 1978 may vary slightly from those presented here.

Scenario for National Compromise

Despite the election outcome, there is still jockeying for position and advantage within Communist ranks and between the Greek Right and Left: Bearing this point in mind, we must now address these questions: Under what conditions might collaboration between Right and Left be initiated in Greece? And who would profit in the long run from the development of an Italian-style "historic compromise" in the country—Karamanlis's traditional Right or the Communists? The answers depend, it seems to this observer, on the development of Greek-Turkish relations.

Greece's moderate Communists, as well as Andreas Papandreou, apparently think that a Greek-Turkish war—or at least a prolonged crisis situation—is inevitable, and they are trying to use this state of affairs to come to power. They would like to duplicate—up to a point—the wartime record of the EAM. Their analysis with respect to the foreseeable future might be summarized as follows. The traditional Right has no more capability of organizing Greece's masses against an invasion by Turkey today than it had in 1941 to mobilize the masses against the German-Italian-Bulgarian invasion. The Communists are better organized among the masses for such a purpose. If the anticipated war should be lost, the new (Communist) Left would control armed resistance to the invader and exploit national feelings against Turkish occupation. On the other hand, if the war should be won, the Communists would emerge reinforced by having supported Karamanlis's government.

The domestic-international linkage in Communist calculations was made quite clear in a memorandum signed by Leonidas Kyrkos that the KKE-Interior sent to Karamanlis on March 18, 1975:

> Mr. President, we would like to submit to your government some thoughts concerning the Cyprus crisis, the threats which our country has to face [from the Turks], and the reorientation which is necessary—in our opinion—in our foreign policy. We have the impression . . . that our country is gradually being driven toward the center of a great international crisis and that the time that is left to us in order to face it successfully is perhaps limited. . . . In the idea of the preparation of the Nation, we include the preparation of the Armed Forces, the union of the army with the people, and the unity of the people above all ideological and political differences. . . . We propose [therefore] the formation of a government of national union, with the participation of all parties and groups of the present parliament, without any

exception, in order that the whole people, as one man, support the common national effort.[37]

And a year later, the Communists used the occasion of the renewed Aegean crisis (over exploration of the continental shelf) to ask the government for the formation of a national guard, a people's army the Communists could hope to control. The Central Committee of the KKE-Interior, meeting in extraordinary session on August 13, 1976, issued the following declaration:

> Our country is facing its greatest outside threat in its postwar history. . . . The continuous provocation of *Sismik I* [the Turkish ship that precipitated the 1976 crisis] has dangerously increased the tension in Greek-Turkish relations. The danger of an armed conflict is real. . . . [We propose] the organization of the nationwide mobilization of all human and material resources for a struggle of long duration and that this mobilization be self-governed with the participation of the people's organizations . . . [specifically, we propose] the setting up of a national guard with the periodic participation of all Greeks of the reserve, without distinctions.[38]

On the same day, Kyrkos made the following statement to *Ta Nea*, the Athens daily newspaper with the largest circulation:

> The crisis in our relations with Turkey can be a prolonged one. . . . Cuba, for instance, has not reached a state of war with the USA. But the mobilization of its people on a solid moral and political basis allowed that country to build structures and institutions, to develop economically and socially to such a degree that the preparation of its national defense also was better than it had ever been.[39]

It is important to note that centrist *Ta Nea* urged the Greek public to adopt a similar path.

Although Andreas Papandreou is also attempting to profit from the Greek-Turkish crisis, his tactics are very different. Instead of supporting the government and trying to climb on its back as the EDA and KKE-Interior are doing, he has violently attacked Karamanlis for not having declared war on Turkey immediately and has accused the prime minister of national treason. Papandreou seems to be seeking to stir up the army against Karamanlis with the hope that a Portuguese-type military coup would raise him and his PASOK to power.

Papandreou's reactions to a minor Greek-Turkish incident in

April 1977 illustrate his tactics. The Turkish coast guard arrested a Greek fisherman between the Greek island of Samos and the Turkish coast in allegedly Greek waters, although the Turks subsequently released the man. Papandreou issued inflammatory declarations clearly designed to push the Greek government to war.

In any case, the course of the Aegean crisis thus far suggests that the calculations of the Left regarding Karamanlis's vulnerabilities in the foreign policy realm may not be unrealistic. The continuing crisis has shown that, like his predecessors, the prime minister lacks a clear-cut program with which to cope with the Greek-Turkish problem. He has taken decisions on a day-to-day basis while the Turks have followed a preconceived plan of action, and the result has been major frustration for Greece.

After assuming office, Karamanlis took a hard stand toward Turkey, but the oil-exploration activities of *Sismik I* in the Aegean in July-August 1976 forced him to retreat. He appealed first to the Security Council of the United Nations, hoping that it would condemn Turkey; however, the Security Council on August 25, 1976, unanimously advised both countries to begin direct, bilateral negotiations on the Aegean issue—an endorsement of the Turkish, not the Greek position. He then took the matter to the International Court of Justice, asking it to prohibit *Sismik I* from looking for oil in what Greece considers part of its continental shelf. But on September 11, 1976, the International Court also rejected Athens' petition, by a vote of twelve to one, with two abstentions.

Nor did any of the other avenues through which Karamanlis sought to improve Greece's diplomatic leverage against Turkey yield more positive results. For example, the Greek prime minister had pursued a policy of Balkan entente designed to partially disengage Greece from the United States and to bring about a rapprochement with the Soviet Union—with the ultimate end of winning the support of the Communist states of the Balkans and of the USSR against Turkey. Yet soon after the Aegean crisis broke out, the Soviet Union, Bulgaria, and Romania announced their neutrality in the dispute—which, under the circumstances, was rather favorable to Turkey. By the beginning of 1977, moreover, the Soviet Union was leaning more and more toward Turkey. Similarly, Karamanlis had endeavored to get Greece admitted to the Common Market in the hope that he could then bring West European pressure to bear on Turkey. But with the possible exception of France, the Common Market countries proved unwilling to give Athens unconditional backing against Ankara, and in the first quarter of 1977 even France made clear that it would not provide such support. Indeed, Paris was cool toward Greece's entry into the Common Market. France's attitude was a major, even catastrophic, defeat for Karamanlis, for he had based his external *and* internal policies on the slogan "Greece-France: Alliance!" and on the early incorporation of Greece into the Common Market with French backing.

In short, Karamanlis has found himself isolated internationally and obliged to retreat before a dynamic Turkish foreign policy. To add to his problems, his authority has been eroding because of increasing evidence of corruption in his government. Beginning on March 27, 1977, the centrist newspaper *To Vêma* published a series of articles that carefully documented not only overwhelming mediocrity but also widespread corruption in all governmental institutions. The government simply ignored the highly incriminating evidence, perhaps because it implicated the prime minister's brother, Ahileus Karamanlis.

Faced with this general situation, Karamanlis in the summer of 1977 sought to work his way out by moving back toward a closer relationship with the United States. Nonetheless, it is possible that to avoid being ousted by internal adversaries dissatisfied with his handling of the country's affairs, he still might conclude that he has no choice but to rely "on the masses" by turning to the Left for support—or to go to war with Turkey and let the chips fall where they may. In either case, the Greek Communists could reap some benefits.

Regardless of Karamanlis's future attitude toward the Greek-Turkish conflict and his relations with the United States and NATO, however, there is one striking feature of this second, post-1974 phase of his rule. Communism in Greece has gotten the chance to regroup its forces and increase its power.

Notes

1. In the 1961 elections, Karamanlis's National Radical Union won 49.6 percent of the valid ballots cast. The Center Union of Georgios Papandreou and Sofoklis Venizelos had anticipated winning the election, but, in alliance with the small Progressive Party of Spyros Markezinis, received only 34.3 percent of the vote. The Communist-dominated Pan-Democratic Agrarian Front got 15.1 percent, much below its 1958 record of 24.3 percent. Disappointed with the election results, both opposition forces complained bitterly of fraud and intimidation at the polls. Furthermore, they attributed

Dimitri Kitsikis

Lambrakis's death in Salonika to deliberate government action. The Communists even went so far as to found a youth movement called Democratic Youth Lambrakis, intended to spread communism among the younger generation. Mikis Theodorakis was leader of the movement. The motion picture *Z*, for which Theodorakis composed the score, was based on the story of Lambrakis's death.

2. Stavros Zorbalas, *Sêmaia tou laou: selides apo tên istoria tou "Rizospatê," 1917-1936* [People's flag: some pages from the history of Rizopastis, 1917-1936] (Bucharest: Politikes kai Logotehnikes Ekdoseis, 1966). See also D. Kitsikis, *Propagande et pressions en politique internationale—La Grèce et ses revendications à la Conférence de la Paix, 1919-1920* [Propaganda and pressures in international politics: Greece and its claims at the Peace Conference, 1919-1920] (Paris: Presses universitaires de France, 1963), pp. 460-480.

3. Georgios Papandreou founded the Socialist Democratic Party in 1933. The party was not active within Greece until after World War II.

4. D. Kitsikis, "Greece," in *International Guide to Electoral Statistics*, ed. Jean Meyriat and Stein Rokkan (The Hague: Mouton, 1969), vol. 1, pp. 163-182.

5. D. Kitsikis, "Parliament and Social Change in Greece up to the Military Coup d'Etat of 1967," *Social History—Histoire sociale* (Ottawa), November 1970, p. 63.

6. Pavlos Nefeloudis, *Stis pêges tês kakodaimonias. Ta bathutera aitia tês diaspasês tou KKE, 1918-1968: episêma keimena kai prosopikes empeiries* [At the roots of bad fortune. The deep causes of the split in the Communist Party of Greece (KKE), 1918-1968: official documents and personal experiences], 2d ed. (Athens: Gutenberg, 1974), p. 116.

7. D. Kitsikis, "Starvation in Greece, 1941-1942: The Political Consequences," *Revue d'histoire de la deuxième guerre mondiale* (Paris), April 1969, pp. 17-41.

8. Petros Rousos, *E megale tetraetia* [The big four years] (Bucharest, Politikes kai Logotehnikes Ekdoseis, 1966).

9. See D. Kitsikis, "The Communist Movement in Greece," *Etudes internationales* (Quebec), September 1975, pp. 334-354.

10. On divisions within the KKE, see Antonio Solaro, *Storia del partito comunista greco* [History of the Greek Communist Party] (Milan: Teti, 1973). Solaro has been in the KKE since 1948.

11. D. Vlantas, "Why I Disagreed with the Communist Party," *Akropolis* (Athens), April 1-5, 1973. Vlantas later published his full memoirs himself in Athens. The fourth volume, entitled *1950-1967*.

Tragôdia tou KKE [1950-1967. Tragedy of the KKE], came out in late 1976.

12. Evanghelos Averoff-Tossizza, *Le feu et la hache: Grèce '46-49* [The fire and the axe: Greece '46-49] (Paris: Editions de Breteuil, 1973), pp. 260-263; and Dominique Eudes, *The Kapetanios: Partisans and Civil War in Greece, 1943-1949* (London: NLB, 1972). Averoff-Tossizza is a former minister of foreign affairs. In the present Karamanlis government, he is the minister of national defense.

Averoff said that the reason for Markos Vafiadis's elimination was his great respect for Tito. Like Tito, Markos was a nationalist Communist. Consequently, Moscow ordered Zahariadis to remove Markos from all his positions. Averoff also indicated that Markos did not agree on military tactics with Zahariadis, who wanted to launch regular army operations in a positional war instead of continuing guerrilla warfare.

Eudes, on the basis of information obtained from Markos himself, confirms the accuracy of this last cause of divergence alleged by Averoff. Markos is supposed to have said to the disagreeing Zahariadis on January 15, 1948, "We are not a regular army, and we are in no position at the moment to operate seriously against urban centers." *The Kapetanios*, p. 309. And in August of the same year, in another violent quarrel, "Markos accused Zahariadis of trying to liquidate the revolution." Ibid., p. 330. On August 21, 1948, claimed Eudes, Zahariadis tried unsuccessfully to murder Markos; Averoff, however, doubted this.

Markos gave more details of his rift with Zahariadis in a series of articles published under the title "Markos Vafiadis' Diary," *Ta Nea* (Athens), December 13-21, 1976.

13. Zahariadis had been approved as head of the KKE by the Comintern in 1931. He was appointed secretary-general in 1934.

14. On Stefanopoulos's statement of government policy, see *To Vêma* (Athens), February 21, 1975; and *Vradynê* (Athens), February 21, 1975.

15. *Akropolis*, October 8, 1976.

16. *Ê Avghê* (Athens), October 5, 1976.

17. Grigorios Palamas (1269-1359), archbishop of Thessaloniki, has been thoroughly studied in the many works of Professor John Meyendorff. On the "Eastern party" and Georgios O Trapezountios (1395-1484), see D. Kitsikis, "From Byzantine to Contemporary Greece," in *Encyclopedia Universalis* (Paris, 1970), vol. 7, pp. 1077-1085.

18. The term *liberal* is used here in its broader sense and is not

restricted to the Liberal Party founded in 1910 by El. Venizelos.

19. D. P. Kabas, "Turkey and the West," *Politika Themata* (Athens), April 2-8, 1977, p. 8. This argument, it should be noted, is reminiscent of the Greek Westernists' interpretation of the Greek-Turkish struggle in the nineteenth century as a conflict between Europe and Asia. Such an interpretation, of course, ignored the fact that Hellenism since antiquity had flourished as much in Asia as in Europe.

20. See, for example, NCNA's press release datelined Peking, August 3, 1976, concerning the entry into the Mediterranean of the Soviet aircraft carrier *Kiev*.

21. For a monographic study of Theodorakis's life, see George Giannaris, *Mikis Theodorakis* (New York: Praeger, 1972).

22. Untitled typed memorandum in Greek, dated April 1972, pp. 2, 4. The author has a copy of this memorandum in his personal collection. An earlier and shorter French-language version was dated March 19, 1972, Sydney, Australia.

23. Ibid., p. 8.

24. *To Vêma*, August 8, 1976.

25. *Apoghevmatinê* (Athens), August 17-18, 1976.

26. For earlier efforts to promote the pro-Karamanlis slogan, see, for example, *To Vêma*, August 8, 1976.

27. *Apoghevmatinê*, September 6, 1976.

28. On the "historic compromise" proposal of Berlinguer, see Giacomo Sani's chapter in this volume.

29. *To Vêma*, February 26, 1977.

30. *Ê Avghê*, March 8, 1977.

31. *To Vêma*, March 4, 1975.

32. Ibid.

33. *Apoghevmatinê*, September 6, 1976. Emphasis in original.

34. *Ê Avghê*, April 5, 1975.

35. Th. Romanos, "The Crisis of the KKE-Interior and the Demand for Renewal of the Communist Movement," *Anti* (Athens), December 31, 1977, p. 26.

36. Bas. Tzannetakis, "The Meaning of the 'Impressive' Presence of the Left Extremists in the Electoral Results," *To Vêma*, November 23, 1977.

37. *Ê Avghê*, March 20, 1975.

38. Ibid., August 15, 1976.

39. *Ta Nea*, August 13, 1976.

6
Finland: The SKP and Electoral Politics

John H. Hodgson

In 1916, Lenin departed from his general advocacy of violent revolution and suggested that socialism might be achieved peacefully in a small country sharing a common frontier with a large country that has already undergone the transformation from capitalism to socialism.[1] Irrespective of whether Lenin had Finland in mind, this country seems to fit his explicit and implicit criteria. Not only does Finland share an 800-mile border with the Soviet Union, but it also boasts a strong labor movement. Moreover, a majority of the members of the Finnish Communist Party (Suomen Kommunistinen Puolue, or SKP) appear to accept the notion of a transition to socialism through the ballot box. Thus, Finland provides an interesting and important case study of the possibilities and problems facing a Communist party committed to a "peaceful path" to socialism.

Operating through the Communist-dominated Finnish People's Democratic League (Suomen Kansan Demokraattinen Liitto, or SKDL), the SKP has achieved considerable electoral success, polling more than 20 percent of the popular vote in seven of the ten postwar Finnish national elections. This performance, surpassed in the West only by the French and Italian Communist parties (see Table 1), has led one noted Western scholar to classify Finland with France and Italy among the world's "unstable democracies."[2] Another study has included the SKP among the thirteen "most influential" of the nonruling Communist parties committed to the "peaceful path."[3]

Indeed, the SKDL shares with the Social Democratic Party and the Center (Agrarian) Party the distinction of having dominated the Finnish electoral scene since World War II, although Finnish politics in the postwar period has been characterized by competition among a minimum of seven parties. In one election (that of 1958), the SKDL emerged with a plurality of seats, but the Social Democrats have proved the most consistent vote-getters, winning a plurality of seats

Table 1: Communist Election Results and Membership—A Comparison

Year of Nat'l. Election	Finland Percent of popular vote	Membership of SKP	of SKDL	France Percent of popular vote	French CP membership[a]	Italy Percent of popular vote	Italian CP membership
1945	23.5	19,000	100,000	26.2[b]	825,000		
1946				25.9[b]	895,000	18.96[b]	2,150,000
"				28.2			
1948	20.0	53,000	150,000			21.0[c]	2,250,000
1951	21.6	45,000	143,000	26.9	625,000		
1953						22.6	2,150,000
1954	21.6	46,000	142,000				
1956				25.9	430,000		
1958	23.2	47,000	140,000	19.2	425,000	22.7	1,800,000
1962	22.0	50,000	155,000	21.7	406,000		
1963						25.3	1,600,000
1966	21.2	47,000	145,000				
1967				22.51	426,000		
1968				20.02	426,000	26.9	1,500,000
1970	16.6	48,000	165,000[d]				
1972	17.0	48,000	165,000			27.2	1,600,000
1973				21.25	455,000		
1975	19.0	42,000[e]	170,000				
1976						34.4	1,600,000

Table 1 (cont.)

[a]Data for the PCF (*Parti Communiste Français*--French Communist Party) represent membership cards delivered -- not total accepted--and therefore inflate the actual membership figure.

[b]Election of a Constituent Assembly.

[c]A Communist-Socialist coalition won 31 percent of the votes in Italy in 1948. Since the PCI usually wins at least 1 percent less votes than seats, its share of the 1948 vote was derived from the share of seats won (22.8 percent).

[d]The substantial jump in SKDL membership between 1966 and 1970 resulted essentially from the admission of the 25,000-member Finnish Democratic Youth League to the SKDL in 1967.

[e]This drop in SKP membership resulted from an exchange of party cards in early 1973. At that time the party rolls were reduced from 47,611 to 35,756 members. Previous exchanges had taken place in 1950, 1958, and 1964.

SOURCES: Election data come from statistical handbooks, from *Le Monde* (Paris), and three books: Jaakko Nousiainen, *The Finnish Political System*, tr. by John H. Hodgson, Cambridge, Mass., Harvard University Press, 1971, pp. 40-41; Philip M. Williams, *French Politicians and Elections, 1951-1969*, Cambridge University Press, 1970, pp. 292-93; and Giaemilio Ipsevich and Enrico Zampetti, *Elezioni 1972 risultati e confronti* (1972 Election Results and Comparisons), Milan, Pan Editrice Milano, 1972, pp. 25, 139, 143, 145-46, 148-49. On party membership, see official party sources plus John H. Hodgson, "The Finnish Communist Party," *Slavic Review* (Columbus, Ohio), March 1970, p. 80; and Annie Kriegel, *The French Communists: Profile of a People*, tr. by Elaine P. Halperin, University of Chicago Press, 1972, pp. 32-35.

in seven elections. The Center Party captured the most seats in two others (1948 and 1962).

The dominance of these three parties has been reflected in the composition of the Finnish cabinet. A coalition including all three ruled for two long periods, 1944-1948 and 1966-1970, and for three shorter periods, 1970-1971, 1975-1976, and most recently since the formation in May 1977 of a majority government headed by Social Democratic leader Kalevi Sorsa. In the 1950s and well into the 1960s, the Center Party exercised prime influence in the government, and the Social Democrats held sway in the late 1940s and the early 1970s. At present, the Center Party is again the backbone of the Finnish cabinet.[4]

A Finnish Model

In pursuing power by parliamentary means, the SKP has rejected the model singled out for emulation by Soviet party leaders at the 20th Congress of the Soviet Communist Party in 1956—the model of 1948 Czechoslovakia. Although admitting that socialism was achieved by "relatively peaceful" means in certain East European countries in the early postwar period, SKP Chairman Aarne Saarinen argues that circumstances surrounding those events were unusually tense and hence atypical. Although Stalinist elements within the SKP resist his views, Saarinen remains optimistic about the prospects for a transition to socialism in Finland more peaceful than that experienced in countries such as Czechoslovakia. As he explains it,

> Finland is to a degree an exception because we have in general a very strong labor movement and the leftist labor movement is relatively powerful. When socialist principles gain ground within the rest of the labor movement—I have in mind particularly the Finnish Social Democratic Party—it is quite possible that a majority of the voters will lean toward support for socialist reforms.[5]

Finnish Communists have nonetheless moved cautiously in nationalistic Finland, particularly in the early postwar years. At that time, the Finnish electorate was hardly ready for Communist or even Socialist slogans—a fact duly noted by Hertta Kuusinen, who before her death in 1974 served for many years as a member of the SKP Politburo and chairman of the SKDL's Parliamentary Group.[6] The populace at large disliked the presence in Helsinki of A. Zhdanov's Allied Control Commission during 1944-1947, and the return to Finland in 1946 of several emigrant Finnish Communists, including

Hertta Kuusinen's first husband T. Lehén, was seen by many observers at home and abroad as an ill wind. In Finland there were rumors about the existence of a "barricade" group of Communists, and abroad there was talk that Finnish political leaders had sold out to Moscow. The fact that Hertta Kuusinen's father had been a member of the Central Committee of the Communist Party of the Soviet Union since 1941 and was a member of the CPSU Presidium (Politburo) under both Stalin (1952-1953) and Khrushchev (1957-1964) added to the uncertainties of a population who had rallied so spontaneously and uniformly to the defense of their country against the incursion of Soviet forces in 1939.[7]

In light of these circumstances, it has been natural for the SKP to shun the Communist label and to campaign under the banner of the Finnish People's Democratic League at election time. The Communists' central role in the SKDL has been unchallenged for three decades. With close to 50,000 members, the Finnish Communist Party is the largest of the member units that comprise the League. (Other units include the 25,000-strong Finnish Democratic Youth League, which joined the SKDL in 1967, and the 20,000-strong Finnish Democratic League of Women.) Perhaps more indicative of the Communist domination of the umbrella organization is the unusually high percentage of SKP members who sit on SKDL executive committees at the local, district, and national levels.[8] The SKP Central Committee has itself acknowledged that the SKDL is beginning to resemble a unified political party, but it still wishes to avoid the appearance of excessive Communist control of the SKDL and looks with disfavor upon suggestions that the SKDL and the SKP form a single political party,[9] although pressures in that direction persist within Communist ranks. At the SKP Congress in 1972, for example, Leo Suonpää—a leading Stalinist—proposed reorganizing the SKDL so as to reduce further the influence of left-wing Socialist (i.e., non-Communist) elements.[10]

Despite the SKDL's significant electoral setbacks in the 1970s (see Table 1) and the shock administered to supporters of the "peaceful path" by the overthrow of the Allende coalition government in Chile in September 1973, leaders of the SKP and SKDL have not abandoned their optimism about the chances for a peaceful transition to socialism in Finland.[11] Whether or not such optimism is justified is, of course, another question—a question that can be answered only if one understands the sources of SKDL strength and the causes of the fluctuations in the League's electoral achievements.

An analysis of this aspect of the problem leads to the conclusion that despite the generally held view that Communist electoral successes primarily reflect economic factors (i.e., are greatest when economic conditions are the worst), in Finland the electoral ups and downs of the Communists are more a function of politics.[12] (Thomas H. Greene has drawn attention to the importance of the political—as opposed to the economic—factor in the electoral fortunes of French and Italian Communists.)[13] Specifically, the fortunes of the SKDL seem to bear an inverse relationship to the vicissitudes of its major rival on the left—the Social Democratic Party. It is in the relative attractiveness of these two parties to the Finnish electorate, particularly to the protest voter, that one can find some realistic basis for assessing the past achievements and future prospects of the peaceful, parliamentary strategy of Finland's Communists.

Factors in Postwar Strength

The parliamentary successes of the SKP are primarily a post–World War II phenomenon, achieved through the Communist-dominated SKDL, although the history of the SKP dates back to its formation in Moscow in the summer of 1918 by Finnish Social Democrats who had escaped to the USSR after defeat in a three-month-long civil war.[14] The SKP was for all practical purposes an illegal organization throughout the 1920s and 1930s, achieving a maximum membership of 2,000, although it was able during the 1920s, operating through two electoral fronts similar to the SKDL (the Socialist Workers' Party of Finland and the Socialist Workers' and Small Farmers' Election Organization), to win an average of 12.7 percent of the popular vote in national elections (reaching a high in 1922 of 14.8 percent, which netted 18 of 200 parliamentary seats). After 1930, when all groups of the extreme Left (including the Socialist Workers' and Small Farmers' Election Organization) were pro-scribed, Communists apparently either abstained from voting or voted for the Social Democratic Party. Only in 1944, as a result of the Finnish-Soviet armistice, did the SKP become a fully legal political organization. This, in turn, paved the way for the formation of the SKDL by Communists and left-wing Socialists for purposes of winning the March 1945 national election. On the eve of that first postwar election, Finnish President J. K. Paasikivi made his famous appeal for "new faces" in parliament.[15] When the returns were tallied, the SKDL had captured 23.5 percent of the popular vote and 49 of 200 parliamentary seats.

An appreciation of the reasons for this remarkable Communist electoral success—virtually a doubling of the party's strength from the levels attained in the 1920s, and this after nearly fifteen years of illegal status—is essential for an understanding of the whole postwar record of the SKDL. Although the inheritance of political loyalties and beliefs from prewar days—what one scholar has called "the Mendelian law" of politics[16]—may have played a role in the resurgence of the Finnish Communists, it alone does not suffice to account for the SKDL's resounding success in 1945. Nor does the absence in 1945 of the intimidation and violence that had characterized the interwar elections in which Communist-supported candidates had been permitted to participate fully explain the jump in Communist strength. Instead, the answer should perhaps be sought in political events that dramatically realigned working-class voting patterns, events such as those to which Richard F. Hamilton refers in his study of French workers.[17] Specifically, the behavior of Finland's workers in the 1945 election may have stemmed from an adverse reaction to Finland's experiences with right extremism and from a growing awareness that changes within the Social Democratic Party had undercut its status as the best political spokesman for worker interests. Both aspects of this proposition call for further examination.

During the two decades preceding the outbreak of World War II, Finland (like Italy and France) experienced movements both of a conservative "right-wing" and of a revolutionary "centrist" nature[18] —i.e., it had its monarchists and parafascists. In the former category was Gustaf Mannerheim, an aristocrat in the age of democracy, who twice served as head of state (1918-1919 and 1944-1946) yet never accepted parliamentary government.[19] To the end of his life, Mannerheim remained faithful in spirit if not in his actions to the Lapua Movement, which from its inception in the early 1930s sought ultimately to destroy all parties and parliamentary government.[20] In 1932, some ten years after the successful fascist march on Rome, there was a revolt by the Lapua Movement forces of Vihtori Kosola in the Finnish community of Mäntsälä that was supposed to be followed by a march on Helsinki in support of demands for a new government that would include Mannerheim as president and his closest friend and chief lieutenant, Rudolf Walden, as prime minister. But this revolt was suppressed without bloodshed, its leaders were arrested, and the Lapua Movement was outlawed.[21]

In the same year (1932), there also emerged a militant new party— the People's Patriotic Movement (Isänmaallinen Kansanliike, or IKL).[22] Because of its attacks on capitalism (a position resembling the anticapitalist themes of Jacques Doriot's Parti Populaire

Français[23]) and on Finland's Swedish-speaking minority, the IKL antagonized Finnish industrialists who had been prominent in the Lapua Movement, and failed to win the blessing of the older generation of conservatives who had supported the latter—e.g., Mannerheim and J. K. Paasikivi. Paasikivi, who had favored a German monarch for Finland in 1918, denounced the IKL as a revolutionary body seeking to establish a fascist dictatorship in Finland. In fact, the IKL leadership did have a deep admiration for Mussolini and Hitler, in particular for fascist Italy. Nonetheless, in the 1936 and 1939 elections the People's Patriotic Movement won 8.3 and 6.6 percent of the vote, respectively, drawing support from civil servants, academics, physicians, and clergy.

In its quest for the Finnish equivalent of the German *Volksgemein-schaft* ("national community"), the IKL ultimately sought a Greater Finland, to be achieved at the territorial expense of the Soviet Union. Both the Winter War of 1939-1940 with the USSR and Finland's cobelligerency with Germany in World War II seemed compatible with the IKL's goal of a Greater Finland. However, the aspirations of the movement collapsed with the defeat of Germany, and the IKL was explicitly outlawed by the terms of the Finnish-Soviet armistice of 1944.

Although some would argue that postwar support for the Communists has no roots in such prewar or wartime political events,[24] the Finnish experience with right extremism—whether the Mäntsälä revolt or the cooperation with Germany's National Socialists—can hardly be discounted as a factor in postwar Communist electoral successes. It helps to explain why Hertta Kuusinen during the first years after her postwar release from prison stressed the themes of antifascism and support of democracy. Such themes were openly accepted by SKDL supporters, who might have been alienated by direct talk of socialism.[25] Moreover, the SKDL was able to marshal considerable support among leftist groups for its demand that those responsible for Finland's wartime misadventures be held accountable. In a broader, comparative frame of reference, it is surely more than coincidence that three of the strongest of Europe's nonruling Communist parties—those of Finland, France, and Italy— have operated in politics that experienced a traumatic struggle with right extremism of one or another variety in the interwar period.

Weakness of Social Democracy

Not only did the Finnish rejection of right extremism provide a favorable environment for the promotion of Communist political fortunes, but—more important perhaps—the whole issue of interpreting the war years gave rise to debilitating controversy within the Social Democratic Party, the SKDL's principal rival for the postwar leftist vote.[26] Dissension within the SDP largely revolved around the person and policies of Väinö Tanner, a man who dominated the social democratic movement for more than a quarter of a century and who was perhaps the most powerful single Finnish political leader of this century. His firm, unyielding grip on his party during the war years and the opposition to his policies within the SDP weakened the electoral appeal of the party in the early postwar period.

The controversy reached back to the Winter War of 1939-1940 with the Soviet Union. Tanner was Finland's foreign minister during these events and was therefore both vulnerable and unreceptive to demands from other Social Democrats that the circumstances of the brief war be thoroughly discussed. In 1940, K. H. Wiik, the party secretary of ten years' standing and a man dubbed "Finland's Karl Marx" by one rightist observer,[27] led the fight to lift the veil of secrecy from events surrounding the brief conflict with the USSR. Instead, in the fall of 1940, Wiik and one other SDP leader, Johan Helo, were expelled from the party and its Executive Committee in a move spearheaded by a small group supporting a program evocative of Germany's National Socialism and closely associated with Tanner. After Finland joined Germany against the USSR in 1941, Tanner publicly demanded that Wiik and his supporters be "crushed" *(on murskattava)*,[28] and six SDP members of parliament (including Wiik), plus Helsinki's city manager, were subsequently arrested, convicted of treason, and imprisoned.[29]

These measures failed, however, to eliminate opposition within the Social Democratic Party to Tanner and to his apparent conviction that German military might was invincible and that Finnish independence could be secured only through the support of Germany. As the war progressed, Mauno Pekkala and J. W. Keto—members of the SDP's Executive Committee—argued for the negotiation of a separate treaty with the USSR and for reliance on support for Finnish independence from the United Kingdom and the United States at an eventual peace conference. When the president of Finland, Risto Ryti, pledged in a June 26, 1944, letter to Hitler that neither he nor any Finnish government appointed by him would sign a separate peace treaty with the USSR, a majority of the SDP Executive Committee sought to have the party disassociate itself from this position by withdrawing from the Finnish cabinet. But Tanner, relying on support from the SDP's Parliamentary Group, blocked this move.[30]

Although President Ryti's pledge was rendered meaningless by his resignation and by Marshal Mannerheim's assumption of the duties of president on August 4, 1944 (followed quickly by the signing of an armistice with the USSR in September), the affair further exacerbated the rift within the SDP. Pekkala and others warned that the Communists—free to operate legally as a result of the armistice with the Soviet Union—would dominate the Left in forthcoming elections unless the Social Democratic Party underwent a radical transformation, including the retirement of Tanner and others most closely associated with war responsibility, and the readmission to the party of Wiik's group, which had been freed and returned to parliament.

Tanner dismissed these proposals as a bid for power by Pekkala, and the SDP Executive Committee also rejected Pekkala's subsequent call for an electoral alliance with the Communists. When the opposition announced its intention of joining an electoral coalition with the Finnish People's Democratic League irrespective of the Executive Committee's decision, Pekkala and Keto were removed from that organ, and all members favoring an electoral alliance with the Communists were expelled from the SDP. Thus, on the eve of the March 1945 election, a sizable number of Social Democrats, disillusioned with their party's wartime leadership and collaboration with right extremism, swung their support to the Communist-dominated SKDL and thereby contributed to its successful political debut.[31]

Political Plateau

Once established, the electoral strength of Finnish communism (i.e., the SKDL) has proved relatively stable. In keeping with generally observable rules of Finnish political behavior,[32] the average fluctuation in the SKDL's share of the vote in the ten postwar elections has been only 1.7 percent (see Table 1).

The explanation for this stability is fairly simple. Finns, like voters elsewhere, tend not only to remain constant in their political loyalties once party identification has been established, but also to vote as their parents do. Indeed, the proportion of Finns who vote as their parents do may run as high as 75 percent.[33] Thus, persons who voted for the SKDL in 1945 have by and large done so ever since, and their offspring have in all likelihood followed their example.

Of course, Communist electoral strength in Finland has not been as steady as the average shift of 1.7 percent from election to election would indicate. The greatest deviations from the mean occurred in 1948 and 1970, when the SKDL registered losses of unusual magnitude in a multiparty system (3.5 and 4.6 percent, respectively). In an effort to explain fluctuations in the 1950s, a number of observers have posited a direct relationship between unemployment and a vote for the SKDL.[34] For example, in examining Finland's 1951 and 1954 parliamentary elections, Erik Allardt sees a correlation between support for the SKDL and unemployment in the given voters' families during the Great Depression.[35] Other studies single out unemployment in the family as the most important determinant of a vote for the Communists in the Finnish city of Tampere in the 1958 parliamentary election. Unemployment was, to be sure, exceptionally high in the entire country on the eve of the polling, and the Communist share of total votes jumped to 23.2 percent from its level of 21.6 percent in 1954.[36]

Without question, in some instances unemployment may be a significant independent (or explanatory) variable determining Communist electoral support in Finland. However, one should be cautious about making this finding a general principle. In fact, time-series data for the years 1948-1975 (encompassing the last nine of Finland's ten postwar elections) show an *inverse* relationship between unemployment (the independent variable) and Communist votes (the dependent variable): i.e., it turns out that the higher the average unemployment recorded in the years preceding an election, the lower the vote for the SKDL.[37] This phenomenon was most evident in the 1970 election, when the SKDL suffered its sharpest decline in voter support. Although it had recently been strengthened by the addition of the 25,000-member Youth League, it captured only 16.6 percent of the vote (as compared with 21.2 percent in 1966) and dropped below the twenty-percent mark for the first time in its history. Yet before this election, Finns had experienced the worst unemployment in the country's history. As one observer commented in 1968, "The unemployment situation in our country has never been this bad before, not even during the period of the so-called Great Depression."[38] The fact that the SKDL received its biggest postwar setback in this economic setting suggests that one might do well—at least in the case of Finland—to look at something other than economics to explain changes in Communist electoral fortunes.

Reasons for the 1970 Setback

A more rewarding approach would be to focus on the question of political alternatives, which, as noted above, figured so prominently in the SKDL's success in 1945. To Finnish workers and farmers, who accounted for 81 percent and 13 percent, respectively, of SKDL supporters on the eve of the 1970 election,[39] the choices were no longer so clear-cut as they had been in 1966, or for that matter throughout most of the postwar period. Marked transformations within the Social Democratic Party and within the Finnish Communist movement as well as the emergence of a new rural political protest movement had further expanded the options open to Finland's protest voters.

Turning first to the Social Democratic Party, it would not be inaccurate to say that the SDP had gradually resolved its internal disputes and had come to present the electorate with a more united and radical posture. During the mid-1950s, it experienced a major struggle between forces led by party secretary Väinö Leskinen, who was associated with a vigorous policy of anticommunism, and those around party chairman Emil Skog. On the eve of the extraordinary SDP Congress of 1957, called in response to pressure from a number of district organizations controlled by Leskinen's forces, Skog was asked to meet with Väinö Tanner, who had reemerged into the SDP limelight after a political retirement that had been forced upon him by imprisonment for "war responsibility."[40] Tanner announced that he had agreed, at the age of seventy-six, to answer the appeal of the opposition group to run as a "harmony candidate" against an opponent acceptable to the Skog group. The result was hardly harmonious, for when Tanner triumphed by a margin of one vote, Skog and his supporters boycotted elections for the party Executive Committee and secretaryship. Soon after the 1958 parliamentary election, the new leadership of the SDP moved to expel the "rebellious" members and sections,[41] and in the spring of 1959, the Skog group organized an independent party around its fourteen members of parliament.

The disarray in the party began to abate in 1963, however, when Rafael Paasio replaced Tanner as SDP chairman. In a "programmatic speech," Paasio called for party unity and, significantly, also noted that the SDP had erred in forgetting that it was first and foremost a party of the workers.[42] The ensuing years produced substantial progress toward intraparty harmony and the successful projection of a more radical SDP image. (A major step in the latter direction was the inclusion of SKDL and SKP ministers in the cabinet formed by Paasio in 1966.)

Some evidence of the success achieved in transforming the political image of the Social Democratic Party can be seen in the responses to polls taken in 1958, 1966, and 1969, in which supporters of all Finnish parties were asked to identify their second choice among Finland's political parties.[43] In 1958, when the SDP was pursuing an essentially moderate, nonradical course and when cleavages within its ranks had weakened its appeal among the dissatisfied and unemployed, the party proved an unexpectedly strong alternative choice (selected by 26 percent of those polled) among supporters of the National Coalition Party, which is located at the right end of the Finnish political spectrum. The share of National Coalition Party supporters who saw the SDP as a viable alternative dropped to 19 percent in 1966 and only 9 percent in 1969. By contrast, in the latter year—on the eve of the 1970 election—the increasingly radical posture of the SDP had made it the first alternative choice of 51 percent of SKDL supporters (as compared with just 30 percent in 1958 and 38 percent in 1966). Clearly, the Social Democratic Party had become a more formidable political rival of the SKDL over the intervening decade.

Schism in the SKP

While the SDP seemed to be moving toward the left politically and closer to internal unity, the Finnish Communist Party was undergoing its first major schism of the postwar period. It was in the throes of a conflict over the issue of maintaining hard-line Stalinist positions on matters of doctrine and political strategy vs. seeking new ways to promote the SKP's fortunes in the Finnish political context.

In the mid-1960s, opposition to General Secretary Ville Pessi and other Stalinist leaders of the SKP began to surface in the party press.[44] A further crack in the conservative leadership of the party occurred in 1966 at the 14th SKP Congress, where Aarne Saarinen was elected party chairman, replacing the veteran Aimo Aaltonen, a man who had sought to cleanse the SKP of "revisionist bedbugs."[45] Saarinen, a relative newcomer to party ranks (having joined the SKP only in 1944), brought to the post a fresh perspective, but one that profoundly antagonized many traditionalists in the party hierarchy. He reformulated the traditional Communist concept of the "dictatorship of the proletariat" by advocating "workers' power" and a form of "democratic centralism" that placed more emphasis on "democracy" than on "centralism," and he went on record as favoring the existence of a number of different parties under socialism.[46] Moreover, under his leadership, the SKP accepted cabinet responsibility after an opposition role dating back to 1948, when the Communists rejected

K.-A. Fagerholm's offer of five portfolios in his government.[47] In 1966, SKDL Chairman Ele Alenius and two SKP members accepted portfolios in the cabinet of SDP Chairman Rafael Paasio.

Ironically, this step toward accommodation with other political forces and greater legitimacy backfired, for the SKDL and the Communists assumed governmental responsibility at a time when unemployment was high and harsh economic measures such as devaluation of the Finnmark were the rule rather than the exception. With Alenius the co-minister of finance, SKP member Leo Suonpää the co-minister of communications and public works (with special responsibility for matters related to unemployment), and SKP member Matti Koivunen the minister of social affairs, it was difficult for the Communists to dissociate themselves in the public mind from unpopular policies and circumstances. The result was a decline in acceptance of the SKDL among its traditional supporters.[48] In large part in reaction to this drop in support, the Communists decided to withdraw from the cabinet of Ahti Karjalainen a year after the 1970 parliamentary election.

Opposition to Saarinen's "reformism," or what he subsequently came to call the blue and white model for socialism (after the colors of the Finnish flag), was strongest in the conservative Communist strongholds of southern Finland and coalesced around the person of Taisto Sinisalo, vice-chairman of the SKP and member of parliament. Throughout this period (from the mid-1960s on), Sinisalo defended traditional Stalinist doctrine against Saarinen and the latter's support of innovations such as "workers' power."[49]

The rift within the SKP widened in the wake of the invasion of Czechoslovakia by Soviet troops in August 1968 and the ensuing termination of Alexander Dubček's experiment in "socialism with a human face." On the morning after the invasion, Saarinen called a meeting of the SKP Politburo, which voted to condemn the Soviet Union as an aggressor in Czechoslovakia.[50] This condemnation was later endorsed overwhelmingly (twenty-four to nine) by the SKP's Central Committee. In September, Vice-Chairman Erkki Salomaa, upholding the party's official position, termed the Soviet presence in Czechoslovakia an "occupation" (miehitys), an occurrence that had caused a deep personal crisis for many Finnish Communists. When Salomaa came under attack from Moscow, the SKDL/SKP newspaper Kansan Uutiset rose to his defense and claimed that his comments reflected the perspectives of Finnish Communists.[51] However, this view was clearly not shared by all SKP elements. Saarinen's speech to the Central Committee before its formal approval of the earlier Politburo action caused the opposition to circulate a mimeographed statement that contained a strong denunciation of his stance.[52] Subsequently, members of the opposition singled out SKP criticism of the Soviet invasion as a major cause of the party's developing internal crisis, and Saarinen agreed that events in Czechoslovakia had "very significantly" exacerbated the conflict within party ranks.[53]

The dispute finally erupted in open confrontation in April 1969, when opposition delegates to the 15th SKP Congress marched out of the conference hall and held a separate meeting to discuss the advisability of forming a new party.[54] When the opposition further refused to participate in the election of SKP officials, Arvo Aalto, a thirty-seven-year-old district secretary from northern Finland, was elected general secretary, replacing Ville Pessi, who had served in that capacity for twenty-five years and who leaned toward the opposition. The opposition began to establish a "shadow organization" throughout the country, and in August 1969 six district executive committees under the control of Sinisalo forces changed the SKP leadership with abandoning the principles of Marxism-Leninism.[55]

A formal rupture was averted, however, through the efforts of a mediation committee, established in May 1969. By the end of the year, the committee had hammered out a written agreement designed to restore some semblance of party unity, and this agreement was formally approved in early 1970 at an extraordinary SKP Congress. Under its terms, the opposition received fifteen of thirty-five Central Committee seats, six of sixteen Politburo seats, and three of eight seats in the party Secretariat. Although the agreement prevented the presentation of rival Communist slates in the parliamentary election that took place one month after the extraordinary party congress (a specter that had been raised in at least four electoral districts), it could not conceal the deep cleavage in the party. The SKDL's attractiveness as a political alternative was severely damaged, and it experienced a sharp drop in popular support and lost five seats in parliament.

In assessing their 1970 setback, Finnish Communists seemed generally aware of the foregoing factors, even if their commentaries were not so candid as Saarinen's analysis of a similar electoral defeat suffered by the Swedish Communists two years before. At that time, Saarinen had observed:

> As a Communist I naturally consider as most regrettable the defeat of our fraternal party in Sweden. But it comes as no great surprise, because within the party as well as on its fringes there exist many different

tendencies which have dissipated the party's energies, have prevented
the appearance of a common front, and have transmitted to the voters
an image of vacillation. The outcome of the election was no doubt also
influenced by the fact that the Social Democratic Party sought after its
defeat in the communal election of 1966 to strike a more radical pose on
policy questions. Many left-wing voters apparently thought it safer
and more certain to cast ballots for the Social Democrats. Obviously the
events in Czechoslovakia also had an important effect on the
electorate.[56]

In a postmortem on the 1970 Finnish election, Ele Alenius, the
SKDL's chairman, admitted that his organization had suffered from
participation in the government, from the spillover effects of the
Soviet invasion of Czechoslovakia, and from the schism within the
Finnish Communist Party. Although more noncommittal about the
changing nature of Social Democracy in Finland, Alenius did
acknowledge the growing strength of a new protest movement
(protestiliike)—the Rural Party (Suomen Maaseudun Puolue).[57] In
1970 the Rural Party campaigned on a platform mixing right-wing
bourgeois and left-wing socialist demands designed to attract swing
voters in the countryside.[58] Drawing 49 percent of its supporters from
farmers and 43 percent from workers, it evidently siphoned voters
from both the Center (Agrarian) party and the SKDL in boosting its
share of the vote from 1 percent in 1966 to 10.5 percent in 1970.[59]

Prospects

The parliamentary election of 1972 confirmed that the SKDL's
slippage with Finnish voters in 1970 was more than a transitory
phenomenon. Although the SKDL was able to regain some lost
ground in 1975 by winning 19 percent of the popular vote (see Table
1), it still has not recovered the position that it enjoyed before 1970.
This state of affairs has produced a marked erosion in the confidence
of Communist leaders.

As the present party leadership is well aware, the SKP and the
SKDL have failed to keep pace with the rapid changes in Finnish
society. Chairman Saarinen acknowledges that the SKP has lost
support among construction and factory workers in urban areas and
among the poorer people of the countryside. To help offset this trend,
he has called for a special effort to win recruits from labor's "new
strata," i.e., white-collar professionals such as nurses.[60]

Furthermore, the reduction of Soviet influence in the SKP may
have made the Communist movement more respectable among

Finland's protest voters, but this increased independence has created serious tensions within the party, which have already affected the electoral fortunes of the Finnish People's Democratic League. On the eve of the 17th SKP Congress in 1975, Saarinen conceded that the SKP had as many problems as—and perhaps even more than—it had had at any time since the mid-1960s.[61] Sinsalo's minority controls close to a majority (eight out of seventeen) of the SKP's district organizations, and in those districts under its influence, it is attempting to force parallel SKDL organizations to submit to its orders. Moreover, Sinisalo has termed the theoretical views of Ele Alenius "an anticommunist doctrine,"[62] and both the Stalinist minority and Moscow have asserted that a recent change in SKDL rules requiring all members, whether Communist or non-Communist, to accept the SKDL's program represents an effort to undermine the role of the SKP as the political vanguard of the working class and to eliminate the SKP by subordinating it to the SKDL.[63] Reflecting on these personal attacks and on an unsuccessful 1973 attempt by Sinisalo forces to unseat him as chairman of the SKDL, Alenius warned in 1975 that continued pressure could make it impossible for the SKDL to cooperate with Finnish Communists of the Stalinist variety.[64] Although such developments have unquestionably affected the popular appeal of the SKDL, in the 1975 parliamentary election it did manage to improve its showing somewhat over 1972 because of voter ennui with respect to the Rural Party, which had been so successful in 1970 at the expense of the Communists and Agrarians, and because of the Finnish electorate's perception, comparable to that on the eve of the 1958 election, of an "embourgeoisement" of the Social Democratic Party.[65]

Despite these difficulties, the SKDL remains one of the three strongest blocs in parliament, and in November 1975, against the opposition of the Stalinists, it once again entered the government. In 1978, it holds three portfolios in the cabinet presided over by Kalivi Sorsa, chairman of the Social Democrats.

This is a long way from saying, however, that the prospects for a peaceful transition to socialism, as envisioned by SKP and SKDL programmatic statements, are promising. Only three times in Finland's history have parties of the working class captured a majority of the 200 seats in Parliament (103 in 1916, 101 in 1958, and 103 in 1966), and only once have they been able to win a majority of the popular vote (51 percent in 1966). The probability of a repeat performance in terms of either seats or the popular vote is low. Furthermore, given the long history of conflict between Finnish

Communists and Social Democrats, cooperation on far-reaching solutions to major social problems will almost certainly remain an unrealized goal.

Thus, a cabinet in which members of the SKDL/SKP hold at most three or four portfolios does not herald radical change. Rather, it suggests "a compromise of compromises," as the Social Democratic prime minister called his government's program soon after Communists entered the cabinet in 1966. If the Finnish case is typical of prospects for the major nonruling Communist parties in the world, the judgment expressed by Peking in the early 1960s, i.e., that "there is no historical precedent for a parliamentary transition from capitalism to socialism,"[66] will be no less valid at the end of the 1970s.

Notes

1. V. I. Lenin, *Polnoe sobranie sochinenii* [Complete collected works], 5th ed., vol. 30 (Moscow: Izdatel'stvo politicheskoi literatury, 1962), p. 122.

2. Seymour Martin Lipset, *Political Man: The Social Bases of Politics* (Garden City, N.Y.: Doubleday, 1959), pp. 30, 32.

3. George W. Rice, "Nonruling Parties and the 'Peaceful Path,'" *Problems of Communism,* July-August 1973, 65-66.

4. For a summary view of Finnish politics, see Jaakko Nousiainen, *The Finnish Political System,* trans. by John H. Hodgson (Cambridge, Mass.: Harvard University Press, 1971), especially pp. 40-41, 180-181, and 262-265. In May 1977 a majority cabinet formed by Kalevi Sorsa, chairman of the Social Democratic Party, replaced the minority government of Center Party leader Martti Miettunen. The Center Party nonetheless still holds the most portfolios (five), including the all-important position of foreign minister.

5. See the interview with Saarinen in *Suomen Kuvalehti* (Helsinki), January 28, 1967, p. 22.

6. See *Vapaa Pohjola* (Helsinki), April 4, 1946.

7. Kuusinen's political career is outlined in two books by the present author: *Edvard Gylling ja Otto W. Kuusinen asiakirjojen valossa, 1918-1920* [A profile of Edvard Gylling and Otto W. Kuusinen through documents, 1918-1920] (Helsinki: Tammi, 1974); and *Escape to Russia: A Political Biography of Otto W. Kuusinen,* published in Swedish as *Den röde eminensen. O. W. Kuusinens*

politiska biografi (Helsinki and Stockholm: Holger Schildts and Forum, 1974) and in Finnish as *Otto Wille Kuusinen. Poliittinen elämäkerta* (Helsinki: Tammi, 1975).

8. On this point, see John H. Hodgson, "The Finnish Communist Party," *Slavic Review* March 1970, pp. 83-84; and Ele Alenius, quoted in *Helsingin Sanomat* (Helsinki), May 16, 1970. In 1975, the SKP accounted for 35-40 percent of the executive committee members at the local level and 60-70 percent at the district and national level. See *Suomen kommunistisen puolueen toiminnasta 16. ja 17. edustajakokouksen välisenä aikana* [Activity of the Finnish Communist Party between the 16th and 17th congresses] (Helsinki: Yhteistyö, 1975), p. 42.

9. See *SKP 16 edustajakokous Helsinki 31.3-2.4.-72. Päätös ja julkilausumat* [The 16th Congress of the SKP, Helsinki, March 31-April 2, 1972. Resolutions and proclamations] (Helsinki: Yhteistyö, 1972), p. 36.

10. *Helsingin Sanomat*, April 2, 1972.

11. On the reaction to the Chilean events, see Arvo Aalto and Jorma A. Hentilä in *Suomen Kuvalehti*, September 28, 1973, p. 31; and Ele Alenius in ibid., September 21, 1973, p. 7.

12. Among those who have argued that Communists are most successful where economic development and educational opportunities are limited are Seymour Martin Lipset *(Political Man*, pp. 45-46, 118-119, 125) and Charles A. Micaud ("French Political Parties: Ideological Myths and Social Realities," in *Modern Political Parties: Approaches to Comparative Politics*, ed. Sigmund Neumann [Chicago: University of Chicago Press, 1956], p. 152).

13. Thomas H. Greene, "The Communist Parties of Italy and France: A Study in Comparative Communism," *World Politics* October 1968, p. 9.

14. For a discussion of the Finnish civil war, see John H. Hodgson, *Communism in Finland: A History and Interpretation* (Princeton, N.J.: Princeton University Press, 1967), pp. 53-80; and Marvin Rintala, *Three Generations: The Extreme Right Wing in Finnish Politics* (Bloomington: Indiana University Press, 1962), pp. 7-70.

15. See *Paasikiven linja* [The Paasikivi line], vol. 1 (Porvoo: WSOY, 1956), pp. 15-16.

16. See Robert E. Lane, "Fathers and Sons: Foundations of Political Belief," *American Sociological Review* August 1959, p. 502.

17. Richard F. Hamilton, *Affluence and the French Worker in the Fourth Republic* (Princeton, N.J.: Princeton University Press, 1967), p. 285.

18. Lipset set up these descriptive categories in *Political Man*, p. 130.

19. See Marvin Rintala, *Four Finns: Political Profiles* (Berkeley and Los Angeles: University of California Press, 1969), pp. 13, 22, 37-39.

20. See Marvin Rintala, *Three Generations*, pp. 183, 193.

21. On the Lapua Movement, see ibid., pp. 164-199; and Rintala, "Finland," in *The European Right: A Historical Profile*, ed. Hans Rogger and Eugen Weber (Berkeley and Los Angeles: University of California Press, 1966), pp. 434-435.

22. Rintala discusses the IKL in his contribution to Rogger and Weber, ibid., pp. 435-441; in *Three Generations*, pp. 221-243; and in "An Image of European Politics: The People's Patriotic Movement," *Journal of Central European Affairs* October 1962, pp. 309-315.

23. On Doriot's party, see Eugen Weber, "France," in Rogger and Weber, *The European Right*, pp. 107-110.

24. See, for example, Erik Allardt, "Traditional and Emerging Radicalism" (manuscript, 1963), p. 38.

25. See note 6 above.

26. The tendency for Communist parties to register electoral gains in countries where rival Socialist parties are weak and disunited was noted by Gabriel A. Almond in his pioneering study, *The Appeals of Communism* (Princeton, N.J.: Princeton University Press, 1954), pp. 387-388. This has certainly been the case in France, where the PCF (French Communist Party) has benefited from the vertical and horizontal rifts in the Socialist Party. See, e.g., Micaud, "French Political Parties," p. 137.

27. Erkki Räikkönen, in *Kustaa Vaasa* (Helsinki), March 22, 1939, p. 37.

28. *Suomen Sosialidemokraatti* (Helsinki), July 31, 1941.

29. See Hodgson, *Communism in Finland*, pp. 181-191.

30. Ibid., pp. 196-202.

31. Ibid., pp. 202-214.

32. On the stability of Finnish voting patterns during normal times, see Tapio Koskiaho, "The Popular Vote and Parliamentary Seats by Party in the Elections of 1907-1966," in *Mitä puoluetta äänestäisin. Tietoja ja tutkimuksia puolueista, politiikasta ja vaaleista* [What party should I vote for? Information and studies about parties, politics, and elections], ed. Olavi Borg (Helsinki: Otava, 1970), p. 161; and Nousiainen, *The Finnish Political System*, pp. 40-41.

33. On the topic of generational political continuity, see V. O. Key,

Jr., *Politics, Parties, and Pressure Groups*, 4th ed. (New York: Crowell, 1958), pp. 234-235. On Finnish voting habits, see also Antti Jaakkola, "Electoral Studies and General Factors Influencing Voting Behavior," in Borg, *Mitä puoluetta äänestäisin*, p. 123; Risto Sankiaho, "Geographic Support for Finnish Parties," in ibid., p. 191; Onni Rantala, "Shifts in Voter Preference," in *Valtio ja yhteiskunta* [Government and society], vol. 16 (Vammala: Vammalan kirjapaino, 1957), pp. 72-74; Pertti Pesonen, *Valtuutus kansalta* [Mandate from the people] (Porvoo: WSOY, 1965), pp. 96-97, 106, 117, 348 (an English-language edition of Pesonen's work was published as *An Election in Finland: Party Activities and Voter Reactions* [New Haven: Yale University Press, 1968]).

34. See, for example, Erik Allardt, *Social struktur och politisk aktivitat* [Social structure and political activity] (Borgå: WSOY, 1956), p. 83; Lipset, *Political Man*, pp. 106, 248; and Erik Allardt, "Patterns of Class Conflict and Working Class Consciousness in Finnish Politics," in *Cleavages, Ideologies and Party Systems*, ed. Erik Allardt and Yrjö Littunen, Transactions of the Westermarck Society, vol. 10 (Turku, 1964), pp. 112, 114, 116-117. Allardt finds this linkage particularly striking in northern and eastern Finland. See "Finnish Communism," in *Suomen Tie* (Helsinki), no. 1, 1961, p. 5; and "Factors Explaining Variation in Strength and Changes of Strength of Political Radicalism," *Helsingin Yliopiston Sosiologian laitoksen tutkimuksia*, no. 15, 1962, p. 10.

35. Allardt, *Social struktur*, p. 84. In "Traditional and Emerging Radicalism," Allardt argues that unemployment is related positively to increases in Communist strength but has little or no bearing on the initial magnitude of that strength.

36. See Pesonen, *Valtuutus kansalta*, pp. 88-91, 95, 297, 399; and Lipset, *Political Man*, pp. 118-119, note 66.

37. The Pearson correlation coefficient (r) is -0.67. Data on unemployment in Finland came from the *Yearbook of Labour Statistics*, published annually by the International Labor Office in Geneva, and from Terho Pulkkinen, *Työttömyyden levinneisyys. Sösiaalipoliittinen tutkimus työttömyyden levinneisyydestä Suamessa vuosina 1948-1953* [Distribution of unemployment. Sociopolitical study of the distribution of unemployment in Finland in the years 1948-53] (Porvoo: WSOY, 1956), pp. 231-234.

38. See the editorial in *Uusi Suomi* (Helsinki), September 15, 1968.

39. Gallup poll results, reported in *Helsingin Sanomat*, November 23, 1969.

40. Tanner was sentenced to a five-and-one-half-year term in 1946

but was released in 1948; he was soon reelected to parliament and to the SDP Executive Committee. In 1957, Tanner was invited by the Finnish president, Urho K. Kekkonen, to try his hand at forming a cabinet, an unsuccessful effort that nonetheless gave Soviet commentators an opportunity to castigate Tanner as a reactionary tool in the hands of the Finnish bourgeoisie. See *Izvestiia*, October 26, 1957.

41. See Emil Skog, *Sosialisti ja patriotti* [A socialist and patriot] (Porvoo: WSOY, 1971), pp. 367-407; and Nousianen, *The Finnish Political System*, p. 27.

42. The full text appeared in *Kansan Lehti* (Tampere) and then in *Suomen Sosialidemokraatti;* excerpts can be found in *Uusi Suomi,* June 27, 1963.

43. See Pesonen, *An Election in Finland*, p. 141; and idem, "Dimensions of Political Cleavage in Multi-Party Systems" (Paper delivered at the 1972 Annual Meeting of the American Political Science Association), p. 15; also Gallup poll results reported in *Helsingin Sanomat*, December 5, 1969.

44. See Ilkka Hakalehto's summary in *Suomen Kuvalehti,* April 3, 1969, pp. 51, 54.

45. See *Uusi Päivä* (Turku), April 26, 1966.

46. See interview with Saarinen in *Suomen Kuvalehti,* January 28, 1967, and his comments in *Kansan Uutiset*, August 31, 1966.

47. On this episode, see the mimeographed release "Pääministeri K.-A. Fagerholmin puhe Tampereen työväentalossa 20.8.1948" [Prime Minister K.-A. Fagerholm's August 20, 1948, speech in the Tampere Workers' Building], K. D. no. 4560 (Helsinki: Valtion Tiedoituskeskus, pp. 4-5.

48. The negative impact of SKDL and SKP participation in the cabinet during 1966-1970 on SKDL voter support was revealed in various opinion polls, the results of which were discussed in an editorial in *Helsingin Sanomat,* September 24, 1972.

49. Sinisalo's views were summarized in an article appearing in ibid., February 15, 1970.

50. See the *New York Times,* September 25, 1968; *Kansan Uutiset,* August 29, 1968.

51. *Kansan Uutiset,* October 3, 1968 (quoted in *Uusi Suomi,* October 4).

52. Excerpts from the mimeographed statement were quoted in *Uusi Suomi,* October 16, 1968. The opposition continues to view Saarinen as an undesirable Finnish Dubček. See *Helsingin Sanomat,* April 15, 1973.

53. See *Helsingin Sanomat,* October 9 and 26, 1969.

54. One delegate suggested naming the new organization the Finnish Communist Workers' Party. See *Uusi Suomi,* April 8, 1969.

55. *Helsingin Sanomat,* August 29, 1969.

56. Quoted in *Uusi Suomi,* September 16, 1968. The Swedish CP polled 3.0 percent of the popular vote in the national election of 1968 (as compared with 6.4 percent in the communal elections of 1966 and 5.2 percent in the 1964 national election). See M. Donald Hancock, *Sweden: The Politics of Postindustrial Change* (Hinsdale, Ill.: Dryden Press, 1972), p. 117. Saarinen's comments, it is worth noting, came a month before the Finnish communal elections of 1968, in which SKDL support dropped 5 percentage points, presaging the setback in the 1970 national election.

57. See *Kansan Uutiset,* May 16, 1970.

58. Olavi Borg, *Suomen puolueet ja puolueohjelmat 1880-1964* [Finnish parties and party programs: 1880-1964] (Porvoo: WSOY, 1965), p. 340.

59. *Helsingin Sanomat,* November 23, 1969, and March 24, 1970.

60. *Kansan Uutiset,* June 18, 1970.

61. See *Helsingin Sanomat,* March 2, 1975.

62. See ibid., May 17, 1975.

63. "Whose 'Variant' Is This?" *Novoe vremia* (Moscow), May 2, 1975, pp. 14-15. See also Arvo Aalto, in *Kommunisti* (Helsinki), nos. 4-5, 1969, p. 140.

64. See *Suomen Kuvalehti,* May 16, 1975, p. 53.

65. On the eve of the 1975 election, only 30 percent of SKDL respondents to a Gallup poll selected the SDP as their second preference (as compared with 51 percent in 1969 and 30 percent in 1958). But 24 percent of the conservative National Coalition Party's supporters found the SDP an acceptable alternative (as compared with 9 percent in 1969 and 26 percent in 1958). See *Helsingin Sanomat,* May 5, 1974.

66. See a Chinese document published in the *New York Times,* July 5, 1963.

7
Sweden, Norway, Denmark, and Iceland: The Struggle between Nationalism and Internationalism

Trond Gilberg

For all nonruling Communist parties, the perennial dilemma of international solidarity and the need to exist within a relatively hostile political environment remains the major problem in the 1970s as it has in the past. On every major issue (and on a host of smaller ones), the party leaders must weigh the pros and cons of close relations with the major centers of international communism against the need for programs and policies with some appeal in the local environment. In West European countries specifically, the Communists must interact and compete with powerful workers' organizations operated by the Social Democrats or other variants of "reformism," and on the left, a plethora of Trotskyite, Maoist, and other radical groups provide stiff competition for whatever radical support exists in the local populations. The schism in the world communist movement in many cases reaches into the heart of the Communist parties themselves, producing pro-Soviet and pro-Chinese factions as well as "centrist" groups that attempt to establish an uneasy balance between the two quarreling factions. To compound the misery of harassed leaderships, the Communist youth organizations in these countries tend to be considerably more dogmatic in ideological terms than their parent organizations and therefore act as a further factor of divisiveness at the centers of political activity.

In addition to the problems associated with *international* communism and a *national* environment, nonruling Communist parties find themselves caught up in the web of international *state* politics. For years, West European Communist parties were largely perceived as mere agents of Moscow; despite the many undertakings of such parties to emphasize their independence from any center, the lingering doubts of West European public opinion about such a drastic transformation are resurrected in every election campaign, often with considerable results. The fact that the once "monolithic" Communist camp now is seriously split, with a severe conflict between the Soviet Union and China, has not by any means resolved the problem of public perceptions.

Furthermore, the actions of some *ruling* parties have severely hurt the efforts of the West European Communist parties (especially the Italian, French, and Scandinavian comrades) to enhance their national images. The Soviet invasion of Hungary in 1956, the Cuban missile crisis in 1962, the Warsaw Pact occupation of Czechoslovakia in 1968, and the widespread suppression of civil rights in the Soviet Union and Eastern Europe—all have tended to reduce the influence of local Communist parties outside the bloc area. It is in this context that the interests of the Soviet *state* have seriously impeded the political advancement of communism. Numerous works have shown, however, that Moscow has little intention of adjusting its foreign policy to accommodate the needs of the international movement or the needs of individual parties abroad; hence, Soviet foreign policy remains a major liability, which is likely to continue to hamper the political efforts of nonruling Communist parties in Europe.[1]

Although the behavior of Communist-ruled states has seriously weakened the domestic positions of many Communist parties in Western Europe, other factors during the 1960s and 1970s have created considerable opportunities for the left-wing organizations in this part of the world. The Vietnam war and the resultant anti-Americanism that swept through many of the countries of the region provided the Communist parties with a ready-made issue that could be used to expand popular support and to infiltrate existing mass organizations. Moreover, U.S. involvement in Southeast Asia lent some credence to Communist charges of U.S. imperialism and produced considerable consternation in normally pro-U.S. quarters —a situation that helped reduce anti-Sovietism and the general feeling of alienation from domestic communism.

During the 1960s and 1970s, too, there has been an economic and social crisis of developed capitalism, which has afforded considerable openings for left-wing radicalism. This crisis has reflected both highly tangible problems, such as the energy issue, and a psychological stocktaking of modernity. The latter has been manifest in movements such as the hippie-and-drug culture and in a "turning off" of existing society, with a subsequent drift toward guruism, mysticism, and otherworldliness. Furthermore, both the working class and the bourgeoisie in Western Europe began to question the basis of the welfare state, albeit from different premises. Working-class leaders expressed fear that increased automation and rationalization would seriously impede the position of the traditional industrial proletariat, but the rank and file of labor railed against the "bossism" of their own leaders. The middle classes increasingly felt constrained by the enveloping welfare state and its severe restrictions on personal initiative and rugged individualism. Such a general questioning of society has certainly provided new and exciting opportunities for all those who deem it their business to question the status quo and, if possible, change it.

The Nordic Communist parties in the 1970s are part and parcel of this conflicting welter of opportunities and liabilities. Their ability (or lack of such) to adjust to rapidly changing circumstances will most likely be the crucial vector of success or failure in this and coming decades.

A true assessment of the likelihood of their success must begin with an examination of the political pasts of the four parties—the Danmarks Kommunistiske Parti (Communist Party of Denmark, or DKP), the Norges Kommunistiske Parti (Norwegian Communist Party, or NKP), the Vänstrepartiet Kommunisterna (Left Party of Communists, or VPK) of Sweden, and the Altydubandalagid (People's Alliance, or AB) of Iceland—as well as those of their allies and rivals on the left of the local political spectrum. For all of these parties and movements, many of the problems and opportunities of the 1970s have been confronted at earlier stages of history, albeit in slightly different form and in somewhat different circumstances. Moreover, there is a definite sense of *déjà vu* in the policies now being promoted by the DKP, NKP, VPK, AB, and assorted other left-wing groups. As is so often the case, the legacy of history still significantly imposes itself on the contemporary struggles of Nordic leftism.

From Revolution to World War

The Danish, Norwegian, and Swedish Communist parties were established in the aftermath of World War I and the successful Russian Revolution. In all three cases, the Communists split off from the traditional Social Democratic parties, whose older leaders refused to accept the new revolutionary slogans so eagerly sponsored by the left wing of their parties and by their youth organizations. The creation of the Communist International as the "general staff of world revolution" further alienated the more revisionist leaders and drew a sharp dividing line inside each of the three Social Democratic parties. "For or against the International, *that* is the question" was one of the slogans of the Norwegian Left, and it reverberated throughout the three Scandinavian countries during those first exciting, but unsettling, years after the Great October.[2]

Political conditions in Iceland varied considerably from those in Scandinavia. The island had come under Danish rule in 1380, and nominal Danish sovereignty continued until World War II. Thus, in Iceland the force of nationalism superseded socioeconomic class cleavages, which were so important in Scandinavia; moreover, the quest for independence clearly had the effect of reducing the fortunes of left-wing groups dedicated to internationalism. Icelandic radicals remained primarily within the traditional political movements, constituting factions within them and campaigning for greater social and economic justice even though egalitarianism was well established in the population and the socioeconomic structure of the population was still rather undifferentiated because fishing and fish processing were the economic mainstays. A formal Communist party was not founded until 1930.[3]

In Denmark and Sweden, the Communist parties came into being as small left-wing offshoots of the mother party and never succeeded in winning over the majority of the socialist membership or a major share of the left-of-center electorate. These parties' dogmatism and staunch support of the Comintern and its twenty-one conditions for membership, combined with the revolutionary program promoted by the Comintern, soon ensured their relative isolation inside the labor movements and in the electorate. By the time the Executive Committee of the International (ECCI) was ready to proceed with its efforts to "bolshevize" the Communist parties of Europe in 1923, the fate of Danish and Swedish communism had been sealed for many years to come. The DKP and the SKP became sectarian movements, firmly loyal to the changing line of the Comintern but strangely out of touch with their domestic scene and with the considerable radicalism that existed in the two countries during the difficult and unstable 1920s.

To turn first to Denmark, two small groups—namely, the Independent Social Democratic Party (USDP) and the Socialist Labor Party (SAP)—split off from the Danish Social Democratic Party (DSDP) almost immediately after the Russian Revolution. In 1919, the Social Democratic Youth (SDU), which was considerably to the left of the USPD and the SAP, declared itself the Left Socialist Party of Denmark (DVSP); the following year, it amalgamated with the SAP and reconstituted itself as the Danish Communist Party (DKP).

After considerable factional infighting, the leadership of the DKP fell to Thöger Thögersen, who presided over its steady decline, among both the general electorate and the Danish working-class movement. During the 1929-1930 period, the DKP underwent several purges, which finally produced a new leadership under Askel Larsen. Larsen was to remain head of the party until World War II—indeed, far beyond.[4]

The situation in Sweden was also rather complicated. As early as 1912, a radical faction had developed in the Social Democratic Party (SAP), under the inspiration of the youth leaders Zeth Höglund and Carl Lindhagen. In 1916, at the Zimmerwald Conference, the Social Democratic Youth League, represented by Höglund and Ture Nerman, firmly adhered to V. I. Lenin's political line, although the Swedish delegates were as yet unwilling to formalize a break with the SAP. A split, however, took place in early 1917. At that time, the left-wing faction of the party and most of the Youth League were expelled from the SAP and promptly organized the Swedish Left-Socialist Party (SSV).[5]

Factionalism plagued the new party from the very beginning. Although a staunchly revolutionary wing was in the majority, there was a rather sizable group with more reformist tendencies; only opposition to the SAP kept them together. When the SSV had to decide for or against membership in the Comintern in 1919, the majority accepted such membership, but the right wing objected and in 1921 broke with the party. In 1923, this faction rejoined the SAP. The majority of the SSV constituted itself as the Swedish Communist Party (SKP) in 1921.[6]

Events were soon to demonstrate the great difficulties that the revolutionaries in the SKP had in adjusting to Leninist discipline in the Comintern. In 1924 Höglund was forced out of the leadership of the SKP because of his independent views in the International. Höglund's successor was Karl Kilbom, who accepted the Comintern's policies of limited cooperation with the Social Democrats, but when Moscow's policies changed to unmitigated hostility to the "social fascists," Kilbom balked. In 1929, the Comintern leadership was instrumental in removing Kilbom; this time, however, the majority of the SKP followed the deposed leader, while Moscow supported Hugo Sillén. There were therefore two Communist parties in Sweden until 1937, when the Kilbom faction formed the Socialist Party. The last leader of the SKP before World War II was Sven Linderot, who succeeded Sillén.[7]

Circumstances in Norway differed significantly from those in the other two Scandinavian countries. There, the left wing of the Norwegian Labor Party (DNA) had gained considerable strength during the period after the international conferences of left-wing forces at Zimmerwald and Kienthal (1915 and 1916, respectively). By 1918 they had gathered enough support to make a successful bid for the DNA leadership. The new Central Committee, elected at the Easter congress of 1918, was firmly in the hands of Martin Tranmael, a dynamic leader whose ideological views were a highly original blend of Marxism, anarcho-syndicalism, and a firm belief in the right of each party to determine its policies on the basis of national conditions. Although the Danish and Swedish parties had accepted the organizational premises of the Comintern, thus subordinating the trade unions and other mass organizations to strict control by the party, Tranmael upheld the principle of collective membership through the unions, and he never retreated from this view.[8]

With ideological and organizational principles this remote from the Leninist precepts reigning in the Comintern, it was only a matter of time before the DNA would experience conflicts with the "general staff of world revolution." At the founding congress of the Comintern in 1919, the DNA representative, who authorized Norwegian membership in the Comintern, expressed reservations about its organizational principles. In 1920, at the Second Congress and later at the congress of the German Independent Social Democratic Party (USPD) in Halle, Tranmael's views clashed with those of the ECCI, and by 1922 the rift between the DNA and the Comintern had grown to unbridgeable proportions. Open polemics then broke out between Moscow and Kristiania (Oslo). Tranmael and his close associates accused the Comintern of deviationism, especially in the execution of the united front policy that had been promulgated at the Comintern congress the previous year.[9]

The final split between the DNA and the Comintern came in late 1923. By that time, it was clear that Moscow had decided to force a split in the DNA so that a loyal Norwegian party could be established. The script worked to perfection. In November 1923, the pro-Comintern faction in the DNA broke out of the ranks at the party congress and, singing "The Internationale," marched out of the hall to constitute themselves as the NKP.[10] Norway had joined the ranks of the other Scandinavian countries, in that a relatively small faction on the left had established itself as the "real" Communist party.

As for the DNA, its flirtation with the Comintern, although earnest in terms of revolutionary commitment, was nevertheless based upon a deep misunderstanding of the Marxist-Leninist principles that reigned in Moscow. After a few years, in which the DNA's rhetoric matched that of the NKP in terms of revolutionary zeal, the party effected a reunification with the small Social Democratic Party of Norway (NSDP), which had been formed by a splinter group of DNA moderates in 1921. After 1927, the DNA joined the ranks of the large and reformist Social Democratic parties in Scandinavia—parties that were to become the dominant factors in their respective political systems to the present day.

The NKP, on the other hand, soon found its niche in the ranks of "bolshevized" parties and participated faithfully in the many twists and contortions that characterized Comintern policies during the 1920s and 1930s. In this respect, it followed the lead of the other two Scandinavian sections of the Third International as reliable, but relatively unimportant, members of the international movement.

Organizationally, the NKP, like its sister Scandinavian parties, experienced considerable turmoil. The first chairman of the newly established party was Sverre Stöstad; however, the most important leaders were Arvid Hansen and Peder Furubotn, both members of the party Secretariat. As the Comintern turned drastically against working-class cooperation in 1928, the right wing of the NKP became isolated in the party, and a massive purge followed. Arvid Hansen's group now took over the leadership of the dwindling party. But by the summer of 1931, the Comintern had decided to remove Hansen because of the growing isolation of the NKP in Norwegian politics, and Johan Egede Nissen became the new chairman. The real power in the party, however, lay in the hands of Christian Hilt, the leader of a so-called "centrist" group in the Central Committee. The last NKP leader before the German occupation was Emil Lövlien, who in the postwar years proved to be the chief "Stalinist" in the NKP (to be discussed later).[11]

As the preceding discussion suggests, the three Scandinavian Communist parties exhibited great "changeableness" during the interwar period. In the years 1921-1927/28, they firmly supported the Comintern's policy of "united fronts," but in the period 1928-1933/34 they were equally devoted to the struggle against "social fascism," which pitted Communists against Social Democrats. With no less facility, the DKP, NKP, and SKP in 1934-1939 shifted to a "popular front" line, according to which the despised Social Democrats of yesterday were now the most valuable members of the great united effort against nazism and fascism. And when Josef Stalin signed the infamous nonaggression pact with Hitler in August 1939, the three parties soon followed his general lead in their policy statements.[12]

This astonishing agility in the tactical field failed to enlist much meaningful political response in the local political environments. For the nonsocialist part of the population, no amount of Communist maneuvering could remove the stigma of "red agents" from the DKP, NKP, and the SKP; for the Social Democrats, such maneuvering and the devious Communist approach to united fronts, which allowed cooperation between parties and organizational leaders while Communist organizers ceaselessly worked at weaning the rank and file of Social Democracy away from their leaders, proved that no real cooperation was feasible. The Communist-sponsored splitting of trade unions and other mass organizations during the hard-line 1928-1933/34 period was not soon forgotten, and the grateful Social Democrats took tough countermeasures, which effectively excluded Communists from all but the most insignificant posts in the labor movement.

It is true, of course, that the degree of electoral failure of the three parties did differ. For example, although the DKP received only 0.4 percent of the total vote in 1926 and 0.2 percent in 1929, its share rose to 1.6 percent in 1935 and 2.4 percent in 1939. In contrast, the SKP's share of the total vote fell consistently, standing at 3.5 percent in 1940.[13]

Icelandic communism had a base different from that of its Scandinavian counterparts. In 1930, a left-wing dissident group of the Social Democratic Party broke away and formed a relatively loose alliance of the left in protest against the reformist policies of the mother party. This group designated itself the Communist Party of Iceland. In 1938, the Social Democrats suffered another split, and the left secessionist group joined the Communists, who promptly changed the name of their organization to the United People's Party-Socialist Party (SA-SF). The very title of this new addition to the Icelandic political landscape indicated its somewhat amorphous ideological nature, but therein also lay its strength—namely, it had an appeal beyond the usual narrow confines of the traditional Communists. In keeping with its ideological amorphousness, the SA-SF programs emphasized tangible economic measures and, above all, national independence from Denmark, a highly popular cause among Icelanders. It was this nationalistic stance that helped to propel the SA-SF into membership in the coalition government established when the island achieved formal independence in 1944 and that permitted it to remain in the government until

1947, when a change in electoral fortunes forced it to move temporarily into the opposition.[14]

Even before World War II, then, the SA-SF had managed to establish and maintain a relatively broad political base—a unique feat in Nordic communism. From the standpoint of ideological orthodoxy, the party was highly suspect; however, the realities of the domestic political scene made a blurring of its ideological outlook the only meaningful path. Such a course prevented the twin scourges of isolation from the mainstream of the local environment and of classification as an "alien agent," a label so frequently attached to the Danish, Norwegian, and Swedish parties during this period. These unique aspects of Icelandic communism were to become even more evident in the postwar era.

The onset of World War II provided the acid test of the Scandinavian Communist parties and their relationships with their respective local environments. As long as Moscow had endorsed, even promoted, the popular front policy, West European Communists could feel reasonably sure that their policies would be generally acceptable to domestic audiences, since the anti-Nazi stance of all left-wing parties found a ready echo in most sectors of public opinion. But after the USSR abandoned this policy and signed the nonaggression pact with Nazi Germany, the DKP, NKP, and the SKP joined the ranks of temporarily bewildered Communists in Western Europe. Two alternatives now lay before the Communist leaderships all over the continent, and both seemed equally unpalatable. On the one hand, the West European Communists could back the Soviet policy change, but by doing so they would almost certainly cause their local populaces to regard them once more as untrustworthy "red agents." On the other hand, they could reject the Kremlin's latest policy move, thereby committing an intolerable breach of international discipline.

Within a few days after the conclusion of the Nazi-Soviet pact on August 23, 1939, the leaderships of the three Scandinavian parties accepted the Soviet lead. When war broke out on September 1, 1939, the three parties issued almost identical statements condemning the war as a product of British and French imperialism and playing down the role of Nazi Germany.[15] Similarly, the Soviet annexation of eastern Poland was described as the long-awaited liberation of the downtrodden masses in the area.[16] The staunchly pro-Soviet stand of the parties on the Winter War between the USSR and Finland created an outcry in all of Scandinavia,[17] and there is little doubt that even the minimal public support that local communism enjoyed was rapidly vanishing. But despite such clear warnings, discipline and subservience to Moscow prevailed.

The German attack on Denmark and Norway on April 9, 1940, afforded another example of the extreme rigidity of Communist policies in this period. Although all other political parties in the two countries aside from the local Nazis went underground to continue the struggle against the occupier, the DKP and the NKP remained legal organizations for several months, and during this time they attempted to gain more influence in the mass working-class organizations while maintaining a cautious dialogue with the Germans. The SKP, watching developments in the two neighboring countries from the safe haven of neutrality, emphasized the need for "correct" relations with the new Germany. In all three countries, public opinion very nearly associated local communism with treason.[18]

With the German attack on the Soviet Union in June 1941, however, the three Scandinavian parties gained opportunities to expand their domestic influence to an unprecedented extent. Overnight the halfhearted "collaborators" changed into the most active protagonists of "decisive warfare" against the occupiers, and the DKP and NKP became major factors in the two resistance movements. This wartime experience, in turn, produced a definite shift toward more nationalistic leaderships in both parties. In the DKP, Aksel Larsen, the supreme tactician who had managed to reverse the downward tide in the party's public support in the 1930s, emerged as one of the most active figures in the underground, and in Norway, Peder Furubotn increasingly came to the fore as a superb sabotage expert who also possessed the diplomatic skills required to negotiate with the social democratic and nonsocialist elements of the resistance.[19] The strong concern with national needs espoused by both the DKP and the NKP was vindicated by the Soviet-backed decision to dissolve the Comintern in 1943.

Because the two Communist parties were among the most active anti-Nazi forces in the underground, they gained immense prestige, which was further enhanced by the enormous sacrifices and burdens carried by the USSR in the common struggle. Cooperation with the Social Democrats reached new heights, and toward the end of the war, both the DKP and the NKP launched major campaigns for final reunification of the forces of the Left.[20]

In Sweden, the early antagonism against the "red agents" turned to tolerance, even considerable support, once the attack on the Soviet Union had taken place. The SKP now became staunchly nationalistic and dedicated to the Allied cause, a popular move in a population that was pro-West, albeit neutral. In 1944, at the party congress, the SKP accepted most of the political program established by the Social Democrats (SAP) and went so far as to emphasize its commitment to the peaceful transition to socialism.[21] For a presumably revolutionary party, this program transformation, with its new emphasis on *national* policies, was a drastic departure from long-standing procedures.

Political conditions in Iceland during the war did not resemble those of any of the Scandinavian countries. True, Iceland remained uninvolved directly in the conflict; in this respect it shared the privileged position of Sweden. But there were foreign troops on Icelandic soil, and this fact eliminated the status of neutrality, a status that Stockholm so assiduously cultivated.

During the war period, however, Iceland did achieve the primary national goal of political independence. In this process, the SA-SF played an important part, which gained it considerable public support. Furthermore, its flexible ideological program, coupled with favorable conditions for radicalism arising out of the difficult economic conditions facing the newly independent state in wartime, propelled the SA-SF into the mainstream of national politics.[22]

The 1917-1945 Period: An Analytical Overview

Before we examine the interaction between the Nordic Communist parties and their local environments in the postwar era, it would seem desirable to pause briefly and try to draw up a general balance sheet for the years from 1917 to 1945. To what extent, for example, did political opportunities exist for the parties during these years? Did they take maximum advantage of the opportunities available? If not, why was this the case?

International communism, with its calls for a new and better world of solidarity, brotherhood, and peace had all the makings of at least a viable alternative to the social and political order that had gone so drastically wrong during the preceding decade; moreover, the revolutionary aspects of this doctrine held potential appeal for those who rejected the existing order but who had no clear vision of alternatives. During the 1920s, periodic inflations seriously undermined the economic viability of the lower middle class and turned many into members of the lumpenproletariat, thus rendering them susceptible to radical political programs. When the Great Depression hit Europe in the early 1930s, millions of unemployed and dislocated individuals should also have provided ready raw material for a mass revolutionary movement.

Why, then, did the Scandinavian Communists fail to capitalize on such favorable opportunities? The reasons are many and varied. First of all, Scandinavian societies, despite their many ills, were not ready to disintegrate into revolutionary turmoil. The political elites of the old order had succeeded in keeping the three countries out of World War I, and rather intelligent social legislation in subsequent years helped reduce the socioeconomic effects of the worldwide depression, which devastated Central and Western Europe. All three countries had political cultures that were basically democratic, with considerable traditions of participatory democracy. Centuries-old cultural and historical traditions stressed individualism, not collectivism, and for many, the extreme Communist emphasis on class solidarity, especially *proletarian* class solidarity, seemed a bit out of line in societies that had only recently emerged from an agrarian socioeconomic status. The atheistic aspects of Marxism-Leninism were alien to many in societies where Lutheranism was a strong cultural (as well as religious) force. There was a basic sense of decency in the relations between rulers and ruled; therefore, politics could not be played as a zero-sum game. All of these factors undoubtedly contributed greatly to the isolation of Lenin's political doctrine from the masses of the proletariat, be it industrial or agrarian.

A second major obstacle was the existence of a well-established working-class movement prior to the foundation of Communist organizations. Here the large Social Democratic parties of Denmark, Norway, and Sweden played a crucial role. These parties displayed many of the traits the Communists lacked, including a belief that society could be transformed by peaceful means rather than through bloody revolution (which was somewhat derisively reserved for other, less civilized peoples). Furthermore, the Social Democrats were nationalists at heart, although their rhetoric paid much attention to internationalism. This aspect of their platforms enabled them to deal with concrete problems of immediate concern for every worker. There was enough organizational flexibility in the DSDP, DNA, and SAP to allow for considerable local and regional autonomy in political organization; this was extremely important in populations imbued with regionalistic spirit and pride. Religion was treated as a personal affair; thus, a religious proletarian could join a leftist party or give it his vote without severe psychological dislocation. Finally, the visible elements of radicalism in all three Social Democratic parties—especially the DNA (which could not really be considered a social democratic organization until the early 1930s)—made them appealing to the genuinely radicalized masses in Scandinavia.

Third, the alien aspects of Marxism-Leninism, especially after the "bolshevization" of Communist parties in 1923-1924, and the astonishing tactical changes in line effected by the DKP, NKP, and SKP during the 1920s and 1930s gave the parties the image of mere puppets dancing on strings pulled by a foreign master. The remoteness of Russia, the general perception of the Soviet Union as backward and possessed of an alien culture, and the excesses of the Stalinist regime during the 1930s—all contributed to the failure of Communist organizational drives and electoral campaigns. Although internationalism had been popular in the Socialist parties and movements before the Russian Revolution, it had been based largely upon groups in countries with rather similar experiences, cultural backgrounds, and developmental levels. After it became clear that internationalism in the post-1917 world was to be a Soviet-controlled affair, the romantic attachment to the idea waned, and only the true believers remained as faithful followers of the Kremlin.

The 1941-1945 period was the first one in which the major handicaps discussed above did not apply, at least temporarily. The local Communists had become ardent nationalists, expending a great deal of energy and suffering many casualties in the common struggle against foreign occupation. There was considerable Communist willingness to cooperate with other political groups in the underground in Denmark and Norway, or in a broad antifascist front in neutral Sweden. The mentor of international communism, the Soviet Union, was now one of the leading forces in the anti-Nazi coalition. Indeed, without the enormous war effort on the eastern front, the defeat of Nazi Germany might well have been impossible. Thus, the Soviet Union for the first time since the Russian Revolution was perceived not as an alien force bent upon the destruction of Scandinavian and other European societies, but rather one of the main forces ensuring their survival. Large segments of Scandinavian public opinion became infatuated with romantic pro-Sovietism, a phenomenon that greatly enhanced the appeal of the local Communists.

Compared to their Scandinavian colleagues, the Icelandic Communists were remarkably successful in the 1930-1945 period. The SA-SF avoided the isolation that the DKP, NKP, and SKP experienced in their national environments and succeeded in achieving governmental participation at a time (and for a sustained period) when few other West European Communist parties had much influence. Similarly, it gained predominance in the trade unions of Iceland, a feat that the Scandinavian Communists looked upon with great envy.

The source of this success was the highly original blend of leftist radicalism and nationalism, coupled with isolationism vis-à-vis the international communist movement, that characterized the policies of the Icelandic party in these years. While alliance with Moscow cut the three Scandinavian parties off from their own environments and populaces, the very remoteness of Iceland helped promote Communist policies that were unencumbered by "foreign" elements. In contrast to the leaders of other West European parties, in which Moscow fueled constant factional struggles until only the most servile fellow travelers survived, the Icelandic Communist leaders never lost sight of their national mission, which, in their opinion, included a quest for broader leftist unity. Thus, they may have shown an ideological laxness, but their aggregative abilities were superior.

Nationalism and International Solidarity, 1945-1960

As the four Nordic parties entered the post–World War II era, they all found themselves in promising situations. The vastly enhanced stature of the DKP, NKP, and SKP in their national constituencies was dramatically illustrated by their electoral successes. In Denmark, the DKP obtained fully 12.4 percent of the total vote in the first postwar election, and in Norway the NKP received 12 percent. Both parties also had representation in the first, interim governments of national unification established in the two countries during the period between liberation and the first elections. In Sweden, the SKP polled an impressive 10.8 percent of the total vote in 1944 at the very end of the war. There was considerable Communist influence in many of the mass organizations of the labor movements in the three countries, and the fame of Communist exploits in the underground garnered sympathy far beyond the normal reaches of the DKP and the NKP. For the first time in their histories, the three parties had a real opportunity of gaining significant power in their societies. In Iceland, as already mentioned, the SA-SF participated in the first coalition government set up after the achievement of independence in 1944 and remained in the cabinet for two years after the conclusion of the war.

But at the height of their popular successes, the Nordic parties and especially the DKP, NKP, and SKP were faced with an excruciating dilemma. The successes of the Scandinavian parties in particular had been due to the staunchly nationalistic policies that they had adopted during the war and to the Soviet military victories on the eastern front; now these very victories ensured for the Kremlin a predominant position in Eastern and Central Europe and the reimposition of the hegemony of the Communist Party of the Soviet Union (CPSU) in the international communist movement. Thus the specter of overwhelming Soviet *state* influence as well as the reestablishment of the old servile relationship with Moscow was resurrected for both Communists and others in Scandinavia. In short, the DKP, NKP, and SKP now had to choose between the "national road" and international solidarity, between broadly based and relatively flexible policies, on the one hand, and ideological conformity, on the other.

In all three parties, the nationalistic policies carried out during the war had aroused some opposition from the more orthodox elements in the organization, who feared that too much cooperation with non-Communist forces would result in dangerous ideological erosion. During 1945 and 1946, when serious negotiations were carried out with a view toward close cooperation with the Social Democrats, these fears became predominant in all three parties, and the early optimism concerning working-class unity soon faded into bitter infighting on the left of the political spectrum. The Communists had no intention of giving up their organizational base and envisioned the unification process primarily as a loose confederation of groups and parties, within which they could maintain their autonomy and even engage in united front tactics vis-à-vis the Social Democrats. The latter rejected this approach and also bitterly upbraided the DKP and the NKP for early collaboration with the Nazis and quislings in their respective countries.

By late 1946 it was clear that the political systems in the Scandinavian countries had settled back into familiar, prewar molds and that unification of the working class would not take place.[23] Instead, Scandinavian communism was launched on a path of increasing isolationism, coupled with unswerving loyalty to the CPSU and to Stalin personally. This trend became even more pronounced after the middle of 1947, when Andrei Zhdanov proclaimed the two-camp view of international relations and the establishment of the Cominform. The Communist parties in Western Europe now increasingly directed their efforts to fighting the Social Democrats politically and to thwarting the creation of new Western defense organizations. In all three Scandinavian countries, the Communist parties and their front organizations assailed the Social Democrats and sought to undermine the prevailing influence of the latter in the trade unions and other mass organizations of the working class.[24] To try to forestall the emergence of new collective security arrangements, the DKP and the NKP became active, indeed leading, participants in the many peace organizations established about this time. After the formation of the North Atlantic Treaty Organization (NATO) in 1949, the Communists also promoted various movements designed to reestablish Danish and Norwegian neutrality in foreign policy. In Sweden, the emphasis was on safeguarding existing neutrality and preventing increased U.S. influence in Europe.

The results of such policies were not surprising. Up to the end of the Stalinist era, the three Communist parties suffered one setback after another, both in municipal and national elections. By the mid-1950s, they had been reduced to the insignificant political sect on the left that they had been in the 1930s. The municipal elections of 1954 in Denmark saw the DKP's share of the vote decline to 3.4 percent. In the parliamentary elections of 1957, the figure dropped to 3.1 percent, and by the 1960 parliamentary elections it stood at 1.7 percent. The NKP's slide toward insignificance had already begun in 1947, when the party polled 9.8 percent of the total vote in municipal elections. In 1949, in the second parliamentary elections after the war, its share of the vote fell to 5.8 percent; in 1953, its share fell further, to 5.1 percent. The SKP, which had fared well in the elections to the second chamber in 1946, soon found itself in the company of its fraternal parties in Scandinavia; by 1952, it could muster only 4.3 percent of the total vote in national elections.[25]

These immense problems confronting the Scandinavian parties in their domestic environments were compounded by the difficult readjustment to total CPSU domination of the international communist movement. After 1947-1948, when the Soviet party sponsored purges of "domesticists, nationalists, Titoists, cosmopolitanists, and Zionists" in all European Communist parties, the DKP, NKP, and SKP underwent major shifts in leadership. The changes were especially drastic in Norway, where Peder Furubotn, the successful wartime underground leader, was purged as a Titoist and Gestapo agent. Emil Lövlien, who had headed the NKP at one point in the 1930s, now became unquestioned party chief once again. In Sweden, Sven Linderot lost his position to Hilding Hagberg in 1953. Aksel Larsen, who had headed the DKP since the early 1930s, managed to hold on to his post, but there were considerable attrition at the next level of the DKP's national leadership and also much turnover at the regional and local levels.[26]

Although the purges and the policies of ideological and organizational rigidity reduced the Scandinavian Communist parties to insignificance in their respective local environments, the new, Stalinist leaders of these parties did ensure complete conformity with the policies and wishes of Moscow, and they thereby remained true to the only constituency they deemed worthwhile, Stalin and his lieutenants in the Kremlin. The Scandinavian Communists railed against the Social Democrats' unwillingness to cooperate in the quest for "working-class unity," against the governments formed by the Social Democrats, against the economic policies of reconstruction, and against the generally pro-Western foreign policies that they decried as total subjugation to U.S. imperialism. Conversely, they hailed the policies of the Soviet Union, in both the domestic and international spheres, as mankind's greatest contribution to peace and progress; they characterized the establishment of people's democracies in Eastern Europe as liberation; and they expressed their fond wish that their countries could soon follow the same path. Gone were the program statements of peaceful transition to socialism. Instead, the NKP and the SKP began once again to discuss the concept "dictatorship of the proletariat." The DKP's Aksel Larsen, by all accounts a much more flexible and undogmatic man than the Norwegian and Swedish Stalinists, clearly had difficulty accepting this complete subjugation to outside masters; thus, the DKP exhibited fewer of the excessive Stalinist traits found in the neighboring countries. But it gained little domestically from such policies, and in relations with Moscow, Larsen's lack of complete "synchronization" brought him much grief.[27]

The death of Stalin in 1953 sent shock waves throughout all European Communist parties, including those in Scandinavia. For some time, however, there was no appreciable change in the relationships between the DKP, NKP, and SKP, on the one hand, and the CPSU, on the other. During the first post-Stalin year, the Scandinavian parties competed with other European Communists in panegyrics to the dead leader, and the supremacy of the Soviet Union as the model for the rest of the world to emulate was never officially in doubt.

Nonetheless, there were quieter attempts at a reassessment, both of domestic policy and the relationship with Moscow. As early as the fall of 1953, the NKP issued a new party program, which discussed national political conditions while paying the usual homage to the CPSU and Stalinism. Similar program revisions also took place in Denmark and Sweden.

These cautious moves toward reassessment became a torrent of questions and growing recriminations after Nikita Khrushchev's

secret speech criticizing Stalin at the 20th CPSU Congress in February
1956 and especially after the events of the fall of 1956—notably, the
popular discontent that led to the ouster of the Stalinist leadership in
Poland and the revolt and subsequent Soviet occupation in Hungary.
These events led to the first serious crisis of international communism, from which it has never recovered. The Scandinavian
Communist press cried for explanations. Why had the fraternal
parties outside the Soviet Union been held in the dark about the
activities of the Stanlin era? How could such monstrous crimes as
those depicted by Khrushchev have taken place in the era of Soviet
socialism? The Scandinavian Communists also had serious reservations about the invasion of Hungary. From now on, the Scandinavian
quest for "national communism" was on.[28]

Nevertheless, the damage inflicted upon the parties by the
revelations about Stalin and the events in Eastern Europe was
considerable. In all three countries, many party members burned
their cards in front of the local headquarters or marched to the Soviet
embassy to tear up their tangible affiliation with local and
international communism. Mass demonstrations demanded the
termination of diplomatic relations with the Soviet Union. The
electoral fortunes of the Scandinavian Communists went from bad to
worse. In 1957, the NKP captured only 3.3 percent of the total vote in
Norway's parliamentary elections, and in 1960, the Swedish party
suffered a major setback, obtaining only 4.5 percent of the vote in the
country's national elections. In the DKP, the events of 1956 had direct
repercussions at the top of the party hierarchy. Aksel Larsen, who had
never been entirely comfortable with Stalinist policies and foreign
subjugation, voiced strong criticisms of the Soviet occupation of
Hungary and hinted broadly at his admiration for the Yugoslav road.
As a consequence, he was excluded from the Central Committee at the
DKP Congress in 1958, and was later expelled from the party
altogether. With Knud Jespersen's elevation to the chairmanship of
the party, Danish communism was, for the moment at least, securely
back in the fold of pro-Moscow servility.[29]

In the wake of 1956, then, there appeared to be a consolidation of
pro-Soviet leaderships in all three Scandinavian parties, but this
appearance was deceptive. Many voices had been raised in question of
existing policies. In Norway, Reidar Larsen, editor of the NKP party
organ *Friheten*, continued to emphasize the need to establish a
national profile for the party, and in Sweden, Carl-Henrik
Hermansson, a member of the Secretariat, became the leading
spokesman for SKP elements with similar views. After the ouster or

demotion of Aksel Larsen and his followers, the DKP never displayed the nationalistic fervor of the two other Scandinavian parties; instead, it faced serious splits and defections. Thus, as the 1950s drew to a close, Scandinavian communism found itself on a course that was to lead to a very different set of experiences in the 1960s.

Primarily because of Iceland's remoteness from the European continent, the SA-SF faced far less of a dilemma in the immediate postwar years from the USSR's enhanced position in Europe and the international communist movement than did the Scandinavian parties; moreover, its response to the dilemma differed markedly from that of the Scandinavian parties. During the Stalinist period, it maintained within its ranks a powerful coalition of Communists and Social Democrats, a coalition that refused to succumb to the Kremlin's demands of political synchronization during these years. It thus managed to stay clear of debilitating witch hunts against "Titoists," "Zionists," and "cosmopolitanists." At the same time, the Icelandic party remained essentially pragmatic in its policies, thus avoiding the shrill, Talmudic castigations of deviant "isms" that reverberated through the Communist party halls of Copenhagen, Oslo, and Stockholm. As a consequence, the party retained its predominant position in the Icelandic labor movement, notably the trade unions, after it departed from the coalition government in 1947, and still had a substantial following among the local electorate.[30]

Because the SA-SF had never been fully integrated into the Soviet-controlled network of Communist parties, the death of Stalin, though a shock, constituted much less of a political watershed than was the case elsewhere. Icelandic communism's advantageous position was dramatically demonstrated in 1956, the year when European communism in general underwent a series of wrenching jolts that sent the fortunes of every party in the international movement plummeting. During that year, the SA-SF entered into a leftist electoral alliance called Altydubandalagid (AB). (In doing so, it dropped its earlier name and henceforth referred to itself as the AB.) The superior organization of the Communist component within the AB ensured it a predominant position within the alliance (although the Communists did not manage to obtain the top post of the body, which went instead to the Social Democrat Hannibal Valdimarsson); and the electoral success of the AB in 1956 was considered primarily a Communist victory. In the aftermath of the election, the AB, with considerable SA-SF influence on its policies, joined a coalition government and stayed in it until 1958.[31]

While most of the other European Communist parties were

agonizing over the question of "national roads to socialism and communism" versus "international solidarity" raised by the Polish October and the revolt in Hungary, then, the Icelandic comrades openly opted for the former by directly participating in a coalition government. Similarly, the Icelandic Communists, preoccupied with national economic development, the conflict with Great Britain over fishing rights, and the continued presence of U.S. troops on the island as well as Icelandic membership in NATO, found the frantic Soviet efforts to reestablish hegemony in the international communist movement, so evident from 1957 to 1959-1960, strangely irrelevant. In short, throughout this entire difficult period of *international* communism, the comrades in Reykjavik succeeded in maintaining their *national* posture.[32]

It should be noted, however, that the AB, although quite successful within the national political milieu, did experience considerable internal problems after its formation. The old difficulty of maintaining a viable alliance between left-leaning Social Democrats and more orthodox Communists was exacerbated by the new formal ties. Hannibal Valdimarsson, who resigned as head of the Social Democrats and became the leader of the AB in 1956, engaged in a constant struggle up to the mid-1960s to exercise some autonomy in the face of persistent attempts by the Communists to increase their influence in the coalition; the result was considerable resentment. The SA-SF component of the AB, frustrated in its attempts to gain complete control over the alliance, even rumbled about the need to reconstitute the AB on a different, more properly conceived ideological basis. Such a change did ultimately take place in the 1960s, but until then the alliance held together and constituted a substantial force in Icelandic politics.[33]

Fragmentation of the Left, 1960-1977

In retrospect, 1960 seems to have ushered in a new phase in the histories of the Nordic Communist parties. Increasingly during the 1960s, international communism was beset by fundamental problems that reduced or removed any advantage that West European Communists may have perceived from membership in a cross-national political movement, and the internal conditions in many West European countries proved unexpectedly favorable for the development of various forms of political radicalism. As each West European Communist party wrestled with its response to this state of affairs, more and more national differences developed. By the late

1970s, any attempt to classify the nonruling Communist parties in this area in a common category is doomed to failure. Instead of attempting such a categorization, the student of West European communism can more profitably deal with the major developmental *trends* that the parties in this area of the world have experienced. For the three Scandinavian parties, these major trends have been rather similar, although their effects have differed considerably. The Icelandic Communists, on the other hand, have undergone experiences and produced policies that defy even such trend analyses. Iceland must therefore be discussed as a special case.

Of the many dramatic events influencing international communism during the last seventeen years, none has had a more profound impact than the Sino-Soviet conflict. The history of the world communist movement up to the late 1950s had revolved around the problem of national roads versus dedication to Moscow, but the 1960s and 1970s have witnessed a bitter debate between the Soviets and the Chinese as to ideological propriety, international solidarity, the preferred model of socioeconomic and political development, and the very idea of a center of communism. The allegiance of all Communists to a supranational solidarity has suffered serious, indeed probably irreparable, damage during this period. Not only has Moscow lost its position as unquestioned leader of the movement, but many have rejected the very idea of *any* central leadership of communism. Polycentrism, national roads to socialism and communism, and Eurocommunism—all have become familiar concepts in Western Europe and elsewhere, indicating the wide variety of strategies and tactics now considered appropriate for the political struggle of Communists. Since the Chinese challenge to Moscow's brand of communism is also ideological, the era of the Sino-Soviet dispute has brought unprecedented arguments about the classics of Marxist-Leninist ideology. From all of this has come a proliferation of organizations and ideologies that has made the political scene of West European leftism exceedingly complicated, even confusing, both to the voter and to the analyst.

In this organizational-ideological welter, however, one can discern two trends. One might be described as leftist fragmentation and the other as pro-Soviet fragmentation.

As regards the former, Denmark has presented the most confusing situation. In 1964, two dissident Communists—Gotfred Appel and Benito Scocozza—formed a pro-Chinese group named the Communist Labor Circle (KAK). The KAK split in 1967, when Scocozza joined a new leftist party, the Left Socialists (VS). With the splintering of the VS in the fall of 1968, another Marxist organization came into being, namely, the Communist League (Marxist-Leninist), or KFML. In 1968 a new youth organization of the Danish Left—the Communist Youth League (KUF)—was established as well. This youth group was supplemented by yet another organization—the Communist Youth (Marxist-Leninist), or KUML—in 1969. Also in 1969 the VS excluded from its ranks a youth group that constituted itself the Socialist Youth League (SUF) and affiliated with the Trotskyite Fourth International. Finally, in the same year a small group of Trotskyites formed the Revolutionary Socialists, which promptly joined the Fourth International.[34]

In Norway, the state of affairs has been nearly as complicated.[35] In 1967, part of the Norwegian Communist Youth League (NKU) broke away from the parent body and established itself as Communist Youth (KU), in sympathy with a pro-Soviet faction in the NKP. The next year, the youth organization of the Socialist People's Party made an ideological break with the parent party and adopted the political program of Maoism. This group is known as the Socialist Youth League (SUF). During 1969 and 1970, the KU and the SUF began to cooperate fairly closely for the implementation of certain programs such as worker participation in the decision-making process in industry. The SUF established itself as a formal political party in 1969 under the name Socialist Youth League (Marxist-Leninist). There also came into existence "Marxist-Leninist study groups," or *ML-gruppene*, which presumably drew together revolutionary elements from many parties and organizations, even including those that had no organizational affiliation. The *ML-gruppene* have since been formally established as the MLG. Moreover, in 1970 a number of dissidents in the NKP broke away and set up the "Marxist-Leninist Front in the NKP" (or MLF).

The year 1973, however, brought a reamalgamation of many of the groups to the left of the NKP with the founding of a new party named the Workers' Communist Party—Marxist-Leninist, or AKP (m-1). This party has its primary strength among the students and intellectuals at the nation's universities.

The Swedish Left has experienced its share of leftist schisms and factionalism as well.[36] For instance, pro-Chinese dissidents within the SKP established the Communist Workers' League of Sweden (SKA) as early as the 1950s. In the 1960s, a Maoist Communist League (Marxist-Leninist), or KFml, was founded. This group split in 1970, when one of its leaders was expelled for misappropriation of funds and thereupon set up, with the support of a fairly large number of the original KFml membership, the KFML (r)—the *r* having been added to the organization's acronym to denote the revolutionary dedication of the new body. In 1973, the KFml designated itself the Swedish Communist Party (SKP), thus assuming the appellation that the original Communist party had abandoned in 1967 in favor of Left Party of Communists (VPK). Somewhat earlier, the VPK's youth organization (VVF) had split from the parent party and had increasingly come under the influence of a pro-Chinese organization named the Marxist-Leninist League of Struggle (MLK). Furthermore, in the 1970s the Swedish Clarity League (Clarté), a student body of long standing, grew more and more Maoist in orientation. To complicate the picture to an even greater extent, the pro-VPK elements in the various youth groups reconstituted themselves as Communist Youth (KU) in 1973. Two Trotskyite groups have also appeared—the Revolutionary Marxists and the Bolshevik Group.

Until quite recently, the Icelandic Communists had forestalled the creation of Maoist splinter movements. Only in 1972 did the Communist Organization of Marxist-Leninists come into being. This organization appears to be very small and has not had the impact of the Scandinavian Maoist groups.[37]

Far more important for Icelandic communism was the split that took place within the AB in 1967.[38] In that year, Hannibal Valdimarsson ran for parliament on a personal slate in direct protest against the Communist-dominated policies of the coalition. The following year, he resigned from the alliance, which then reconstituted itself as the People's Alliance Party. As a consequence of this process, the Communists severed their organizational ties with other, affiliated groups. Ragnar Arnalds became head of the reconstituted Communist party, but the most influential members of the group have been Ludvik Josefsson and Magnus Kjartansson, who had several important posts in the coalition government in which the AB participated during 1971-1974 (more on which later). Although the breaking away of Valdimarsson and his personal followers did not amount to a leftist split per se, it did bring more ideological clarity and consistency into the AB, and for this reason the affair can definitely be considered a move of the AB to the left politically. Despite this ideological and organizational "clarification," though, the AB remained nationalistic, pragmatic, and relatively undogmatic. For example, during the years when Josefsson and Kjartansson held major positions in the coalition government, they emerged as the most outspoken supporters of Icelandic nationalism, especially with respect to the explosive issue of fishing limits and British violations of what Reykjavik defined as the Icelandic territorial zone.

This history of leftist organizational factionalism clearly shows the debilitating effects of the Sino-Soviet split on Nordic communism. The existence of a competing center of international communism has tended to undermine the claims of the DKP, NKP, VKP, and AB to represent the only really revolutionary elements in Scandinavia and Iceland. Now they find themselves decried as mere "running dogs of capitalism" and as subdivisions of Soviet imperialism—a tired and aged sect of bureaucratic leaders out of touch with political reality, unable and unwilling to provide the leadership needed in an era of increasing class struggle. For parties that pride themselves on their ideological rectitude, such charges have been extremely hard to accept, and the Communist parties continue to fight back in ideological and political terms. The civil war on the Nordic left shows no sign of abating.

Although the leftist fragmentation has mainly given rise to pro-Chinese, Maoist groups, there have been splits favoring Moscow as well. Such splits have taken place in Iceland, Norway, and Sweden, where the Communist party leaderships have refused to accept the Kremlin's efforts to enlist them in the anti-Peking front fashioned by pro-Soviet forces. In Denmark, there has been no need for the establishment of splinter groups to promote Moscow's views, for the DKP has been solidly in the hands of staunchly pro-CPSU elements in the 1960s and 1970s.

In Iceland, the "unorthodox" methods of the Communists in the AB resulted in the departure of a pro-Soviet faction from the party in the late 1960s and the founding of the Organization of Icelandic Socialists (Samtok Islenzkra Sosialista, or SIS). This body remained fairly small throughout the 1960s.[39]

It should also be noted that Hannibal Valdimarsson's group, known as the "Hannibalists," has moved even further away from its former close ties with Communist organizations, as the establishment of the Organization of Leftists and Liberals (OLL) under Valdimarsson's leadership attests. This group, whose name reflects the nature of its policies, has reduced the AB's opportunity to attract left-leaning elements of the Icelandic political spectrum.[40]

In Sweden, pro-Soviet forces around former chairman Hilding Hagberg have long predominated in the north of the country, particularly in the district of Norrbotten, where the Hagberg faction publishes the only Communist daily in the country. From the late 1960s to the mid-1970s, there were frequent skirmishes between the Hagberg group and the party leadership around C. V. Hermansson over such issues as relations with the Social Democrats and views on the international labor movement, and these disputes ultimately brought about a formal split and the creation of a new, pro-Soviet party in the spring of 1977.

In Norway, the centrist policies of NKP Chairman Reidar Larsen in 1967 produced a direct challenge by the pro-Moscow leaders around Jörgen Vogt, the former editor of the party organ, *Friheten* ("Freedom"). The effort proved unsuccessful, but although Larsen denounced the views expressed by the group, he refused to expel its members. Nevertheless, subsequent retirements reduced the group's significance until 1975, when Larsen confronted the NKP with a proposal to dismantle its organizational apparatus and join a broader left-wing party. At that point, the older, stalwart members stepped in to remove Larsen and thus stem the "slide" of the party away from ideological orthodoxy. Larsen and several of his followers, in turn, left the party.[41]

Although the emergence of Maoist splinter groups and pro-Soviet factions has sapped the strength of the Scandinavian Communist parties on one of their flanks, the formation of leftist Socialist parties in Denmark and Norway in the late 1950s and early 1960s has reduced support for the DKP and NKP on the other. The Danish Socialist People's Party (SF) was formed by Aksel Larsen, onetime DKP leader, in 1959; the Norwegian SF was established in 1961 by dissident Social Democrats. Although the electoral fortunes of the two SF parties have varied greatly in the 1960s and 1970s, they have succeeded throughout this entire period in draining off considerable support from both the Communists and Social Democrats. The Danish and Norwegian Communists have alternated between open hostility toward and wary collaboration with the SF parties. But most of the time, the DKP and NKP have felt that they were receiving less than their just due from any cooperation, and in the end the two sets of parties have remained considerably removed from each other in doctrine and practice.

Perhaps the most innovative effort to bridge the Communist-SF gulf was undertaken in Norway in the early 1970s. Before the parliamentary elections of 1973, the NKP entered into an electoral alliance with the SF and a faction of the social democratic DNA that had left the party in protest against the pro–Common Market policies of the national leadership. This alliance, entitled the Socialist Electoral Alliance (SV), succeeded in obtaining sixteen seats in the parliament, one of which was held by NKP Chairman Reidar Larsen. After the successful showing in the 1973 elections, the SF component of the SV began to press for organizational unification of the main groups inside the SV, and, somewhat surprisingly, the NKP leadership under Larsen expressed its willingness to go along. During 1974 and into 1975, Larsen's stance produced a great deal of acrimonious debate within the party. Many felt that organizational unity of the Left was the only meaningful way to deal with the fragmentation and loss of influence threatening the seemingly successful SV, but others fundamentally objected to the dismantling of the NKP organization. In the end, as has already been mentioned, the latter faction won out, and at the NKP congress in 1975 Reidar Larsen lost his position as party leader to Martin Gunnar Knudsen. The SV subsequently voted to remove the NKP from its roster, and Reidar Larsen left the NKP to become one of the leaders of the now-truncated SV. Although the NKP made rather hazy promises about electoral and policy cooperation with the SV, the debate over possible NKP amalgamation with the SV had engendered much bitterness,[42] and the wounds from that debate do not appear to be healing very rapidly.

The problems faced by the NKP in connection with its relationship to the SV have been exacerbated during the last two or three years. The SV, which had included the NKP in the electoral campaign of 1973, was reconstituted as the Sosialistisk Venstreparti (SV) after the truncated NKP left it in 1975. The new SV participated in the recent parliamentary elections (September 12, 1977), but the results were disastrous. It obtained only 4.1 percent of the total vote, as opposed to the "old" SV's 11.2 percent in 1973. The NKP all but disappeared; it obtained only 0.4 percent of the vote and was thereby bested even by the Red Electoral Alliance, which received 0.6 percent. The losses of the Norwegian Left were apparently picked up by the Social Democrats (DNA), whose share of the total vote rose from 35.2 percent in 1973 to 42.4 percent in 1977.[43]

As the foregoing discussion makes clear, organizational difficulties, fueled by a long tradition of factionalism and ideological battles, still plague the Nordic, and especially the Scandinavian, Left. The issues that underlie the schisms fall into several categories: the question of internationalism, nationalism, and polycentrism; the Sino-Soviet dispute; relations with the United States and other "imperialist elements"; membership in NATO and the European Economic Community; and relations with the non-Communist national environment. Since the positions that the Nordic Communist parties have taken on these matters help to explain their successes and failures in the recent past and will go a long way toward determining their prospects in the future, it is desirable to look at these positions in some detail.

International Issues

The debate concerning the international communist movement

has been over whether there is one center of world communism, whether there are several centers, or whether there are multiple national communisms. The many Maoist groups listed above split away from the parent parties because their members considered official party policy to be excessively submissive to the CPSU and the Kremlin's foreign and domestic policies. Similarly, the pro-Moscow factions in the AB, NKP, and VKP resented the *lack* of party commitment to the Soviet Union. Nevertheless, most members of the parent parties have remained within the official party organizations and have supported the international policies of their respective leaderships.

These official policies, however, have differed considerably. The DKP leadership under Knud Jespersen has remained a staunch supporter of the CPSU throughout the 1960s and 1970s, even in the aftermath of the invasion of Czechoslovakia, which had disastrous results for Danish leftism in the wider national electorate, at least in the short run. After some hesitation and many consultations with Moscow, Jespersen accepted the Soviet explanation that the intervention had been necessary, since socialism was directly threatened in Czechoslovakia. The DKP also has supported the CPSU position on China and Albania, has faithfully echoed the frequent calls for an international Communist party conference, and has maintained views rather similar to those of the CPSU on the Yugoslav and Romanian "deviations." In short, the DKP has been the most orthodox and faithful supporter of Moscow in the Nordic countries.[44]

Such faithful service has not been performed by the other major Communist parties. The Icelandic party has traditionally maintained an isolationist stance and has had little involvement in the broader trends of the world movement. Nevertheless, during the 1960s and 1970s the AB has spoken out repeatedly against the schisms in the movement and has expressed grave reservations about the tendency of larger parties to attempt to control the smaller ones. For example, the Soviet invasion of Czechoslovakia engendered a virtual outpouring of Icelandic denunciations, and the AB went so far as to threaten expulsion of any party member who upheld relations with the "occupying powers" and their official party organizations.[45] It has adhered to this extreme position ever since. Indeed, the Icelandic Communists have only occasionally sent observers to the congresses of other Communist parties or to regional meetings of such parties. Whenever the AB leadership comments on international affairs, it tends to quote the views of the Yugoslav and Romanian parties as appropriate. In keeping with these views, the Icelanders have refused to take sides in the Sino-Soviet dispute and on the question of

Albania, except to reiterate their stand that each party is entitled to its own policy.[46]

The NKP and the VPK have likewise officially refused to take sides in the Sino-Soviet dispute; both parties have emphasized national communism and the need for flexibility and political programs appropriate to the national context. In Sweden, the VPK since the mid-1960s has attempted to capitalize on domestic radicalism by emphasizing national policies, and in the international movement the Swedes became forceful proponents of the view that there can be no single international center and model for others to follow. The invasion of Czechoslovakia, the litmus test of communist internationalism, triggered an angry outburst from party leader Hermansson, who termed the intervention "totally unjustified" and hurried to demand that Sweden break diplomatic relations with the Soviet Union in protest.[47] The VPK leader also visited other West European party leaders to attempt to establish a "united front" of those who condemned the invasion. Such policies led to bitter ideological struggles in the VKP, as a result of which the pro-Soviet wing under Hilding Hagberg broke away and formed its own organization in the spring of 1977.

During the Larsen era (1965-1975), the NKP took much the same positions with regard to the international communist movement that the Swedish party did. Larsen also condemned the invasion of Czechoslovakia in strong terms, and has stuck to his guns on this issue since. During the decade when he was chairman of the party, the onetime editor of *Friheten* continued to emphasize the need for national communism, stressed that the Sino-Soviet dispute represented an unnecessary splitting of the leftist and progressive forces of the world, and expanded the party's ties with the Yugoslavs, Romanians, and Italians. He made highly publicized tours of China and fought off a challenge from a pro-Soviet faction in the late 1960s; during the 1970s, his so-called "centrist" policies on international communism earned him repeated attacks from Maoist factions, which ultimately split off and set up new groups and parties on the Norwegian Left.

Although Larsen lost the chairmanship of the party in 1975, his deposal was the result of controversies over domestic and organizational matters, not over the NKP position on international communism. In regard to the latter, it appears that the NKP is continuing Larsen's policy, even without the former leader on board.[48]

The Norwegian and Swedish positions on international communism are closely related to NKP and VPK views on the state policies of major Communist powers. In this sphere of concern, both parties have predictably emphasized the need for each country to determine its own foreign policy. Consequently, they roundly condemned the actions of the Soviet *state* in Czechoslovakia. Similarly, both the NKP and the VPK have emphasized the need for all European states, regardless of socioeconomic and political systems, to work out solutions of military security and economic cooperation in their *own* interests, not conforming to "big power chauvinism." Their position here is remarkably close to that of the Yugoslavs and Romanians.[49]

Despite the tendency of the Norwegian and Swedish Communists to castigate the Soviet Union occasionally for imperialistic tendencies, however, there appears to be an irreducible minimum of support for Soviet foreign policy below which even these two parties cannot or will not go. Thus, they sometimes speak of the Soviet Union in terms of its "progressive policies" and its efforts to enhance peace. Moreover, the general tone of discussion in both parties and in their major press organs is cautiously pro-Soviet. This favorable treatment of Soviet foreign policy was especially evident during the early 1970s, when Hermansson was trying to make certain accommodations to the "Stalinists" in the Norrbotten regional party in Sweden and when Larsen was battling the many Maoist challenges to his leadership of the Norwegian party.

In light of the Icelandic party's traditional emphasis on nationalism and neutrality on all major foreign policy questions, it is hardly surprising that the AB's publications show little of the cautious pro-Sovietism on matters of state foreign policy apparent in the Norwegian and Swedish Communist press. Instead, they stress the Icelandic party's opposition to U.S. influence in Iceland and Europe and its strong support for Icelandic nationalism and neutrality.[50]

The Danish Communists, predictably, have expressed warmer support for official Soviet foreign policy than have the other major Nordic Communist parties. Not only does the Danish Communist press habitually quote from *Pravda* and *Izvestia*, but its commentaries about even domestic developments in the Soviet Union tend to be highly favorable. Thus, the DKP belongs firmly in the ranks of the rather uncritical admirers of the Soviet Union.[51]

Although there has been considerable variation in the views of the Nordic Communist parties with regard to international communism and the USSR, one can detect little such differentiation when it comes to their perceptions of the "main enemy" and how to deal with that enemy. The four parties are uniformly opposed to "U.S. imperialism," to the development of "capitalist" regional organizations and "imperialist" military systems such as NATO, as well as to all other attempts to incorporate the four countries into Western cooperative efforts of any kind. By the same token, they all support various and sundry national liberation movements, any manifestation of anti-Western—especially anti-U.S.—feeling in the Third World, and "progressive" political forces in Europe and elsewhere.

In Denmark, Norway, and Iceland, the Communists' struggle against U.S. influence has been conducted as a perennial campaign against membership in NATO. In the first two countries, this campaign has been especially virulent at times when individual NATO partners have pursued policies not to the liking of large segments of the populaces of Scandinavia. Perhaps the best examples of such policies have been U.S. involvement in Vietnam and the suppression of opposition by the authoritarian "colonels' regime" (1967-1974) in Greece. The possibility of Spanish membership in NATO has served as another rallying cry against participation in the alliance; here, long-standing memories of Nazi occupation and continued abhorrence of the Franco regime have created widespread popular aversion to such a development until recently. After the 1974 revolution in Portugal, the Danish and Norwegian Communists strongly backed the Portuguese Communist Party (PCP) and accused NATO and the United States of foul play in the gradual dismantling of the PCP's influence in the country.[52] To date, however, the DKP and NKP campaigns to reestablish Danish and Norwegian neutrality through withdrawal from NATO have been unsuccessful. Moreover, there is relatively broad agreement in the two countries on the desirability of continued membership, and it appears likely that this consensus will prevail in the near future, thus making futher anti-NATO efforts unpromising.

In Iceland, the situation has been considerably different. Icelandic membership in NATO is resented by many, both because of the large U.S. presence stemming from the air base at Keflavik and because of Iceland's ongoing controversy with Great Britain, another NATO member, over fishing rights and extension of Icelandic territorial waters to protect its critical fisheries industry. Thus, the AB has managed to couple the question of membership in NATO with genuine appeals to nationalism and vital economic interests, thereby mounting a most effective campaign. As a consequence, Iceland during the 1970s has renegotiated its diffuse arrangement with the United States (though the United States made some concessions, the air base remains intact), and it has waged the so-called cod war against Great Britain, which has severely strained the relations between these two NATO members.[53] Nevertheless, Iceland has remained a member of the NATO alliance, despite many threats to the contrary, and seems likely to continue to do so in the near future.

For the VPK, the question of participation in regional defense organizations does not arise, for as a neutral country Sweden does not maintain any special relationship with NATO. Therefore, the Swedish Communists have concentrated on agitation for continued neutrality, coupling their arguments on this point with charges that Swedish capitalism effectively aligns the presumably neutral country with "Western imperialist interests."[54] All in all, however, this issue is not one on which they can make a lot of political capital in Sweden.

The development of the EEC as a major economic (and potentially political) regional organization provided the Nordic Communists with a highly exploitable political issue in the early 1970s. During these years, the governments of Denmark and Norway applied for full membership in the EEC, while Iceland and Sweden attempted to negotiate special trade agreements with the EEC. The four Communist parties in these countries uniformly opposed membership or any other association with the regional organization. In all cases, the EEC was described as an ultracapitalistic organization dominated by the big countries, especially West Germany (still something of a bogeyman, particularly in Denmark and Norway, because of the memories of World War II), and claims were made that membership or other association would be disastrous to the continued existence of a national culture. It was also argued that involvement in the EEC would be highly detrimental to the interests of *all* wage earners as well as fishermen, farmers, and small industrialists. Finally, the proposition was often advanced that Nordic peoples should not be directly associated with others whose democratic credentials were less solid (a reference both to the Germans and to the Italians and other "Mediterranean" peoples).[55]

The issue of EEC membership or association had all the ingredients necessary to draw together large numbers of individuals not necessarily directly associated with Communist organizations. Intertwined in it were important elements of nationalism, even chauvinism; furthermore, persons not normally associated with left-wing political causes had very tangible economic interests at stake. It was possible, too, to associate EEC membership with fears of undue influence from a resurrected Germany. Insofar as the United States lent tacit support to the expansion of the organization, the fairly substantial amount of anti-Americanism displayed by the Nordic peoples at this time (to be discussed later) could also be brought into play.

In the end, the campaigns were rather unsuccessful in Denmark, Iceland, and Sweden. Denmark became a full member of the EEC, and the other two countries negotiated certain trade agreements with it. Nonetheless, the issue did allow the three Communist parties to broaden their appeal beyond their normal confines in the political spectrum, and it appears that this advantage is still of considerable importance for the three parties in terms of public support.

The most successful anti-EEC campaign was carried out in Norway. Here, very special conditions set the stage for one of the most interesting political developments in postwar Scandinavian history.[56] Because of the special economic circumstances in Norway, a great many Norwegians felt that their economic livelihood would be threatened by membership in the EEC; in this category could be found most of the farming class, the fishermen of the coastal districts, and many small industrialists. As a result of both ideological alienation and cultural separatism, significant elements of the Norwegian working class, including much of the rank and file of the trade union organization (LO), also rejected the proposal to join the EEC. Conversely, the bigger industrialists, the banking interests, and the top leadership of the Social Democratic Party (DNA) as well as the Conservatives consistently favored EEC membership.

Thus, the coalition against membership included the most disparate political elements, from staunchly conservative and nationalistic farmers through parts of the urban and rural intelligentsia to the extreme left wing of Communists, Maoists, and Trotskyites; it also embraced a sizable segment of the DNA and the LO. The NKP became one of the most active, albeit not the most important, elements in the coalition, and in the process elaborated a nationalistic, even to some extent chauvinistic, program. This was the issue that was to prove to the Norwegian public that the NKP was not a lackey of a foreign power, but rather a staunch defender of national interests, be they political, economic, or cultural.

The anti-EEC effort proved spectacularly successful. An "advisory" referendum, called to sound public opinion on the issue, rejected the idea of membership by a margin of 55 percent to 45 percent. The NKP hailed this outcome as an endorsement of its policies and confidently predicted a great future for its national policy.[57] However, such was not to be. The success of the anti-EEC coalition stemmed from the fact that the coalition had support from elements that were far from socialist—let alone communist—elements that had nothing in common with the NKP or other leftist elements aside from the Common Market issue. Once that issue had been resolved to their satisfaction, the NKP appeared destined to find itself once more in relative isolation.

The public uproar over Norwegian membership in the EEC does seem to have had one at least temporary effect on the electorate, namely, to push public opinion somewhat to the left. This was evident from the relative success of the SV (the leftist electoral alliance) in the 1973 parliamentary elections. Furthermore, the rebellion of much of the rank and file of organized labor against the LO leadership on the EEC issue opened up further possibilities for Communist infiltration of the labor movement. The long-run effect of this state of affairs remains to be seen.

Another issue that provided Communists everywhere with a ready-made choice to expand their political influence beyond the ordinary reaches of leftist circles was the U.S. involvement in Vietnam from the mid-1960s on. This involvement became intensely unpopular with large segments of Nordic (indeed European) public opinion. Here again, most of the necessary ingredients for a potential mass movement were present. The issue engendered a sense of outrage at the United States for pitting its might as a global power against a small, seemingly genuine liberation movement. Furthermore, there was a great deal of romanticism about the elusive North Vietnamese jungle fighters and their ability to thwart the sledgehammer approach of the Americans.

The Nordic Communists, especially the DKP, NKP, and VPK, attempted to capitalize on this issue by becoming major participants in—indeed, initiators of—numerous broad anti-American "Vietnam movements." But their Vietnam campaigns proved considerably less successful than the effort to keep Norway out of the EEC. In all the Scandinavian countries, the main Communist parties had stiff competition in the "Vietnam movements" that sprang up during the 1960s. To the left were the Maoist groups. They were highly active and managed to obtain important posts in many of the mass organizations. To the right were the Scandinavian Social Democrats. They also took a strong interest in the issue and gained control of a considerable number of cross-party groups and action committees. Since the Social Democrats held governmental power in the three Scandinavian countries for substantial periods during the 1960s, they could bring more clout to the Vietnam committees than could the Communists or any other leftist organization. In the end, the three Scandinavian Communist parties found themselves isolated once again, criticized from the left for insufficient revolutionary vigilance against U.S. imperialism and outmuscled on the right by the powerful Social Democrats.

National Environment Issues

During the 1960s and 1970s, the Nordic Communists made fundamental decisions on a number of specific problems of strategy and tactics. How should political power be achieved—through "mass action" or electoral victories? How should Communist parties relate to other political organizations in a pluralistic society? Should they cooperate with them or ostracize them? If the former, what shape should cooperation take—united fronts from above, united fronts from below, "action unity"? What attitude should Communist parties adopt toward the non-Communist Left—one of hostility or of cooperation? If the latter, what form should cooperation take—agreements on issues on a case-by-case basis or a more formalized arrangement, including possible organizational unification? How should Communist parties deal with national culture—reject it, as a disciplined member of the *international* system of communism, or defend it, as a *national* political party dedicated to the preservation of the "progressive" elements of the cultural heritage?

Each of the four parties has clearly opted for the status of a national political party dedicated to a "national road" to socialism and communism. Each has participated actively in elections at the national, regional, and local levels and, when elected, has attempted to use the democratic political process for maximum benefit for their detailed and pragmatic political programs. At the same time, all four have become major spokesmen for nationalism, Nordic cooperation, and isolation from the wider European political system, as evidenced by the anti-NATO and anti-EEC campaigns.[58] The historical context of national development, the traditions of democracy and civil rights, and pride in the political and socioeconomic achievements of four small countries in the frozen North have also figured prominently in the parties' political platforms over the last eighteen years. On this basis, the parties have in certain cases launched political cooperation with conservative forces (e.g., the anti-EEC campaign in Norway), while at other times they have attempted to validate their revolutionary credentials with the extreme Left by sponsoring various campaigns against the Social Democrats and the SF parties of Denmark and Norway. In day-to-day politics, the DKP, NKP, VPK, and AB have emphasized the need to reduce the "stranglehold" of multinational concerns on the local economy, have pushed for a more "equitable" tax system, have stressed increased worker participation in industrial decision making, and have sponsored schemes designed to enhance nationalization of large plants and the main banks. On highly emotional issues such as the expansion of Icelandic and Norwegian territorial waters, the AB and the NKP (as well as the Norwegian SV) have endorsed the extension of such limits as squarely in "the national interest," thereby gaining broader public support. In the debate over governmental control over oil exploration and extraction in the North Sea, the NKP has taken an extreme nationalistic line, even in the generally nationalistic Norwegian discussion of the issue. All in all, the four parties have produced rather similar policies in their quest for a new image of national responsibility.[59]

The biggest problems for the Nordic Communists have stemmed from the proliferation of political organizations on the left of the national political spectrums. Once again, the approaches of the four parties to this question have had certain similarities. In almost all cases, the parties have rejected the splinter groups to their left as "sandbox radicals," "extremists," or victims of "left-wing infantilism." Since most of the leftist organizations have castigated the local Communist parties as "state capitalists" or "lackeys of Soviet imperialism," the Communist parties had little choice but to respond in like manner, and the result has by and large been an acrimonious debate among the Left, which can only enhance the Left's reputation as irresponsible and starry-eyed dogmatists. As already noted, however, the Communists in Iceland avoided a major challenge from the left until very recently; hence, the ideological debate there has been much less acrimonious. In any case, the ideological charges and countercharges seemed strangely unreal in the traditionally pragmatic Nordic political systems.

Although the Nordic Communist parties have reacted in a rather uniform manner to the leftist challenge, their responses to the problems posed by powerful parties and organizations to their immediate right have varied. In Sweden, the somewhat declining fortunes of the Social Democrats (SAP) provided the VPK with the opportunity to play power politics during the 1970-1976 period insofar as Communist support was necessary for the continuation of a SAP government. Thus the Swedish party could extend its political influence considerably beyond its existing popular support. However, the defeat of the SAP by a center-right coalition in the 1976 parliamentary elections altered the situation radically, and the split of the VPK in the spring of 1977 raises serious doubts about whether the rump party will again be able to play a balancing role in parliament in the foreseeable future.[60]

In Denmark and Norway, the DKP and NKP have had to contend with both the Social Democrats and the SFs. Their initial reaction to the establishment of the Danish and Norwegian SFs was rejection: they held that the working class needed unification, not fragmentation, and they voiced fear that the new parties, though ostensibly dedicated to socialism, would turn out to be nothing but "the left wing of the bourgeoisie." This rather sharp rhetoric was based on the assumption that the SFs would make serious inroads into the right wings of the DKP and the NKP, thereby further isolating the latter two parties. That assumption turned out to be well founded.

Once their initial dismay had subsided, however, the Danish and Norwegian Communists took a more pragmatic approach to the Socialist People's parties. In Denmark, although the formation of the Left Socialists (VS) in 1968 further hampered the DKP's chances of registering electoral gains, by 1973 the DKP, fighting both the SF and the VS, polled enough votes to get six seats in parliament, largely at the expense of the SF. The NKP, although often disagreeing with the local Socialist People's Party, also established electoral alliances with it. Thus, in the 1971 municipal elections, there was limited NKP-SF cooperation, and in the 1973 parliamentary elections, both parties participated in the electoral alliance of the Left—the SV—with good results. Throughout 1974 and 1975, as has already been mentioned, the NKP toyed with the idea of dissolving its organization and merging with the SV, but the party congress of 1975 decided against such a move. In the wake of this decision, Reidar Larsen, who had headed the NKP until the 1975 congress, resigned his NKP membership and became one of the leading figures of the SV.[61]

Throughout the 1960s and 1970s, then, the Scandinavian Communist parties have striven mightily to enhance their images as national and radical parties, as entities dedicated to social justice, individual rights, democracy, and national independence. To this end, they have talked a great deal about the need for unity of the Left. But when the opportunity of achieving some increment of unity has arisen (as it did in Norway in 1974 and 1975), they have shied away from the final, decisive step and have opted for continued existence as a separate unit, even though this decision might mean continued political isolation.

Even the VPK, long a symbol of the success of the more "open" Communist policies during the last two decades in Scandinavia, has suffered several setbacks on this issue. First of all, C. H. Hermansson, who had drawn the ire of the more orthodox party faction in the Norrbotten district, felt compelled to make concessions to this group in the early 1970s, and the ensuing policies tended to make the VPK less palatable to the Swedish electorate than had previously been the case. When Hermansson stepped down as party leader in 1975, to be succeeded by Lars Währner, the controversy became sharper than ever. In the spring of 1977, the long-standing feud between the "nationalistic" leaders of the VPK and the "Stalinists" of the Norrbotten area resulted in a formal split in the VPK. The new party that resulted from this split is called the Workers' Communist Party (APK) and is headed by Rolf Hagel. Hilding Hagberg, the former leader of the Communist party, was instrumental in forcing through the split, and his son, Harry Hagberg, edits the only Swedish Communist daily, the *Norrskensflamman*.[62]

The split in the VPK appears to stem almost entirely from disagreements about international communism and relations with the CPSU. As we have already observed, these go back to the time of the Soviet invasion of Czechoslovakia in 1968, and the recent break represents a logical conclusion to the protracted struggle that has raged since then. It leaves Sweden with four parties claiming to be "the real Communists," thus exacerbating the problems of Swedish leftism in general.

It is too early to gauge the relative strengths of the VPK and the new APK. The VPK undoubtedly kept control over the bulk of the membership, but the APK's strength lies in the discipline and regional concentration of its support (the province of Norrbotten and the city of Gothenburg). The APK seems likely to play a considerable role inside the Swedish Left.

Unlike its Scandinavian counterparts, the AB in Iceland has enjoyed predominance in the country's Left. At the same time, it has also shown a great deal of skill in fashioning policies with broad national appeal and in cooperating not only with other leftist elements, such as the "Hannibalists," but also with nonsocialist parties, e.g., the Progressives. In regard to policies, the AB has struggled hard to raise the standard of living in the face of a debilitating inflation; this position has been quite popular with most Icelanders, especially the organized working class. Other practical measures with considerable attractiveness to the general public have included programs to expand the offerings of the welfare state to *all* citizens regardless of political views and the campaign to maintain the proud traditions of Icelandic culture in the face of "Americanization" and other forms of Western pop culture.[63] These policies have, in turn, facilitated collaboration with forces to the right of the party on the Icelandic political scene. Indeed, the AB once again participated in a coalition government in 1971-1974. Out of this kind of political collaboration, the Icelandic Communists have gained a reputation for sobriety and responsible political behavior, characteristics seldom ascribed to their colleagues in Scandinavia.

Influence

During the 1960s and 1970s, the confusing organizational splits and mergers, resplits and remergers have tended to limit the appeal of the Nordic Communist parties to their respective national electorates, and the Maoist challenge on the left has undermined their claims to be the sole representatives of the revolutionary forces of the Nordic countries. At the same time, the opportunities open to protest parties on the national political scene have multiplied. Scandinavian Social Democracy has exhibited a general malaise, there has been a polarization of political life—especially in Denmark, Norway, and Sweden—and the electorate has displayed a growing fragmentation and an increased willingness to desert old allegiances in search of new views and policies. Moreover, the general reassessment of the welfare state that appears to be now under way in Scandinavia and Iceland has brought on a period of political instability, a situation potentially beneficial to those who attack the status quo. Finally, anti-Americanism and distrust of the regional arrangements in Europe, particularly the EEC, have made neutralism and a benevolent attitude toward the Soviet Union less abhorrent to many than was the case during the cold war years.

How have the Nordic Communists fared under such circumstances? Tables 1 and 2 demonstrate the difficulties and successes that they have encountered in trying to build mass support. Table 1 traces the electoral fortunes of the DKP, NKP, VPK, AB, and their political competitors in the Nordic Left since World War II; Table 2 presents figures on party memberships during the 1967-1977 decade.

As Table 1 indicates, the assorted Communist parties in Scandinavia have not been able to garner significant electoral strength; consequently, only in special cases—as in Sweden during much of the 1970s, when the VPK provided the necessary margin of support for the Social Democrats in parliament—have any of the parties enjoyed importance in the national political context. Moreover, the electoral clout of the parties has tended to decrease in

Table 1: Electoral Strength of the Nordic Left in Parliamentary Elections, 1944–1976/77

(in percent of total vote)

A. Denmark

Year	Social Democrats[a]	Comm.[b]	SF[c]	VS[d]
1945	32	--	--	--
1947	40	--	--	--
1950	39	--	--	--
1953 (April)	40	--	--	--
1953 (Sept.)	41	--	--	--
1957	39.4	3.1	--	--
1960	42.1	1.1	6.1	--
1964	41.9	1.2	5.8	--
1966	38.2	0.8	10.9	--
1968	34.2	1.0	6.1	--
1971	37.3	1.4	9.1	--
1973	25.6	3.6	6.0	--
1975	29.9	4.2	5.0	2.1
1977	37.1	3.7	3.9	2.7

Table 1 (Cont.)

B. Norway

Year	DNA[e]	NKP[f]	SF[g]	SV[h]	Red El. Alliance[i]
1945	40.7	11.8	--	--	--
1949	45.4	5.8	--	--	--
1953	46.4	5.1	--	--	--
1957	48.1	3.3	--	--	--
1961	46.5	2.9	2.4	--	--
1965	43.0	1.4	6.0	--	--
1969	46.4	1.0	3.4	--	--
1973	35.2	--	--	11.2	0.04
1977	42.4	0.4	--	4.1	0.6

C. Sweden

Year	Soc. Dem.[j]	VPK[k]	SKP[l]	KFML(r)[m]
1944	46.6	10.3	--	--
1948	46.1	6.3	--	--
1952	46.1	4.3	--	--
1956	44.6	5.0	--	--
1960	47.8	4.5	--	--
1964	47.3	5.2	--	--
1968	50.1	3.0	--	--
1970	45.3	4.8	--	--
1973	43.6	5.3	0.4	0.2
1976	42.7	4.8	0.3	--

Year	Hannibalists[n]	SIS[o]	People's Alliance[p]	Soc. Dem.[q]
1963	--	--	16.0	14.2
1966	--	--	17.6	15.7
1971	9.0	--	17.1	10.5
1974	4.3	--	18.3	9.3

[a]*Socialdemokratiet* (Social Democrats)
[b]*Danmarks Kommunistiske Parti* (Denmark's Communist Party)
[c]*Socialistisk Folkeparti* (Socialist People's Party)
[d]*Venstresocialisterne* (Left Socialists)
[e]*Det Norske Arbeiderparti* (The Norwegian Labor Party)
[f]*Norges Kommunistiske Parti* (The Norwegian Communist Party)
[g]*Sosialistisk Folkeparti* (Socialist People's Party)
[h]*Sosialistisk Valgallianse* (Socialist Electoral Alliance); in 1977, *Sosialistisk Venstre-Parti* (Socialist Left Party)
[i]*Röd Valgallianse* (Red Electoral Alliance)
[j]*Arbetarepartiet-Socialdemokraterna* (Social Democrats)
[k]*Vänsterpartiet Kommunisterna* (Left Party of Communists)
[l]*Sveriges Kommunistiska Parti* (Communist Party of Sweden)
[m]*Kommunistiska Forbundet Marxist-Leninisterna (Revolutionärerna)*--(Marxist-Leninist Revolutionaries)
[n]*Samtök Frjalslyndra og Vinstri Manna* (Union of Liberals and Leftists)
[o]*Samtök Islenzkra Sosialista* (Organization of Icelandic Socialists)
[p]*Althydubandalagid* (People's Alliance Party)
[q]*Althyduflokkurin* (Social Democratic Party)

SOURCES: *Statistical Yearbook of Denmark*, selected years; *Statistical Yearbook of Norway*, selected years; *Statistical Yearbook of Sweden*, selected years; *Yearbook on International Communist Affairs*, Stanford, Cal., Hoover Institution Press, selected years; and *Yearbook of Nordic Statistics*, Stockholm, the Nordic Council, 1974.

recent years because of the fragmentation of Scandinavian communism. The public appears in part to look upon Communists as hopeless splitters and dogmatists and in part to be bewildered by, and unable to keep track of, the organizational changes.

The Icelandic party, in contrast, has demonstrated its ability to transcend narrow ideological and organizational boundaries. Indeed, its very form, described officially as an alliance of leftist forces on a Marxist basis, testifies to its broad base of support. The AB has captured between 15 and 20 percent of the total national vote for a considerable period of time, and it is one of the larger parties in the parliament (Allting). Clearly, large segments of the population see it as a respectable and responsible party.

There are major discrepancies between membership claims made by party spokesmen and membership estimates made by others, but as the figures in Table 2 demonstrate, the sizes of the parties vary greatly. In all cases, however, the ratio of members to total population of the country is low. This state of affairs is not inconsistent with Marxist-Leninist ideology, which emphasizes the elite aspect of party membership. Of course, the figures for the revolutionary Left as a whole would run somewhat larger, since many groups to the left of the Communists have come into being since the mid-1960s; nevertheless, the Maoist splinter groups can at best boast memberships in the hundreds. It should also be noted that the recent split of the VPK has undoubtedly had some effect on the size of its membership and that of Sweden's revolutionary Left as a whole, but no reliable figures are yet available from which to gauge the impact of this development.

As for influence in the labor movement, there is also a sharp distinction between the Scandinavian Communist parties on the one hand and the Icelandic Communist party on the other. In each of the Scandinavian countries, the national council (LO) of the trade unions and most of the national unions are securely in the hands of the Social Democrats. Communists control a few locals, primarily on the waterfront, in construction and metal working, and among forestry workers. Thus, Communist strength in the unions is, on the whole, negligible. The main competition for the Social Democrats comes from other left-wing parties. In Norway, for example, the AKP(m-l) has some support in several large unions and important locals.[64]

The AB has been the predominant influence in the Icelandic trade union federation (ASI) for years, and a Communist, Bjorn Jonsson, has headed the federation since 1973.[65] In addition, Communists

Table 2: Membership in Nordic Communist Parties

	Membership	Percent of Total Pop.
Denmark		
1967	6,000	0.13
1968	6,000	0.13
1970	6,000	0.12
1971	5,000	0.10
1973	5,000–7,000	0.10/0.14
1975	8,000	0.16
1977	7,500–8,000	0.15/0.16
Iceland		
1967	1,000	0.5
1968	1,000	0.5
1970	1,000	0.49
1971	1,000	0.49
1973	2,000–2,500	0.95/1.19
1975	2,500	1.15
1977	2,200	1.00

Table 2 (cont.)

Norway

Year		
1967	2,000–3,000	0.05/0.08
1968	2,000–3,000	0.05/0.08
1970	2,000–3,000	0.05/0.08
1971	2,000	0.05
1973	2,500	0.06
1975	2,500–5,000	0.06/0.13
1977	2,500	0.07

Sweden

Year		
1967	29,000	0.37
1968	29,000	0.37
1970	24,000	0.30
1971	17,000	0.21
1973	17,000	0.21
1975	17,000	0.21
1977	17,000	0.2

SOURCES: *Yearbook on International Communist Affairs*, Stanford, Cal., Hoover Institution Press, selected years; Central Intelligence Agency, *National Basic Intelligence Factbook, January 1977*; national statistical yearbooks, selected years.

control the most important locals, such as the General Workers' Union of Reykjavik.

It should also be reiterated that the Scandinavian Communists have failed to gain sway over the many mass movements that have developed in Denmark, Norway, and Sweden since the beginning of the 1960s. Although the NKP did manage to obtain significant influence in the movement against Norwegian membership in the EEC, its success in this undertaking stemmed largely from the considerable hostility to EEC membership among the rank and file of the social democratic DNA; moreover, the NKP derived few lasting benefits from its role in this movement.

The Future

In sum, then, the Scandinavian Communists have failed to achieve great influence in their respective national political systems and thus have failed to accomplish their alleged mission of establishing socialism; although the Icelandic Communists have not attained the latter goal, they have succeeded in gaining a position where they can make their weight felt on the political scene. But what are their prospects in the years ahead?

To answer this question, one must begin with a brief analysis of why the Nordic Communists have not managed to profit more tangibly and more lastingly from the opportunities that have confronted them. In the case of the Scandinavian countries, our discussion has underlined the debilitating effects of ideological and organizational splits, ideological rigidity, the stigma of foreign connections, and the competition from other left-of-center groups. All these things clearly played a major role in isolating the DKP, NKP, and VPK. However, the fundamental explanation may lie elsewhere—namely, in the fact that Scandinavian societies have on the whole managed to combine humaneness and economic soundness with long-standing traditions of political democracy. The Scandinavian countries have long been seen as models of political democracy, in which a common commitment to the rules of the democratic game, with universal respect for the institutions of the state and the localities, bridges the many cleavages typical of any modern society. In all three countries, the bureaucracy has the reputation of being efficient and incorruptible, and citizens generally accept a degree of state interference in their lives that the populace in, for example, the United States might consider intolerable—primarily because most Scandinavians have a high level of trust in appointed and elected officials and hence refuse to look upon politics as a zero-sum game. Scandinavia's welfare-state social programs have been held up as the envy of the world and have clearly produced considerable satisfaction among large segments of society during most of the postwar period. The economic policies of all three countries have created highly developed industrial societies with some of the highest living standards in the world. In each country, the relative homogeneity of the local population has ensured that ethnic and racial conflict are minimal. Societies with such characteristics are not generally prone to radicalism. Rather, they tend toward political moderation and stability.

Despite these various handicaps, of course, left-wing forces in Scandinavia have enjoyed a modest upsurge since the mid-1960s. Several factors help account for this trend. As has already been mentioned, anti-Americanism growing out of the Vietnam war, and substantial opposition to membership in the Common Market contributed significantly to the revival. The decisive stands of the NKP and the VPK against Soviet policies and "proletarian internationalism" as defined in Moscow may also have had a beneficial effect in Norway and Sweden. But the most important influences have clearly been the problems that the Social Democratic parties of Scandinavia have experienced in recent years and the "crisis of confidence" in the welfare state among the populaces of the area.

Since the mid-1960s, the Scandinavian Social Democratic parties have been caught in a classic dilemma. Although they began as class-based groups with a definite organizational base and body of support, their advent to power confronted them with the need to produce policies relevant to all of society, not just to one class. By the 1950s, therefore, they were seeking to establish themselves as "people's parties," with appeal to elements beyond the industrial proletariat and rural smallholders. This policy brought about a certain erosion of the traditional support of these parties and a splitting away of leftist elements. The Danish and Norwegian SF parties, to be sure, benefited the most from this development, but the local Communists made some gains as well. More important to the fortunes of the Communists was the reaction of the Social Democrats to this decline of their support on the left. The Social Democrats rushed (somewhat frantically) to reaffirm their commitment to "proper" leftist policies, which made Communist positions seem more "mainstream" than they had previously and reduced the stigma that many persons had perceived in extending electoral support to them.

During this same period, a general reevaluation of the welfare state has been going on in the Scandinavian countries. Many individuals have increasingly considered the extensive system of regulations, taxes, and other monetary contributions necessary to maintain the solvency of the welfare state to be excessive, and it seems clear that these countries may have reached the "taxable limit" of their populations, beyond which public support will dwindle or in fact turn into political rebellion. One indication of this has been the relative success of the "tax denial party" established in Denmark in the early 1970s under the leadership of Mogens Glistrup.[66] There has also been growing opposition to the bureaucratization of life, to the subjection of larger and larger areas of human activity to regulations and restrictions, albeit of a benevolent kind. One example was the formation of a Norwegian nationalist party, the ALP, dedicated to the dismantling of the state bureaucracy and to a return to the "old Norse way" of rugged individualism.[67] Any questioning of the existing system always provides openings for those who would like to change that system; hence, the Scandinavian Communists have profited to some extent from the discontent.

That these various factors will offset the disabilities under which the Scandinavian Communists have labored for many years and afford them opportunities for major new advances, however, remains highly doubtful. The impact of some—for example, U.S. involvement in Vietnam and the EEC issue—has already faded. Perhaps most critical, the current malaise in Scandinavian societies has developed as a result of middle-class concerns and a demand for reversion to a less collectivist society. The Communists clearly favor even *more* collectivism, *more* regulations, and *less* leeway for individual enterprise than do the Social Democrats; hence, the present wave of protest is not ultimately likely to redound to the benefit of the many leftist groups in the three countries. Instead, it may well work to the advantage of the local right-wing forces. Particularly with the recent splits in the NKP and VPK, the future continues to look fairly bleak for Scandinavian communism.

The Icelandic Communists have managed to avoid most of the difficulties that have beset their Scandinavian counterparts—as their relatively positive political record bears witness. Moreover, Iceland has provided a much more fertile ground for domestic communism than have the Scandinavian countries. Especially during recent years, the republic's economic situation has proved much less satisfactory than that in Scandinavia, and its economy has perennially been at the mercy of the fish catch, a notoriously insecure and unpredictable source of wealth.

If, then, the AB maintains its nationalistic stance on major issues, it will in all probability retain its appeal to the Icelandic general public as well as to the island's working class. That, in turn, will ensure preservation of its status as one of the most successful Communist parties in Western Europe.

Notes

1. A good discussion of the Soviet role may be found in Vernon V. Aspaturian, *Process and Power in Soviet Foreign Policy* (Boston: Little, Brown, 1971), especially Chapter 10.

2. See, for example, Olav Scheflo, "Die Fragen der Kommunistischen Partei Norwegens" [The questions concerning the Norwegian Communist Party], *Die Kommunistische Internationale* (Hamburg), no. 23 (1923), pp. 107-114.

3. *Yearbook on International Communist Affairs 1969* (Stanford, Calif.: Hoover Institution Press, 1970).

4. Peter P. Rohde, "The Communist Party of Denmark," in *Communism in Scandinavia and Finland*, ed. A. F. Upton (New York: Anchor Press/Doubleday, 1973), pp. 9-12.

5. Åke Sparring, "The Communist Party of Sweden," in ibid., pp. 62-68.

6. Ibid.

7. Ibid., pp. 69-72.

8. The DNA position on organizational matters can be found in *Pervyi Kongress Kominterna* [The First Congress of the Comintern] (Moscow: Partiinoe Izdatel'stvo, 1933), pp. 28-30.

9. Knut Langfeldt, *Moskvatesene i Norsk Politikk* [The Moscow theses in Norwegian politics] (Oslo: Universitetsforlaget, 1961), pp. 51-56.

10. The proceedings of the DNA congress were reported in *Arbeiderbladet* (Oslo), November 6, 1923.

11. For a discussion of the purge that established Lövlien as the leader of the NKP, see *Arbeideren* (Oslo), February 9, 1934.

12. One example of this is an article in ibid., September 15, 1939, which completely accepted the Soviet view of the international situation.

13. See the appropriate national statistical yearbooks and Upton, *Communism in Scandinavia and Finland*, pp. 10-11, 67-84.

14. *Yearbook on International Communist Affairs 1969*, pp. 429-430.

15. E.g., *Arbeideren*, September 15, 1939.

16. Ibid.; see also decisions of the NKP Central Committee, November 11-13, 1939, in ibid., November 14-19, 1939.

17. Ibid., December 1, 1939.

18. For a good survey of this problem, see Åke Sparring et al., *Kommunismen i Norden og Krisen i den Kommunistiske Bevegelse* [Communism in the Nordic countries and the crisis of the Communist movement] (Oslo, 1965).

19. E.g., Furubotn's letter to the Norwegian government in exile in London in *Vårt Partis Politikk under Krigen* [Our party's policy during the war], an NKP document collection published in Oslo in 1945-1946, pp. 14-18.

20. Rohde, "The Communist Party of Denmark," pp. 20-22.

21. Sparring, "The Communist Party of Sweden," pp. 80-82.

22. *Yearbook on International Communist Affairs 1969*, especially pp. 429-430.

23. See, for example, statements at the 1946 NKP Congress, as reported in *Friheten* (Oslo), June 8, 1946.

24. See, for instance, ibid., August 23, 1947.

25. These statistics are drawn from official Danish, Norwegian, and Swedish statistical yearbooks of the appropriate years.

26. Rohde, "The Communist Party of Denmark," pp. 22-23.

27. Larsen was eventually forced out of the DKP. See ibid., pp. 24-26.

28. With respect to the NKP, for example, see Reidar Larsen's commentary in *Friheten*, June 22, 1956.

29. *Yearbook on International Communist Affairs 1969*, p. 265.

30. This position was reflected in the national elections in 1963 and 1967, when the Icelandic party obtained 14.2 percent and 15.7 percent of the total vote, respectively; in the 1950s the electoral support was of the same order.

31. *Yearbook on International Communist Affairs 1970* (Stanford, Calif.: Hoover Institution Press, 1971), pp. 202-204.

32. An example of the *national* concerns of the Icelandic Communists can be found in the pages of *Thjodviljinn* (Reykjavik), the main party organ.

33. The organizational change took place in late 1968; see ibid., November 5-12, 1968.

34. This summary was derived from a study of the following publications: *Land og Folk* (DKP daily), *Fremad* (Danish Communist Youth League), *Kommunistisk Orientering* (KAK), *Kommunist* (KFML), *Ungkommunisten* (KUF), and assorted pamphlets. All the

regularly issued items are published in Copenhagen.

35. This summary is derived from a study of the following publications: *Friheten* (NKP weekly), *Orientering* (SF), *Arbeiderbladet* (DNA daily), *Klassekampen* (AKP-ml), *Fremad* (KU), and assorted pamphlets. All the regularly issued items are published in Oslo.

36. This summary is derived from the following publications: *Ny Dag* (VPK biweekly), *Norrskensflamman* (the Norrbotten Communist daily), *Socialistisk Debatt* (Norrbotten theoretical quarterly), *Gnistan* (SKP—Stockholm), and assorted pamphlets.

37. *Visir* (Reykjavik), August 9, 1972. See also the Maoist publication *Stettabarattan* (Reykjavik).

38. *Thjodviljinn*, November 5, 1968.

39. E.g., *Visir*, April 20, 1970.

40. In the 1974 elections, the OLL obtained only 4.3 percent of the total vote.

41. See *Arbeiderbladet*, November 1-3, 1975, on this question; see also Per Egil Hegge, " 'Disunited' Front in Norway" *Problems of Communism*, May-June 1976, pp. 49-59.

42. See, for instance, Hegge, " 'Disunited' Front in Norway"; and articles in *Friheten*, *Orientering*, and *Arbeiderbladet* in November 1975.

43. The results of the election can be found in *Arbeiderbladet*, September 13-15, 1977.

44. See my "Patterns of Nordic Communism," *Problems of Communism*, May-June 1975, pp. 20-36.

45. The resolution forbidding contact with the Warsaw Pact countries was discussed in *Morgunbladid* (Reykjavik), October 8, 1968.

46. *Ny Dag*, August 22-26, 1968.

47. The VPK answered in kind through the pro-Soviet *Norrskensflamman*, June 29 and August 31, 1973.

48. The resolution of the NKP Congress in November 1975 seems to indicate such continuity. See *Friheten*, the first half of November 1975.

49. This judgment is based on a close examination of *Friheten* and *Ny Dag*.

50. See, e.g., *Thjodviljinn*, April 29 and June 14, 1973.

51. See, for instance, Jespersen's remarks at the DKP Congress in 1973, in *Land og Folk*, March 3-4, 1973.

52. See, e.g., *Friheten*, May 6-11, 1974.

53. During some of the hottest episodes of the "cod war" with

Great Britain, *Thjodviljinn* demanded a national protest movement and got a great deal of cross-party support. See, e.g., *Thjodviljinn*, May 22, 1973.

54. See, e.g., *Norrskensflamman*, September 18, 1974.

55. Derived from the DKP's *Land og Folk* and the NKP's *Friheten*, first half of 1972.

56. *Arbeiderbladet*, September 12-13, 1973, discussed the effects of the EEC campaign on the 1973 national elections.

57. This view was articulated in the NKP "kickoff" of the electoral campaign for the 1973 national elections, in *Friheten*, April 9-14, 1973.

58. See, for example, the May Day manifesto of the NKP in ibid., May 1-7, 1971.

59. This was perhaps most forcefully demonstrated by the NKP in its anti-EEC campaigns in 1971 and 1972.

60. The nonsocialist coalition appears unstable at this point, and a possible resignation may propel the Social Democrats to power once more.

61. See, e.g., *Land og Folk*, August 21, 1968; and *Friheten*, March 12-17, 1973.

62. Based on discussions with Mats Bergquist of the Swedish Embassy in Washington, D.C., and the issues of *Norrskensflamman* in May 1977, which discussed this subject practically every day.

63. See, e.g., *Thjodviljinn*, April 29, 1973.

64. Editorial in *Arbeiderbladet*, November 25, 1975; here it is also admitted that the AKP(ml) is gaining ground among industrial workers.

65. *Yearbook on International Communist Affairs 1976* (Stanford, Calif.: Stanford University Press, 1976), p. 177.

66. Glistrup's Progress Party obtained 14.6 percent of the total vote in the February 1977 elections in Denmark.

67. It should be noted, though, that this party is now clearly on the wane in Norway; in the 1977 elections it did not obtain representation in parliament.

8
Great Britain: Revolution or Gradualism for the CPGB?

David Lynn Price

The propaganda of the Communist Party of Great Britain (CPGB) resounds with rhetoric of the "revolutionary situation" in the country. On the face of things, some evidence exists. The United Kingdom has chronic economic problems such as inflation, a crisis of confidence in sterling, an unsatisfactory industrial performance, and turbulent industrial relations. Having lost an empire, it is still trying to adjust to its reduced world status; there appears to be no sense of purpose or direction, an aimlessness emphasized by the weakening of organized religion. But does all this amount to a revolutionary situation?

More probably, the foregoing factors constitute forces for change in accordance with a historical pattern. To be sure, the speed, complexity, and extent of contemporary change are unprecedented. Nevertheless, the differences between contemporary change and historical change do not convincingly suggest a prerevolutionary condition, for the classic catalysts of revolution—deprivation and unfulfilled but rising expectations—do not exist in contemporary British society. The CPGB has chosen to ignore this distinction, thus sharpening its intellectual dilemma.

Performance

Traditionally, the CPGB has been divided over political strategy. Should it be true to Marxist-Leninist precepts and seek power by any means, or should it cooperate with political forces in the existing system in the hope of forming a united front prior to the dismemberment of that system? Thus, the CPGB has been an actor in search of a role since its formation in 1920.

Until World War II, the party was uncompromisingly in favor of the "revolutionary overthrow of capitalism"; it was also completely subservient to the orders of the Soviet Union or the Comintern. At that stage of its development, the British party was a rigid Stalinist organization, with an authoritarian leadership that tolerated no internal dissent. In the mid-1930s, some of the party's members did feel that it was isolated from the working class politically and ideologically, and to improve its image it sought the support of the Labour Party and the trade unions.[1] But both were hostile.

During World War II, the battle against fascism and nazism gave the party a political legitimacy it had not hitherto enjoyed. By 1944, its membership had risen to 56,000, as compared with 4,000 in 1920.[2] However, if the CPGB believed that its support of the war effort would earn it great political goodwill, it was disappointed. The election of a Labour government and the introduction of a welfare state in 1945 undermined the position of the CPGB, for a parliamentary party showed that it could do more for the working class than a professed revolutionary party could. In effect, there had been a revolution from above. Furthermore, although the Comintern had been dissolved in 1943, thus distancing the CPGB from Moscow, there was still the suspicion that the Soviet Union really ran the CPGB. Hence, the party's fortunes remained low.

The 1950s brought new travails. Nikita Khrushchev's revelations in February 1956 of some of the atrocities of the Stalin era and the Soviet invasion of Budapest later that year reduced the CPGB membership by a third; nevertheless, a Committee on Inner Party Democracy reiterated the principles of the CPGB's organization, thus ending any prospect of internal reform for at least the time being.[3]

Over subsequent years, the party's membership dropped steadily, standing at 25,293 in 1977 (the population of Great Britain is 54,421,000).[4] As of the 1970s, it certainly has no appeal to youth. Only 9 to 15 percent of the party members are under 25, and the main party leadership is aging and out of touch with changes in British society. For example, at the 1975 congress, 45 of the 425 delegates were under 25; 233, between 25 and 40; and 146, over 40. Thus, their average age was 36.25 years, as compared with an average of 34.8 years for the delegates to the last previous congress in 1973. Although those under 25 constituted only 10 percent of the total, the proportion of those over 40 reached about 34 percent.[5] The situation of the youth wing of the CPGB also underscores the party's lack of attractiveness to the young. In 1967, the Young Communist League (YCL) had a membership of 6,000, but by the end of 1976 the figure had declined to barely 2,000.[6] By and large, this poor performance is due to competition from the New Left, which has put forth platforms more compelling to youth than the YCP has. At the same time, young people mature, take jobs, marry, have families—in short, they grow out of youthful enthusiasms.

Nor has the CPGB been notably successful in attracting members from several other segments of British society. Since its inception, the party has paid special attention to the role of women. Indeed,. it has a separate women's department, a newspaper for women, and women's district committees. Yet at recent congresses, women have formed only about 15 percent of the forty-two-member Executive Committee, and the rank-and-file membership probably does not contain a much higher proportion of women. The immigrant community has proved particularly sterile for the party. Britain's Caribbean, African, Indian, and Pakistani populations have chosen to form their own ethnic-cultural groups. As a result, the CPGB has few immigrant members, and its Executive faithfully reflects this aspect of its social composition.[7]

The "industrial proletariat" constitutes the backbone of the party. Nearly 40 percent of the delegates at recent party congresses come from the blue-collar trades—engineering, shipbuilding, power and construction work, mining, and railway labor. Moreover, the party's traditional support is located in the heavy industrial areas—Scotland, South Wales, and London's East End. Scotland has 7,000 members; London, 5,000; and Wales, 2,000.[8] These are areas that have undergone dramatic technological change, leading to the decline of traditional industry, high unemployment, and the introduction of capital-intensive, not labor-intensive, manufacturing industries.

Since 1969, however, the CPGB, following the example of unions, has taken more interest in the white-collar workers. (The Executive Committee, it should be noted, has a majority of white-collar, as opposed to manual, workers.) If inflation and technological change continue to erode the real incomes of white-collar workers, there could be a qualitative improvement in both the labor movement and the CPGB, with increased intellectual rigidity the likely result.

In the postwar years, the party has repressed its apocalyptic visions, and it has now become a party of caution and ambivalence. How, then, does it campaign as a respectable political party while upholding the canons of Marxism-Leninism? And how are the principles of Marxist theory to be applied to a generation that has known only affluence?

The CPGB has accepted that it has no chance of competing with the Labour Party as a mass movement, so it has compromised by generally supporting Labour policies. This stance puts the party in an uncomfortable position, for the right wing of the Labour Party (the "reformists") and the CPGB are bitter opponents. Thus, as one observer has astutely remarked, the Communists say that *"once the Labour Party is purged of reformism* and socialism is being built," they "do not seek exclusive leadership of the united left," but "they and Labour will be the political organization of the working class."[9]

In practical terms, the CPGB, like the Labour Party, seeks to campaign on issues that affect the working class. It advocates social reform, an improved standard of living, trade union rights, public ownership, abolition of NATO, opposition to U.S. "imperialism," and the creation of Welsh and Scottish parliaments. This platform obviously entails a strategy of democratic militancy, and such a strategy has drawn criticism from the party's orthodox wing as a betrayal of the Leninist ideal.

By trying to reconcile two traditions, the party has ended up satisfying neither. Its constitutional approach has had abysmal results. In the last six elections, not one Communist candidate has been elected, and the highest number of votes that the party has collected was 62,112 in 1966. Most of its votes have come from Scotland, South Wales, and London's East End, where it has the largest concentrations of members and where it places most of its candidates.[10] Despite these electoral failures, the party still insists that electoral success is vital for the advance toward socialism.

Internal Problems

It seems fairly clear that the CPGB's program has no appeal for the British electorate, but that program alone does not account for its inability to attract greater support. Much of the explanation lies in characteristics of the party itself.

As a party, the CPGB has four levels: the National Congress; the Executive and its committees and departments; the districts; and the branches, which are both residential-based and factory-based. The highest authority is the National Congress, which meets every two years; delegates to the congress are representatives from districts and branches. But in practice the congress serves as a virtual rubber stamp for the party leadership. It operates in completely undemocratic fashion, and opposition is rare. Between congresses the Executive Committee provides continuity; it meets every two months to discuss party activities. The Executive selects a Political Committee—the party's nerve center. The latter includes the party general secretary; the assistant secretary; the chairman; the national organizer; the industrial organizer; the editor of the party organ, *Morning Star;* and others, among them prominent trade unionists. Members of the Political Committee are appointed, not elected.

Although the CPGB is disciplined and active at the center, the Political Committee delegates very little, and it discourages any independent undertakings. This inflexibility is one of the weaknesses of the party at the level of the shop floor, for although the party places a great deal of emphasis on branch activity in the factories to strike at the heart of the capitalist industrialist system, the circumstances of each factory are bound to differ. The traditional party rigidity at this level has provoked some radicals to raise questions about the usefulness of shop-floor activity altogether.

Besides these structural drawbacks, the CPGB has suffered from divisions within its ranks. During the first half of the 1960s, criticism of party policy came primarily from direct-action propagandists such as Reg Birch. The quarrel arose over industrial agitation. According to the CPGB, factories were the key point of industrial struggle, but Birch and the dissenters pointed out that this was a paradox. How could one promote industrial militancy while supporting the Labour Party's program of public ownership? Ultimately, the CPGB's ambivalence drove these alternative strategists out of the party. In 1966, Birch left the CPGB and set up the Communist Party of Britain (Marxist-Leninist), a Maoist group.

From the late 1960s up to 1973, the dissent of Stalinist hard-liners, who objected to the party's tentative efforts to put some distance between itself and the Soviet Union (more on which later), enlivened national congresses. The 34th Congress in November 1975 was relatively tranquil, with all policy proposals being unanimously endorsed, but this tranquillity masked continuing disagreements behind the scenes. In January 1976, John Gollan, former party general secretary, gave some hint of these disagreements in an article he wrote seeking to describe the party's attempts to assert its independence of Moscow.[11] The essay rebuked the Soviet leadership for the persecution of dissidents and admitted that the CPGB had been "insufficiently critical" of the Soviet Union during the Stalinist purges. Then on February 11, 1976, the party experienced a severe blow. Jimmy Reid, who had become nationally known when he directed the work-in by employees of the bankrupt Upper Clyde Shipbuilders group in 1971-1972, resigned after a career of twenty-six years in the party. His reasons for leaving were not specific, but he criticized the party for dogmatism and sectarianism.[12]

As the CPGB struggled during 1976-1977 to produce a revised

version of the 1951 document *The British Road to Socialism* that would follow Eurocommunist lines (to be discussed subsequently), the tensions between Stalinists and less orthodox elements increased. On July 17, 1977, Sid French, a leading Stalinist who had spearheaded the opposition to the new draft manifesto, decided to break away and set up his own splinter party, the New Communist Party (NCP). The NCP's ideological justification for its existence was that "the Communist Party of Great Britain has capitulated to anti-Sovietism and is now trying to foist a social democratic programme on the working class."[13] In reality, there was nothing original about the NCP's program, because it remained faithful to the traditional Marxist-Leninist doctrines—dictatorship of the proletariat, democratic centralism, and the likelihood of armed struggle.

Support for the NCP was limited—about fifty members attended a public meeting to discuss the split—and the reaction of the CPGB was predictably hostile. The latter held that "the forming of a breakaway organization . . . would only bring joy to the enemies of the working class."[14]

Certainly, the NCP's dissidence did nothing to improve the image of British Communists, but it is questionable whether the NCP has obtained any advantage either. The party is small, has no access to the media, and alienates public opinion by its pursuit of a "Soviet Britain." Moreover, the USSR's silence vis-à-vis the NCP is unpromising for a professed Stalinist minority. In his late fifties, French has been a Communist for more than forty years, and his earlier activities failed to attract many recruits. Hence, it is unlikely that he and the NCP will bring fresh intellectual vigor to the British Left. As a newspaper commentary stated, "one does not know whether to admire his tenacity or to deplore his self-delusion."[15]

Relations with Other Domestic Forces

As part of its domestic strategy, the CPGB advocates unity of the Left. The prime target of the party's attentions is the Labour Party. From the CPGB's standpoint, a liaison with Labour would enhance its access to the labor movement and open increased possibilities, through block voting, of using industrial action for political ends.

However, the Labour Party to date has proved essentially unreceptive to the CPGB's wooing. To be sure, the Labour Party did remove the CPGB from its proscribed list in 1973, and the CPGB can rely on some Labour Members of Parliament and some members of the Labour Party's National Executive to attend and speak at rallies and to contribute to the CPGB organ. But the Labour Party officially remains hostile to the CPGB. Equally important, there is often an uncompromising hostility between the Labour supporter and the Communist activist at the level of the shop floor in heavy industrial areas.

In its search for political unity, the CPGB has attempted to work with other "progressive" organizations on single issues. Among these organizations have been the Young Liberals, the Campaign for Nuclear Disarmament, the Anti-Apartheid Movement, and the United Nations Association; the issues have included Chile, South Africa, NATO, industrial relations, comprehensive education, and wage freezes. Most of these efforts have produced some measure of success.

However, when the party has sought to cooperate with the ultra-Left in any fashion, dissension and hostility have been complete. In large measure, this state of affairs stems from a divergence in view with respect to the correct path to power. During the 1960s, the CPGB, caught up in its dedication to the parliamentary road, failed to recognize the social, political, and intellectual changes in train; consequently, neither the party nor the YCL played any significant role in the student movement. Today, moreover, the CPGB is primarily concerned with aligning itself with the mainstream of the Labour Party rather than with building a genuine mass movement for direct action. Thus, the ultra-Left castigates the party for insufficient dedication to revolution.

The ultra-Left also engages in direct competition with the CPGB for support. This challenge from the left comes mainly from Trotskyite groups. They are the Workers Revolutionary Party (WRP) and the Socialist Workers Party (SWP). The former has about 2,000 members, and the latter, about 3,500.[16]

There is particularly strong friction between the CPGB and the WRP at the factory level. The former recruits among the management, but the latter courts the lathe operator. Ideological skirmishes are frequent. The WRP considers the CPGB to be Stalinist and attacks it for obstructing Trotskyite activities in industry; furthermore, the WRP often asks the CPGB rank and file to reject their "right-wing" leadership. For its part, the CPGB in recent industrial confrontations has denounced Trotskyites and others for provoking unnecessary violence, which damages industrial relations and compromises not only the Labour Party but also the labor movement in general, to whose leadership the CPGB aspires.

In its dogfights with the Trotskyites, the CPGB has been at pains to present a moderate image and to establish its credentials as a democratic party. This effort, however, has in effect reduced the meaning of its slogan of "unity of the Left" to alliance with the Labour Party. Given the disparity in strength between the two parties, the CPGB has thus found itself in a weak position.

Despite its failures to bring about cooperation with other political forces and despite its stagnation at the shop-floor level the CPGB exercises its greatest influence through the labor movement. Although it does not control any individual union, it has played a major role in nearly all the labor-government confrontations of recent years.

In the 1970s, however, the CPGB's showing in trade union elections has been quite modest, and in some cases disastrous. For example, although the CPGB is most influential in the Amalgamated Union of Engineering Workers (AUEW), the elections to the union executive in 1975 resulted in a massive victory for the moderates. The election of Bob Wright, a prominent left-winger who had Communist support, as assistanct general-secretary in November 1976 reversed the trend, but the party still has by no means recovered its losses.

Internationalism

If the CPGB's domestic policy suffers from paradoxes, its international stance embodies even greater contradictions. In broad terms, the CPGB's world view is simple: United States and NATO bad, Soviet Union and the Warsaw Pact good. It follows that the European Economic Community (EEC) is vilified as a "capitalist club," while the Council for Mutual Economic Assistance (CMEA) and centralized socialist economies are regarded as models. Nevertheless, at recent congresses, the CPGB has espoused a Titoist line toward the Soviet Union—a position that provoked opposition from Stalinist hard-liners, as mentioned earlier. This limited independence first emerged in 1968, after the Warsaw Pact invasion of Czechoslovakia, and has developed steadily, to a point where the CPGB guardedly welcomed the outcome of the East Berlin meeting of European Communist parties in June 1976. Commenting on the effectiveness of such meetings, the Executive Committee stated: "Last month's conference in Berlin and the preparations for it indicated that some methods utilized hitherto in the international Communist movement were no longer appropriate."[17] This was strong language for the CPGB and clearly reflected the CPGB's discomfort at too close a relationship with the Soviet Union. A sign of things to come had already been given during Gordon McLennan's visit to Moscow for the 25th Congress of the Communist Party of the Soviet Union (CPSU) in March 1976. "Our aim," he said, "is the construction of socialism in Britain which would guarantee personal freedom, the plurality of political parties, the independence of the trade unions, religious freedom, freedom of research, cultural, artistic and scientific activities."[18]

In adjusting to the concept of Eurocommunism, the CPGB has probably made its most important ideological decision since it distanced itself from Moscow in 1968. Like its French, Italian, and Spanish counterparts, the CPGB has come to terms with two objective realities: "the crisis of the Soviet myth and the complexity of Western society which makes the classic type of revolution almost impossible."[19] Thus, since 1976 the British party has been grappling with the distinctive features of the new Eurocommunist doctrines: commitment to the construction of socialism in freedom, a multiparty system, and recognition of the rights of different parties to take turns in power; rejection of the concept of a leading party and of the Soviet revolutionary example as a model for the West; and, finally, criticism of Soviet repression of domestic dissidence.

During the acrimonious exchange, in mid-1977, between Moscow and the Spanish Communist Party over the attack of the Soviet magazine *New Times* on Santiago Carrillo, the Spanish party's secretary-general, and his outspoken views on Eurocommunism, the CPGB was generally reticent. But in a rare public comment, the party did take a critical line toward Moscow and also gave some indication of the way the party might develop ideologically. In early July, Gordon McLennan, the CPGB's general secretary, commented at length in the *Morning Star* on the Eurocommunism controversy. McLennan was not explicit, but he clearly blamed the *New Times* for the original breach of fraternal etiquette. "It is to be regretted," he said, "that there has been a departure from this essential basis of discussion between Communists." To emphasize his point, he added that "it must be clearly understood that each party is independent and sovereign and will not only decide its own analysis but will work out its policy in its own country, and no one else can do it." Picking up on the observation of many outsiders that the treatment of dissent in the international communist movement compared with that of dissent in the Catholic church, he stated that "there can be no excommunication from a non-existent centre."[20]

At the party's 35th annual congress in November 1977, McLennan sounded similar themes in his report to the 1,500 delegates. For instance, he indicated in no uncertain terms that the British party itself would chart the course that it pursued. Moreover, the congress adopted a new version of *The British Road to Socialism* that embodied characteristically Eurocommunist commitments to respect democratic freedoms and to accept the verdict of the ballot box and the rights of other political parties.[21]

On the face of it, this apparent increase in flexibility is encouraging for the British and European political scene. But like most Communist parties, the CPGB has a track record of internal inflexibility and intolerance of opposition. Furthermore, will CPGB criticisms of Soviet and East European repression intensify to the point where the party dissociates itself from these regimes? Such a decision would undoubtedly entail fundamental changes in the party.

No less important, the CPGB has carefully avoided associating itself with any specifically West European bloc of parties. At the November 1977 party congress, General Secretary McLennan dismissed the term *Eurocommunism* as neither useful nor accurate. he went on to say that though "we warmly welcome the advance of communist, socialist and democratic forces in Western Europe and their growing unity, . . . we independently decide our policy for Britain." If that policy "coincides in some important respects with that of other communist parties in Europe and elsewhere, it is because many of the objective conditions they face are similar to ours."[22]

It should also be noted that even if the CPGB adopts a formal stance in favor of Eurocommunism as the Spanish, French, and Italian parties have, its position will remain ambivalent. The CPGB has repeatedly declared that in an East-West crisis it would support the Soviet Union, but only if there is "imperialist aggression."[23] In addition, it continues to work for the unity of international communism, for whose triumph it sees the Soviet Union and Eastern Europe as fundamental. As McLennan put the matter in his July 1977 commentary in *Morning Star*, "the success of the Soviet Union and other Socialist countries, the liberation movements and the working-class movements in capitalist countries makes even more possible a transition to Socialism without foreign military intervention and without civil war."[24]

Moreover, this ambivalence is not likely to improve the CPGB's standing with the British electorate. British voters would be asked to believe that, in domestic matters, the CPGB would allow other parties to exist as a legal opposition if it came to power and would make way for any party that defeated it. But no ruling Communist party has ever done so, and in light of the CPGB's mixed attitude toward the USSR, the party's dedication to such a course would be hard to make convincing.

Prospects

The CPGB general secretary's statements on Eurocommunism in July 1977 and November 1977 were clearly intended to preempt any potentially divisive debate. However, it does not seem likely that this effort will prove entirely ·successful in stifling discussion, for the party's youth and student departments have shown a keen interest in Eurocommunism. The same month as McLennan's initial commentary appeared, the CPGB youth wing organized a nine-day Communist University in London, which was attended by well over 1,000 students. Although the main item for discussion was the new draft of *The British Road to Socialism,* another important subject was the party's attitude toward Eurocommunism. Participants in the debates at this event approved the party's slow progression toward a more moderate image similar to that of the Italian, French, and Spanish parties.[25]

In the future, the more cosmopolitan attitudes of the youth organizations could present problems for the CPGB. A number of young Communists are pro-European and derive support from a group known as Communists for Europe, a body of former party members and other left-wing sympathizers set up in 1975. The pro-European Communists criticize anti-Europeans as unrealistic, "little England" protectionists and urge British Communists to play an active role in the European Community. They maintain that such an initiative would help to forge links with other European Communist parties and pave the way for the preparation of a common socialist program in Europe.

For its part, the CPGB remains officially committed to British withdrawal from the EEC, and it has placed itself firmly behind the anti-European MPs in the Labour Party. As in the past, this ambivalence will probably continue to weaken the party. On the one hand, the CPGB acknowledges the existence of Eurocommunism; on the other hand, its opposition to the EEC places it in the position of custodian of British nationalism—no kind of posture for a declared adherent of an international movement.

But this nationalist garb in which the party has now clothed itself is unlikely to arrest its steady domestic decline. The CPGB is ideologically uncertain, it is losing members, it cannot attract young people, and its electoral performance has been disastrous. From within government, the Labour Party's left wing promotes policies that are more radical than those of the CPGB. As a militant party, the CPGB has been upstaged by the direct-action Trotskyites. In an era of change, the CPGB's central leadership remains inflexible. And the emergence of Eurocommunism may force the party into yet another tortuous adjustment, creating yet another ideological ambivalence. The CPGB has inherited an unwieldy doctrinal tradition, and faced with social and political change, it has felt compelled to make partial compromises that could lead to political impotence and eventual dissolution.

Notes

1. Peter Shipley, *Revolution in Modern Britain* (London: Bodley Head, 1975), p. 23.

2. Richard F. Starr, ed., *Yearbook on International Communist Affairs 1974* (Stanford, Calif.: Hoover Institution Press, 1974); idem, ed., *Yearbook on International Communist Affairs 1975* (Stanford, Calif.: Hoover Institution Press, 1975).

3. *Daily Worker* (London), November 3, 1956.

4. *The Times* (London), October 4, 1977; Richard F. Starr, ed., *Yearbook on International Communist Affairs 1977* (Stanford, Calif.: Hoover Institution Press, 1977).

5. *Yearbook on International Communist Affairs 1974* and *Yearbook on International Communist Affairs 1975*.

6. *Economist Foreign Report* (London), November 5, 1976.

7. *Morning Star* (London), June 4, 1973.

8. Ibid., May 14, 1973.

9. Shipley, *Revolution in Modern Britain*, p. 117. Emphasis added.

10. *Daily Telegraph* (London), November 1, 1975.

11. *Marxism Today* (London), January 1976.

12. *The Times*, February 13, 1976.

13. Ibid., July 19, 1977.

14. *Morning Star*, July 25, 1977.

15. *The Observer* (London), July 24, 1977.

16. *Yearbook on International Communist Affairs 1974*.

17. *Morning Star*, July 12, 1976.

18. Ibid., March 2, 1976.

19. *Times Europa* (London), March 6, 1977.

20. *Morning Star*, July 4, 1977.

21. On the congress, see *The Times,* November 13 and 14, 1977; *Daily Telegraph,* November 14, 1977.

22. *The Times,* November 14, 1977.

23. Ibid., April 23, 1977.

24. *Morning Star,* July 4, 1977.

25. *The Times,* July 11, 1977.

9
The Challenge of Eurocommunism

Kevin Devlin

> For years, Moscow . . . was our Rome. We spoke of the Great October Socialist Revolution as if it were our Christmas. That was the period of our infancy. Today we have grown up.
> —Santiago Carrillo at the East Berlin Conference of European Communist and Workers' Parties, June 29, 1976.

The first European Conference of Communist Parties was held in Karlovy Vary, Czechoslovakia, in April 1967; the second took place in East Berlin in June 1976. A brief comparison of the two offers one measure of the changes that have come about in European communism—East, West, and East-West, over the past decade.[1]

By 1967, the monolithic unity of European communism was already a thing of the past, owing largely to the disruptive impact of the Sino-Soviet conflict and to the wave of "revisionist" adaptation to environmental realities that affected many West European parties, to varying degrees, in the early 1960s. The clearest proof of this was the list of absentees: the Karlovy Vary conference was boycotted by the Albanian, Yugoslav, and Romanian parties from the East, and by the Dutch, Icelandic, and Norwegian parties from the West, and the Swedes sent only an observer. Nevertheless, those that did attend maintained the tradition of unanimous solidarity under the exemplary leadership of the CPSU. So the project went through expeditiously, if not altogether smoothly. The call for a pan-European conference came from the loyalist French and Polish parties in January 1967; the only preparatory meeting was held in Warsaw in February; and in April, the conference itself unanimously adopted a collective document calling in general terms for a long-range effort to exploit détente but suggesting by its very generality the already divergent political interests of both East and West European Communist leaderships.[2]

The contrast with the second European conference is striking, not least with regard to the time and effort consumed in bringing the latter about. The first calls for another pan-European meeting—and for a world conference to follow—came from pro-Soviet party leaders (West German, Hungarian, and Bulgarian) in November 1973. A twenty-eight-party consultative meeting took place in Warsaw nearly a year later, in October 1974, after months of secret interparty negotiations—the first of many preliminary events in a long preparatory process. The conference itself did not take place until late June 1976, a full year behind schedule—and then, as we shall see, it was not the kind of conference that the Soviets and their supporters had obviously wanted, but instead one that marked the "institution-alization of diversity" in the European Communist movement.

The "scenario" adumbrated in the Kremlin seems fairly clear. The conference of Communist parties—addressed to "the struggle for peace, security, cooperation, and social progress in Europe"—was to be held in East Berlin "no later than mid-1975"; it was to be linked primarily with the international Conference on European Security and Cooperation scheduled for Helsinki in the summer of 1975, and secondarily with the thirtieth anniversary of the victory of the antifascist alliance in World War II. By producing a collective ideological interpretation of détente in Europe, the Kremlin hoped, the conference would lessen the effect of the concessions that the East Europeans would have to make in Helsinki with regard to "Basket 3" (the freer movement of information, ideas, and persons); at the same time, it would at least implicitly reaffirm the status of the CPSU as primus inter pares (or *impares*) in the European communist movement.

In retrospect, it appears that the Soviet leadership made a fundamental miscalculation in seeking to obtain the participation of as many parties as possible—and more specifically, to bring in the Yugoslavs and Romanians, who had boycotted the Karlovy Vary conference. One concession upon which the Yugoslavs, backed by other independent parties, insisted, proved to be of crucial importance. This was the new procedural principle of "decision making by concensus," adopted at the start of the Warsaw meeting. Indeed, the prolonged preparatory process that followed—involving at least sixteen meetings over twenty months—could be described as the story of repeated and ultimately largely fruitless efforts by the loyalist majority to reduce the effect of that initial concession.

After the Warsaw meeting and the first preparatory session proper, held in Budapest in mid-December 1974, a curtain of official secrecy descended over the proceedings, but the outlines of the confrontation over the character and content of the conference document were clear enough.[3] For the independent parties—notably, the Yugoslav, Romanian, Italian, Spanish, British, and Swedish CPs, later joined at least on some issues by the French—it was a matter of resisting repeated attempts (made through the East Germans, who as hosts were charged with producing the successive draft texts) to secure the adoption by the European Communist parties of something like a "general line," expressed in ideological terms. Against this pressure the independent parties stood by their demands: if there was to be a collective document at all,[4] it must be based upon genuine consensus; it must emphasize the principles of autonomy, equality, and noninterference in interparty relations (with the important corollary that no special status should be accorded to the CPSU); it must contain no criticism of any party, present or absent (e.g., the Chinese); it must deal with political action, not with ideology; and in any case it was not to be binding upon any party.

The early stages of this debate took place at sessions of the so-called working group,[5] which met in East Berlin in mid-February and again in early April 1975. This phase ended in deadlock. At the April session, the East Germans produced a first draft, which a Yugoslav party source described as calling for "a joint stand of all Communist parties in their actions and ideology";[6] it was rejected by the independent parties.

Continuing Deadlock

At this point, an attempt was made to find a way out of the impasse by handing the problem over to a balanced "subgroup" of eight parties—four independent ones (Yugoslavia, Romania, Italy, and Spain) and four loyalist ones (the Soviet Union, East Germany, France, and Denmark). The subgroup met three times—in mid-May, early July, and mid-July 1975[7]—but failed to reach agreement: a second draft text, produced by the East Germans in July, was no more acceptable to the independent parties than the first had been. In an interview given at the end of August, Sergio Segre of the Italian Communist Party (PCI) said that "only a few small steps forward" had been made, and that both East German drafts "contained statements of political and ideological principle that were frankly unacceptable—and not only to the PCI." He went on to provide some useful details:

> On the concept of détente, agreement is general, but we risk running aground on the first and third chapters of the document. The first chapter consists of an analysis of Western capitalism and contains a series of assessments of the function of the Socialist and Social Democratic parties. The third . . . concerns the strategy of the Communist parties, and here it is said that they play a vanguard role, pursue identical objectives, and are guided by a single ideology. We believe, and we are not the only ones, that these parts of the document do not reflect the reality of the Communist movement and the orientations that were expressed by its components on various subjects—for example, Portugal.[8]

Segre's reference to Portugal was a timely reminder that events themselves—and particularly the ferment of change affecting all of the southern European countries in different ways—were making it more and more difficult for the European Communist parties to adopt a collective analysis of the continental situation. During the spring and early summer of 1975, the corner-cutting pursuit of power by the Portuguese Communist Party (PCP), in alliance with the leftist military and in conflict with Mario Soares's Socialist Party (PS), became a source of deepening disunity and even polemics.[9] The Italian and Spanish CPs, whose domestic fortunes were directly and negatively affected by the Portuguese drama, openly criticized PCP policies and made their sympathy for the PS equally clear (the more reticent Yugoslav and Romanian party presses made much the same point by giving favorable publicity to Soares and not the "Muscovite" Alvaro Cunhal).[10] On the other hand, the independent British and Swedish CPs went along with most other Communist parties in giving fraternal support to the PCP. But it was the French party (PCF) that characterized itself above all others by its systematic and vociferous support of Cunhal, even though the latter's undisguised contempt for constitutional democracy (most memorably expressed in an interview with Oriana Fallacci)[11] was in conflict with principles proclaimed domestically by the PCF—for example, in the impressive "Declaration of Liberties" published in May 1975.[12]

Although the PCF's stand on Portugal involved it in counterproductive polemics with its French Socialist ally/rival, the PCI repeatedly linked its criticism of the PCP with its strategic emphasis on a multiparty, gradualist approach to a pluralistic socialist order in which "bourgeois" liberties would be guaranteed and extended—a perspective it applied not only to Italy but to advanced Western societies in general.[13] The interparty debate over Portuguese developments therefore raised issues of regional significance (while making it more difficult to achieve consensus on them); these included "national paths," the nexus between socialism and democracy, the "vanguard role" of the national Communist party, and—not least—relations between Communist and Social Democratic parties.[14]

The debate was not confined to the Western parties. Until August 1975, Soviet comment on Portuguese events and the issues raised by them was relatively restrained, probably because of preoccupation with the Helsinki conference. Once the East-West summit was over, however, Soviet and East European commentaries on Portugal and on the "ideology of transition" in general became more outspoken and more hard-line.[15]

Of particular significance was an article that Konstantin Zarodov, editor-in-chief of *Problems of Peace and Socialism* (Prague), contributed to the August 6 issue of *Pravda*.[16] Commemorating a seventy-year-old work by V. I. Lenin, Zarodov insisted on the unchanged necessity for "a revolutionary democratic dictatorship of the proletariat," led "from above" by the Communist party, and stressed that it should be based on a "political" majority not an "arithmetical" one. The rebuke to "modern conciliators" (i.e., Communist parties seeking electoral progress through broad political alliances) was clear: "This Leninist idea . . . completely debunks the still fashionable opportunistic conceptions which make out that possession of the levers of power should be . . . the results of some kind of nationwide referendum."

The Zarodov article (and a series of similar, earlier ones by Boris Ponomarëv, Aleksandr Sobolev, and others) could be viewed as an effort by a more conservative element in the Soviet leadership to "balance" the strategic emphasis on détente by reasserting the CPSU's revolutionary legitimacy. Yet it also involved reasserting the CPSU's magistral right to impart ideological and political lessons to other Communist parties.

Most Western CPs ignored the article, but there were strong reactions from the Italian,[17] British,[18] and French parties. Of these, the last was the most significant. In an initial response, Secretary-General Georges Marchais emphasized at a press conference on August 8 that "PCF policy in all spheres is determined in Paris and not in Moscow," and that his party's attitude toward "the future of democracy and personal and collective freedoms . . . does not stem from any existing model or models." Four weeks later (and the delay added weight to the riposte), the PCF unexpectedly returned to the attack with a front-page *l'Humanité* article by Central Committee member Jacques Chambaz, who criticized Zarodov for presenting the conclusions that Lenin drew from the Tsarist Russian situation in 1905 as being "valid everywhere and always, and hence also in France." In particular, the PCF's goal of an "advanced democracy" was "incompatible with the idea of scholastic distinctions setting an arithmetical majority against a political majority."[19] This considered rejection of Soviet ideological arguments can now be seen to have heralded much more significant changes in PCF-CPSU relations.

It was against this background of rumbling polemics and divergent political interests that the eight-party subgroup failed, both in regular sessions and in a series of bilateral talks that continued through September, to end the deadlock over the conference document. The confrontation would have to be transferred back to the wider forum.

Meanwhile, the Spanish CP (PCE) struck a weighty blow for the independent grouping by adopting, at its Second National Conference in early September 1975, a resolution detailing its position on the pan-European conference.[20] This resolution stated that "the differences existing among the Communist parties of Europe on essential questions, such as that of the democratic way of socialism," were such that "it would be negative to seek through ambiguous formulations to convey an impression of false unanimity." In the PCE's view, the conference "could have a positive outcome even without a final document"; but if there was to be a final document, it could cover questions only on which there was consensual agreement. In any case, "the PCE could not approve a document of a programmatic and ideological type which could [even] appear obligatory for all the parties."

Moscow's Vacillations

At this point came the first of several successive, dramatic shifts in Soviet attitudes toward the conference project. It was signaled by the British CP's announcement in late September that a delegation would attend a meeting in Berlin on October 9-10 "to consider the next stage in the preparations for the conference." The fact that the independent British party was able to add that it would "continue to work for the successful holding of the conference before the end of this year"[21] suggested that "the next stage" would involve concessions by the conservative majority to the independent minority.

And so it proved. The meeting of October 9-10, with twenty-seven delegations present (the San Marino CP having excused itself), was confronted with a third East German draft that was evidently very different from the first two: it seems to have been essentially devoted to the uncontroversial subject of post-Helsinki détente, covered in the original second chapter. Commenting with satisfaction on the outcome, *l'Unità* (October 11) said that although the latest "synthesis" still required further "elaboration and clarification," it had been agreed that it could be "taken as a basis for discussion with the aim of arriving at a document that can receive the agreement of all the parties." It was further agreed that on the basis of the discussions of October 9-10 "and of the observations and proposals that can be put forward by all the participating parties," the full Editorial Commission would meet in November to draw up the final draft "on the basis of the agreement of all the parties."[22]

The apparent victory of the consensus principle and the concomitant agreement to refer the synthesized result back to all the central committees for approval seemed to mark the institutionalized recognition—in a new way and on a new level—of the principle of the autonomy of each Communist party. It also meant that the lowest common denominator would be very low indeed.

One party that accepted this with notably bad grace was the PCF, as Jean Kanapa made clear in an address at the session and in interviews afterward.[23] In his speech, he complained that as the months passed, "the political content of the document has been reduced, impoverished. That has not been our doing." On the demand of "numerous parties," the text would now be limited to the post-Helsinki "struggle for détente, peaceful coexistence, disarmament, and cooperation." His party regretted this limitation and in particular the failure to produce a collective analysis of "the grave crisis affecting the capitalist countries, the workers' struggles for democracy and socialism, and the possibilities for a broad union of democratic forces." The PCF therefore demanded that the document should at least note that since peaceful coexistence "does not in any way signify the social and political status quo, each Communist party pursues its class struggle . . . in full independence and without outside interference."

At this juncture, however, the Soviet position unexpectedly changed again—"zig" being followed by "zag," so to speak. For when the twenty-eight-party Editorial Commission met on November 17-19, the outcome was very different from what had clearly been anticipated in October. The meeting did not adopt a revised draft or set a date for the conference. Instead (the British *Morning Star* reported on November 20), it decided that an "editorial group" open to all parties would meet in December "to continue work on the draft, taking into account the points brought up"; the Editorial Commission would meet again in January to discuss the result and "consider" setting a date for the conference.

The postponement (and the reversion from "Editorial Commission" to "editorial group") showed that something had happened to block the consensual agreement that was in sight a few weeks earlier. And it was a last-minute development. Only a few days before that mid-November session a Yugoslav spokesman had declared: "Barring the unexpected, we are on the way to creating a [conference] document, a political communiqué, which will suit everyone."[24]

What had happened? Later statements by Spanish, British, Italian, and Yugoslav party spokesmen cast some light on the matter. In an interview published in the PCE organ *Mundo obrero* immediately after the November session, the leader of the Spanish delegation, Manuel Azcárate answered the editorial question "What is the reason for the postponement of the conference?"

> Let us recall that from the start of the preparatory process there was manifested a tendency to present to the conference a document which would be a sort of "general line" for all European parties. Various parties, including the Spanish CP, declared roundly that that was impossible. Considerable progress had in fact been made toward a concrete document limited to certain themes on which the parties, each acting in full independence, were in agreement. If that path had been followed, perhaps the recent meeting would have brought the preparatory work to a close.
>
> That was not the way it happened. The tendency to press for a document of what may be called an "ideological type" reasserted itself. Faced with this, the position of a certain number of parties was maintained very firmly.
>
> The only solution lies in continuing the discussion. On the other hand (and I do not think that this is a coincidence), my impression is that certain parties which plan to hold their conferences [sic[25]] in the near future, and which earlier had shown interest in having an early conference, now prefer to have it postponed. . . .
>
> In any case, as far as we are concerned, this process of preparation is helping to reemphasize, in a new form, a very important principle: the independence of the Communist parties.[26]

A later statement by the British delegate Reuben Falber substantially confirmed Azcárate's account. He indicated that the basic confrontation had all along been between the parties pressing for "a document which could be interpreted as laying down a general line" and those opposed to such a pronunciamento. At the October session "agreement appeared to have been reached . . . providing for a final document which would be limited in scope and [which would] primarily deal with united action in carrying forward the struggle for peace and détente in Europe." The British delegation therefore went to the November session "hopeful that the final draft would then be agreed and the date fixed for an early conference. The whole character of the document, however, was again called into question. Some wanted it shortened and still more limited in scope, while others favored a more extensive and basic document."[27]

There were other, less direct allusions to the reverses at the November session. In an interview in *l'Unità* of November 23, G. C. Pajetta elaborated on the PCI's known positions, saying of the November meeting only that it had not had "a positive result" and that there was still "a long way to go." A statement by the Yugoslav chief delegate Aleksandar Grličkov was significant precisely because it ignored the November session. Without referring to the clearly controversial draft text submitted by the East Germans—their fourth such effort—Grličkov noted that the *third* East German draft, produced at the October meeting, had "for the first time provided a working basis for all participants . . . since the chief element of discord was eliminated. This element was the discussion of issues—which, after all, are not part of the agenda and which refer to ideological problems in the Communist movement—that are more or less known to be issues in dispute." The fact that the preparatory process had been so prolonged, he suggested, "is in itself proof of the efforts being made to express the interests, concepts, and policies of all parties."[28] This studied optimism was the more striking because of the contrast with the stand taken by less official Yugoslav commentators.[29] The Yugoslavs, it seemed, had decided to treat the November draft as a merely temporary deviation from a consensus-paved path to which the pro-Soviet majority would be obliged to return because of the unyielding stand of the independent parties.

This confidence was not groundless. In December, there occurred another shift in Soviet position, back toward a "softer" line. These successive shifts, indicative of uncertainty in the Kremlin, could be connected with changes in the CPSU delegation: at the October meeting, the chief delegate had been Boris Ponomarëv; in November, he was replaced by Konstantin Katushev; and in December, the latter was in turn replaced by an ascendant protégé of Brezhnev's, Vadim

Zagladin. A few days before the December 16-19 session of the "editorial group," Zagladin flew to Rome for what appears to have been a "turning point" meeting with leaders of the PCI. "Informed" reports from various capitals subsequently indicated that in these talks Zagladin expressed the CPSU's willingness to drop controversial ("programmatic") sections of the November draft and to reconsider passages dealing with certain debatable issues (e.g., the relationship between the blocs, an analysis of the situation in Western Europe, and the Communist parties' relations with other forces).[30]

Even on this basis, however, progress toward a consensual document would be slow (a "marathon" editorial session on January 13-22, 1976, evidently brought agreement on much of the text but left major issues unsettled).[31]

The Emergence of Eurocommunism

In the meantime the prolonged confrontation over the conference document had helped to develop among the major Western Communist leaderships an increased awareness of convergent interests—and of their ability to band together in defense of those interests. Of special importance here was the dramatic change that took place in the positions of the traditionally loyalist French CP in late 1975 and early 1976. The shift was marked by a more emphatic commitment to pluralistic democracy and civic liberties—and by a consequent, sometimes almost ostentatious, readiness to criticize the Soviet regime, which led to unprecedented polemical exchanges between the PCF and the CPSU.

The change in the French Communists' posture took place within the framework of preparations for their 22d Congress (scheduled for February 4-8, 1976) and was accompanied by the emergence of a strategic alliance among the French, Italian, and Spanish CPs. This alliance was formalized by the adoption of bilateral communiqués proclaiming the parties' commitment to the pluralistic-libertarian ideals of what was soon to be known as "Eurocommunism."[32] The PCI-PCF statement, which Berlinguer and Marchais issued in mid-November 1975 after talks in Rome, could justly be termed a manifesto of Eurocommunism. It committed the two CPs to support "for the plurality of political parties, for the right to existence and activity of opposition parties, and for democratic alternation between the majority and the minority." The eventual building of a socialist order in Italy and France would be characterized by "a continued democratization of economic, social, and political life," and existing bourgeois liberties would be "guaranteed and developed." The statement went on: "This goes for freedom of thought and expression, of the press, of assembly and association, of demonstration, of free circulation of persons at home and abroad, of inviolability of private life, of religious freedom." It also pledged "complete freedom of expression for all currents of philosophical, cultural, and artistic opinion." Within a regional and not merely national context, the two parties vowed to promote "the common action of the Communist and Socialist parties, of all the democratic and progressive forces of [Western] Europe."[33]

The sincerity of these pluralistic/libertarian commitments could be questioned (and was widely questioned, particularly in France). The present point, however, is that the PCF-PCI manifesto represented an implicit challenge to the East European regimes—a challenge that the PCF soon made explicit. The French Communists were already embarked on a course of cautious criticism of the Soviet handling of internal dissidence. On November 1, *l'Humanité* expressed editorial concern over the fate of the Soviet dissident Leonid Plyushch, reportedly interned in a psychiatric clinic; if this were true, the editorial intoned, the PCF would register "total disapproval."[34] On November 12, PCF Politburo member Jean Kanapa indicated disagreement in *l'Humanité*'s pages with the Soviet refusal to grant Andrei Sakharov an exit visa to collect his Nobel Peace Prize: "Liberties are indivisible, and include in particular freedom of movement as well as freedom to publish all writings." A more decisive step toward criticism of Soviet repressive policies came on December 12, when the PCF Politburo issued a statement expressing its "most formal reprobation" of Soviet labor camps, as depicted in a television documentary film that the Politburo clearly accepted as genuine.[35]

Other issues, notably the PCF's abandonment of the doctrine of the dictatorship of the proletariat, added fuel to the polemical flames, but the PCF obviously relied on recurrent criticism of Soviet repression as the most crucial tactic in its image-building campaign to sell "socialism in French colors." "Socialism is synonymous with liberty," Marchais told an interviewer on January 7. "This idea is valid in all countries, under all circumstances. . . . There is a divergence between us and the CPSU with regard to socialist democracy."[36] Despite taunts from the French Socialists, the Communists would not, however, go a logical step further to conclude that where liberty was violated, as in the USSR, true socialism did not exist.[37] The new look had its limitations.

The new posture of demonstrative independence was emphasized at the 22d PCF Congress in early February, when Marchias explicitly criticized Soviet repression in his opening speech. Referring to "certain developments in the Soviet Union," he said: "We cannot admit that the Communist ideal . . . should be stained by unjust and unjustifiable acts. . . . This is why we express our disagreement when violations of human rights occur in a country that made its socialist revolution 58 years ago."[38]

Events at the CPSU Congress

A few weeks later, the 25th Congress of the CPSU gave Marchais another chance to draw attention to the widening gap between the two parties—by declining to attend in person. In a radio interview on February 27, he said that he had made this unprecedented decision "because there is a divergence between our two parties on the problems of socialist democracy . . . [and also] on the evaluation of French foreign policy." Then, when asked about the prospect of a meeting between himself and Brezhnev, he went significantly further: "The conditions for such a meeting do not exist today, and for the moment there is no question of it."[39]

In place of Marchais, Gaston Plissonnier headed the French delegation to the Soviet congress. His address—delivered February 28—was unprovocative, but it was followed by a rather theatrical challenge. After speaking to the congress, Plissonnier led his delegation to the Kremlin press center to give a press conference, at which he declared:

> The abandonment of the notion of the dictatorship of the proletariat [by the PCF] is not negotiable. . . . We have not come to Moscow to negotiate. . . . As for proletarian internationalism, if this is reduced to a mere identity of views among Communist parties, it would be better to finish quickly with this rudimentary form. . . . The PCF does not share Leonid Brezhnev's assessment of French foreign policy.[40]

The other two major Eurocommunist parties also used the 25th Congress, in instructively different ways, to reaffirm their positions. Like Marchais, Santiago Carrillo of the Spanish CP did not attend the congress (in his place the aged President Dolores Ibárruri, resident in Moscow, delivered an unprovocative speech). Instead, he went to Rome with a delegation of other Spanish opposition leaders for talks with Italian politicians, serenely explaining that this was "more important." While in Rome, he gave the Milan newspaper *Corriere della Sera* an interview in which he expressed very outspoken views about the Soviet regime and its relations with the Western parties.[41] Soviet socialism, Carrillo said, was "in the primitive stage," and Western socialism, when it came, would have to be profoundly different: "In the West we can have socialism only if the democratic and pluralistic systems are respected, and if it is based on majority consensus, with a readiness to give up power if this majority ceases to exist." Asked whether he did not fear that this idea of communism would be condemned by Moscow, he replied: "By what right could they condemn us? They can criticize us, as we criticize them. Condemnation is excommunication from a church, and the Communist movement was a church but now no longer is one."

Berlinguer of the PCI, on the other hand, did attend the congress—and used the occasion to present the PCI's Eurocommunist positions, offering some very challenging formulations (without, however, criticizing his hosts).[42] Subsequently, Berlinguer met Brezhnev, Mikhail, Suslov, and Ponomarev for an "exchange of opinions" on the communist movement, inter alia. The joint communiqué was unrevealing, but the key sentence bore an "Italian" stamp: "The common wish was expressed to continue broadening international cooperation between the two parties on the basis of fraternal friendship and reciprocal respect for their independence"—no mention of proletarian internationalism.[43] Although the French seemed to feel the need to draw repeated attention to a newly assumed posture of independence, the Italians could strengthen a substantive independence gradually developed over two decades by acting *suaviter in modo, fortiter in re.*

On the Soviet side, Ponomarëv and especially Suslov must have signed the PCI-CPSU communiqué with more reluctance than Brezhnev; for by this time, there was growing evidence of differences and uncertainty in the Kremlin over how to deal with the conference project and the related challenge posed by Eurocommunist ideas. A survey of the congress speeches strengthens this impression.[44]

Continuing Confrontations

The developing debate between loyalists and Eurocommunists found more explicit expression before and after the 25th Congress in statements and articles by regime spokesmen—notably, Soviet, East German, Bulgarian, and Czechoslovak[45]—and in Western Communist reactions. The debate generally concerned such doctrinal issues as proletarian internationalism, the dictatorship of the proletariat, and "general laws" for the building of socialism. Another controversial question was the extent to which Western Communist parties should seek political progress through alliances with other forces. But behind these lay a more basic issue: the challenge to Soviet authority posed by major Western parties increasingly determined to give priority to their own political interests over those of the Kremlin and to reinforce their claim to independence by selective criticism of Soviet policies. This challenge was the more significant in that it came at a time when the Soviets were making obvious efforts to strengthen integration among the East European regimes in many areas—a fact that had much to do with the vigorous Yugoslav interventions in the debate on the side of the independent Western parties.[46]

Against this background of generally indirect ideological polemics, preparations for the pan-European summit made fitful headway in the early months of 1976. After the ten-day editorial session in January, when the fifth East German draft was discussed, there was growing evidence that the tide was now flowing in favor of the independent parties. In a *Rinascita* article of early February, the Italian delegate Antonio Rubbi claimed that agreement had been reached on "the fundamental lines" of the document, although "there still remain questions to be clarified and discussed."[47] He pointed to one of these questions in criticizing Soviet and East German spokesmen who saw in solidarity with the USSR/CPSU the essence of proletarian internationalism or who held that "there cannot be an anti-Soviet communism or a communism turned against existing socialism, against the Warsaw Pact, against Comecon and the community of socialist countries" (quoted by Rubbi from an article by V. Korionov in *Pravda*, of January 24, 1976). Rubbi put forward a compromise formula (which would be substantially adopted in the final document), stressing the need to distinguish between the "*a priori* anticommunism" of imperialists and reactionaries and "criticism of individual aspects and particular or even fundamental options of the socialist countries."

A more revealing account was given by Sergio Segre in his report to a PCI Central Committee commission in mid-February. Segre said that although work still remained to be done, "the agreement that now seems to be taking shape on the draft document agreed upon at the Berlin meetings of December and January is consistent with the stand defended from the first by the PCI." This stand, he went on, "had as a premise the fact that a document acceptable to all could only be one that identified the points of convergence, without claiming to delineate general lines and strategies, to take on a binding character, or to tackle themes—such as ideological [issues]—on which there exist diverse and divergent positions."[48]

Another preparatory meeting took place from March 16 to 18 and ended with the announcement that the results would be "discussed at a session of the Editorial Commission." The change in nomenclature indicated again (as it had, deceptively, in October-November 1975) that considerable progress had been made toward an agreed text.

Shortly afterward, however, there came reports that such progress had been put in question by a new development—a memorandum presented by the French delegation at the mid-March session. The reports from Belgrade, Moscow, and Paris all told substantially the same story.[49] The memorandum reportedly criticized the current draft for its lack of a "class analysis": it demanded a more militant document, with particular reference to the "crisis of capitalism" and its consequences for Western Communist parties. The reports also linked the memorandum with the PCF's current criticism of Soviet attitudes on French foreign policy. Finally, the memorandum warned (and the PCF later confirmed) that the French had not yet decided whether to attend the conference.

As these plausible reports indicated, the lines of confrontation on various issues had become more complex as the unprecedented debate developed, often cutting across the familiar division into "central-izers" and "autonomists." Thus, if the French now joined the Italians, Spanish, and Yugoslavs in emphasizing independence, they strongly disagreed with them on other questions—notably, NATO.

Nevertheless, the central issue was still whether the new rule of consensus would prevail. In a three-part interview in a Yugoslav newspaper at the end of April, Grličkov was officially confident that it would; because of the progress made, he said, there now existed "realistic possibilities for the conference to be held in June."[50]

At the Editorial Commission session from May 4 to 6, the remaining differences continued to be ironed out: the communiqué said that the "final" meeting of the commission would be in early June and that the conference itself could take place "in the near future." But there were still clouds around the summit. On May 12, Grličkov reported to the LCY Executive Committee that "an important step forward" had been made in coordinating views on certain parts of the draft through "satisfactory formulations," but that the questions on which agreement had *not* been reached were mainly "issues of principled and fundamental significance."[51] A few days before, he had expressed the hope that the remaining problems would be "solved" at the session in early June—adding that in this connection he expected "other parties to take the LCY's position into account, *and to accept it.*"[52]

In late May, the last act of the long drama was heralded by a flurry of interparty diplomacy, involving bilateral communiqués by the independent parties and Soviet visits to Bucharest and Belgrade. Of decisive importance were the talks Katushev had in Belgrade with LCY Secretary Stane Dolanc at the beginning of June. According to a Yugoslav source, "Brezhnev's messenger ended by unexpectedly accepting all the demands which until that moment the Soviets had opposed."[53] On the eve of the conference, Grličkov confirmed that at the May session the LCY presented "seven decisive amendments . . . on which we particularly insisted," implying that they had eventually been accepted. One, dealing with proletarian internationalism, "was concerned with whether it was possible to describe any one country as a major factor, or the main force";[54] the implicit reference to the Soviet Union was obvious.

The final session of the Editorial Commission adopted the consensual text (produced by Soviet acceptance of the Yugoslav demands) on June 10-11, before adjourning until June 24. This last interval was allowed to let the individual party leaderships give formal approval to the final draft—but perhaps also to await the outcome of the Italian parliamentary elections of June 20, which clearly could have affected the timing of the conference had the results propelled the PCI into negotiations to participate in a coalition government. Although this did not come about, the PCI got an unprecedented 33.7 percent of the popular vote in the elections, only narrowly failing to overtake the Christian Democrats, and this near victory was an important factor in strengthening the positions of the independent parties vis-à-vis the Moscow loyalists. During the campaign preceding the election, the PCI was more outspoken than ever in proclaiming its autonomy and differentiating its stance from that of the loyalist parties. In a mid-June interview, for example, Berlinguer said that he had no fear of meeting the "unjust" fate of Dubček because "we are in another area of the world"; and, asked whether NATO could constitute a "useful shield" for the construction of socialism in liberty, he readily agreed: "I feel more secure being on this side." Again, on the eve of the elections *l'Unità* (June 18) published a letter that unidentified leaders of the Prague Spring had sent to the PCI, praising its commitment to a socialist order based on pluralistic democracy and saying that its positions helped East

Europeans who wanted "a socialistic society in which there no longer exist inequalities, privileges and unjustices"—a reminder of the relevance of Eurocommunist ideas for the "socialist opposition" in the East.

At Last, the Conference

When the delegates reassembled on June 24, it was to announce that the conference would take place on June 29-30. On the eve of the opening, Brezhnev and Tito held private talks in East Berlin. There was an irony of history here, for that day was the twenty-eighth anniversary of the Cominform's "excommunication" of Yugoslavia. Now the great heretic had returned to "conciliar communism" essentially on his own terms. After nearly two years of complex interparty confrontations, the newly promoted Marshal Brezhnev had been outmaneuvered by that indomitable veteran, Marshal Tito.

Consensus, of course, involved concessions on both sides; nevertheless, it seems indisputable that with regard to the conference document, the independent parties had their way on almost every major point.[55] It was a lowest-common-denominator text based on the new principle of consensus (itself a formal recognition of the equality and autonomy of all Communist parties); it contained no criticism of the Chinese and no praise of the Soviets; it dealt with political action and not with ideology; and it was not binding upon the participants (in fact, it was not even signed by any of them). The victory of the independent parties on these central issues was emphasized by the unexpected arrival of a twenty-ninth delegation, that of the independent Dutch party, which had boycotted all the preparatory meetings. Thus, in the end the only absentees were the isolationist Icelanders and the intransigent Albanians.

The document was more important for what it did not say than for what it did say. Most striking was the fact that the sacrosanct formula, "proletarian internationalism," was omitted and replaced by a distinctly "Italian" formulation:

> [Communist parties] will develop their internationalist, comradely *and voluntary* cooperation and solidarity on the basis of the great ideas of Marx, Engels, and Lenin, strictly adhering to the principles of equality and the sovereign independence of each party, noninterference in internal affairs, and respect for their *free choice of different roads* in the struggle for *social change of a progressive nature* and for socialism [Emphasis added].

Again, no special status was accorded the CPSU or the USSR. The only minor concession to tradition here was a reference to campaigns by imperialist and reactionary forces "against the Communist parties and the socialist countries, beginning with the Soviet Union"; and even this was qualified by a preceding phrase with the Italian stamp: "The Communist parties do not consider all those who are not in agreement with their policies or who take a critical attitude toward their activity as being anti-Communists."[56] Also of note was the "Western" emphasis on Communist parties' dialogue and collaboration with "all other democratic forces, each of these forces fully retaining its identity and independence." Finally, for the first time in a collective Communist document, there was recognition of "the movement of nonaligned countries . . . [as] one of the most important factors in world politics"—an important point for the Yugoslavs.

It is true that the long list of political objectives was broadly in harmony with Soviet foreign policy goals. Still, one should remember that the differences between independent and conservative Communist parties are generally concerned not with foreign policy but with ideology, domestic policies, and interparty relations.[57]

The main interest of the conference, however, lay not in this largely anodyne text but in the "institutionalized diversity" of positions manifested in the speeches. Thus, loyalist speakers, having reluctantly agreed to the dropping of proletarian internationalism and the abandonment of special status for the CPSU/USSR, proceeded to insist on the continued validity of both. In this regard, Brezhnev himself was more subtle and flexible than, say, Todor Zhivkov of Bulgaria or Yoldas Bilen of Turkey; and his performance at the conference could be viewed as, in part, a reassertion of his authority over ideological hard-liners such as Suslov.

At the other end of the spectrum, non-Communist journalists found their liveliest "copy" in the speeches of the Eurocommunist trio of Berlinguer, Marchais, and Carrillo.[58] The most provocative, to loyalist ears, was Carrillo: he explicitly rejected Soviet authority, made an obvious reference to former Soviet support for Enrique Lister's splinter party, and suggested that socialist states should set an example by withdrawing their troops from foreign countries.

The most complete statement of Eurocommunist positions came from Berlinguer, who called on all present to accept the qualitative change in interparty relations: "Methods which are now outdated [must] be abandoned." The new methods he proposed included the free confrontation of ideas in open debate, with the consequent right of criticism (in this connection, he made the only public reference at the conference to the invasion of Czechoslovakia—a disappointing result for the former Prague Spring leaders who, like a group of Soviet dissidents, sent an open letter to the delegations protesting against regime repression).[59] Stressing that the Italian road to socialism lay "within the framework of the international alliances to which our country belongs" (i.e., NATO and the EEC), he noted that other West European Communist parties now shared the PCI's perspective of a socialist society based upon "the principles of the secular, nonideological nature of the state and its democratic organization; the plurality of political parties and the possibility of alternation of government majorities; the autonomy of trade unions; religious freedom, freedom of expression, of culture, and of the arts and sciences."[60]

If such an open display of radical divergences made the East Berlin conference the first of its kind, Marchais of the PCF suggested that it was also likely to be the last of its kind. "Conferences like this one do not appear to us to correspond any longer to the needs of our time," he said. "Since any elaboration of a strategy common to all our parties is henceforth absolutely ruled out, it seems opportune to seek new forms of collective encounters, more lively, flexible and effective," which could produce frank discussion of topical problems and which would "not always end with the adoption of a document."[61] The French and the other independent parties made clear, too, their opposition to loyalist plans for a world communist conference, which the Kremlin had obviously envisaged as a sequel to the European one.[62]

Assessment and Aftermath

On balance, those observers who evaluated the conference as a victory for the independent parties were undoubtedly correct. But it is important not to overestimate the scope of that victory—as, for example, the dissident East German intellectual Robert Havemann did when he declared: "The great significance of the Berlin conference for European communism lies in this—that an end has been put to hegemonic efforts by one party. This hegemony of the CPSU has been removed not only from the parties of the capitalist West but from all parties, including those of the East."[63]

A first indication of the limitations of the autonomists' "victory" was provided by the blatant censorship that the East European media applied—particularly with respect to Western Communist speakers—in their coverage of the conference[64] (the only exception was *Neues Deutschland*, which as "host organ" was obliged to publish all the speeches in full, as *Pravda* had at the Moscow international conference of 1969). At the same time, these media, with Soviet journals in the lead, opened a campaign to present the conference in triumphal terms, as having strengthened the unity and cohesion of the communist movement on the basis of proletarian international- ism; the Bulgarians were particularly zealous in arguing the corollary that the USSR "inevitably serves as the universal model for other socialist revolutions."[65]

The Yugoslavs reacted with polemical vigor to this "falsification of the consensus reached in Berlin,"[66] but Western parties at first generally ignored signs of recidivism (although one PCI spokesman complained about "partial and sometimes distorted interpreta- tions").[67]

However, as the clearly regime-inspired polemics continued, with criticism of "opportunism," "bourgeois democracy," and "anti- Sovietism," and with a corresponding insistence on "general laws," the French CP launched a counterattack. In mid-October, it sent Pierre Juquin to a rally demanding the release of specifically named political prisoners in the USSR, Czechoslovakia, and Latin America; speaking for the party, he declared: "We shall never accept that methods in violation of human rights should be used in any country in the name of socialism."[68] And when Hungarian Politburo member Desö Nemes argued that any socialist regime, "irrespective of the national form it assumes," must perform "the historic function of the dictatorship of the proletariat," Jean Kanapa of the PCF rejected the East European model as irrelevant to French conditions and did so in offensive terms:

> If one considers that in order to install socialism in France it is
> necessary to have recourse to the dictatorship of the proletariat, as was
> done in Hungary (and also in the Soviet Union and elsewhere), [then] it
> is necessary to state that one must ban opposition parties, establish
> censorship, deprive part of the population of the freedoms of
> expression, association, demonstration, etc., and one must tell the
> French workers, "This is one of the consequences of what the
> Communists propose to you," because the dictatorship of the
> proletariat, no matter what its form, is exactly (not entirely, but
> exactly) this.[69]

The divergence of political interests that lay behind such polemical exchanges was clear enough. On the French side of the Kanapa- Nemes clash, there was an obvious effort to build up the PCF's electoral credibility by dissociating it from unpopular practices of the

Communist regimes, and also to strengthen its position vis-à-vis its Socialist ally/rival. On the East European side, a factor of growing importance was the obvious concern of authoritarian regimes over the "subversive" effect of Western Communist ideas on their populations. That effect was already being evidenced in the welcome given to Eurocommunist ideas and positions by East European dissidents in a position to do so—e.g., Andrei Sakharov and Roy Medvedev of the USSR, Robert Havemann and Wolf Biermann of the GDR, or Edwar Lipínski and Adam Michnik of Poland. The only Communist leader, East or West, who has spoken forthrightly about this important but sensitive factor is Carrillo of the Spanish CP. In an interview given (provocatively) to the Italian dissident-Communist daily, *Il Manifesto*, he said there should be no illusions about the fact that the USSR would "view with concern" the emergence in Western Europe of pluralistic socialist regimes "not dependent upon the USSR itself, and [with] a political structure different from that of the peoples' democracies. There is no doubt that the latter will look more and more toward [West] European models of socialism, if we reach that point."[70]

The challenge that Western Communist ideas pose to Soviet authority and to Soviet interests is therefore obvious enough. But this challenge has limitations, which it is also important to recognize.

First, if Eurocommunism is a regional phenomenon of sociopolitical adaptation that affects virtually all West European CPs to some degree—as evidenced by the Brussels conference of eighteen West European parties in January 1974 and by the frequent thematic conferences that have been taking place since late 1973—the explicit challenge comes from a handful of parties. At the forefront of these stand the "Big Three" of Italy, France, and Spain, whose leaders met in Madrid and issued a joint declaration of views in early March 1977. Other Western parties do not go so far.[71]

Second, even the most independent and "revisionist" of the Western parties are concerned—as they seek *alliances de convenance* with Social Democracy—to maintain their identity as *Communist* parties, as national components of the international revolutionary movement. While endeavoring to extend their autonomy, they want to avoid anything like an open break with Moscow;[72] and this, in turn, sets limits on their critical independence. Dissident Communists such as Roger Garaudy and Pierre Daix of France, or Franz Marek of Austria, may urge the Western CPs to undertake thorough analyses of the Eastern regimes and to draw the conclusion that the latter are *not* socialist—but they urge in vain.[73] Again, the

differentiated character of the criticism by the Western CPs weakens
the claim that it is principled criticism: contrast the PCI's
championing of imprisoned leaders of the Prague Spring with its
embarrassed reaction to the shooting of an Italian Communist truck
driver at the Berlin Wall in July 1976, or its criticism of Soviet
treatment of political prisoners with its failure to respond to the
persecution of Polish workers after the Ursus-Radom riots of June
1976. It is to be noted, too, that the most thorough criticism directed at
the regimes concerns not the present but the past, and especially the
Stalinist past.[74]

The depth of this desire to retain links with the world revolutionary
movement was aptly demonstrated in the reaction of the Spanish
party to the Soviet attack on its secretary general, Santiago Carrillo, in
late June 1977.[75] A communiqué unanimously adopted by the PCE
Central Committee declared support for Carrillo's "Eurocommunist" positions, rejected Soviet criticism of them, and accused Soviet
critics of using the method of "excommunication" instead of a
"scientific analysis of problems." At the same time, it treated the
assault on Carrillo as directed not only at the Spanish party but also at
"all Communist parties that favor a democratic road to socialism and
socialism in democracy."[76] Moreover, Carrillo and the PCE evinced
no wish to push the confrontation to the point of a rupture with the
CPSU, and they responded favorably to efforts to reduce tensions
between the two parties. Indeed, Carrillo himself went to Moscow in
early November 1977 to attend the celebrations in honor of the
sixtieth anniversary of the October Revolution—although he subsequently found himself barred from delivering his prepared speech
during the activities marking the occasion.

Furthermore, as noted earlier, the independent Western CPs
generally support the USSR on issues of foreign policy; and this is of
importance to a Soviet leadership that fairly obviously puts *raison
d'état* before *raison d'idéologie*. On this level, however, some
significant departures from the pattern are to be noted. The line of the
Italian and Spanish parties on NATO and the EEC is now strikingly
deviant. Since its 14th Congress in March 1975, the PCI has officially
opposed any "unilateral change" in the East-West power balance—a
stipulation that is explicitly applied not only to Italy's membership
in NATO but also to Yugoslavia's nonalignment. As for the Spanish
CP, its foreign affairs spokesman, Manuel Azcárate, has said that "the
problem of the U.S. bases [in Spain] can be solved only in the process
of overcoming the blocs," and that entry into the EEC is the "only
alternative" for a democratic Spain.[77] Finally, the PCF now publicly
criticizes the Kremlin on one key issue—its benign attitude to the

foreign policies of President Giscard d'Estaing. In all three instances, the element of political opportunism is obvious—as is the fact that on most foreign policy issues the three parties habitually support the Soviet line[78]—but then, Eurocommunism might be described as the tendency for Western CPs to give priority to their own political interests in the course of adaptation to their sociopolitical environments.

It is precisely because of this tendency that the major West European parties—with the exception of the deeply divided Finnish CP, coping with its internal conflict in the geopolitical shadow of the Soviet regime—seek to maintain and if possible extend their freedom of maneuver vis-à-vis Moscow. This was demonstrated by their reactions to the death of Mao Tse-tung. Both *l'Unità* and *l'Humanité* devoted four pages to the passing of what Marchais called "one of the greatest figures in history."[79] The French Communist tributes were particularly significant in that the PCF's attitude to Maoism had been, until shortly before Mao's death, one of vigorous criticism.[80] Now the French were concerned not only to play down this past hostility but to indicate a readiness for rapprochement with the Chinese—a move the Spanish and Italian parties had already made.[81] "We profoundly regretted that these divergencies changed our relations," said the PCF Central Committee's message of condolences to Peking. "This was not our doing, and it is not our desire."[82]

Equally significant was the mild reaction of the PCI and PCF, particularly the latter, to the Chinese rejection of their condolence messages. Jean Kanapa said that this would not change the PCF's "deep-rooted conviction that, no matter how grave our divergences may be, they should not result in a deterioration of relations . . . and that in the future another form of relations between our parties can be established—relaxed, comprehensive and friendly."[83] This benign response strengthened the impression that the Franco-Italian "signals" to Peking were primarily prompted not by the hope of renewing relations with the Chinese but rather by the desire to affirm PCI-PCF autonomy vis-à-vis the Soviets—in short, less a move toward Peking than a move away from Moscow. Thus, when Sergio Segre was questioned about the affair, he dismissed the suggestion that the PCI still kept up "a special, or at least preferential, relationship with Moscow," and added: "If there is a priority in the development of our relationships, today this clearly applies to parties in the geographical area facing problems similar to those of Italy— not only Communist parties but also Socialist and Social Democratic parties."[84]

Political developments in Italy, France, and Spain will surely continue to strengthen this tendency; accordingly, one may also expect a continuation of intermittent polemics between the major Western CPs and Eastern regimes, whether on ideological questions or through Western Communist reactions to image-harming events in the East. But the Eurocommunist parties, as argued earlier, have no interest in severing relations with the ruling parties. It is therefore most unlikely that they will go beyond sporadic, dissociating criticism to anything like a thoroughgoing analysis of the failings of the Eastern regimes.[85]

On the other hand, the CPSU, though clearly concerned about the destabilizing influence of Western Communist ideas on the East European bloc, would also seem to have no interest in a serious deterioration of relations with these parties—the more so since the challenge of Eurocommunism is not posed only, or even primarily, to Soviet authority.[86] For its developing role in strategically important countries of southern Europe has made Eurocommunism a factor of growing, if still largely potential, importance in what the Kremlin may hope will eventually lead to the controlled destabilization of the adversary NATO alliance. But that is another story.

Notes

1. The complete names and initial designations of the East European Communist parties mentioned in this chapter are: Albanian Party of Labor (Partia e Punes e Shqiperise, or APL or PPSh); Bulgarian Communist Party (Bulgarska Komunisticheska Partiya, or BKP); Communist Party of Czechoslovakia (Komunistická Strana Ceskoslovenska, or KSC); Communist Party of the Soviet Union (Kommunisticheskaia Partiia Sovetskogo Soiuza, or CPSU or KPSS); Hungarian Socialist Workers' Party (Magyar Szocialista Munkaspart, or HSWP or MSzMP); League of Communists of Yugoslavia (Savez Komunista Jugoslavije, or LCY or SKJ); Polish United Workers' Party (Polska Zjednoczona Partia Robotnicza, or PZPR); Romanian Communist Party (Partidul Comunist Roman, or PCR); Socialist Unity Party of Germany (Sozialistische Einheitspartei Deutschlands, or SED), East Germany; Turkish Communist Party (Turkiye Komunist Partisi, or TKP).

2. The divergence of political interests was dramatically emphasized sixteen months later by the reaction of most West European parties to the invasion of Czechoslovakia by Warsaw Pact forces. In speeches at a PCI Central Committee plenum on August 27 and 29,

1968, Secretary General Luigi Longo criticized the failure of "some socialist countries" to pursue the strategy of détente set forth in the Karlovy Vary document, owing (he suggested) to preoccupation with the subversive effect of "ideological aggression."

3. For an analysis of the early stages of the preparatory process (up to May 1975), see Kevin Devlin, "The Interparty Drama," *Problems of Communism*, July-August 1975, pp. 18-34.

4. At different times, spokesmen for the Yugoslav, Romanian, Italian, and Spanish parties expressed the view that the conference need not adopt any document—presumably as a bargaining position to strengthen the demand for *their* kind of document.

5. The "working group" consisted of as many delegations as chose to attend a particular editorial session (e.g., sixteen in February 1975 and twenty in April). In this connection, nomenclature was significant: when the delegations later met as the "Editorial Commission"—as in November 1975 and May-June 1976—it was a signal that consensual agreement was in sight.

6. See Devlin, "The Interparty Drama," p. 32. Giancarlo Pajetta of the PCI reportedly described this first draft as having been "written in German, but translated from the Old Russian—of the Cominform era." See "Great and Unclear Divergencies among the PC's of Europe," *Il Manifesto* (Rome), May 17, 1975.

7. During a private conversation in September 1976, Sergio Segre of the PCI told the writer that one of these subgroup sessions (presumably the final one) had lasted eight days.

8. *L'Espresso* (Rome), August 31, 1975. In a later *L'Espresso* interview, in mid-October, Segre said that after the last eight-party meeting, "the margin of disagreement was so wide that some even thought it impossible to reach a settlement."

9. See K. S. Karol, "The Portuguese Obsession," *Le Nouvel observateur* (Paris), June 2, 1975.

10. In late 1974, Yugoslav and Romanian delegations attended a congress of the Portuguese Socialist Party in Lisbon—but not one of the Communist Party.

11. This interview was published in *L'Europeo* (Milan), June 15, 1975.

12. See *l'Humanité* (Paris), May 16, 1975.

13. As Piero Pieralli of the PCI Secretariat put it: "We affirm once more that all we have done and said, all we shall do or say, with regard to Portugal, is based on what we consider to be questions of principle—on the way in which we think the essential, crucial issues of the struggle for democracy and socialism in Western Europe must

be tackled." "A Pigheaded Demand," *Rinascita* (Rome), August 20, 1975.

14. The importance of Communist-Socialist relations in southern European countries and of the disunity among Communist parties on this subject was demonstrated by reactions to Soares's proposal in late August 1975 for a conference of Socialist and Communist leaders of Portugal, Spain, France, and Italy to discuss "the transition toward socialism in society while preserving democracy." The Italian and Spanish CPs promptly joined the Socialist parties concerned in accepting the proposal; the Portuguese CP rejected it; and the French CP eventually expressed a heavily qualified and polemical acceptance that amounted to a rejection. See "The Response of Georges Marchais to Mário Soares," *l'Humanité*, October 23, 1975.

15. A good example is Ivan Hlivka's article in *Pravda* (Bratislava), August 26, 1975: "Unfortunately from time to time it happens in our movement that certain comrades, under the fabricated pretext that they want to win the broadest possible circles of allies for their party, criticize the socialist countries and particularly the Soviet Union at any price. And often they also criticize those revolutionary movements that follow a path of revolution reminiscent of the victorious path followed by fraternal socialist countries up to now. Such a practice objectively harms the revolutionaries and the revolution." In this article, Hlivka also denounced "any neutrality toward the current policy of China"; again, the relevance to the struggle over the conference document was obvious.

16. Was it a coincidence that Zarodov's article appeared on the day that a PCI delegation headed by Pajetta arrived in Moscow to discuss "questions concerning the international situation and the international Communist movement"? The Communist-line daily *Paese sera* (Rome) of August 11 had no doubt that the circumstances made the article "a severe doctrinal warning" addressed to the PCI and other parties taking "pluralistic and autonomous paths."

17. The *Pravda* article was criticized in *l'Unità* (Rome) statements of August 9 and 12: "The attempt to dictate rigid and general rules is groundless. . . . The relationship between democracy and socialism is understood by us in an extremely different fashion from the way in which it is outlined in the doctrinaire thinking of Zarodov."

18. A British CP spokesman, George Matthews, commented: "The policy of the British Communist Party is independently decided by our party and by no other. The time has long since passed when Communist parties subscribed to a single political center." *Morning Star* (London), August 14, 1975.

19. *L'Humanité*, August 9 and September 4, 1975.

20. The writer has been unable to obtain the text of the PCE's resolution. This account is synthetically based upon reports in *l'Unità* of September 25, 1975; *Il Manifesto* of September 20; Frane Barbieri's article in *Il Giornale* (Milan) of September 23; and a sixpoint summary given by Manuel Azcárate of the PCE Executive Committee during a private meeting in October 1975.

21. *Morning Star*, September 27, 1975.

22. In his speech at the session of October 9-10 (text in *l'Unità*, October 14, 1975) and in a later Central Committee report (ibid., October 30, 1975), Pajetta expressed the PCI's wary satisfaction over the way things now appeared to be going. His CC report stressed that the conference would be "based on the principle of consensus insofar as it relates to the drawing up of a joint document and full freedom of debate. This signifies not only the full and explicit recognition of every party's equality and independence but also the renunciation of any organizational bond and the rejection of directives which could represent an obligation not arising from direct responsibility to the workers' movement and people of one's own country." Of the PCI's role in the preparatory process, he said: "We were faced with a complex document which in our opinion tried to cover too many issues, for which we thought the process of joint research and agreement was not yet ripe. We asked for brevity in the formulations and a reduction in the number of subjects covered, even at the cost of a conclusion which might seem too succinct and too limited in subject matter." See also Pajetta's interview, "No Common Strategy," *Le Nouvel observateur*, October 19-25, 1975.

23. Text of speech in *France nouvelle* (Paris), October 20, 1975; interviews in Agence France-Presse (AFP) dispatch of October 11, 1975, and *l'Humanité*, October 13, 1975.

24. Jure Bilić, secretary of the LCY Executive Committee, in an interview with the fortnightly publication *Oko* (Zagreb), reported by the Yugoslav Telegraph Agency (TANJUG), November 13, 1975.

25. Pending congresses included those of the French, Soviet, Polish, Bulgarian, and Czechoslovak parties; but it seems obvious that Azcárate was referring primarily to the 25th CPSU Congress, scheduled for late February 1976.

26. "Conference of the Communist Parties of Europe: A Declaration by M. Azcárate," *Mundo Obrero*, November 25, 1975. The December 2 issue of the British CP daily, *Morning Star*, published almost the complete text of Azcárate's statement; no other East or West European party newspaper seems to have mentioned it.

27. *Morning Star,* December 19, 1975.

28. Interview with the editorial staff of *Komunist* (Belgrade), reported by TANJUG, November 30, 1975. Grličkov serenely took it for granted that interparty differences were now such that the elaboration of "joint strategy and tactics for Communist parties—and even the very idea of harmonizing their foreign policies—is today an anachronism."

29. For example, in a Radio Zagreb broadcast on December 15, 1975, Milika Sundić charged that "some parties want the end of the conference to be accompanied by the publication of a 'strong' communiqué containing some obligations for all parties," and called this "a deviation from what had been agreed on at the beginning of the preparations." In an earlier broadcast of December 10, Sundić was even more direct: criticizing Leonid Brezhnev by name, he assailed the CPSU's insistence that "there is only one way to socialism and only one acceptable prescription for cooperation, particularly for the socialist countries."

30. Reporting "the new Soviet *volte-face*" in a dispatch from Moscow published in *Le Monde* (Paris), December 30, 1975, Jacques Amalric said of the harder-line November draft: "Moscow demanded in effect that the document . . . solemnly condemn 'the hegemonic pretensions of the United States over Western Europe' and denounce 'the dangers that NATO poses for the European socialist community.' The Soviet Union also demanded that the final document give a very restrictive definition of the leftist alliances in which the Western Communists could take part."

31. After the ten-day January session, the Yugoslav delegate Grličkov told Austrian journalists that there had been no agreement yet on the principles of interparty relations, the role of nonaligned countries, relations between Communist and Social Democratic parties, disarmament, and the assessment of "the crisis of modern capitalism" (Reuters and AFP reports from Vienna, February 1, 1976). The list could obviously have been extended—e.g., to the assessment of NATO and the EEC, or to such concepts as "anti-Sovietism" and "proletarian internationalism."

32. The November 1975 communiqué (PCI-PCF) was preceded by a similar PCI-PCE statement in July 1975 and followed by a PCF-PCE communiqué later in November.

33. *L'Humanité* and *l'Unità,* November 18, 1975. The pattern of bilateral "Eurocommunist" communiqués was later extended to several minor West European parties (e.g., the British) as well as to

to the distant Japanese CP. At its congress in July 1976, the JCP went further along the road of doctrinal deviation than any West European party by eschewing not only the dictatorship of the proletariat but also "Marxism-Leninism"—the latter being replaced by "scientific socialism."

34. In January 1976, after Georges Marchais had intervened with the Kremlin, Plyushch was released and allowed to go to Paris.

35. *L'Humanité*, December 13, 1975. Noting that "there have in fact been in the Soviet Union trials of citizens prosecuted for their political stands," the Politburo said that it was "against all repression affecting the rights of man, and notably the freedom of opinion, expression, and publication."

36. *Le Monde*, January 9, 1976.

37. In a report on the "evolution" of the PCF issued in late January 1976, a national secretary of the Socialist Party, Lionel Jospin, said that condemnation of Soviet labor camps did not constitute a "real turning point" in PCF-CPSU relations: this would come only if French Communist leaders were to "draw the logical conclusions from what they are affirming" and state that "since freedom is synonymous with socialism, there is no socialism where there is no freedom." Ibid., January 29, 1976.

38. *L'Humanité*, February 6, 1976. The same day's issue of the Czechoslovak organ *Rudé právo* (Prague) carried an editorial that, without mentioning the PCF, denounced the rejection of the doctrine of the dictatorship of the proletariat as "rightist revisionism," saying that those who disavowed the doctrine could not be called Socialists.

39. *L'Humanité*, February 28, 1976.

40. *Le Monde*, March 2, 1976. It may be noted that these provocative remarks were not reported in *l'Humanité* in the covering dispatch of March 1, which merely said that Plissonnier and Kanapa had again put forward the views of the PCF at the Moscow press conference.

41. Giovanni Russo, "The Eurocommunism of Santiago Carrillo," *Corriere della Sera* (Milan), February 26, 1976.

42. Berlinguer—whose speech was published in full in *Pravda* (Moscow)—said that his party was working for an Italian foreign policy "which, *within the framework of the international alliances of our country* [i.e., NATO and the EEC], would make an active contribution to détente and firmly defend the sovereignty of the Italian people against *any foreign interference* in our internal affairs"; the PCI, he added, was struggling to achieve a "pluralistic

and democratic" socialist society that would guarantee "all the individual and collective liberties, [including] religious liberties and freedom of culture, the arts, and science." *L'Unita*, February 28, 1976. Emphasis added.

43. Ibid., March 2, 1976.

44. Brezhnev himself was unabrasive in his emphasis on "proletarian internationalism" and "general laws" and in his veiled warnings against "concessions to opportunism" *(Pravda*, February 25, 1976); but other Soviet speakers were more direct in their attacks on "right-wing opportunism" and on "attempts to 'modernize' Marxism . . . and to cut it up into national slices" (P. Masherov, alternate Politburo member, quoted in ibid., February 26). On the other hand, as the congress opened, *New Times* (Moscow) published an article in which Vadim Zagladin spoke approvingly of the diversity of ways to socialism as being advantageous to the USSR; his only stipulation was that "one must not throw away the baby with the bathwater, and socialism, notwithstanding all its diversity, must remain socialism." Reported in *l'Unità*, February 28, 1976.

45. Czechoslovak CC Secretary Josef Kempny was particularly outspoken in a speech criticizing "the transformation of Marxist-Leninist parties into opportunistic parties of a Social-Democratic nature." *Nová svoboda* (Ostrava), March 15, 1976.

46. One interesting example of the Yugoslav-Eurocommunist alliance may be noted. In mid-March 1976 a booklet attacking "revisionism" and "opportunism" was published in Moscow. The author was one Veniamin Midtsev, an obscure "collaborator" of the foreign affairs section of the CC—CPSU, who made his target clear by devoting a third of the work to criticism of the PCI ideologist Luciano Gruppi. An editorial in *l'Unità* (March 19, 1976) scornfully refuted Midtsev's "aberrant" dogmatism. But the Yugoslav reaction was even more vigorous: on March 23, commentaries on Radio Zagreb and Radio Belgrade denounced the booklet as an attempt to impose on other Communist parties "the theory of limited sovereignty."

47. A. Rubbi, "Interpretations and Reality," *Rinascita*, February 6, 1976. A few days earlier, in an interview in *Le Nouvel observateur* of February 2, Giancarlo Pajetta had said that the draft document was "now ready" and that "nothing has been decided that is contrary to our preoccupations or to what we judge it necessary to affirm through such a conference."

48. *L'Unità*, February 14, 1976. Another indication of concessions being made to the independent parties came from Jean Terfve of the Belgian CP. In an interview about the 25th CPSU Congress, he said that the Soviets accepted "without great difficulty" the idea that

Western CPs could develop a "unitary strategy," adding: "This is, by the way, said explicitly, with the agreement of all, in the document drawn up in the course of the preparations for the conference. . . . As to whether [the Soviets] accept this strategy with enthusiasm, that is another question." *Le Drapeau Rouge* (Brussels), March 12, 1976.

49. See AFP dispatch from Belgrade, March 23, 1976; Paolo Garimberti's report from Moscow in *La Stampa* (Turin), March 26, 1976; Jacques Amalric's report from Moscow in *Le Monde*, March 28-29, 1976. It should be noted, however, that some weeks later a PCF Politburo statement (May 21, 1976) denied an AFP report that the French party had proposed certain "tough" amendments to the conference document, calling the report "entirely imaginary."

50. *Nova Makedonija* (Skopje), April 30, May 1 and 2, 1976.

51. *Borba* (Belgrade), May 13, 1976. Grličkov was presumably referring primarily to the continuing dispute over proletarian internationalism and "anti-Sovietism," but perhaps also to the difficulties posed by the PCF's stand.

52. *Politika* (Belgrade), May 8, 1976. Emphasis added.

53. Quoted in Frane Barbieri's dispatch from Belgrade, published in *Il Giornale*, June 20, 1976. See also François Fejto's report from Belgrade in ibid., July 17, 1976, giving what are said to be extracts from the protocol of the talks.

54. Radio Belgrade television interview, June 26, 1976. In a conversation with the author in September 1976, Sergio Segre of the PCI accepted the suggestion that Katushev's visit to Belgrade was "the final turning point."

55. The text of the document is published in *New Times*, no. 28, July 1976, pp. 17-32.

56. This formulation was significantly reminiscent of that used by Antonio Rubbi of the PCI in his *Rinascita* article of February 6, 1976. Note that although it apparently refers primarily to non-Communist criticism of Communist parties, it could also be taken to justify Western Communist criticism of East European regimes.

57. For an interesting "balance sheet" of the conference, drawing broadly similar conclusions, see Heinz Timmermann, *Die Konferenz der europäischen Kommunisten in Ost-Berlin: Ergebnisse und Perspektiven* [The conference of the European Communists in East Berlin: result and perspectives], Berichte des Bundesinstituts für ostwissenschaftliche und internationale Studien, no. 28 (Cologne, 1976).

58. The 800-odd journalists covering the conference were able to follow the entire proceedings through closed-circuit television and to

interview delegates, the holding of an "open" conference having been another basic demand of the independent parties.

59. Reported in *l'Unità*, June 30, 1976.

60. Ibid., July 1, 1976.

61. *L'Humanité*, July 1, 1976.

62. In September 1976, Sergio Segre of the PCI told the author that he thought the precedents established at the European conference (e.g., consensus) would also apply to any future world meeting, adding that he believed the Soviets, as "realists," would quietly drop the world conference project since they knew that the major West European parties would not attend.

63. *Der Spiegel* (Hamburg), July 5, 1976.

64. See J. L. Kerr, "The Media and the European CP Conference: A Study in Selective Reporting," *Radio Free Europe Research* (Munich), RAD Report 171, August 11, 1976.

65. CC member N. Iribadzakov in *Rabotnichesko delo* (Sofia), August 11, 1976.

66. Vlado Teslić in *Borba*, August 14, 1976. See Zdenko Antic, "Belgrade Attacks East European Views on Berlin CP Conference," *Radio Free Europe Research*, RAD Report 180, August 18, 1976.

67. A. Rubbi, "Berlin, Beyond the Polemics," *Rinascita*, July 30, 1976.

68. *L'Humanité*, October 22, 1976. The rally at which Juquin spoke was organized by a committee of French mathematicians campaigning specifically for the liberation of two Soviet, one Czech, and three Latin American political prisoners. Rejecting Soviet and Czechoslovak criticism of Juquin's participation in "this dirty enterprise" (TASS), the PCF reprinted 7 million copies of his speech.

69. *France nouvelle*, October 5, 1976. Kanapa was replying to Nemes's article in *Problems of Peace and Socialism* (September 1976) on the "lessons" that Western Communists should draw from Hungarian experience.

70. *Il Manifesto*, November 1, 1975.

71. For example, the Danish CP dropped the formula of the dictatorship of the proletariat at its congress in September 1976, as the Portuguese CP had done two years earlier, but neither would think of making this a ground for disputes with the ruling parties, as the French have.

72. The most obvious exception is the Icelandic CP, which for years has in effect had no relations with the CPSU and other ruling parties.

73. It is significant that the most radical indictment of the East

European regimes produced by the PCI's publishing house was written by a dissident Polish Communist (in exile). See Włodzimierz Brus, *Sistema politico e proprietà sociale nel socialismo* [The political system and social characteristics of Socialism] (Rome: Editori Riuniti, 1974).

74. Of some interest, Italian and French Communist writers have recently produced notably objective histories of the Soviet Union under Stalin. See Giuseppe Boffa, *Storia dell'Unione Sovietica* [The history of the Soviet Union] (Rome: Mondadori, 1976); Jean Elleinstein, *Histoire du phénomène stalinien* [History of the Stalinist phenomenon] (Paris: Grasset, 1975); and his four-volume *Histoire de l'U.R.S.S.* [History of the USSR], 2d ed. (Paris: Editions sociales, 1972-1975).

75. Although several items in the Soviet media during this period contained criticism of Carrillo, the main condemnation took the form of a review of Carrillo's *Eurocomunismo y el Estado* [Eurocommunism and the state] (Barcelona: Editorial Grijalbo, 1977). This review appeared in *New Times* (Moscow), no. 26, June 1977, pp. 9-13, and Tass publicized it on June 23.

76. *Mundo obrero*, June 29, 1977.

77. Statements made at a private meeting of social scientists and politicians in Cologne in October 1975, at which the writer was present. It may be noted that Spanish-Italian-Yugoslav resistance was probably responsible for the omission from the European conference document of the customary attacks on the United States and NATO.

78. In conversations with "leading PCI policymakers," Michael Ledeen recently "asked them to describe the conflicts, if any, between their party and the Soviet Union in the area of foreign policy. They answered with a single voice: no such conflicts exist." See his "The Soviet Connection," *Commentary* (New York), November 1976, pp. 51-54.

79. See issues of September 10, 1976.

80. At the 22d PCF Congress in February 1976, Marchais—although stressing the party's new independence of the Kremlin and criticizing Soviet repression—was still denouncing the "profoundly reactionary . . . senseless and dangerous" policies of Peking. *L'Humanité*, February 5, 1976.

81. In September 1971 Secretary-General Carrillo led a PCE delegation to Peking in a not very successful attempt to resume normal relations with the Chinese CP. A month before Mao's death, Giancarlo Pajetta revealed that on that occasion Carrillo took with him a message from the PCI, "to let them know that we desired

meetings with leaders of the Chinese CP, in Italy or in China" (*l'Unità*, August 11, 1976). The offer was ignored—as were other Italian Communist approaches to Peking, made through the Romanians and the Vietnamese—but Pajetta made clear that it still stood.

82. *L'Humanité,* September 10, 1976.

83. *Le Monde,* September 17, 1976.

84. *Corriere della Sera,* September 15, 1976. Cf. Santiago Carrillo's statement in an interview in *La Stampa* of December 14, 1975: "Contacts with the state parties of the East can remain; there can be cooperative relations; but the priority lies in the West."

85. The small British CP has perhaps come nearest to encouraging open debate on these regimes. In January 1976 its monthly organ, *Marxism Today* (London), carried a twenty-seven-page anti-Stalinist article by former General Secretary John Gollan, and "discussion contributions" by readers were invited. The debate opened in the March issue and ran for a number of months—generally with a "ration" of two letters criticizing the Soviet regime and one defending it in each issue.

86. See Heinz Timmermann, "Eurocommunism—A Challenge for East and West," *Deutschland Archiv* (Cologne), December 1976, pp. 1276-1298.

Index